OUR
GAME

Henry Holt and Company   New York

OUR GAME

An American Baseball History

CHARLES C. ALEXANDER

FOR RACHEL CAMILLE ALEXANDER

Copyright © 1991 by Charles C. Alexander
All rights reserved, including the right to reproduce
this book or portions thereof in any form.
Published by Henry Holt and Company, Inc.,
115 West 18th Street, New York, New York 10011.
Published in Canada by Fitzhenry & Whiteside Limited,
195 Allstate Parkway, Markham, Ontario L3R 4T8.

Library of Congress Cataloging-in-Publication Data
Alexander, Charles C.
Our game: an American baseball history/Charles C. Alexander.—
1st ed.
p.   cm.
Includes bibliographical references and index.
1. Baseball—United States—History.   I. Title.
GV863.A1A4   1991
796.357'0973—dc20   90-20585
                                                     CIP

ISBN 0-8050-1594-9

Henry Holt books are available at special discounts
for bulk purchases for sales promotions, premiums,
fund-raising, or educational use. Special editions
or book excerpts can also be created to specification.
For details contact:
Special Sales Director, Henry Holt and Company, Inc.
115 West 18th Street, New York, New York 10011

FIRST EDITION

Book Design by Claire Naylon Vaccaro
Printed in the United States of America
Recognizing the importance of preserving
the written word, Henry Holt and Company, Inc.,
by policy, prints all of its first editions
on acid-free paper. ∞
10 9 8 7 6 5 4 3 2 1

Contents

Preface

I've undertaken to write neither an "anecdotal history" of baseball, à la books by such authors as Joseph Durso, Douglas Wallop, and Harvey Frommer, nor anything so detailed as David Voight's and Harold Seymour's multivolume histories. There are anecdotes; there is detail. I've sought, though, to maintain a balance in that regard, as well as in more general matters of explanation and interpretation. I wanted to cover the history of baseball—as game, sport, business, and social institution—in a way that would interest baseball-lovers of all kinds, be sound enough to satisfy specialists, and prove serviceable as a compact, inclusive one-volume history.

I've subtitled this book "An American Baseball History," at least in part to forewarn readers that it contains virtually nothing about the rich baseball history of Japan. And while baseball in Canada, the Caribbean, and Central America receives some attention, the focus is on the origins, development, and significance of baseball within the United States. If I haven't been able to explain why—as Jacques Barzun wrote many years ago, "whoever would know the mind and heart of America had better learn baseball"—I at least hope that whoever finishes this book will have come to realize that baseball history reveals much about life in this country over the past century and a half.

My treatment is chronological, because history pretty much happens that way, not topically or thematically. It seems to me that, as far as possible, history ought to be narrated in real time, which means giving some sense of the crowded, disordered nature of the past. Thus I've integrated a number of different themes and topics into a chronological frame extending from roughly the 1830–1840s up to the 1990 baseball season.

Much of what I know about events in baseball history over the past forty-five years comes from personal observation and recollection—in other words, from being a fan. Two good personal and professional friends—Warren F. Kimball, of the graduate faculty in history, Rutgers University, and Eugene C. Murdock, of the emeritus faculty, Marietta College—have also been devoted followers of the game since childhood. Once again they were willing to give my work a close, critical, and corrective reading, bringing to bear their strong knowledge of both baseball and U.S. history. It's always a pleasure to thank them for letting me impose on their time, expertise, and good natures.

I also appreciate the interest and indulgence of upwards of one thousand students who've taken my American Baseball History course since I started offering it at Ohio University in 1985. This book strongly reflects the way my thinking has developed as I've taught that course year by year.

And, as always, I owe thanks to JoAnn Erwin Alexander—for nearly everything. But then, after thirty years, she already knows that.

C.C.A.   ATHENS, OHIO

August 1990

I see great things in baseball;
   it's our game,
  the American game.

—Walt Whitman

1.
The
New York
Game

Within less than three years, the people of the United States would be locked in an epochal civil conflict that would kill more of them than any other war in their history—past or future. But on Tuesday, July 20, 1858, for the couple of thousand Americans who paid a stiff fifty cents each to get into the Fashion Race Course near the village of Flushing on Long Island, and then jammed the little grandstand and elbowed each other around the track railing, the most important thing about to happen was a game of baseball.

One team, representing the city of New York and consisting of players drawn from baseball clubs in Hoboken, New Jersey; Morrisania (just north of the Harlem River in the Bronx); and the Gothams, Empires, and Eagles from Manhattan itself, would meet an all-star outfit made up of players from the Putnam, Excelsior, Atlantic, and Eckford clubs in the independent city of Brooklyn. It was the first match in what was planned as a three-game series, bringing together most of the best players in the country.

Early in the afternoon, spectators began reaching the site by horseback, carriage, and the special trains run for the occasion by the little Flushing Rail Road. Others walked as many as five miles. The players arrived with their full club memberships in horse-drawn omnibuses decorated with flags, bunting, and streamers; the Excelsiors came by the Fulton Avenue Line in a huge conveyance pulled by fourteen gray horses bedecked in feathered bridles.

The interclub Committee of Management, having prohibited the sale of anything stronger than beer, was delighted with "the very decorous conduct of the immense numbers on the ground." The presence of a couple of hundred well-dressed ladies supposedly added to the wholesomeness of the event.

At 2:30 the game started on the grass diamond laid out inside the racetrack. Batting first, the Brooklyns scored three runs. They added two more in the second inning, while the New Yorks counted once. Each team scored twice in the third inning; then New York made four runs in the fourth to tie the game at 7–7. Brooklyn came back with four in the fifth inning, only to see New York rally for seven scores in its turn at bat. Each club tallied two more runs in the sixth inning and one in the seventh. Brooklyn scored four times in the eighth, but the New Yorks piled up five more. Although the outcome was decided when the Brooklyn players failed to score in the top half of the ninth inning, they courteously took the field so their opponents could have an equal number of times at bat. The New Yorks also made their three outs without scoring, so that the final count was New York 22, Brooklyn 18.

After cheering each other on the field, the players adjourned to the little clubhouse atop the racecourse grandstand to exchange champagne toasts and raise their glasses to the Niagara Club, several of whose members had traveled all the way from Buffalo to watch the event. The president of the Excelsiors hoped for a better outcome in the return match the following month.

Reporters from several Manhattan newspapers as well as the *Brooklyn Daily Eagle* covered the game. Frank Pigeon of the Brooklyns won praise for his play in the "short field" (shortstop), as did Harry Wright in center field for New York. Outfielders Green and O'Brien of Brooklyn had excelled "particularly in catching the ball on the fly," while New York's Davis "made a miss on a ball, which, if he had held it, would have immortalized him as a fielder." The only moment of controversy had come late in the game, when Wadsworth of New York swung at the ball and somehow managed to hit it off his forefinger. The Brooklyn pitcher tossed over to first, but the umpire, seated under an umbrella at a table about twenty feet from the home base, had ruled no play.

All in all, thought the *New York Times*, it had been a fine match, one that would be "long remembered with pleasure by all lovers of this noble and invigorating game." Indeed it had been the most-talked-about and watched baseball event up to that time—something of a landmark in the evolution of the "New York game" from a pleasant recreational activity, based on the ancient English children's game of "rounders," into a mature competitive sport.

Europeans had played varieties of stick-and-ball games for centuries before the earliest American Colonial settlements. Children here, like their European forebears and contemporaries, frequently amused themselves at games with names such as "one o' cat," "three o' cat," and particularly rounders, also commonly called "town ball." What all of those games had in common was that a boy with a stick or "bat" would try to hit a small ball tossed to him by another boy, and then run to a base or bases (depending on the game) before he was "put out."

Until the early 1800s, such games remained almost exclusively children's amusements. In a country such as the new United States, one that valued hard work and possessed no true leisure class, few adults had either the time or inclination for idle diversions. Thomas Jefferson might acknowledge the usefulness of horsemanship and hunting skills, but "Games played with the ball," he wrote a friend in 1785, "stamp no character on the mind." Two years later the faculty at the staunchly Presbyterian College of New Jersey (later Princeton) adopted a resolution prohibiting "a play at present much practiced by the small boys among the students and by the grammar scholars with balls and sticks in the rear campus. . . ." The boys, the faculty felt, should seek to entertain themselves in ways "both more honorable and more useful."

Yet across the country, in villages and towns and on the many open fields and empty lots in its few cities, youngsters continued to play games that went by the generic designation "base ball." No doubt boys in the hamlet of Cooperstown, New York, also played such games; one of them may even have been named Abner Doubleday. In 1839, according to what would become official legend seventy years later, young Doubleday devised the basic rules for a new kind of baseball, an indigenously American version. At that time, though, the twenty-year-old Doubleday was already more than one hundred miles away at West Point, in his second year as a cadet at the U.S. Military Academy. When he died in 1893, Doubleday was known for his distinguished record as a Union officer in the Civil War and as a postwar promoter of street railways. He left no record of having ever played baseball.

By the 1830s–1840s small numbers of adult young men in the northeastern seaboard cities, evidently less interested in watching and wagering on horse races or cockfights than were many of their peers, began to spend part of their off-work time playing the bat-ball games of their boyhoods. They were mainly small merchants, clerks, lawyers, occasionally physicians—upwardly mobile, solidly middle-class urbanites (what a much later generation would call "yuppies"). As early as 1831 a group of young Philadelphians formed the Olympic Club and played a refined version of town ball, featuring a rectangular playing field with five bases. In the Boston area still another version of town ball was so popular that it came to be called the "New England game."

One group of young New York professionals who liked to bat and throw a ball around on summer afternoons followed the suggestion of Alexander Joy Cartwright, a shipping clerk, that they organize themselves as the Knickerbocker Base Ball Club. Three years later they decided to leave the Murray Hill area of Manhattan, where they'd been meeting, for more space and seclusion at the lovely Elysian Fields, part of the Stevens estate outside Hoboken. On Saturday afternoons during the summer, they would take the ferry across the Hudson River to Hoboken, climb to their playing site, and amuse themselves for a couple of hours at any of various forms of "base ball."

By 1845–1846 the Knickerbockers were regularly playing a particular kind of "base ball." Their new game provided for nine-member teams with fixed batting orders; four bases, positioned in diamond configuration, placed forty-two paces apart; and delivery of the ball underhand from a distance of fifteen paces to a "striker," who had to hit the ball between the lines stretching to the first and third bases. If he missed the ball altogether in three swings at it, he was declared "out." When three outs had been made, the teams would exchange places at bat and afield; when both sides had made their three outs apiece, an "inning" had been played. The winning team would be the first to make twenty-one "aces," or scores. Maybe the most pronounced departure from other bat-ball games was the elimination of "soaking," whereby fielders could put out base runners by throwing the ball and hitting them. In the Knickerbockers' game, the ball always had to reach a base *ahead* of a runner.

Nobody actually "invented" baseball, but the game the Knickerbockers played did mark the beginning of what, within a few years, was being called the "New York game." The Knickerbockers arranged matches under their new rules with a number of other clubs; soon Knickerbocker-style baseball had become the favorite bat-ball pastime in the New York area. The Knickerbockers had wanted a game that would offer lots of hitting and base-running yet could easily be concluded in two hours or less. It was supposed to be fun, a form of play for men who weren't really athletes and weren't trying to be. They differed from other American males of their age range only in that they occupied a somewhat above-average social position, were willing to engage in a limited amount of exercise away from work, and sought that exercise in a kind of activity that traditionally had been child's play.

They were friends and associates, willing to sweat a little as a pretext for some gentlemanly socializing. Besides charging annual dues, they also levied fines on members who used profanity during games or argued with whoever had agreed to serve as the umpire. Part of what they collected went toward paying for the beer and hearty dinner that usually followed their games, and for such occasions they sometimes invited along wives and girlfriends to share in the festivities.

Alexander Cartwright, the instigator of the Knickerbocker Base Ball Club, stayed around only until 1849, when he departed to seek his fortune in California in the great gold rush. On the long trip overland he taught Knickerbocker baseball to people on wagon trains, to soldiers, saloon-keepers, miners, even Indians—anybody who seemed interested. Although he failed to find quick riches in California, he and Frank Turk, another former Knickerbocker, did organize San Francisco's first baseball club. After voyaging to China, Cartwright settled in the Hawaiian Islands, where he continued to spread the gospel of baseball. Founder of a successful trading company and later a bank, a hospital, and the Honolulu fire department, he died in 1892 as one of the most prosperous and respected persons in the Islands. His connection with baseball's beginnings, though, was almost totally forgotten.

By the late 1850s, what the Knickerbockers had intended as little more than a pleasant pastime for themselves and other young gentlemen had become a serious competitive undertaking for substantial numbers of American men. In the city of New York, in much of New Jersey, in Buffalo, Rochester, Washington, Baltimore, and numerous other places, even in faraway New Orleans, baseball had emerged as the favorite form of team athletics. Brooklyn was a particular baseball hotbed, boasting dozens of clubs; in March 1858, fourteen clubs from Brooklyn and Manhattan formed the National Association of Base Ball Players (NABBP). In that first and three subsequent meetings (during which time NABBP's membership more than doubled), the delegates formulated a set of bylaws and produced the first standardized set of rules for baseball.

Essentially they adopted the Knickerbocker rules, the principal change providing that whoever was ahead after nine innings would be the winner, rather than whoever first scored twenty-one "aces." The distances between bases, moreover, were officially set at ninety feet. A proposal (from the Knickerbockers) to eliminate outs on one-bounce catches of outfield flies was turned down, despite complaints such as that of the influential weekly *Porter's Spirit of the Times* that nothing "is more annoying to an admirer of good fielding than to see a splendid hit to the center field . . . entirely nullified by the puny effort of waiting until the force of the ball is spent on the ground and then taking it on the bound." Although the Knickerbockers went ahead anyway and banned one-bounce catches in their own matches, the NABBP didn't adopt the new fly rule until 1864.

Much of the thinking behind the proposed requirement for a clean catch on outfield flies had to do with a desire to make baseball an unimpeachably "manly" game. If baseball had already become an acceptable activity for fully grown men, then it was also beginning to move away from its origins in the male gentry. Especially in Brooklyn, club members frequently included skilled workmen—shipwrights, cobblers, coopers, and stonecutters. A majority of the players on

Brooklyn's powerful Eckford club made their livings with their hands, although they were, to be sure, among the highest-paid workmen in the country.

As they attracted a following of spectators (who with growing frequency found themselves paying admissions), baseball games featured heightened partisanship and emphasis on winning. The rivalry among the Eckfords, Atlantics, and Excelsiors in Brooklyn was particularly intense. A three-game series in 1860 between the Atlantics and Excelsiors for the putative city championship drew crowds of eight to twenty thousand. With each team having won a game, the deciding contest, late in August, ended unexpectedly when the Excelsiors' captain, disgusted by heckling from the pro-Atlantics spectators, took his team off the field despite enjoying an 8–6 lead.

The Excelsior Club was the most significant in the pre–Civil War years in promoting and exhibiting baseball to people in the hinterlands. In the spring of 1860 the Excelsiors first toured the western part of New York State, winning all six games from local teams, then traveled as far south as Baltimore, again going without defeat. James Creighton, the Excelsiors' star pitcher, was the most admired player of his time and also probably the first player to be paid by his club. Winning had become a more important consideration for the Excelsiors than abiding by the NABBP's strictures against professionalism. Baseball had come a long way since the early years of the Knickerbockers.

The Knickerbockers themselves were more and more an anachronism. Persisting in their genteel approach to the game, they never sought publicity or made much of an effort to attract spectators. When the leading Brooklyn and Manhattan clubs began to talk up championship matches, the Knickerbockers quietly withdrew from such discussions. While their name would continue to carry a certain cachet in New York baseball circles, the game was rapidly moving away from the easygoing ways of the Knickerbockers and toward something more intense and keenly competitive. In short, baseball, as played by most of the clubs in and around New York and Brooklyn, had become less a "game" and more a modern organized sport.

As baseball progressed, the British game of cricket lost whatever chance it may have had of becoming a mass-appeal sport in the United

States. Although that outcome wasn't inevitable, given the particular circumstances in which baseball came to flower in the middle decades of the nineteenth century, it's hard to envisage how things might have worked out differently. Baseball, as Melvin Adelman has said, "ful- filled the requirements of the sporting universe created by the changing social and urban environment of the antebellum period."

The 1840s and 1850s brought growing concern over the nation's physical health, a concern articulated mainly by and for the benefit of the swelling numbers of middle-class city-dwellers. Americans, so the argument went, were sickly, lacking any interest in "physical culture," and therefore in danger of betraying the virile, heroic heritage of their Revolutionary forebears. Outdoor recreation was not only desirable for the crowded urban masses but, according to the physical fitness propagandists, absolutely necessary to forestall national decline.

Of course, it wasn't necessary for people to take up baseball to get the exercise everybody supposedly needed and few (apart from the majority that still worked in agriculture and other physically demanding occupations) appeared to be getting. Americans could, for example, have taken up gymnastics or cricket, both of which already had a firm hold in particular segments of the population. But therein lay much of the problem. Gymnastics was a recent import, brought over by German immigrants beginning in the late 1840s, and unable to escape its central European connections. Cricket, widely played in Philadelphia, New York, Boston, and elsewhere in the East, never managed to overcome its associations in American thinking with British ways, especially British class-consciousness.

To be sure, as early as the 1830s considerable numbers of spectators turned out for cricket matches in the eastern seaboard cities; for a time the exploits of New York's St. George Club eclipsed those of any of the baseball outfits. Both working-class immigrants as well as the scions of prominent Anglo-Saxon families played cricket avidly, and in 1859 the American tour of the All-England Cricket Team became a major national event.

Yet part of the explanation for the failure of cricket in the United States had to do with that very tour, which showed the British sport at its best and, if anything, discouraged athletically minded Americans from trying to master it. The All-England team's proficiency brought home the sheer difficulty of playing cricket, especially for people who hadn't grown up with it and didn't really understand such an abstruse, tradition-laden, indisputably foreign, and already well-organized sport.

Cricket also suffered from being the favorite game among the ruling class of a country toward which great numbers of Americans continued to feel distrust and resentment. As a pastime of the English upper crust, cricket seemed incompatible with the egalitarian, democratic ways of the great Western republic. Thus the strident American nationalism of the period, in combination with the complexity and sophistication of cricket, meant that the British game would continue to find its followers mainly among a shrinking number of Americans with close ties to Britain.

Then, too, baseball as a game offered certain intrinsic, structural advantages over cricket. With the ball in play anywhere on the field, and with a side remaining at bat until each of its eleven team members had been put out, cricket matches frequently lasted for days. Comparatively speaking, a baseball game was over in a hurry, rarely taking up more than part of an afternoon. As both European visitors and native observers frequently pointed out, Americans had become an extraordinarily time-conscious people, impatient with delay, more and more regulating their lives by the clock at both work and play.

Moreover, Steven Gelber has written, baseball was an activity that "in many ways . . . replicated and legitimized the social and intellectual environment of the work place." In its orderly inning-by-inning progression, its synthesis of teamwork with individual achievement and expression, its increasing emphasis on records and numbers for measuring both collective and personal performance, and its corporate competitive framework (involving teams, associations, and eventually leagues), baseball was particularly suited to the young male American working in a professional or business occupation. Baseball provided, in Gelber's phrase, "a leisure analog to his job," a form of recreation with distinctly "modern" overtones.

Finally, baseball was inexpensive, fun to play at any skill level, and inchoately adaptable. Playing fields were abundant; equipment was minimal (basically a ball and bat) and, if not affordable, then easily fashioned by players themselves; and neophytes could always find other beginners with whom to play. Lacking cricket's institutionalized history, baseball could be changed as seemed appropriate to make it more appealing to both players and spectators.

Baseball, it seemed, had come along at just the right moment in American history. It was time, said *Porter's Spirit* in 1857, "to set up a game that could be termed a 'Native American Sport.' " Early in 1860 English-born Henry Chadwick, who covered sporting events for the *Brooklyn Eagle* and had only recently become a convert from cricket, published the first book on American baseball. Mainly a compilation of articles Chadwick had written over the past three years for his newspaper, *Beadle's Dime Base Ball Player* offered a testimonial to baseball's healthful, character-building benefits, provided the NABBP's up-to-date rules, and included rudimentary team and player statistics from the 1859 season.

Chadwick also briefly discussed baseball's lineage, which he unequivocally traced to rounders. Yet he also assured his readers that "though of English origin," American baseball represented such an improvement over rounders "as almost to deprive it of any of its original features beyond the mere groundwork of the game."

Porter's Spirit was convinced that baseball "must be regarded as a national pastime." Chadwick went further, maintaining that "this invigorating exercise and manly pastime may be now justly termed the American game of Ball. . . ." The weekly *New York Clipper* pronounced baseball "the National game amongst Americans; and right well does it deserve that appellation." By 1860 those boosters and numerous others were trumpeting baseball as something indigenously American, the great national sport the country had supposedly long needed.

Cricket would undergo something of a renaissance in the 1870s, but its appeal would always remain limited—to immigrants from the British Isles, to a certain number of people in the largely Anglophilic eastern upper classes, and, much later, to newcomers from parts of the world that had once been British colonies. For the great majority of Americans, cricket would simply cease to matter.

By 1861 a number of British-born cricket players, such as Harry Wright, New York's twenty-three-year-old center fielder in the famous 1858 all-star baseball series, had taken up baseball in a serious way, as had an even greater number of native-born young men for whom the game, once only a spare-time activity, had become a consuming passion. The summer months were no longer a period of sweltering drudgery in offices and shops but now a season full of spirited, virile competition, in which one proudly wore the colors of one's club. If in most places baseball remained a game, in the New York area it was already an organized sport, featuring standardized rules, quantified performance, accumulation of records and documents, and an overall governing framework.

The American Civil War had significant but less-than-devastating effects on baseball. Although about two-fifths of all the baseball clubs in Brooklyn and Manhattan ceased to function (particularly hard hit were the numerous "junior" clubs, made up of less-skilled players), most of the better-organized "senior" clubs managed to carry on despite losing some members to military service. The armies both North and South consisted mostly of volunteers, and it was fairly easy to avoid the conscription laws both sides eventually enacted. As a consequence, plenty of able-bodied baseball players remained at home. Big crowds continued to attend matches between the major outfits. An estimated fifteen thousand, for example, watched an Atlantics-Eckfords meeting in September 1862, on the same day that news reached the New York area of one of the war's bloodiest battles, at Antietam Creek in western Maryland.

A popular notion taking root in the decades after the war was that Union soldiers had served as baseball evangelists, carrying knowledge of the game into the southern parts of the country either as they extended their areas of occupation or during confinement in southern prison camps. In fact southern boys, like youths everywhere else, had long played various bat-ball games, while baseball in a club-competitive format already flourished in the prewar years in such cities as Baltimore, Richmond, and New Orleans. Baseball was even played before the war in the distant seaport of Galveston, Texas (contrary to a local fable that Abner Doubleday also instigated baseball there while on a brief postwar military assignment).

Given the appalling conditions in Confederate prison camps, moreover, it seems unlikely that many Union P.O.W.s possessed sufficient health and energy to demonstrate baseball to their captors. One frequently published print of well-clad and ostensibly well-fed Yankees playing baseball in a neat prison compound at Salisbury, North Carolina, could have little relation to reality, given the thirty-four percent death rate among the more than ten thousand men held there—worse even than the infamous prison at Andersonville, Georgia.

Sometimes rebels did learn the New York game while imprisoned, as happened on Johnston's Island in Lake Erie. Typically soldiers played baseball (often cricket as well) within their own armies during the long periods of winter inactivity in the relatively mild climate of the South. The United States Sanitary Commission, the huge extra-governmental medical relief agency organized in the North, officially encouraged soldier participation in amusements and sports, including baseball and cricket.

By the summer of 1865, with four years of civil carnage finally at an end, baseball had not only recovered but entered upon a new period of growth. The New York game had finally eclipsed Philadelphia and New England town ball; in the City of Brotherly Love, the Olympic Club was now part of a lively baseball scene that also included such clubs as the Keystones, the Adriatics, and the powerful Athletics. In 1864–1865, despite occasional threats from Confederate forces striking northward, several games took place in Philadelphia between the city's leading clubs and clubs from Brooklyn, Manhattan, and New Jersey.

Meanwhile the National Association of Base Ball Players continued to make rule changes that would supposedly improve baseball's appeal for both players and spectators. Besides doing away with the one-bounce catch on outfield flies, the NABBP recognized the increasing skill of pitchers by requiring that they deliver the ball (still underhand) with both feet on the ground, confine their motions to a small space, and throw "fair balls" to the "striker." Already authorized to call strikes if the man at bat refused to swing, the umpire could now award the striker first base if the pitcher threw three "unfair" balls. Thus began a process of tinkering with strike-ball combinations that would go on for another twenty-five years.

The first intercollegiate baseball game took place three years after the end of the war, at Worcester, Massachusetts, between Harvard and Yale. (In 1859 Amherst College had defeated Williams College 73–32 in a match played by New England town-ball rules.) In the summer of 1870 the Harvard team traveled by railroad to various places in the "West," including Chicago, Milwaukee, and St. Louis, and won twenty of twenty-five games against college and local clubs. That tour did much to establish baseball as a major sport in the colleges, although within a couple of decades the new rugby-derived game of American football would become the foremost campus enthusiasm.

Although early post–Civil War baseball remained nominally an amateur endeavor, carried on by clubs of genteel sportsmen who observed certain standards of behavior both on and off the playing field, in fact baseball, particularly as it functioned in the major American cities, had become more and more a matter of trying to put the best available talent on the field, with the primary object of winning. Most people seemed to have understood and approved of the changes taking place, which among other things brought a widening gap between those who participated and those who watched.

During the war William H. Cammeyer drained the property in eastern Brooklyn on which he'd operated a skating pond in winter, erected a board fence around it, and opened the Union Grounds as the country's first enclosed baseball facility. He charged ten cents a head to see the Eckfords, Atlantics, Excelsiors, and other Brooklyn clubs in action. A year later two other Brooklyn entrepreneurs sought to emulate Cammeyer's success by building an enclosure called the Capitoline Grounds, in the western part of the city. When the players demanded and received a share of the Union and Capitoline receipts, Chadwick later wrote, "that was really the beginning of professional baseball playing."

Yet professionalism also manifested itself in other ways. Plenty of talented players were prepared to follow the lead of the Brooklyn Excelsiors' James Creighton in taking some form of remuneration for putting their skills at the service of particular clubs. (Creighton himself died in the fall of 1862, at the age of twenty-two, from internal bleeding after he somehow ruptured his abdomen batting a home run against Morrisania.) William Marcy Tweed, the notoriously corrupt boss of New York City, had players for the Mutuals Base Ball Club added to the city payroll so they could compete with the strong Brooklyn clubs and, not incidentally, advertise the Tammany Hall political organization. With civic pride in the burgeoning young city of Chicago suffering from a 49–4 beating administered to the local Excelsiors by the touring Nationals from Washington, D.C., amateur clubs began openly paying some of their players.

Meanwhile such major Chicago businesses as Field, Leiter, Palmer (later Marshall Field) and the Pullman Palace Car Company, as well as dry goods stores, insurance companies, and other concerns, put young men on their payrolls as bookkeepers and clerks primarily to play for company teams. One such hired player was seventeen-year-old Albert Goodwill Spalding, star pitcher for the local Forest City nine of nearby Rockford, who took a job with a Chicago wholesale grocer at $40 a month, with his hours arranged to give him plenty of time for baseball. Initially troubled by the idea of taking money mainly for his baseball skills, young Spalding soon decided that if actors, singers, and musicians got paid for entertaining the public, then it wasn't "wrong to pay a ball player for doing exactly the same thing in his way."

In 1867 the NABBP included more than three hundred member clubs, drawn from seventeen states and the District of Columbia; about a hundred thousand Americans played baseball in organized competition. As yet only a relative few were actually playing for money, but those men were doing quite well for themselves. For 1868, reported the *New York Times*, the country's top seven or eight clubs had totaled about $100,000 in admissions. Players on the three leading Brooklyn clubs earned $600 to $900 per season, paid from the gate receipts after Cammeyer and other operators of ball grounds took their cut. That was good money, especially for a young man, in a period when neither clerks nor manual workers earned more than about $500 a year.

As baseball spread across the country and became largely (in varying degrees) professionalized, two particularly troublesome matters surfaced—one having to do with players' loyalty, the other with their competitive integrity. Many clubs sought to strengthen themselves by enticing rival players to desert their teams. Originating in the prewar years, the practice of "revolving" (as it was called) became acute in the late 1860s as the winning ethic became dominant. During the past three seasons, reported the *Brooklyn Eagle* in 1869, one man had played with six different clubs.

Although the Brooklyn and Manhattan teams signed a few "revolvers," they generally kept hands off each other's players. The newer clubs in the areas west and south were the worst offenders, prompting numerous complaints in the New York sporting press about unscrupulous players who, as Chadwick put it, "have gone off to other clubs without so much as a by your leave." The NABBP officially condemned revolving but was helpless to do much else.

It was probably inevitable that as baseball grew in popularity and commercial success, accusations of game-fixing—"hippodroming," in contemporary parlance—would begin to surface. Operators of baseball grounds sometimes conspired with one or both teams in fixing the outcome of particular games to build up attendance at subsequent games, as in two-out-of-three series. The practice of players and proprietors sharing receipts, said Chadwick, carried with it "a tendency to evil habits. . . ." It would be far better, as far as Chadwick and other observers were concerned, to go ahead and pay the players straight salaries.

As for the effects of gambling, most of the sporting press came to agree that if some people were determined to bet on baseball, then nothing much could be done about it. But everybody agreed that efforts to bribe players to do less than their best on the field couldn't be tolerated if baseball were to survive. Allegations of collusion between players and gamblers were numerous, but only one such episode actually came to light.

In 1865 William Wansley, a player with the New York Mutuals, bribed teammates Thomas Devyr and Ed Duffy to throw a game to the Eckfords. The Mutuals expelled all three. Devyr was reinstated two years later; after that the NABBP gave the Mutuals Club as a whole a clean bill of health. Yet rumors of dishonesty persisted, with the Mutuals, the Atlantics of Brooklyn, and the Athletics of Philadelphia being the most frequently mentioned clubs. Reconciled to spreading professionalism, Chadwick nonetheless lamented that when a player made baseball his principal means of livelihood, "he becomes a more prominent object for the attack of the blacklegs."

Whatever misgivings Chadwick and others might harbor about

players' honesty and the erosion of genteel sportsmanship, professionalism had become entrenched. While a few of the older clubs—
the Brooklyn Excelsiors, Philadelphia Olympics, and Morrisania
Unions, among others—decided to stop paying their players and revert
to pure amateurism, in the major cities the best baseball was played by
clubs that paid at least some of their members.

Late in 1868 the NABBP, still the closest thing to an overall
baseball authority in the country, tacitly recognized its inability to
stem the tide of professionalism when it officially recognized two
classes of players, professionals and amateurs. Two years later, two-
thirds of the delegates to its national convention voted against a resolution that deemed professionalism "reprehensible and injurious to the
best interest of the game," whereupon the advocates of a "game for
recreative exercise" withdrew. For all practical purposes the NABBP
was dead.

By that time a group of young men representing a club in Cincinnati had demonstrated to much of the United States just how well the
game of baseball, in the hands of avowed, salaried professionals, could
be played. The polite pastime of early Knickerbocker Club days was
about to emerge as a full-blown professional sport. As played at the
most expert level, it would always remain so.

2.
The
Professional
Game

The Cincinnati Base Ball Club, organized in July 1866, was a fairly recent addition to the sporting scene in what local promoters proudly called the "Queen City of the West" and detractors had dubbed "Porkopolis." Like many other baseball clubs at that time, its membership was far larger than the number of men who actually played the game with any regularity. Several hundred of the most prominent and civic-minded Cincinnatians paid dues to the club, which soon merged with the local Union Cricket Club and thereby acquired the services of William Henry "Harry" Wright, who'd been the Unions' instructor and number one bowler.

Born in Sheffield, England, in 1835, Harry Wright had come to the United States as an infant with his parents and grown up in New York City. After ending his schooling at fourteen, he worked for a jewelry manufacturer and bowled for the famous Dragonslayers of the St. George Cricket Club, headquartered on Staten Island and coached by Harry's father, Samuel, who'd been a professional cricketeer in England.

Soon, though, Harry Wright as well as his brother George, twelve years younger, found themselves drawn to the baseball they watched being played by the Knickerbockers at the Elysian Fields, where the Dragonslayers also frequently held their matches. Harry joined the

Knickerbockers, while George, by the time he was fifteen, was already good enough to play for the Gothams' senior squad.

Neither Harry nor George Wright felt compelled to interrupt his ballplaying for the sake of saving the Federal Union. As the Wrights continued to play baseball in the Civil War years, they also maintained their ties to cricket. In 1865 Harry was even willing to return to cricket full-time for the $1,200 the Unions of Cincinnati offered him, while George played cricket for both the St. George and Philadelphia clubs, as well as baseball for the Gothams, Morrisania Unions, and Washington, D.C., Nationals.

In 1868 Harry Wright agreed to serve as player-captain of the Cincinnati Base Ball Club for the same $1,200 he'd drawn from the Union cricketeers; and that decision turned out to have profound consequences for the development of the game the members of the Knickerbocker Base Ball Club had started playing for their own amusement in the 1840s. For one thing, Wright permanently altered baseball attire when he had his men abandon the pantaloons players everywhere had worn up to then, in favor of flannel knickers and woolen stockings. Combined with jockey-style caps (already sported by some baseball clubs, while others still wore flat-brimmed hats) and half-sleeved flannel blouses with soft collars, the Cincinnati garb established the basic elements of the baseball uniform that would still be worn more than a century later. Because their stockings were a bright red, their followers quickly started calling them the "Red Stockings."

For another thing, Wright insisted that his players take their baseball as seriously as he did. His regular practice sessions were more than the usual leisurely round of throwing, batting, and socializing. Wright drilled his men in what to do when certain situations arose during a game, encouraged them to keep in good condition, and generally functioned more as a "manager" than anybody up to then had.

The club's most dynamic member was a twenty-six-year-old lawyer named Aaron B. Champion. Not much of a player himself, Champion exemplified a familiar American type emerging in the mid-nineteenth century—the hard-driving civic booster who identified his own well-being with that of his town and sought to publicize its virtues and promote its growth. One way to advertise Cincinnati, Champion believed, would be to field the best possible baseball club. The local talent was pretty good, good enough to produce seventeen victories against only one loss in 1867. That one loss, though, was a 53–10 trouncing by the Nationals of Washington, whose star player was shortstop George Wright.

With assurances from Champion and associates that he could spend whatever he needed to, Harry Wright headed east in search of talent and returned with four professionals who would help make the still nominally amateur Red Stockings one of the country's most powerful clubs. Ranging as far east as Brooklyn and west to St. Louis, Wright's 1868 team won forty-one out of forty-eight games. A hard-fought series with the Morrisania Unions, for whom George Wright now played, ended inconclusively when the Unions refused to play the deciding game, thereby holding on to their mythical national championship.

In 1869 the Red Stockings "threw down the gauntlet of defiance to the National Association of Base Ball Players . . . by a manly declaration that henceforth it would be known as a professional organization." That was the way Albert G. Spalding, recalling his own excitement upon reading about the Red Stockings in Rockford, Illinois, later described their action. The Cincinnati club was far from the first to pay its players; it may not even have been the first all-professional club. It was, though, the first to announce publicly that it had gone all-professional, the first to put its players under season-long contracts, and the first to issue stock to finance its operations.

Only one native Cincinnatian—first baseman Charlie Gould—would wear a Red Stockings uniform in the coming season. Gould and right fielder Cal McVey, from Indianapolis, were the only non-Easterners on the ten-man squad that included George Wright, who joined his brother Harry in the Queen City for a salary of $1,400, the most money anybody had ever made for playing baseball. Already one of the most-admired players in the East, George Wright, at twenty-two, hadn't yet raised the muttonchop whiskers he would later sport. He stood 5-9½, weighed around 150 pounds, and, besides being a fast runner and outstanding batter, was unequaled in throwing prowess at shortstop, where he inaugurated the practice of positioning himself back of the baseline. As a result of his exploits with the Red Stockings, Wright would become baseball's first nationally celebrated player.

The Red Stockings swept away everything (or nearly everything) before them. They won fifty-six games without a loss, not including several unofficial exhibitions against lesser clubs that captain Wright wouldn't count. (They did tie one game when the Troy, New York, Haymakers deserted the field after six innings so a group of New York City gamblers could keep their stakes.) The meeting with the New York Mutuals—before some seven thousand fans at the Union Grounds in Brooklyn, with another couple of thousand gathered at the Gibson Hotel in Cincinnati to hear the outcome by telegraph—was perhaps the finest baseball game played up to then. Cincinnati pitcher Asa Brainard allowed the Mutuals only two runs, an extraordinary feat in that day, while the Red Stockings rallied for two in the ninth to win 4–2.

After being received by President Ulysses S. Grant and defeating the Nationals in Washington, the Red Stockings went home (thrashing the Wheeling club along the way) to be welcomed by thousands of Cincinnatians and presented with a twenty-seven-foot bat, appropriate for "the heaviest batters in the country." Aaron Champion declared that he would rather be president of the Cincinnati Base Ball Club than president of the United States.

Late in the summer of 1869 the Red Stockings traveled by steamboat and railroad to California, making the last part of the journey on the newly completed Union Pacific–Central Pacific transcontinental link. People in and around San Francisco got a taste of baseball at its best before the Red Stockings returned home to close their season by beating the Mutuals again, as well as the powerful Athletics of Philadelphia. After deducting traveling costs and meeting a $9,300 payroll, Champion reported a profit for the club of $1.25.

Yet the Queen City had gained the kind of national exposure Champion and other boosters had yearned for. Proud Cincinnatians had embraced as their own a group of hired professionals, nearly all of whom had come from somewhere else. Amateur baseball clubs would never again be able to command respect and allegiance equaling that of the successful professional clubs. The Red Stockings' sensational season, Spalding later wrote, "demonstrated at once and for all time the superiority of an organization of ball players, chosen and trained and paid for the work they were engaged to do, over any and all organizations brought together as amateurs. . . ."

In the spring of 1870 the Cincinnati club ran up twenty-seven straight victories, scoring more than one hundred runs on three occasions. In New York they easily disposed of the Mutuals, then met the Brooklyn Atlantics at the Capitoline Grounds. The nine thousand people who paid fifty cents apiece to get in saw a historic game that stood 7–7 at the end of nine innings. Following the customary practice, the Atlantics prepared to leave the grounds, only to have Harry Wright prevail on the umpire to order extra-inning play. In the bottom of the tenth George Wright killed an Atlantics rally by intentionally trapping a pop fly and starting a short-second-first double play (a maneuver subsequently negated by the infield-fly rule). The Red Stockings pushed over two runs in the eleventh, but in the bottom half of the inning, the Atlantics tied the game again, then won it when Charlie Gould threw wildly to third trying to cut off a base runner. The greatest unbeaten streak in baseball history—eighty-three games—had finally ended.

The Red Stockings lost several more times that season, an indication that other partly or fully professional clubs had already caught up to them. In Cincinnati the baseball mania of the previous year had started to cool. The club barely broke even again, and, given its inability to accommodate more than a couple of thousand at its home grounds, it wasn't likely ever to make much money. That November the club stockholders ousted Champion, amid much grumbling about mismanagement and mercenary players. Sensing that their best days in Cincinnati had passed, the Wrights, together with Cal McVey and Charlie Gould, joined a new club in Boston, which quickly purloined the nickname Red Stockings. The remaining Cincinnati players ended up with the Washington Olympics.

Meanwhile the National Association of Base Ball Players had fallen apart over the issue of professionalism. Led by the Excelsiors of Brooklyn and the Knickerbockers of New York, thirty-three amateur clubs formed their own "Amateur National Association," and for four years they tried to buck the trend toward professionalism. Even after

the amateur association disbanded in 1874, the Knickerbockers and a
few other clubs carried on for a while with dues-paying young men
who played intrasquad and occasional interclub games, pretty much as
such clubs had done in the forties and fifties. Among the amateur
outfits of the early 1870s was the once-celebrated Cincinnati Base Ball
Club, which, having established the superiority of the out-and-out
professional game to the satisfaction of millions of Americans, had
quietly reverted to baseball for the fun of it.

The country's professional baseball players, less attached to particular clubs than to their new profession, formed their own organization. In March 1871, in New York City, delegates from ten professional clubs, representing about one hundred players, brought into
being the National Association of Professional Base Ball Players
(NAPBBP). If one stressed "professional" in the title of the new body,
then it looked like a radical departure in baseball history. What was
more significant, as things turned out, was the fact that avowedly
professional players still thought in terms of a loose "association" in
which they, as players, would have the decisive voice.

Nine clubs paid their ten-dollar membership fees and thus qualified to compete for the "national base ball championship," symbolized
by a bright pennant. Although the NAPBBP retained the rule against
"revolving" adopted under the NABBP, contracts were usually informal. Some of the clubs had individual or partnership financial backing; others were cooperative ventures financed by stockholders. No
comprehensive schedule was adopted; each club would arrange its own
playing dates, provided it met every other club five times. The club
with the greatest number of wins at the close of the season (November
1) could claim the championship pennant.

Of course, the new professional association wouldn't have been
possible if not for the intricate railroad system that had come into being
in the northeastern quadrant of the United States. Basically completed
in the 1850s, northeastern rail service rapidly improved in the early
post–Civil War period with the construction of numerous trunk lines.

Besides the railroads, other kinds of new technology—the telegraph, typewriter, and adding machine, and later the telephone—
undergirded the rise of professional baseball within an organized
competitive structure. Along with printing innovations that reduced

production costs and generated a mass readership for daily newspapers, such inventions made it possible to communicate results in-
stantly, inform a growing sporting public of the game-by-game progress
of different clubs, and keep track of the statistical data that soon
became a familiar part of baseball's appeal. All of that, in turn, facili-
tated the growth of sportswriting as a distinct form of journalism.

The NAPBBP survived its inaugural season despite the midyear
withdrawal of the Fort Wayne, Indiana, club (replaced by the
Brooklyn Eckfords) and the necessity for the other clubs to come to the
aid of the Chicago White Stockings after their new lakefront ballpark
burned in the great fire that all but destroyed that city in October. The
homeless White Stockings managed to finish the season on the road,
compile the second-best winning percentage in the Association, and
even show a $2,000 profit, but over the winter they dropped out of the
NAPBBP.

Chicago's loss to the Athletics on the last day of the 1871 season
gave the Philadelphia entry twenty-two wins. Harry Wright's Boston
Red Stockings won as many games and claimed a tie for the championship, but inasmuch as the Athletics had lost only seven games to
Boston's ten, the rest of the clubs recognized Philadelphia as the
pennant winner.

At that point, the professional players still controlled the
NAPBBP, but as David Voight has observed, "it was to be a short-lived
worker's paradise." In succeeding seasons the players proved unable to
enforce schedule commitments or otherwise manage their Association
in a competent, reliable fashion. That was one fundamental weakness
of the NAPBBP; the other was absolute domination by Wright's Boston
club after that first closely competitive season.

Wright was far ahead of the other captain-managers of his day.
Besides schooling his players on what to do, he tailored the talents of
each man to the club's particular needs. When aspiring youngsters
inquired about how they could become successful professionals, he
advised them to "live regularly, keep good hours, and abstain from
intoxicating drinks and tobacco." They must also, he said, be punctual
for practice and serious about their playing. "Professional ball playing
is *business*," he wrote one hopeful, "and as such, I trust you will regard
it while the season lasts."

Wright's methods produced four consecutive NAPBBP champions from 1872 to 1875. The last was the most powerful, running up a 71–8 record, scoring 832 runs, compiling a .326 team batting average, and finishing 173 percentage points ahead of the second-place Athletics. Harry Wright, at the age of forty, took part in only one game that season; but George Wright batted .337 and scored 105 runs, and second baseman Roscoe "Ross" Barnes batted .372, with 116 runs. Albert G. Spalding, having joined the Red Stockings for the NAPBBP's inaugural season, became the outstanding pitcher in the country. In 1875, still in his mid-twenties, a robust 6-1 and 170 pounds, Spalding pitched in all but four of Boston's games, winning fifty-seven and losing only five, besides batting .318.

Such records on individual performance appeared regularly in the sporting press; Henry Chadwick's annual baseball guide, which had originally listed only "average runs per game" for different players, now listed five different season categories for batters and three for pitchers. Chadwick's box score, moreover, had become the standard method for keeping track of a game in progress and encapsulating it the next day in print. Baseball statistics had become a vital part of the way people enjoyed, understood, and appreciated America's first modern team sport.

Following the 1873 championship season (the Red Stockings' second), Harry Wright and young Spalding conceived the idea of a British tour to promote the American game of baseball among people still wedded to cricket. Amazingly, the tour was scheduled for the middle of the 1874 NAPBBP season, necessitating arrangements that allowed both the Red Stockings and the Athletics, who also took part in the tour, to cram their games in at the beginning and the end of the season. Although it was a financial failure, the tour did put on display "the cricket of the American continent," as one British newspaper described baseball. Not for the last time, American baseball promoters failed to make much of an impression on their British cousins.

The game the Americans exhibited in Britain and played professionally under the NAPBBP hadn't changed greatly since the codification of rules in the late 1850s. One-bounce catches on fly balls in fair territory had been discarded under the old NABBP, but one-bounce outs on foul balls were still allowed. Consequently first and third basemen played on top of their bases, so as to be able to move quickly for foul bounces. The pitcher still delivered the ball to the "batsman" or "batter" (the term "striker" had pretty much passed out of usage) from forty-five feet. The ball still had to be pitched where the batter indicated—"high ball" or "low ball"—and if the pitcher missed the called-for location nine times, the batter was entitled to "take his base."

Although the rules still specified that the pitcher's arm must remain below his belt, Spalding and others had learned to throw in three-quarter-underhand fashion, with a great deal of speed and often with a wrist snap that produced varieties of drops and curves—an innovation credited to Arthur "Candy" Cummings of the Brooklyn Excelsiors. Thus, at least at the professional level, the confrontation between pitcher and batter had already become the game's essential feature.

Nobody wore gloves of any kind in the early seventies, not even the catcher, who consequently positioned himself at least ten feet behind the home base. Catchers started wearing wire masks later in the decade, but the physical toll on the man behind the bat—in the form of broken fingers and wounds inflicted on various parts of the anatomy—continued to be heavy. Umpires, by contrast, still stood or sat some distance off to the side. Players might have professionalized themselves, but the game official was still usually a local citizen willing to take on what was a thankless task and sometimes, given the professional preoccupation with winning, a stressful one.

The regulation baseball in the NAPBBP was smaller and harder (at least at the start of a game) than what had commonly been used in the 1850s. In weight and size, it was the same ball that would be in use more than a century later—five and a quarter ounces, nine and a quarter inches in circumference. By the 1870s, such balls were being mass-produced by various manufacturers and sold in "sporting goods" stores in all the major cities, including one Harry and George Wright had opened in New York City.

The men who made up the club rosters in the NAPBBP still came almost entirely from the lower-middle and skilled working classes, and the great majority came from the northeastern part of the United States, with New York, Brooklyn, and Philadelphia being the most

common birthplaces. A few, such as Spalding and Cal McVey, hailed
from the midwestern states, while others had been born in England,
Scotland, Wales, or Ireland. English and Scottish names predominated; the great tide of Irish-descended baseball players wouldn't
arrive until the eighties and nineties. (Lipman Pike, who captained
four clubs in the NAPBBP, was the first Jewish professional ballplayer.)

The pay those early professionals received averaged around
$1,000, with leading players commanding at least twice that much and
the one or two substitutes on each club receiving as little as $500. As
the biggest money-maker in the Association, Boston also had the
biggest payroll—$20,685 by 1875.

The game the professionals played had great spectator appeal in
terms of particular "crucial" contests, which sometimes drew crowds
of ten to twelve thousand. On a season-by-season basis, though, the
NAPBBP was a poorly organized, poorly administered, unprofitable
way to run professional baseball. In 1875, of thirteen clubs competing
in the Association, only seven managed to put in a full season.

Young Albert G. Spalding, among others, believed that he understood what was wrong with the NAPBBP. Professional baseball, he
said late in 1875, should be controlled by businessmen who would be
in charge of "conducting the details of managing men, administering
discipline, arranging schedules and finding ways and means of financ-
ing a team." That winter Spalding parted ways with Harry Wright's
Boston club and signed as player-captain with the Chicago White
Stockings, who'd reentered the NAPBBP in 1874. Spalding was soon
followed by teammates Barnes, McVey, and James "Deacon" White, as
well as by Adrian Anson, the Athletics' powerful young first baseman.

The driving force behind Chicago baseball was William A.
Hulbert, director of the White Stockings club. Hulbert, a portly man
in his mid-forties, had never played the game, but he believed in its
direct profit potential as a professional sport, as well as its usefulness
for boosting general business activity in Chicago. Hulbert intended
not only to build a winner in the fire-ravaged, still-rebuilding city, but
to form a whole new baseball organization. Quickly obtaining support
in St. Louis, Louisville, and Cincinnati, Hulbert on February 2, 1876,
convened interested parties from those cities as well as New York,

Philadelphia, Boston, and Hartford. Meeting at the Grand Hotel in Manhattan, Hulbert and associates founded the National League of Professional Base Ball Clubs.

The operative words were "league" (not "association") and "clubs" (not "players"). By assessing each club $100 per year, the National League would be able to maintain a permanent central office with a president and secretary-treasurer. At Hulbert's urging, the club representatives elected Morgan G. Bulkeley, a well-known Hartford banker, as League president, and Nicholas E. "Nick" Young, a Washington congressional clerk who'd been secretary-treasurer in the NAPBBP, to the same position in the National League.

The new League would consist of eight clubs: Chicago, New York, Boston, Philadelphia, Cincinnati, St. Louis, Louisville, and Hartford. Besides mandating a regular playing schedule, the club representatives agreed on a standard division of gate receipts between hosts and visitors and, in a notable advance over NAPBBP practices, specified a $5-per-game fee for umpires. Seeking to project an image of Christian propriety, they forbade any club to schedule Sunday games or sell alcoholic beverages on its grounds. To keep out the riffraff and presumably attract well-behaved customers, they also set the basic admission price at fifty cents (equivalent to at least six late-twentieth-century dollars), with an allowable surcharge for covered grandstand seats.

Hulbert's bold initiatives destroyed the NAPBBP, leaving such clubs as the Brooklyn Atlantics, the Washington Nationals, and the New Havens out in the cold. Professional players either held on with their old clubs when they affiliated with the new League, scrambled to fill the few open spots, dropped down to one of the half-dozen or so "minor" professional associations that had come into being in recent years, or caught on with independent pro clubs. The level of play in the National League for 1876 was probably a notch higher than it had been in the NAPBBP.

The scrapping of the NAPBBP and the appearance of the National League hardly inaugurated a baseball millennium. The National League was a considerably more centralized, regularized organization in which essential power had unquestionably passed from players to the financiers and directors of the professional clubs; yet in its early history the League was able to achieve neither stability nor, for most of its members, consistent profits.

As had been generally predicted, the Chicago powerhouse Hulbert had put together easily won the first National League pennant, with a 52–14 record to St. Louis's 45–19. Barnes led the League with a .429 batting average and 126 runs, while Spalding pitched all but five of his club's victories. Chicago and maybe one or two other clubs made money; but the New York Mutuals and Philadelphia Athletics, representing the two largest cities in the country, finished sixth and seventh, respectively, did poorly at the gate, and refused to make the trip west for their final games of the season. In response to the first serious challenge to the authority of the new organization, the other club directors, at Hulbert's urging, voted to expel both New York and Philadelphia—despite an emotional plea for mercy from Harry Wright. Thus the League would begin its second season with only six clubs and without its two potentially biggest money-makers.

Boston, still led by Harry Wright, with George Wright still at shortstop and Deacon White, back from Chicago, playing various positions and leading the League in batting, won the 1877 pennant. At Chicago, captain Spalding had given up pitching for first base, which was one reason the White Stockings slumped to seventh place. Spalding retired altogether following the 1877 season, having found wider fields for his talents. Besides purchasing stock in the Chicago club, he'd opened a sporting goods "emporium" in the city, in partnership with his brother Walter (and later still another brother). Hulbert's influence brought them a windfall in the form of exclusive rights to supply baseballs for the National League.

What Spalding sold to the League that year and for decades thereafter was essentially the same "dead ball" used in the Association. It consisted of a hard rubber core wrapped in wool yarn and covered in stitched horsehide. It didn't carry as well off the bat as the balls of previous decades and, left in play inning after inning, tended to soften and deaden still further. The dead ball, in combination with increasingly skilled pitching, made for a gradual decline in batting statistics over the next several years.

Those and other statistics were officially published at the end of each season, beginning in 1877, by A. G. Spalding and Brothers.

Henry Chadwick, at first a harsh critic of the League for its "cloak-and-dagger tactics" in subverting the Association and abandoning several clubs, was soon mollified when Spalding named him editor of *Spalding's Official Base Ball Guide*, a position he would continue to hold until his death in 1908.

Within little more than a decade, Spalding's firm had absorbed such competitors as Reach and Company and Wright and Ditson, and had opened its own plant at Chicopee, Massachusetts. Proclaiming as his motto "Everything is possible to him who dares," the young entrepreneur was on his way to gaining a virtual monopoly in the manufacture and distribution of quality sporting equipment. Meanwhile Spalding was steadily increasing his stock holdings in the Chicago club. By the time he became its president following Hulbert's death in 1882, he was a powerful voice in League affairs.

Facing another season as a six-club circuit, still minus New York and Philadelphia, the struggling League endured its worst trial late in 1877. The previous August the Louisville Grays had built a big lead over Boston, only to blow it late in September and finish seven games behind Harry Wright's club. Even before the season closed, the Louisville *Courier-Journal* began hinting and then stating bluntly that star pitcher Jim Devlin and other Grays had deliberately lost the pennant.

Hulbert, now League president, convened the club directors to investigate the *Courier-Journal*'s charges. At the end of October the League officially expelled Devlin, shortstop Bill Craver, outfielder George Hall, and substitute Al Nichols; three of the four players had confessed under Hulbert's dogged questioning. The quartet had conspired with a New York gambler named McCloud to lose games when they were favored, and then to split McCloud's winnings with him. Devlin got about $150; the other three divided an equal amount.

The banishments gutted the Louisville club, which dropped from the League over the winter. Accusations of bribery and dishonest playing had become common in the sixties, and had continued to come up frequently in the years of the NAPBBP. Like most business executives in the late nineteenth century, Hulbert and his colleagues were at best paternalistic autocrats who treated their employees as little more than children. Yet if the National League were to survive as a professional organization in which people could have any confidence, then decisive, ruthless action against confessed fixers was a necessity.

Devlin persistently sought reinstatement, writing Harry Wright, "I am living from hand to mouth all winter I have not got a Stitch of Clothing or has my wife and Child." Hulbert gave the pitcher $50 while muttering, "Damn you, you have sold a game, you are dishonest, and this National League will not stand for it." Subsequently the club directors officially resolved never to rescind the action taken against the Louisville quartet.

For 1878 Indianapolis replaced Louisville, while Providence and Milwaukee also entered the League, in place of Hartford and St. Louis—a reshuffling scarcely likely to strengthen anybody financially. At the same time, the club bosses moved to extend their authority over professional baseball as a whole by proclaiming something called the "League Alliance." For a $10 membership fee, "minor" professional leagues could place themselves under the protection of the National League, which meant basically a recognition of territorial rights, players' contracts, and "black lists" of players under suspension or banishment. Thus was laid the foundation for what would later become "Organized Baseball."

On limped the League, through 1878 (which brought still another Boston championship) and into the next season. By 1879 Milwaukee and Indianapolis were gone; Cleveland, Buffalo, Troy, and Syracuse joined to restore the original eight-club structure. Half the cities in the League were simply too small to operate profitably. Providence, now managed by George Wright, won the 1879 pennant behind the superb pitching of nineteen-year-old John Montgomery "Monte" Ward. Yet the champions drew fewer than 43,000 people at home and lost money.

As did runner-up Boston, for the fourth straight year. In response, Arthur Soden, president of the Boston club, slashed salaries, advertising outlays, and travel expenses. The once well-accommodated Red Stockings were reduced to staying in third-rate hotels and eating on an allowance of seventy-five cents per day. The players took out their resentments in rebellion against Harry Wright's managerial regimen, and Soden fired the dedicated baseball pioneer following a sixth-place showing in 1880.

Soden's iron hand typified the way the National League club owners felt and acted toward their highly skilled employees. Before the 1880 season, for example, they announced that henceforth injured players wouldn't be paid unless they were "conscientious, earnest, [and] deserving." Players were generally overpaid anyway, thought League secretary-treasurer Nick Young, and, besides, they squandered whatever money they had. "It comes and it goes," he wrote Harry Wright, "and at the end of the season they are hard up as usual, and have little or no idea what has become of it, unless, perchance, some one had induced [them] to invest in a large gold watch."

In September 1879, in Buffalo, the presidents of the various clubs moved to tighten their control over the players. Specifically, they sought to eradicate "revolving," which had continued to cause frequent roster shuffles in the years since the formation of the League. The device they hit upon, originally known as the "reserve rule" and agreed to secretly, gave each club an exclusive right to sign a player from one season to the next. At first the rule covered only five players per club, a little less than half a roster. In the years to come, though, the annual "reserve list" would be steadily expanded to include everybody under contract in a given year.

The reserve rule (or "reserve clause," as it was called later on, when it was openly incorporated into players' contracts) aimed both to stabilize club finances and keep labor costs under control. The object of the reserve rule, Spalding later conceded, was "to prevent competition for the best players . . . and to keep those clubs together." In the immediate circumstances, rumor had it, the object was to keep the Chicago club, the only regular money-maker, from cornering most of the talent in the League. If so, it didn't work.

In 1879 Syracuse had its fling in major-league baseball and gave way to Worcester, Massachusetts, as Hulbert and his confederates still righteously refused to readmit the miscreants from New York and Philadelphia. The 1880 Worcester club finished fifth, 26½ games out of first place, but even second-place Providence ended up fourteen games behind Chicago. Rebuilt by Hulbert, Spalding, and Adrian Anson, the White Stockings were the finest collection of baseball players the sport had seen. Over the next six seasons (1881–1886) they would gather four more National League pennants.

Anson, who'd become captain (field manager) in 1878, was no Harry Wright. He had little interest in tactics, preferring to assemble the best men he could get and then send them out to play the game. A native Iowan, blond and blue-eyed, sporting a carefully waxed handlebar mustache, Anson stood an inch over six feet and weighed two hundred pounds in his prime. If he'd played fifty or sixty years later, "Cap," as his players called him, would have hit many, many home runs. As it was, he amassed 3,041 base hits and a .334 batting average in twenty-two years in the National League (not counting five in the NAPBBP). If George Wright had been the leading player of the seventies, Anson was probably the best of the eighties.

But not by much. Besides such top-notch players as shortstop Tommy Burns, third baseman Ed Williamson, outfielder Abner Dalrymple, and catcher Frank "Silver" Flint, the White Stockings had Mike "King" Kelly, arguably the most popular and colorful competitor baseball had seen. The Troy, New York, native had started playing professionally in 1873 with the local Haymakers, when he was only thirteen; just before the reserve rule went into force, he jumped the Cincinnati club for bigger money in Chicago. Remarkably versatile even for that period's less-specialized game, he played every position except pitcher during his seventeen-season major-league career, although he was behind the bat or in the outfield most of the time.

Kelly did everything well, but his basepath derring-do and head-first dives into bases especially thrilled his admirers, who yelled "Slide, Kelly, Slide!" and hailed him as "the King of the Diamond." The first great player of Irish-Catholic ancestry, Kelly attracted numerous sons (and daughters) of Erin to the Chicago ballpark and wherever else he played. In keeping with the winning imperative of professionalism, he mastered the rules and took advantage of every possible loophole, as well as the inability of the sole umpire to watch everything at once.

Kelly's assortment of tricks included cutting inside bases to reduce the distance to his destination, and bumping or holding opposing base runners. On one occasion he did such a convincing pantomime of making a catch against the fence in near-darkness, on a ball that went out of the park, that the umpire signaled the third out and the game over. Another time he was sitting on the White Stockings bench when an opponent's pop foul looped in his direction; jumping to his feet and yelling "Kelly in for Flint," he caught the ball. Under the rules as then written, the umpire had no choice but to call the batter out.

That day the King may have been nursing a hangover, as was frequently the case. Darkly handsome, a dapper dresser, always a favorite with both spectators and teammates, and a hugely talented athlete, Kelly was also an irresponsible drunk whose binges were the curse of Anson's life as a manager. Sometimes Kelly didn't show up for games; other days he took the field drunk. On one of those days he muffed an easy fly ball, then cheerily yelled in to Anson, "By God, Cap, I made it hit me hand, anyhow." How good Kelly may have been with more professional commitment and self-discipline can only be conjectured. Kelly as he was was plenty good.

In 1881 Kelly and his teammates again finished comfortably ahead of Providence (with Anson batting .399 to lead the league). Next season, though, the Grays, now managed by Harry Wright, battled the White Stockings the whole way. Anson's club ended the season by sweeping three games from Buffalo, which had transferred the series to Chicago in the expectation of making bigger profits there than at home, and those three victories provided the final margin over Providence. When Harry Wright vigorously protested the switching of game sites and much of the sporting press backed him up, Anson and Spalding (the new club president) agreed to a postseason series with the Grays, won by Chicago.

By the early eighties the stubborn business depression that had held on through most of the previous decade had finally passed, and the country was entering a period of unprecedented peacetime economic growth. In the generally prosperous times, the National League gained a somewhat firmer footing, even though it still included Worcester and Troy, hardly major-league cities. Detroit was now also a member, having replaced Cincinnati after the 1880 season.

In their continuing campaign to sell the League as upright and God-fearing, the club presidents voted to expel Cincinnati when the operators of the Queen City franchise wouldn't pledge to stop holding games on Sundays and selling liquor on the grounds. Although Cincinnati had fielded a terrible team in 1880, it was potentially one of the strongest cities in the League. Operating profitably, though, meant

appealing to the city's big German population, which favored the
Continental Sabbath, liked Sunday-afternoon amusements, and liked
beer with its baseball.

Thus because of the League's persistence in its Sabbatarianism
and anti-liquor policy, the city that could boast of being the birthplace
of professional ball had to go its own way. That way soon led to the
formation of another professional league, an organization that would
first challenge the National League's monopoly in major-league baseball, then reach an uneasy peace that in turn would break down when
the players decided to take matters into their own hands.

3.
The National
Pastime
and the
Serfs'
Revolt

The League Alliance created by the National League in the late seventies hadn't stopped independent entrepreneurs from operating profitable professional clubs outside the Alliance, or from violating the League's territorial claims. The Inter-State League, for example, installed a franchise in New York City over the National League's insistence that, despite its expulsion of the New York club after the 1876 season, it still possessed exclusive rights to operate there.

Obviously the National League had failed to exploit to the fullest the profit potential in professional baseball. While the League had brought in such weak sisters as Syracuse, Worcester, Troy, and Providence, it continued to shun New York and Philadelphia, dropped St. Louis and Louisville, expelled Cincinnati, and ignored such promising baseball markets as Brooklyn, Pittsburgh, and Baltimore. Led by O. P. Caylor, a Cincinnati sportswriter, a group of well-to-do baseball enthusiasts determined to change all that.

In the fall of 1882 they met in Cincinnati and founded the American Association of Base Ball Clubs, which they intended to promote as a full-fledged major league. Franchises were awarded to six cities: Cincinnati, Philadelphia, Baltimore, St. Louis, Pittsburgh, and Louisville. The American Association delegates copied the National League's playing rules and constitution, though remaining silent on the reserve rule (which hadn't yet been formalized in the League). Inasmuch as the principal financial backers of four of the Association franchises were saloon and brewery owners (three with distinctively German backgrounds), the Association sanctioned the sale of liquor on the grounds as well as games on Sundays in those cities—Cincinnati, Louisville, and St. Louis—where local laws didn't prohibit such Sabbath amusements. Finally, the base admission price for Association games was set at only twenty-five cents.

Dennis McKnight of St. Louis, elected president of the Association, invited any and every National League player to come over to the new circuit. Only one, catcher Charles "Pop" Snyder of Boston, defied the reserve rule and signed with an Association entry; others threatened to do so and won pay increases from League clubs. Forty-six men with earlier National League experience found their way onto Association rosters, but the Louisville Eclipse, good enough to finish in third place, consisted entirely of a strong semipro club that had operated there for several years.

Even though just about everybody agreed that the level of play in the new circuit was distinctly inferior to that in the National League, the Cincinnati Reds, winners of the first Association pennant with a 55–25 record, boldly challenged both Cleveland, fifth-place finishers in the League, and the mighty Chicago White Stockings, League champs for the third year in a row. Despite president McKnight's expressed disapproval of interleague play, the Reds first dropped three of five games to Cleveland, then surprised even their own supporters by winning the opening game against Cap Anson's club behind the shutout pitching of Will White, the first major-leaguer to play in spectacles. After Chicago's Larry Corcoran bested White the next day, the White Stockings moved on to keep other postseason commitments, leaving Cincinnati boosters bragging that their Reds were the equal of anybody in the National League.

All-out war between the two organizations loomed during the off-season of 1882–1883. In New York, John B. Day headed a group called the Metropolitan Exhibition Company that took advantage of the situation to obtain franchises from both the League and the Association. Dropping Troy and Worcester, the League also reentered Philadelphia, where the Phillies (as the new club quickly came to be called) would compete for customers with the Association Athletics. Meanwhile McKnight and his cohorts established an eighth franchise in Columbus, Ohio's capital but only its third-largest city.

The initiative for peace came not from the "beer league," as the Nationals scornfully referred to the Association, but from the senior circuit. Abraham G. Mills, who'd become League president on William Hulbert's death in the spring of 1882, invited McKnight as well as Elias Mather, president of the Northwestern League (a strong minor circuit), to a parley in New York City. Mills argued that the competition for talent had given the players the upper hand, just as they'd enjoyed before the adoption of the reserve rule in 1879. Ruin awaited all unless a settlement was reached.

McKnight and Mather acknowledged sharing Mills's fears. Eventually they signed a "National Agreement" that extended the reserve rule to all three leagues, set a minimum $1,000 salary for each of eleven players annually reserved by each club, and affirmed that no "revolver" would be signed by any other club. The National League officially recognized the Association's "major" status; the Northwestern League was designated a "high minor" circuit. The three leagues also agreed to adopt the same Spalding-supplied baseball used in the National League from its inception. Other operating leagues and associations were invited to put themselves under the National Agreement. By the end of the year eight more circuits had joined what was now officially designated "Organized Base Ball."

Quickly ratified by the club owners in all three leagues, the National Agreement made possible professional baseball's most profitable season. In 1883 each major league drew more than a million customers, although the profits were smaller in the Association, with its twenty-five-cent seats. But with the sole exception of the Association's New York Metropolitans, everybody made money. Christian Von der Ahe, the florid and flamboyant German-born owner of the St. Louis Browns, boasted that he'd cleared $70,000 on "mein poys."

The Athletics, led by the strong batting of native Philadelphian Harry Stovey, edged Von der Ahe's Browns by one game. Cincinnati was a near third, with Will White pitching forty victories for the second straight year. Embarrassed in a preliminary postseason series with the Phillies, the Athletics decided not to challenge the

Boston Red Stockings, who'd finally dethroned the Chicago White Stockings.

In fact, the times were so good that still another group of baseball capitalists proclaimed their intention of starting up still another putative major league. The National Agreement had been in force less than six months when, on September 12, 1883, the Union Association was formed in Pittsburgh. Declaring that they'd respect all existing contracts in the National League and the Association, the Unions nonetheless refused to "recognize any agreement whereby any number of ballplayers may be reserved . . . beyond the term of their contracts. . . ." That fall the "wreckers," as League president Mills termed the Unions, appealed to players from the other circuits to refuse to sign 1884 contracts and to join the reserve-less new league. In turn the National League and American Association owners officially resolved to blacklist anybody who did so.

Led by Henry V. Lucas, a young St. Louis railroad heir who loved baseball so much that he built his own ballpark on his suburban estate, the Unions challenged the other two leagues head-on in St. Louis, Chicago, Cincinnati, Philadelphia, Washington, Baltimore, and Boston, and also franchised a club in Altoona, Pennsylvania. Adopting the livelier Wright and Ditson ball, they promised spectators plenty of base hits and runs. They also claimed to have enlisted many recruits from National and Association clubs, although except for infielder Fred Dunlap (from Cleveland), pitcher Charley Sweeney (from Providence), and one or two others, the fear of blacklisting served to intimidate players into staying put.

Encouraged by their National League counterparts to move into new territory before the Unions got there, the Association owners rashly expanded to twelve clubs; new franchises were placed in Indianapolis, Brooklyn, Toledo, and Washington. Thus the 1884 season began with twenty-eight teams in three leagues, all pretending to offer top-quality baseball.

Whatever slim chances the Union Association may have had at the outset were destroyed by Lucas's entirely too-successful efforts to field a winner in St. Louis. His Maroons ran away from the rest of the clubs, wrapping up the championship by late July and finishing with a 94–19 record. Cincinnati, Baltimore, Boston, and Washington managed to play out the season; but the remaining four clubs gave way, sooner or later, to Milwaukee, St. Paul, Kansas City, and Wilmington, Delaware.

In the American Association everybody completed the schedule except the Washington club, which transferred to Richmond, Virginia, in August. All eight clubs survived in the National League, but they, like professional baseball as a whole that strange year, saw profits turn into deficits. Only one of the six minor leagues starting the season made it to the end of the summer.

But if fewer people paid to watch baseball in 1884, what they saw was often memorable. In the American Association the New York Metropolitans, owned by the same people who owned the city's National League franchise and bolstered by players transferred from the League's Giants as needed, finished comfortably ahead of the collection of unknowns that made up the Columbus team.

Providence won going away in the National League on Charles "Hoss" Radbourne's pitching heroics, which were amazing even by the standards of that time. Ill-tempered and contentious, Radbourne was twenty-nine years old at the start of the 1884 season, stood 5-9, and weighed about 165 pounds. After turning down an offer from the Unions, he had a run-in with manager Frank Bancroft and found himself relegated to number two pitcher behind Charley Sweeney. A hard-drinking Californian, Sweeney ran up seventeen victories, got into a row of his own with Bancroft, and jumped to the St. Louis Unions. At that juncture Radbourne offered to pitch every remaining game until the Grays clinched the pennant, if the club's owners would agree to his release after the season.

Given that assurance, Radbourne started (and finished) thirty-five of the Grays' last thirty-seven games and ended with sixty victories (of the club's eighty-four) against twelve defeats. It was an unprecedented performance, and one never to be equaled. Radbourne followed up those herculean efforts by pitching three straight victories over the American Association's "Mets" in what was billed as the first "World's Championship Series"—or simply "World Series." A happy Radbourne decided to stay at Providence after all, but his mighty right arm never recovered from the travail of the 1884 campaign.

In the off-season Henry Lucas abandoned the sinking Union

Association in return for the admission of his St. Louis Maroons to the National League. Cleveland was abruptly dropped. League president Mills opposed the move and found himself voted out in favor of the mild-mannered Nick Young. Chris Von der Ahe was even more unhappy over the new National League franchise in St. Louis, until given assurances that the League would maintain its fifty-cent ticket price and continue to prohibit its clubs from playing Sunday baseball or selling liquor at the ballpark—all of which would badly handicap Lucas's operation. Meanwhile the Association strengthened itself by trimming back to eight entries: New York, Brooklyn, St. Louis, Cincinnati, Baltimore, Louisville, Philadelphia, and Pittsburgh.

As it happened, Von der Ahe had no reason to fear the National League's incursion into St. Louis. Lucas's Maroons, no more than a good minor-level outfit when they'd overwhelmed the rest of the Unions, were the worst in the League. After two seasons, Von der Ahe again had the city to himself, with Pittsburgh deserting the American Association to replace the defunct Maroons. Meanwhile Von der Ahe's Browns, finishing fifteen games in front of Cincinnati in 1885, began a run of four consecutive championships, the first team to accomplish that feat since Boston's club in the old NAPBBP.

The St. Louis Browns, a largely Irish-American team, became the darlings of their largely German-American constituency. Mostly young players with only Association experience, they weren't lavishly salaried. The *Sporting News*, the newly founded local baseball paper published each week by the brothers Alfred and Charles Spink, reported in 1886 that Von der Ahe paid his three outfielders $1,800 each, his four infielders $2,000, and his two pitchers and two catchers $2,200. First baseman Charles Comiskey drew an extra $500 as team captain, which in those days meant that he was field manager, business manager, and traveling secretary rolled into one.

Only twenty-three when Von der Ahe made him captain, Comiskey was a native Chicagoan who never became more than an average major-league player. Although later, as a celebrated baseball owner and impresario, he promoted the legend that he'd originated the practice of playing wide of first base, in fact every first and third baseman moved away from the bag after 1883, when the one-bounce catch on foul balls was ruled out. Comiskey was, though, one of the smartest players of his time, and a smart handler of men as well. Not the least of his accomplishments was staying on good terms with the mercurial and overbearing Von der Ahe.

"Vile of speech," "insolent in bearing," "about the toughest and roughest gang that ever struck this city"—so the 1885 Browns impressed editor Francis C. Richter of *Sporting Life*, a weekly tabloid published in Philadelphia. "I believe that kicking is half the game," Comiskey told a reporter in St. Louis. The Browns were the most consistently argumentative, loudmouthed (not to say foulmouthed) group of athletes baseball had seen up to that time—a team that pushed the win-at-any-cost professional ethic to its limits. They were good ballplayers, too, especially James "Tip" O'Neill, a hard-hitting outfielder; pitchers Bob Caruthers and Davey Foutz; and third baseman Arlie Latham, whose ability to rile the opposition earned him the title "The Freshest Man on Earth."

Alongside the rollicking Browns, the Chicago White Stockings, who returned to the top of the National League in 1885, were almost staid. To gain a fourth pennant in six years, Chicago had to pile up eighty-seven wins against only twenty-five losses; bolstered by transfers from the Metropolitans (just as the Mets had been bolstered the previous season), the New York Giants fell only two games short of that lofty record. It was Anson's finest team. Besides Kelly, Gore, Dalrymple, and Williamson, all holdovers from the 1880–1882 champions, Anson and A. G. Spalding had added Fred Pfeffer, a Louisville native and one of the period's foremost second basemen, and Jim McCormick, a burly right-hander who pitched fifty-three victories for the White Stockings—the last time anybody would win that many.

The American Association, still viewed as a lesser league by most nonpartisan observers (insofar as there were any), loudly claimed parity following the 1885 World's Championship Series. Actually it was a standoff, Chicago winning three games and St. Louis three after an opening-game tie that was called when it became too dark to continue play.

Before the next season began, Von der Ahe, as quoted in the broken English with which the sportswriters loved to caricature him, supposedly told his minions: "Of you vin de 'scampionship,' I gif you a suit of clothes and a benefit game extra, and of you don't you vill have to eat snowballs all winter." Whether or not such admonitions from "der Boss President" had any effect, the Browns were even harder to beat in 1886. Far outdistancing Pittsburgh and Brooklyn, they won ninety-three games, more than any baseball club ever had. Caruthers and Foutz combined for seventy-one wins.

The White Stockings were also better, finishing with a 90–34 record. John Clarkson, a handsome Harvard University dropout, emerged as the new Chicago pitching mainstay. At that, the White Stockings had to fight off the powerful Detroit Wolverines, who fell short by only two and one half games.

In midseason 1886, with the White Stockings in St. Louis for a series against the Maroons, a local writer had asked Anson how he thought the Browns would fare in the National League. Maybe fifth place, replied the Chicago captain. Later on he turned down a bet of $1,000 apiece offered by Caruthers and Foutz that the Browns would beat the White Stockings in the postseason series.

A good thing for Anson, too. In Chicago the local favorites took two of three games. Back in St. Louis, though, the Browns won three straight, the last victory coming when, in the tenth inning with the score tied, Clarkson threw a high ball that glanced off Mike Kelly's hands and sailed to the backstop. The Browns' Curt Welch trotted home with the run that gave the Browns $13,920 to split from the winner-take-all gate receipts. The third World's Championship Series drew well in both cities—an average of seven thousand per game.

Angered by the decisive loss to the upstart Browns, the ongoing escapades of "King Kelly" and others on the club, and the failure to make any money at all from the World Series, president Spalding wouldn't even pay the White Stockings' train fare back from St. Louis. That winter he made up his mind to dismantle his great team. It astonished the sporting public when Boston was willing to pay $10,000, an unprecedented price, for Kelly. In short order the almost equally bibulous Jim McCormick, as well as Gore and Dalrymple, were sold off. Clarkson would follow in 1888, sent to Boston for another $10,000.

Deprived of four of his mainstays, Anson could get his 1887 club no higher than third place, while Detroit took its first pennant, by a four-game margin over the Philadelphia Phillies, now managed by

Harry Wright. Built on the "big four" of first-baseman Dennis "Dan" Brouthers, shortstop Dave Rowe, third baseman Deacon White, and infielder-outfielder Hardie Richardson (all obtained as a package in 1885 for $7,000 from the poverty-stricken Buffalo franchise), manager W. H. Watkins's Detroit team also included power-hitting Sam Thompson in right field and speedy Ned Hanlon in center.

The Browns won another easy Association championship. Von der Ahe and Frederick K. Stearns, whose star-studded team still had failed to return a profit in Detroit, then arranged a gruelling fifteen-game World's Championship Series. Played not only in the home ballparks but in eight other cities, the 1887 Series produced ten victories for Detroit, five for St. Louis, and about $12,000 for each club after expenses. Its outcome supposedly restored the National League's dented prestige, at the same time that it infuriated Chris Von der Ahe.

That winter "der Boss" sold outfielder Curt Welch and shortstop Bill Gleason to Philadelphia and his splendid pitching tandem of Caruthers and Foutz to Brooklyn, along with catcher Al "Doc" Bushong. Comiskey still was able to assemble enough of a team to win a fourth pennant, although the much-strengthened Brooklyns made it fairly close. The new Browns' pitching stalwart was a local boy, twenty-one-year-old Charles "Silver" King (ne Koenig), who pitched sixty-two complete games and won forty-two of them.

Finishing at the bottom of the Association in 1888 was Kansas City, which had replaced the New York Metropolitans over the winter. The loss of its New York franchise was a major blow to the Association and showed the perniciousness in what would come to be called "syndicate baseball." After the Association Mets' pennant-winning 1884 season, John B. Day and partners in the Metropolitan Exhibition Company, deciding they could make more money with a strong National League team, continually shifted talent from the Mets to the New York Giants, with predictable results. While the Mets had gone into decline, the New York National Leaguers, managed by Jim Mutrie (who'd also led the 1884 Mets), became a perennial contender.

In 1888 the Giants (whose nickname supposedly derived from Mutrie's frequent praise for "my big fellows, my giants") were nine games better than Anson's young Chicago team. Detroit's champions faded to fifth place. By that time the National League had discarded Buffalo and Providence (which despite its two pennants had never made much money), in favor of Indianapolis and Washington.

The Giants were sparked by the pitching of Tim Keefe and Mickey Welch and the everyday efforts of Monte Ward (the onetime Providence pitching star, now a shortstop), first baseman Roger Connor, and catcher Bill "Buck" Ewing. Undoubtedly the best at his position up to that time, Ewing possessed a compact, rugged physique, a powerful throwing arm, a fine batting eye, and speed on the basepaths. The Cincinnati native also usually gets credit for inventing the rounded, heavily padded catcher's mitt. Other catchers quickly discarded their *two*, simultaneously worn, fingerless gloves for one Ewing-style mitt. That innovation, together with the wire masks catchers all wore and the light chest-crotch pad most had adopted, made life behind the bat somewhat less hazardous.

The city of New York got excited over the 1888 Giants as it hadn't over the Mets or any baseball club. More than thirteen thousand people saw a Memorial Day doubleheader at the Polo Grounds (as the Giants' ballpark was called, a few polo matches having been held there), situated at 111th Street between Fifth and Sixth avenues. Attendance boomed during the August–September pennant drive, and at the end hundreds of Manhattan's leading citizens gathered at the Star Theatre in a benefit that raised $6,000 for the Giants players. Lew Dockstadter's Minstrels, a celebrated blackface act, shared the program with the actor DeWolf Hopper, who gave what was perhaps the first in his countless renditions of "Casey at the Bat"—the poem Ernest R. Thayer had recently published in San Francisco.

A few days later the pride of New York started a five-of-nine-game World's Championship Series with the Browns. Following games in New York, Brooklyn, and Philadelphia, the series ended in St. Louis, where the Giants won for the fifth time in seven tries.

By the late 1880s professional baseball—at least at the major-league level—was in generally better shape than it would be at any time for the remainder of the century, but all wasn't sweetness and light. The National Agreement was never more than an uneasy peace, and tempers flared in the Association when Cleveland switched back to the National League after the 1888 season, replacing the debt-ridden Detroit franchise. Once again the Association had to bring in Columbus to fill out its eight-club structure.

Yet most clubs were operating in the black, and despite the reserve clause, average salaries had doubled from 1881 to 1889. Top players were paid at a level that would be almost unthinkable ten years later. Buck Ewing's salary grew from $1,000 in 1881 to $5,000 by 1889; Mike Kelly's from $1,300 to $4,000; Monte Ward's from $1,700 to $4,250; and Deacon White's from $1,600 to $3,500. Eight years after jumping from Worcester to Cincinnati when the Association club offered him a princely $800, even a journeyman infielder such as Warren "Hick" Carpenter could command $2,300 from the Queen City franchise.

The game on the field was in rapid flux throughout the eighties, too; by the last years of the decade it had acquired a more "modern" look—which is to say it more closely resembled twentieth-century baseball. Almost every off-season brought significant rule changes, most involving adjustments in the pitcher-batter, defense-offense relationship, as well as scoring changes affecting the statistical compilations that had become a vital part of the sport—not least for the players themselves.

One of the most significant rule changes, which went into effect for the 1882 season, moved the front of the pitcher's box back to fifty feet (from forty-five). Three years later (before the 1885 season) the restriction on the pitcher's motion that had made for underhanded and then three-quarter-underhand deliveries was done away with; from then on the overhanded "speed pitcher" was in his element. The next year a base on balls was set at seven pitches outside the strike zone (reduced from nine).

In the off-season of 1886–1887, the joint League and Association rules committee proved especially busy and imaginative. A rubber home plate would now replace the stone object previously used; the Spalding-Reach baseball was mandated for all leagues operating under the National Agreement. The host club would now have the exclusive choice of which team would bat first (a matter decided by coin toss up to then), and the batter's prerogative to call for the location of a pitch was finally disallowed. At the same time, the rule-makers sought to prop up sagging batting averages by giving the batter four strikes, not charging a hit batsman with a time at bat, setting a base on balls at five balls, and scoring a base on balls as a base hit.

The predictable result was a big increase in batting averages—from an overall 1886 mark of .251 in the League and .243 in the Association, to 1887 averages of .269 and .273, respectively. The Browns' Tip O'Neill reached an all-time major-league high .492 that year.

The rule-makers backtracked before the 1888 season, eliminating the base-on-balls hit and returning to three strikes. The next year they finally settled on three strikes and four balls as representing the maximum to which batter and pitcher should be entitled. And before the 1890 season, in one of the most far-reaching changes of all, they provided that a player might be substituted for at any time during the game and for any reason. Up to then, once a game started, a substitute could come off the bench only if a starter was injured—and then only with the consent of the opposing team's captain. Thus on those occasions when a pitcher just couldn't get the other side out, the usual procedure had been to have him switch positions with a teammate, referred to as the "change pitcher."

Players of that period had to do their work under circumstances unknown to later generations of big-leaguers. Although most club owners put their men up at decent hotels, the more impecunious booked third- and fourth-rate accommodations, which even by late-nineteenth-century standards were pretty shabby. The playing fields were characteristically stony and sometimes lopsided, soggy in the spring and early autumn, baked hard in July and August, with grass that was kept only reasonably under control by horse-drawn mowers. Even the best ballparks had no dressing facilities for visiting players, who suited up at their hotels, then took horse-drawn conveyances to and from the ballparks, along the way enduring barrages of insults—and sometimes rocks, vegetables, and rotten eggs as well—from local hoodlums.

Once at the grounds, players sat on open benches about halfway between the stands and the foul lines. Besides abusive spectators (frequently made more so by the liquor sold in Association parks), they had to contend with umpires who were often incompetent, however honest and conscientious they might be.

Until the late eighties, men played barehanded or with skintight fingerless gloves. Of course they erred often in trying to handle a small, hard object that sometimes came at them like a cannon shot. On June 13, 1885, for example, the Louisville team in the Association committed twenty errors in losing 14–2 to the Philadelphia Athletics. In the four games played in the Association that day, scorekeepers charged fifty-one errors, while National Leaguers made sixty-nine. Four days later the Brooklyn Association club made a record twenty-eight miscues in losing 18–5 to the St. Louis Browns. After that dreadful performance, Brooklyn president Charles H. Byrne understandably fined his players $50 each.

In 1886, in winning their fifth pennant in seven years, the Chicago White Stockings committed 475 errors in 124 games. That season the Browns, the best team the Association ever produced, made 494 errors in 139 games, and the Athletics mishandled the ball a staggering 637 times. The best club fielding percentage recorded in the eighties was Cleveland's .936 in the National League (1889).

In the late 1880s, small gloves worn on the nonthrowing hand were coming into general use. Some players wore the rounded Decker glove, patented by Harry Decker, a catcher, infielder, and outfielder in the National League and American and Union associations; but the glove that ultimately became standard for outfielders and infielders (except for first basemen, who settled on something similar to the Decker glove) was one patented by Arthur Irwin, a veteran infielder. Fitting over all five fingers and lightly padded at thumb and heel, the Irwin model had a maximum width of about nine inches. Little different from what one might slip over the hand on a cold day, it was literally a "glove," with which the fielder absorbed the ball's impact while, if possible, securing it with his other (bare) hand.

If bad umpiring was one of the players' complaints, then umpires, in their turn, were subject to steady harassment and vilification on the ball grounds from players and "cranks" (as dedicated spectators were called), and in the press by hotly partisan sportswriters. After 1882, when the newly formed American Association started the practice, umpires served on full-time staffs at salaries of $1,000 to $1,500 per season. Now appearing in the blue coats and caps that would become the classic umpire's attire, the officials may have looked more expert, but in fact they lacked training for their particular work and were frequently ex-players, or "played out ball tossers."

Having to cope with numerous rule changes, working alone, unavoidably out of position much of the time, umpires emerged as the arch villains of the ballfield. Menaced by vengeful mobs, cursed, shoved, kicked, spat upon, and sometimes beaten up by bullying players, umpires went about their duties as best they could, unappreciated by the baseball public and little protected by league officials. "One thing there is that affords a baseball umpire consolation," remarked the *Sporting News* in 1888, "and that is the thought that he can die only once, and then never more."

The ballparks (or grounds, as they were still usually called) were all built by private capital on whatever vacant property was available and usable. Thus they all had irregular dimensions and various other odd features dictated by the size and shape of the building site. For example, in its early years the Congress Street Grounds in Chicago, where the White Stockings played from 1882 to 1895, had fences that were only 216 feet from home plate down the foul lines—which mainly accounts for the twenty-seven and twenty-two home runs hit by Ed Williamson and Abner Dalrymple, respectively, in 1884.

Yet however cozy their foul-line dimensions might be, the parks all had expansive center fields where overflow crowds—typically drawn on Saturdays (and Sundays where baseball was permitted on the Sabbath)—could be accommodated at the base admission charge or less. In deepest center there were often parking areas inside the fence for carriages, buggies, and wagons.

Late-nineteenth-century parks were usually located not far from the city centers because most customers reached the game sites on horse-drawn trolleys, soon to be replaced by electrically driven cars mounted on rails. Some owners went to extra efforts to make their facilities as comfortable and attractive as possible. At his Sportsman's Park in St. Louis, Chris Von der Ahe was one of the first owners to provide toilets for women patrons, while Henry V. Lucas of the rival Maroons hung bird cages inside his Palace Park of America to amuse the customers. The South End Grounds, occupied by the Boston National Association and National League teams from 1871 to 1894, was distinctive for the medieval twin spires rising from its double-decked grandstand.

The Association parks featured open bars, usually located behind the top row of the grandstand, where thirsty patrons could stand with foot on rail and sip beer (sometimes wine by the glass and whiskey by the shot as well) while they watched the action down on the field. Meanwhile vendors in white aprons balanced trays of beer mugs as they worked the aisles.

The ballparks were constructed entirely of wood, which meant that they were firetraps; hardly a season passed without a bad fire in some League or Association facility. Given the low costs of materials and labor in that period, rebuilding was usually accomplished with little delay, sometimes in the middle of the season. Ballpark fires came to be one of the normal risks investors took when they put money into a baseball franchise.

The major-league baseball of the eighties featured plenty of talented athletes, men who could have performed in the fastest company at any time in the sport's history. They were the best in the country—at least the best white players; except for one club in one season, the major leagues had always been exclusively a white man's preserve. In the eighties and nineties the same came to be true throughout Organized Baseball.

Black Americans, especially those living in the northeastern cities, had been caught up in the same baseball craze that affected whites. Despite the impoverished condition of most blacks before and after Emancipation, by the beginning of the Civil War a number of all-black clubs were already operating in the New York area and around Philadelphia. In 1862, for example, a Newark, New Jersey, daily reported a "a base ball match between the Hamilton Club of this city and the Hensen Club of Jamaica, L.I., both composed of the descendants of Ham." A few matches between black and white clubs actually took place, but in 1867 the National Association of Base Ball Players officially refused to admit clubs "composed of one or more colored persons," on the grounds that they might become the source of discord and possible division within the membership.

Black baseball clubs went ahead on their own, competing against each other in matches such as one in Brooklyn, in October 1867, between the Excelsiors of Philadelphia and the Uniques of New York for the "colored championship." In the next decade baseball-playing spread through the black population everywhere, but while neither the National Association of Professional Base Ball Players nor the National League ever adopted any official ban on black players, in both organizations "gentlemen's agreements" kept blacks out.

In other leagues, though, racial scruples weren't so strong. In 1883, the first year of the National Agreement, two black players performed in the Northwestern League: John "Bud" Fowler (ironically, a native of Cooperstown, New York), who pitched, caught, and played the outfield for Stillwater, Minnesota, and Moses Fleetwood "Fleet" Walker, who caught for Toledo, Ohio. When the American Association added Toledo in its expansion to twelve clubs for 1884, Walker, a former student at Oberlin College and the University of Michigan, became the first black person on a major-league roster. Walker appeared in forty-two of Toledo's 104 games and batted .263. Late in the season the shorthanded Toledo club also hired his younger brother Welday Walker, who got into five games.

After Toledo and three other franchises were dropped from the Association for 1885, the Association club owners apparently arrived at their own gentlemen's agreement not to sign black players. Fleet Walker did spend several more years in various minor leagues on otherwise all-white clubs, as did Fowler and perhaps as many as a dozen other black players. In 1886 Walker played for Waterbury, Connecticut, in the Eastern League, while left-hander George Stovey of Jersey City was the league's top pitcher. Infielder Frank Grant played for Meriden, Connecticut, in the same league until that franchise collapsed, then joined Buffalo in the new International Association (later International League). *Sporting Life*'s Buffalo correspondent described Grant as "the best all-around player Buffalo ever had."

In 1887 the National League and the American Association even gave formal recognition to the League of Colored Base Ball Clubs, which included teams in New York, Philadelphia, Boston, Cincinnati, and four other eastern and midwestern cities. Such a league might have flourished under a kind of "separate but equal" policy within Organized Baseball, developing players and selling them to the major clubs, just as other minor leagues did; but the League of Colored Base Ball Clubs lasted only a month before disbanding forever.

Grant, Stovey, and other late-nineteenth-century black players would have excelled in the major leagues if they had ever been allowed to prove themselves. From the late eighties on, however, their chances rapidly diminished in the face of ostracism and threats of boycotts by opposing all-white teams. In the middle of the 1887 season the International League club owners formally agreed "to approve no more contracts with colored men." While that was happening, Cap Anson refused to put his Chicago White Stockings on the field at Newark for an exhibition game if George Stovey went to the box for the locals. Stovey didn't pitch that day, the excuse being "sickness," although the real explanation soon came out. Two months later the St. Louis Browns wouldn't take the field at West Farms, New York, for an exhibition against the all-black Cuban Giants, disappointing the seven thousand people who'd paid to see the game.

American race consciousness intensified throughout the remainder of the century, but the "color line" wasn't drawn everywhere at the same time within Organized Baseball. In 1889 the Cuban Giants (who were actually all U.S.-born) and the all-black Gorhams of New York City joined the Middle States League, which re-formed the next year as the Eastern Interstate League, then broke up in midseason. Having added Frank Grant, the Cuban Giants resurfaced in 1891 in the Connecticut State League, representing Ansonia, but that minor league, too, disbanded halfway through the season. From then on the Cuban Giants, based in Trenton and Hoboken, New Jersey, operated as one of the country's best-known black independent clubs.

In 1895, five members of the independent Page Fence Giants played briefly with Adrian in the Michigan State League, and three years later another outfit called the Acme Colored Giants represented Celeron, New York, in the Iron and Oil League until, with a record of 8–41, they dropped out. Until 1946, when Jackie Robinson appeared with Montreal in the International League, no black person would again play on any club within Organized Baseball.

Marked by frequent outbreaks of racial violence and a movement throughout the southern United States to deny blacks their voting rights and segregate them from whites in virtually every area of social life, the 1880s and 1890s brought a national "capitulation to racism," in the memorable phrase of the historian C. Vann Woodward. Baseball, having worked its way into the fabric of American society, reflected in about equal parts what was good and bad about life in the United States. The gradual elimination of nonwhites from Organized Baseball was a small piece in a broad post-Emancipation pattern of racial exclusion.

Just how much baseball had become part of the institutional character of American society was evident in the welcome accorded Albert G. Spalding, his Chicago White Stockings, and a group of "All-American" players from other National League clubs when they arrived in New York harbor in April 1889, at the end of a seven-month around-the-world tour. Having demonstrated American baseball to people in Australia, Ceylon, Egypt, Italy, France, and England, Spalding and his company were honored guests at the renowned Delmonico's restaurant in Manhattan and later in lavish festivities in Chicago.

At Delmonico's, prominent baseball officials, bankers, and local politicians were among the three hundred banqueters. Young Theodore Roosevelt, just appointed to the U.S. Civil Service Commission, was on hand, as was Samuel Langhorne Clemens, then at the zenith of his literary persona as Mark Twain. After a nine-course meal, the world travelers heard themselves acclaimed as "gladiators . . . covered with their American manhood," apostles of "manly sports," members of "a race fit for peace and war," and the like. Clemens proclaimed baseball "the very symbol, the outward and visible expression of the drive and push and rush and struggle of the raging, tearing, booming nineteenth century. . . ."

It didn't matter that Spalding's tour had been a quixotic venture, sparking little enthusiasm for the game or demand for his sporting goods in other lands. For many millions of Spalding's countrymen, baseball had become almost a necessary part of existence—"the one unalloyed joy of life," as the famous criminal lawyer Clarence Darrow would remember its being during his youth in Kinsman, Ohio.

Prizefighting had only begun to move out of the shadows of quasi-criminality. Football was at once an elite sport for the relative few who could attend college and, as played in the eighties and nineties, an extraordinarily brutal form of athletic competition. Basketball wouldn't be invented until 1892, and then would take a long time to emerge from its YMCA-recreational origins; tennis and golf were still upper-class amusements and, in the eyes of probably a majority of Americans, "unmanly" ones at that. In its broad appeal to both spectators and participants, baseball had no serious rivals as the "National Pastime."

Yet underneath the veneer of good times toward the end of the 1880s, both proprietors and players nurtured major discontents. In most respects, the men who controlled the baseball franchises were typical late-nineteenth-century businessmen. They carried on their businesses according to certain fundamental precepts: Profits always had to be maximized; in turn, profits depended on maintaining a stable work force and keeping labor costs down. The reserve clause, a standard provision in players' contracts beginning in 1887, served effectively to bind men to particular clubs as long as their services were desired; yet growing profits in the aftermath of the Union Association's collapse had enabled owners to pay their uniquely skilled employees at unprecedentedly high levels. Entirely too high, many owners feared.

In 1885 the players, operating in a climate of labor vulnerability and anxiety following the passing of the Union Association, formed the Brotherhood of Professional Base Ball Players. The moving agent behind the Brotherhood was John Montgomery Ward, the twenty-five-year-old captain of the New York Giants. Besides being a top-notch player, Ward was a graduate of Columbia University who would go on to obtain his law degree from that institution. At a time when Spalding's annual *Guide* was inveighing against uncouth players for whom the saloon and the brothel were "the two great obstacles in the way of success," the handsome, articulate, gentlemanly Ward had won the respect of both his professional peers and their employers.

Within a year the Brotherhood had enlisted 107 League and Association players and organized chapters in each city in the majors. Ward also effectively cultivated such leading baseball writers as Tim Murnane in Boston, Ren Mulford in Cincinnati, and Francis Richter of *Sporting Life* in Philadelphia. Claiming to be working only for justice and in behalf of "intelligent and well-behaved" ballplayers, the Brotherhood launched an attack on the reserve clause.

In a cogent article in *Lippincott's Magazine*, Ward asked, "Is the Base Ball Player a Chattel?" Players had no real rights as employees, Ward argued, pointing out that in the sale of Mike Kelly by Chicago, Kelly had been neither consulted about the deal nor offered part of the record $10,000 price Boston paid. While Ward didn't go so far as to propose scrapping the reserve clause, he did want it modified to allow players some say in what happened to them.

Ward was one of the "All-Americans" in Spalding's entourage of globe-circling baseball missionaries. When their boat docked at New York, members of the Brotherhood met Ward with the angry news that in his absence the club owners had instituted a salary-classification scheme under which players would be paid from $1,500 to $2,500, and no more. When the owners wouldn't meet with the players' grievance committee and ignored their protests against the salary ceiling, Ward and the other Brotherhood leaders decided to create a league of their own, to be run in accordance with the players' own best interests.

As Brotherhood representatives conferred with prospective financial backers in various cities and also campaigned to get players to put their own money into the new league, the owners appeared more arrogant than ever. Struggling to recover from a broken ankle suffered on the global tour and misset by a London physician, Ed Williamson, the popular White Stockings shortstop, could get nothing in the way of medical expenses from Spalding beyond the $157 the Chicago club president had paid out before they got home. Cap Anson, by now a stockholder in the club, refused to intercede on Williamson's behalf. Meanwhile the Louisville players in the Association, fed up with numerous fines levied by owner John Davidson, staged a two-day strike in Baltimore.

In what turned out to be the last World's Championship Series of the nineteenth century, Ward and his New York Giants took five of nine games from Brooklyn, narrow winners in the Association over St. Louis. When the last Brooklyn batter was retired to seal the Giants' 4–2 ninth-game victory, some 3,500 New Yorkers spilled onto Manhattan Field (Eighth Avenue and 155th Street), where the Giants had relocated the previous July, to raise their war cry, "We are the people!" But if they rejoiced in their favorites' second straight championship, the better-informed among them knew that the bitter conflict between players and owners cast doubt on big-league baseball's future in New York and everywhere else.

Six days after the 1889 World Series ended, the Brotherhood of Professional Base Ball Players formally announced that in 1890 it would operate its own independent league. Disregarding the National Agreement's territorial provisions, the Brotherhood went forward with plans to place seven of its eight clubs in direct competition with National League franchises. The "Players League," as the new circuit was to be called, would have affiliates in New York, Brooklyn, Boston, Philadelphia, Chicago, and Pittsburgh, as well as Cleveland (which had switched from the Association only a year earlier), but would stay out of Indianapolis, which was leaving the National League anyhow. The new National League member would be Cincinnati, welcomed back after a ten-year absence. Buffalo, which had lost its National League franchise in 1885, was the eighth Players League entry.

Under the visionary program put into effect by the Brotherhood, each of the eight franchises contributed $25,000 to a central fund. Any individual club profits above $20,000 were to be pooled and distributed equally to all eight clubs. Of the $20,000 profit allowed each club, $10,000 would go to the investors, the remainder to be divided among that club's players. All players were guaranteed salaries at least equal to what they'd made in 1889, as well as equal representation with the financiers on the League's board of directors. Yet for all its past complaints about players' having no voice in when and where they were sent, the Brotherhood made compulsory player assignments to constitute the eight club rosters.

It soon became clear that the best baseball to be seen in 1890 would be in the Players League. Of 124 men who appeared in ten or more games in the new circuit, 81 were former National Leaguers, 28 had played in the American Association, and only 15 had been recruited directly from the minor leagues. Moreover, the Players League attracted most of the cream of the talent from both major leagues. Besides Monte Ward, who joined Brooklyn, such stellar performers as Charles Comiskey, Silver King, and Tip O'Neill (Chicago); Buck Ewing and Roger Connor (New York); Mike Kelly, Dan Brouthers, and Harry Stovey (Boston); Deacon White (Buffalo); and Sam Thompson (Philadelphia) went with the Brotherhood. Louis

"Pete" Browning, who'd twice led the Association in batting, joined the Cleveland Players and hit .387, tops in the Brotherhood's league.

A number of rising young players—Ed Delahanty (Cleveland), Jimmy Ryan (Chicago), George Van Haltren (Brooklyn), and Jake Beckley (Pittsburgh), to name a few—also staked their futures on the success of the new organization. Among the lesser lights in the Players League was a skinny catcher with Buffalo who'd played the past four years at Washington. Born Cornelius Alexander McGillicuddy, he'd shortened that to "Connie Mack" for the convenience of box-score printers.

Cap Anson, wedded to the Chicago operation by stock ownership and his personal loyalty to Spalding, stayed in the National League and managed a team of mostly no-names to a close runner-up finish behind Brooklyn, which had switched to the National League and managed to retain Bob Caruthers and Dave Foutz. John Clarkson stayed on to pitch for Boston; Mickey Welch did the same for the Giants; and the dashing Tony "The Count" Mullane, one of the Association's top pitchers for seven years, struggled through a poor season in the Reds' first year back in the National League. Otherwise, with the possible exception of outfielder Mike Tiernan of the Giants, not a single first-rank player was left.

The Association, having lost Brooklyn, Pittsburgh, Cleveland, and Cincinnati to the National League in the previous five years, now consisted of St. Louis, Columbus, Louisville, and Philadelphia, plus new, poorly capitalized entries from Brooklyn, Toledo, Rochester, and Syracuse. Before the season was out, the Brooklyn Association team, unable to compete with the Brooklyn Players and Nationals, had relocated in Baltimore. Most of the other Association franchises were in deep trouble.

The typically small crowds that showed up for National League and Association games in 1890 saw a host of players with unfamiliar names, most of whom wouldn't have been in either circuit that year but for the Brotherhood revolt; many of them wouldn't be again. In some instances, though, the talent scarcity provided opportunities for future stars who otherwise might have remained in the minors for several more years. That was the case with a big right-hander from

Ohio's Tuscarawas Valley named Denton True Young, nicknamed "Cy" because of the "cyclone" fastball he showed at Canton in the Tri-State League. Purchased by Cleveland for $300 in August, Young beat Anson's Chicago club in his first start, and before the season ended, he'd added eight more victories at the beginning of the winningest career any pitcher would ever have.

Everybody lost money in 1890. While its club owners offered the defectors big pay increases to return to their old affiliations, the National League scheduled as many games as possible in conflict with Players League dates. That resulted in one particularly bizarre incident in New York. There the Players League investors had leased another piece of the Coogan property between Eighth Avenue and the Harlem River, and had hurriedly put up a ballpark under the rock cliffs called "Coogan's Bluff," right next to the Giants' park on Manhattan Field. On May 12 the Giants' Mike Tiernan drove a ball over the canvas fence that separated the two parks, into the Brotherhood Park outfield; and as he trotted around the bases, spectators in both places cheered the National Leaguer's blow.

The sixth-place New York Giants drew 60,667 customers and avoided financial collapse only because Spalding, Arthur Soden of Boston, John T. Brush of Cincinnati, and Al Reach of Philadelphia bought $80,000 worth of stock in John Day's club. Pittsburgh, winners of only twenty-three of 136 games, pulled a grand total of 16,064 people into its Recreation Park, while Cleveland could attract only 47,478. Philadelphia, third in the National League standings, led the circuit in attendance with 186,000.

No Players League club did as poorly at the gate as the Pittsburgh and Cleveland Nationals. The Cleveland Players, next to last in the final standings, attracted 54,430 to their home games. Led to the pennant by captain Mike Kelly, Boston drew nearly 200,000 but still lost money. Total National League attendance was 813,678, a figure the Players topped by some 165,000. Careful contemporary estimates put National League losses at $300,000, the Players League's at $340,000. No attendance or financial figures are available for the American Association, but the contemporary consensus was that Association clubs had done a lot worse at the gate than the Nationals and Players. With their smaller financial bases, Association franchises could afford their losses even less than their National League counterparts.

Confused and disgusted by three leagues, the vituperation flying back and forth, and the numerous player desertions and additions, the customers had stayed away in droves. Few people cared that National League winner Brooklyn and Louisville, best in the Association, met in a postseason series, which neither club was sufficiently brazen to call a World's Championship Series. After seven games, with the series tied 3–3–1, bitter cold in Brooklyn ended what turned out to be the last such interleague competition of the century.

Financially, the 1890 baseball season was a debacle, and at its end most of the Players League financiers were ready to throw in the towel. Maneuvering to drive a wedge between the "capitalists" and the "renegades," the National League club owners were willing to negotiate with their peers, but never with the players. The Buffalo and New York Players clubs couldn't meet their payrolls for the last part of the season; the Cincinnati investors turned that city's franchise back to the League; and League president Edwin A. McAlpin resigned. By the end of the year the Players League was in ruins. In a wake at Nick Engel's Saloon in New York, Ward and a few associates toasted the end of their dream.

It was a unique episode in baseball history, an experiment in quasi-socialism that, had it somehow managed to endure, might have changed the sport's entire structure. The "Brotherhood war," as it came to be called, should have left no doubt in anybody's mind that, as Ward said a few years later, "baseball is a business, not simply a sport." In the Brotherhood and its league, the ballplayers had tried something drastic to redress what they saw as a gross imbalance in their circumstances vis-à-vis their employers. The serfs' revolt didn't work, and not until the 1970s would club owners have to face a comparable threat to their power.

4.
Baseball Feudalism and the Rise of the American League

The Players League was extinct by the end of January 1891; its financial backers (with the exception of the Buffalo group, which ended up with nowhere to go) had merged their holdings with franchises in either the National League or the American Association. The National League's structure remained intact, but the Association undertook a thorough reorganization, abandoning Toledo, Syracuse, and Rochester; keeping Baltimore (where the Brooklyn Association club had moved during the previous season); and setting up new operations in Boston, Cincinnati, and Washington. A new National Agreement, concluded by the National League, the American Association, and the minor-level Western Association (soon renamed the Western League), created an overall governing body called the National Board, made up of the presidents of the three leagues, one of whom would be its chairman.

What many expected to be a peaceful arrangement that would return baseball to normality actually lasted about two weeks. The 1889 League and Association reserve lists and various stipulations on particular men were supposed to determine where the Players League defectors would be assigned for the coming season. The Pittsburgh Nationals, though, signed infielder Louis Bierbauer, slated for the Philadelphia Association team, and thereby prompted an outcry against the "pirates" in Pittsburgh (a pejorative that quickly caught on as the team's new nickname). Meanwhile Harry Stovey, instead of joining the Boston Association club to which he was assigned, simply walked over to the office of Arthur Soden, president of the Boston National Leaguers, and signed to play in the senior circuit.

The newly constituted National Board ruled in favor of the League in both cases, whereupon the Association owners convened, fired president Allan W. Thurman (who'd voted against the Association's claims on the two players), elected Louis Kramer of Cincinnati their new leader, and voted to notify Nick Young, president of the League and chairman of the National Board, that the freshly signed National Agreement was dissolved.

To the dismay of the *Sporting News*, *Sporting Life*, and numerous other informed observers, the League and Association were again at war. By terminating the National Agreement, announced the League, the Association "has annulled the approval of the contracts its clubs have made with players, and its clubs have released all their players from reservation." The Association people denied the charges, but that didn't keep the League from going after their best players. Again, as in the first League-Association war, the Union Association episode, and the recent Players League challenge, quality players found themselves courted with offers of more money.

More ravaged by the Brotherhood strife than the better-capitalized Nationals, the Association clubs were less equipped than they'd been in 1882 to bid for players. Pete Browning, Harry Stovey, Dave Foutz, Bob Caruthers, and Arlie Latham, among others originally assigned to Association clubs, jumped to the League. About the only big names corralled by the junior circuit were Mike Kelly, who signed as player-manager of the Association Boston Reds (and then was loaned to Cincinnati to strengthen that shaky franchise), and Dan Brouthers, who also decided to play in the Association at Boston.

It was another bad year for most people who'd put money into major-league baseball; twelve of the sixteen franchises ran deficits. Even Mike Kelly's presence wasn't enough to sustain the Association in Cincinnati. In August, Chris Von der Ahe, the St. Louis president who also owned about three-fourths of the Cincinnati franchise, turned over the club to Association headquarters, which moved it to

Milwaukee. Kelly returned to Boston, moved back into the house given him by the local Association club before the season—and then blithely jumped to the local National Leaguers. Kelly's defection killed negotiations then going on in Washington to end the war.

Although National League clubs weathered the latest storm better than their rivals, allegations of "hippodroming" against the New York Giants added to the League's troubles. Jim Hart, who'd recently become president of the Chicago club upon Spalding's nominal retirement, charged that Giants manager Jim Mutrie, on John Day's orders, had refused to play Buck Ewing, Roger Connor, and pitching mainstay Amos Rusie in a season-ending five-game series at Boston. Day, declared Hart, had sought to ensure a pennant for Arthur Soden and his Boston associates, who owned substantial stock in the Giants as a consequence of the rescue mission Spalding had organized for the New York club during the Brotherhood conflict. Boston won all five games from the Giants and finished three and a half ahead of Chicago.

Hart didn't mince words: "Were I under indictment for murder, with the circumstantial evidence against me as strong as it appears to be against the New York Club, I should expect to be hanged." The Chicago president filed an official protest with League headquarters. In November, Nick Young and the League's board of directors threw out Hart's protest, finding plausible reasons in each instance why the three Giants stars hadn't appeared in the Boston series.

The affair again pointed up the hazards in permitting part-ownerships in franchises by people who also controlled other franchises. However obnoxious that practice might appear to later generations, the baseball businessmen of the nineties weren't prepared to do anything about it. As Hart no doubt was aware, Spalding, still the biggest stockholder in the Chicago club, owned even more Giants stock than Soden did! Interclub stock ownership—baseball's version of the increasingly common "interlocking directorates" in the larger business world—would become an increasing aggravation in the National League.

Meanwhile the Boston Reds, managed by fielder's glove inventor Arthur Irwin, won handily in the Association, even without the services of Mike Kelly. In the bitter atmosphere of the moment, a post-season series between pennant winners was out of the question, so disappointed Boston cranks had to console themselves with having three champions in three leagues—Players, National, and American Association—within two baseball seasons.

In the fall of 1891 the Association's leaders put up a brave front, even going so far as to establish a franchise in Chicago to challenge Spalding's hold on that rich baseball territory. But in doing so, Harold Seymour has written, "The owners were behaving like young boys whistling in the woods when dark approaches." In fact the Association was too debt-ridden to carry on. Von der Ahe, facing the prospect of having to spread his money among several weak franchises to keep the circuit going, was receptive to overtures from the League offered by Cincinnati's John T. Brush, Brooklyn's Charles H. Byrne, and Cleveland's Frank DeHaas Robison when they visited him in St. Louis.

Von der Ahe's willingness to consolidate with the League doomed the Association. In December 1891, in Indianapolis, four Association clubs—St. Louis, Baltimore, Washington, and Louisville—joined the National League to form a single twelve-team major-league organization. The League agreed to compensate investors in the other Association franchises—Boston, Philadelphia, Columbus, Milwaukee, and the new one in Chicago—for a total of about $135,000. That debt, assumed equally by all twelve clubs in the enlarged League, would be paid off from a ten percent deduction from all gate receipts. The ten-year-old American Association of Base Ball Clubs then formally disbanded.

After sixteen seasons, the National League finally sanctioned Sunday baseball in those cities—Cincinnati, St. Louis, Chicago, and Louisville—where state laws or municipal ordinances didn't prohibit it. Although the regular base admission remained at fifty cents, League clubs could charge as little as a quarter for uncovered "bleacher" seats and standing room. As for liquor sales on the grounds, that was again left up to local discretion.

On March 1, 1892, the National League owners and minor-league representatives formulated still another National Agreement. The major innovation in the new pact was provision for a player draft. No longer willing to recognize a minor club's unqualified right to reserve players (and to thereby hold on to them until a major club paid its asking price), the League persuaded the minors' representatives to accept classification into "A" and "B" leagues. In return for reservation rights, "A" clubs would be permitted to draft players in the off-season from "B" clubs for $500 each; National League clubs could draft "A" players for $1,000 each. The lower-classified minors would have no reservation rights at all.

If the National League moguls were arrogant in their dealings with the minors, they treated their players with something approaching contempt. With neither a rival major league to compete for their services nor a surviving union to represent their collective discontents, the players had no choice but to accept a reimposed salary limit—now set at $2,400.

In addition to arrogance and contemptuousness, the National League operators exhibited an extraordinary obtuseness. Apparently it never occurred to them to structure their twelve-club monopoly into eastern and western divisions of six teams each. Such an alignment would have held down travel costs, intensified intercity rivalries, and prolonged spectator interest by setting up an annual postseason series between the division winners to decide the League championship. Instead the League lumbered along season after season with its unwieldy top-to-bottom competitive format, which meant that season after season at least half the teams were hopelessly out of the pennant race by mid-July.

For 1892 the owners announced that the season would be split, with the winners of each half meeting in a championship series. They thereby invited allegations that whoever won the first half would deliberately slack off and let somebody else win the second half to ensure postseason play and extra money for the competitors. The Boston club, now familiarly known as the Beaneaters, ran up a 52–22 record over the first half; Cleveland's Spiders, getting thirty-six wins from big Cy Young and twenty-eight from little George "Nig" Cuppy, took the second half with an almost identical record. In the playoff for the pennant, Boston reasserted itself, winning five games while Cleveland could manage only a twilight-necessitated tie.

Directing the Beaneaters to their second straight National League title was Frank Selee (pronounced See-lee), a mild-mannered New Englander, then thirty-three years old, destined to become the least-known highly successful manager in baseball history. Selee came to Boston in 1890 from Omaha, where he'd just won a Western Association pennant. A canny judge of talent and a clever strategist, he sat on the bench in street clothes, the first nonplayer actually to run his team from the bench once the game started.

At Boston, Selee combined the best youngsters assembled during the Brotherhood war with several returning Players Leaguers to make up what was possibly the best baseball team up to that time; anyway, their 102 victories in 1892 were the most ever recorded. Mike Kelly, worn down by many years of hard play and high life, caught only about half the time and batted a pathetic .189 in his next-to-last major-league season. (Two years later the onetime "King of the Diamond" would die at thirty-six.) But Selee got strong infield play from Tommy Tucker at first base, Yale College product Billy Nash at third, and Herman Long at shortstop, and timely hitting from outfielders Bobby Lowe, Hugh Duffy, and Tommy McCarthy. Jack Stivetts and Charles "Kid" Nichols, two young right-handers, pitched thirty-five wins apiece.

Despite reductions in players' salaries (sometimes exceeding fifty percent) before the 1892 season started and another round of cuts in midseason, all the National League clubs lost money, with the exception of Boston and Brooklyn. Under Monte Ward's leadership, the Trolley Dodgers (so called because several pedestrians had recently been run down by trolleys in Brooklyn) finished third. The consensus among the club owners was that the quickest way to boost attendance would be to give customers more batting, base-running, and scoring. The aggregate League batting average in 1892 had been only .245, down ten points from the previous season.

In the off-season the League adopted possibly the most significant changes in baseball's rules since the Knickerbocker clubmen began playing their new game in the mid-1840s. In fact, "modern" baseball ought to be dated not from the beginning of the twentieth century, as popular lore conveniently assumes, but from the season of 1893. Under the new rules, the pitching distance was lengthened from fifty feet to sixty feet, six inches; the rectangular pitcher's box was eliminated; and, as he delivered the ball to the batter, the pitcher was required to keep his back foot anchored to a twelve-by-four-inch rubber slab (enlarged to twenty-four by six inches in 1895).

The results were everything the rule-makers could have desired. The 1893 season brought the sharpest increase in batting figures in the sport's history: a thirty-five-point rise in the overall National League average and almost a thousand more runs. While every pitcher experienced some trouble throwing from ten and a half feet farther out, younger men such as Cy Young, Kid Nichols, and Amos Rusie adjusted fairly easily. They gave up more hits and runs but continued to win lots of games.

For others, though, the extra ten feet on their pitches made for badly diminished skills. As examples, Boston's Jack Stivetts dropped from thirty-five wins in 1892 to nineteen in 1893, Cleveland's Nig Cuppy from twenty-eight to seventeen, Brooklyn's George Haddock from twenty-nine to eight, Philadelphia's Gus Weyhing from thirty-two to twenty-three (and to sixteen in 1894), and Chicago's Bill Hutchinson from thirty-seven to sixteen (and fourteen in 1894). Although earned run averages weren't figured in that period, historical statisticians have determined that the e.r.a. for the League as a whole jumped from 3.28 in 1892 to 4.66 in 1893, then soared to 5.32 the next year, the highest ever computed.

The new pitching rules provided only that there would be a rubber slab, not that the slab would be set in a pile of dirt to give the pitcher a little compensating leverage as he threw from the greater distance. Although evidence is scanty, what seems to have happened is that, as early as the 1893 season, pitchers and groundskeepers in various places got together to devise the wholly extralegal pitcher's mound—a critical element in the craft of the "moundsman" ever since.

Mound or no mound, pitchers remained at a disadvantage for the rest of the decade. Strangely, the biggest batting surge came not in 1893 but in the second year after the pitching rules were changed. For 1894 the entire League averaged .309; the third-place Philadelphia Phillies, with such sluggers as Sam Thompson and Ed Delahanty, compiled a majestic .349 team mark. Baltimore (.343) and six other clubs topped .300.

Hugh Duffy's .438 was the highest individual average ever made except for Tip O'Neill's in 1887, when bases on balls had counted as hits. Besides Duffy, three other players (Thompson, Delahanty, and Tommy Turner, all Phillies) topped .400. In a 132-game season,

Philadelphia's fleet little Billy Hamilton (besides batting .399) scored nearly two hundred runs; five teams scored at least a thousand times that year.

Inasmuch as nobody claimed the ball had changed, nothing really explains why batters should have clouted more lustily in 1894 than in the previous season. (A change in scoring rules that no longer assigned a time at bat for a sacrifice bunt made some difference, but hardly enough to account for the 1893–1894 batting anomaly.) Clout lustily they did, and play lustily as well.

The general abuse of umpires got worse in the 1890s. In 1893 Selee's Boston club, maybe reflecting his own low-keyed civility, won a third straight pennant with a minimum of umpire-baiting. Throughout the League, though, many players had come to assume that intimidating the arbiters (or at least trying to) was a useful, even necessary tactic—an essential part of the professional game. Inasmuch as the individual club owners showed little interest in curbing their players and League president Young (a naturally timid soul to begin with) knew his job depended on not antagonizing the owners, the League's umpires could do little but try to endure.

In the nineties, the highest salary any of them would ever receive was $2,100—good money, but hardly adequate compensation for what they had to put up with. When he quit the League umpiring staff in midseason 1895, onetime Giants pitching star Tim Keefe described baseball as having become "absolutely disagreeable. It is the fashion now for every player to froth at the mouth and emit shrieks of anguish whenever a decision is given which is adverse to the interests of the club."

The decade was probably the roughest, toughest, generally most disorderly time in the history of the National League. Many years later, when baseball men got together to reminisce about the old days, their talk almost invariably centered on the exploits of the Baltimore Orioles, who supplanted Boston as League champions in 1894–1896. The Orioles weren't the best baseball team ever—they probably weren't even the best team in the nineteenth century—but they gained an enduring reputation as the rowdiest assortment of ballplayers ever brought together on one club. They were also one of the most successful.

During ten years in the American Association, Baltimore's entries had never done better than two third-places. In 1892, in the consolidated twelve-member National League, the Orioles finished ten games behind the eleventh-place club. In the middle of that season, though, Ned Hanlon came over from Pittsburgh to manage the team.

After buying a big block of Orioles stock and getting himself elected club president, Hanlon enjoyed a free hand. In a succession of deals, he acquired big Dan Brouthers from Brooklyn to play first base, Hugh Jennings from Louisville for shortstop, Joe Kelley from Pittsburgh and Walter "Steve" Brodie from St. Louis for left and center field, respectively, and Willie Keeler from New York for the other outfield position. Combining those newcomers with holdovers Wilbert Robinson, a sturdy veteran catcher, John "Sadie" McMahon, a beer-loving but talented pitcher, and John McGraw, an erratic, hot-tempered little third baseman, Hanlon had the makings of a champion.

Drilled and grilled in "baseball as she is played" (in Hanlon's phrase), the Orioles climbed to eighth place in 1893 and then, the next year, won Baltimore's first pennant in any league. In doing so they antagonized opposing players, cranks, writers, and most of all umpires with their truculent, swaggering style. The respected Boston writer Tim Murnane protested that the Orioles, exhibiting a readiness "to maim a fellow for life" in their ruthless pursuit of the pennant, were "playing the dirtiest ball ever seen in this country." Their everyday tactics, as cataloged by Murnane, included plowing into basemen, holding and bumping base runners, interfering with the catcher on pop fouls, and (in catcher Robinson's case) throwing equipment in front of opponents trying to score.

That no-holds-barred baseball, together with what people around the League complained was a systematic effort to terrorize and intimidate the umpires, had much to do with the Orioles' success—or so they themselves believed. Keeping the umpires alert with "artful kicking," claimed John McGraw, could earn his club as many as fifty extra runs a season. But the Orioles were also good ballplayers—smart, mostly fast, resourceful, and determined. "We talked, lived and dreamed baseball," said McGraw many years later. Although Selee's Bostons and other teams had earlier used the hit-and-run play, the

Orioles developed that particular maneuver into a fine art, especially as executed by McGraw, a leadoff man with unequaled ability to coax walks or get hit by a pitch, and Keeler, a 5-4 left-handed batter who uncannily "hit 'em where they ain't." The Orioles' hit-and-run became the most effective weapon in the game.

Of the Orioles' three straight pennants, the toughest was the first—a gruelling struggle with the Giants, now led by Monte Ward, and Selee's Boston champions. The city of Baltimore, long denied a winner, celebrated robustly and feted, fed, and fawned over Hanlon and his men. After a year without any kind of postseason competition, William H. Temple, a wealthy Pittsburgher, came forward with a proposal for a series between the first- and second-place finishers, the winner to receive most of the gate receipts as well as a big silver loving cup donated by Temple.

It was still a poor substitute for the closely followed World's Championship meetings between League and Association winners in the mid-eighties, but the League was willing to give its official sanction to a seven-game series between Baltimore and New York. Demanding a guarantee of half of the receipts, the Orioles almost didn't take the field. When they did they paired off with Giants players in informal fifty-fifty splits, and played listlessly and carelessly. Ward's club swept four straight games, with Amos Rusie and Jouett Meekin, who'd each won thirty-six games that season, throttling the heavy-hitting Orioles.

In 1895 and 1896 the Orioles had an easier time, beating out the Cleveland Spiders in both seasons. Their casual approach to Temple Cup competition continued in 1895, when they were dispatched by Cy Young and his mates in five games in a series marked by extraordinarily bad behavior (even for the nineties) by both Cleveland and Baltimore cranks. After the Orioles were showered with vegetables, beer bottles, seat cushions, and a variety of other objects during three games at the Cleveland park, hoodlums in Baltimore attacked the Spiders' horse-drawn bus with rocks, bricks, and dirt clods. As soon as the fifth and final game ended in Baltimore, the Spiders hurriedly left town with their $580 shares out of the Cup receipts.

Although tales of the rough-and-rowdy "old Orioles" became a staple of baseball folklore, the Cleveland Spiders may actually have been a more ferocious lot. Oliver "Patsy" Tebeau, Cleveland's first baseman-manager, was a more combative leader than Ned Hanlon, who under League rules couldn't leave the bench in his street clothes. Cy Young, a tough but usually even-tempered competitor, concentrated on his mound chores and left the nonathletic part of the fray to his teammates, but they hardly needed Young's help.

One day in 1896 in Louisville, for example, the Spiders created such a ruckus that the local club president had the whole starting nine arrested and hauled into court. Found guilty of disturbing the peace, Tebeau, outfielders Jimmy McAleer and Jesse Burkett, and shortstop Ed McKean paid fines ranging from $50 to $100 each. The reputation of the Spiders' home crowds—"Cleveland hoodlums," Cap Anson called them—matched that of the ball club.

Yet for all that, the Cleveland National League club never did better than two second-place finishes and one Temple Cup triumph. In 1896 Baltimore finally proved its mettle in postseason play by sweeping the Spiders four straight games behind right-handers Bill Hoffer and Joe Corbett (the latter the younger brother of heavyweight boxing champion Gentleman Jim Corbett). Turnouts in both cities were so low that the Orioles came away with only $200 apiece, the losers $117.

That gate was symptomatic of the League monopoly's persistent financial woes; only in 1894 did a majority of its members (nine, to be exact) show a profit. Attendance sagged the next year under generally bad economic conditions; the crowds never reappeared in the same numbers. The Spanish-American War, which began coincidentally with the 1898 baseball season and was over by midsummer, provided a convenient if unconvincing explanation for the fact that, even with economic recovery, only five clubs could meet their expenses that year.

Much of the League's trouble had to do with the absence of a winning team in New York City after 1894. Even at that early date, it should have been apparent that without a successful operation in baseball's biggest market and the nation's communications center, everybody else would find it hard to make profits. Early in 1895 thirty-four-year-old Andrew Freedman, a wealthy real-estate speculator and bondsman who was intimately involved with the Tammany Hall political organization, bought John Day's controlling interest in the Giants for $48,000. A lifelong bachelor who centered his attentions on his business affairs, Freedman generated controversy almost from the beginning of his career as a club owner, while the Giants became one of the League's consistent losers.

Although criticism of Freedman sometimes carried anti-Semitic overtones, he was actually just about everything his growing number of enemies around the League charged. Overbearing, egotistical, short-tempered, capricious, he tolerated no resistance to his authority as club president. Monte Ward had the good sense to quit and return to his legal studies at Columbia, so that he was spared Freedman's incessant meddling in on-the-field matters. After dismissing player-manager George Davis a third of the way into the 1895 season, Freedman hired and fired at a dizzying pace: fifteen more managerial changes up to 1902, including the venerable Cap Anson, who lasted only twenty-two games in 1898.

Freedman's exploits also included barring unfriendly sports-writers from the ballpark and using his influence to have umpire John Heydler fired from the League staff. Amos Rusie, arguably the best pitcher in baseball, sat out the entire 1896 season in a $200 salary dispute with the Giants' president. In July 1898 Freedman stormed onto the field to demand the ejection of Baltimore's Bill "Ducky" Holmes after Holmes, an ex-Giant, yelled to a heckling spectator, "Well, I'm glad I'm not working for a sheeny anymore." When umpire Tom Lynch wouldn't go along, Freedman had Giants manager Bill Joyce take his team off the field, whereupon Lynch declared a forfeit to Baltimore.

The difference between Freedman and the rest of the National League "magnates" (as they liked to see themselves called in the press) was only a matter of degree. Each club owner operated his ball club like a medieval fiefdom. If the owners did little to inhibit their players' unruly behavior, they also did little to improve their circumstances. Although team captains received $500–$600 extra and outstanding players frequently got something under the table, the official $2,400 salary limit remained in force. The owners wouldn't try to curb spectator rowdiness, wouldn't do anything to improve umpiring, wouldn't build dressing rooms for visiting teams, and of course wouldn't consider modifying the reserve clause.

A few players eventually got fed up and went on to other things.

Early in the 1892 season, when Baltimore cut the salary of Charlie Buffinton, already the victor in 230 major-league games at the age of thirty, the pitcher went home to Fall River, Massachusetts, and never appeared again in Organized Baseball. John Montgomery Ward, one of the National League's highest-paid performers, gave up playing at the age of thirty-four in the afterglow of his New York Giants sweep of Baltimore in the first Temple Cup games. Winner of ninety-three games in six seasons (1896–1901) with the Boston Beaneaters, Welsh-born Ted Lewis retired at twenty-nine to begin a long career as an educator, most notably as president of Dartmouth College. And Bill Lange, a husky outfielder who averaged .330 in seven seasons with Chicago, was only twenty-eight when, in 1899, he married into a wealthy family in his native San Francisco and put aside baseball for business and civic affairs. Lange was as good a center fielder as the game had ever seen, according to Clark Griffith, Lange's teammate at Chicago in the early part of Griffith's own career of sixty-odd years in baseball.

Yet whatever its drawbacks, a career in professional baseball held an irresistible allure for millions of young males throughout the United States. Many of those aspiring millions played the game within what, by the 1890s, had become a vast infrastructure below (or outside) Organized Baseball. Neighborhood "sandlot" clubs, with players ranging anywhere from fifteen to fifty years old, competed once or twice a week in cities everywhere. The urban sandlotters had their counterparts in a multitude of village and rural aggregations, commonly called "town teams." At the end of each academic year, resort hotels operating from upstate New York to Maine sponsored teams stocked mainly by Ivy League college players, nominally employed as waiters and busboys but expected to spend most of their time on the ballfield.

In baseball at those levels, the line between professional and amateur was always indistinct. "Semipro" became a generic designation for virtually any adult, noncollegiate competition unaffiliated with Organized Baseball. That included everything from the summer resort teams, to loosely formed sandlot and town clubs, to the considerably organized competition sponsored by urban manufacturers and insurance and retail concerns, Appalachian and western mining companies, New England and southeastern textile mills, and southern lumber companies. Such employee baseball teams were some of the earliest manifestations of what, decades later, would be called "welfare capitalism."

Devotees of simon-pure amateurism focused their criticism on college athletes hired to play summer baseball for hotels and other businesses; otherwise nobody much cared if boys and men worked at something else full-time and picked up a few dollars extra playing on weekends. John McGraw, for example, technically became a professional at about fifteen, when he collected five dollars for pitching (and winning) a game for East Homer, New York. Hugh Jennings, McGraw's future teammate and bosom pal at Baltimore, was even younger when he discovered that on Sundays, when he wasn't laboring in the coal mines at Pittston, Pennsylvania, he could sell his baseball skills.

The dream of a becoming a big-leaguer was most compelling for working-class youths such as McGraw and Jennings, who stood to make four or five times as much in a half-year of ballplaying as in a full year of regular work. The eighties, and even more so the nineties, brought a flood of Irish-American and German-American players, young men who came largely from northeastern and midwestern cities and mining and mill towns, but also frequently from villages such as Truxton, New York, where McGraw grew up, or River Point, Rhode Island, which produced Boston's hard-hitting Hugh Duffy. (Before the twentieth century, only a few Californians and Southerners reached the major-league level.)

If baseball at that level, in the era of the National League's monopoly, wasn't profitable most of the time for most franchises, the sport nonetheless remained very near the center of life in the twelve League cities. Of course, that was particularly the case when the local favorites were battling for a pennant. On September 22, 23, and 25, 1897, the biggest crowds in Baltimore's National League history— some fifty-one thousand in all—saw their adored Orioles lose three times to Boston and miss a chance for a fourth straight title. It was small consolation for the Baltimore faithful that Ned Hanlon's club won four of five sloppily played games from the Beaneaters in the Temple Cup series. Always seen by both players and cranks as an anticlimax to the pennant race, and thus never much of a gate attraction, Temple Cup competition received its *coup de grâce* from the club presidents when they met in Philadelphia later that autumn.

After that the Baltimore club's fortunes waned, even as the legend of the "old Orioles" began to grow. In 1898 Baltimore finished a full six games behind Boston, as Frank Selee became the second man in baseball history (after Cap Anson) to direct five pennant winners. Matching their 102 wins of 1892, the Beaneaters fielded an everyday lineup without weaknesses. The outfield of Charles "Chick" Stahl, Billy Hamilton, and Hugh Duffy was the best in baseball, as was the infield of Brown University's Fred Tenney at first, Bobby Lowe at second, Herman Long at shortstop, and the brilliant Jimmy Collins at third. The team had the best catcher since Buck Ewing, according to some baseball seers, in Marty Bergen—a tragically troubled young man who, early in 1900, would take his own life after murdering his wife and two children. In 1898 Selee used an unprecedented four-man pitching rotation, headed by Kid Nichols with twenty-nine wins and including Ted Lewis (twenty-six), Vic Willis (twenty-four), and Bill Klobedanz (nineteen).

The 1899 season proved the last for the League in its twelve-club incarnation, and also brought the full ripening (or rottening) of syndicate baseball. No longer able to overcome Boston with the club he managed in Baltimore, Ned Hanlon, together with Orioles vice president Harry Von der Horst, bought a half-interest in the Brooklyn franchise. At the same time, Frederick A. Abell and Charles Ebbets, principal stockholders at Brooklyn, bought half of the Orioles.

Now president and manager at Brooklyn while he retained the presidency of the Baltimore club, Hanlon loaded his Brooklyn roster with Joe Kelley, Hugh Jennings, pitcher Jim Hughes, two-time batting titlist Willie Keeler, and other Baltimore mainstays. When John McGraw and Wilbert Robinson refused to leave Baltimore, Hanlon named the twenty-six-year-old McGraw to manage the Oriole remnants, with Robinson to assist him.

Meanwhile the brothers Frank and Stanley Robison, owners of the Cleveland franchise, also bought a controlling interest in the St. Louis Browns from Chris Von der Ahe, whose life had taken a succession of bad turns. The onetime kingpin of the American Association had watched his franchise deteriorate steadily in the absence of Charles Comiskey, who joined the Cincinnati Reds following the Brotherhood war. Trying everything to draw customers, Von der Ahe staged bicycle races, installed a merry-go-round, and built an artificial lake and shoot-the-chute at Sportsman's Park—all to no avail. Two divorces, a big fire at the ballpark, bad real-estate investments, and other reverses finally forced "der Boss President" to sell his beloved "Prowns."

The Robisons, convinced that St. Louis was rich territory, proceeded to strip the Cleveland club of manager Patsy Tebeau, the great Cy Young, batting star Jesse Burkett, and everybody else they thought might strengthen their new property. It was syndicate ball with a vengeance, and the 1899 Cleveland Spiders were probably the worst team to start and finish a major-league season. Certainly their record of 20–134 gave them the worst winning percentage for a full schedule. About a third of the way into the season, with hardly anybody showing up for the Spiders' games, the Robisons simply locked the Cleveland ballpark and transferred remaining home dates to other League cities. Thus the previously proud and pugnacious Spiders became the Orphans or Wanderers, as the writers now dubbed them.

In Baltimore, John McGraw's presence made for a different outcome. McGraw was a small man of limited athletic ability who by grit, guile, and bellicosity had made himself into one of the National League's top performers. In 1899 he not only played the best ball of his career, batting .391, scoring 140 runs, and, one way or another, reaching base about three-fourths of the time; he also managed an assortment of leftovers and pickups to a strong fourth-place finish. The Orioles might have done even better if McGraw hadn't been lost to the club for three weeks late in the season because of his wife's death. McGraw's success with the 1899 Orioles established his reputation as the smartest young manager in the business.

As they were favored to do, the players Hanlon had assembled brought Brooklyn its first National League championship, by a comfortable eight games over Selee's Boston club. St. Louis, made up mostly of former Cleveland players, could do no better than fifth place. Yet the Brooklyn champions' home attendance—about 270,000—was less than what the tenth-place 1898 team had drawn. Philadelphia and Chicago, finishing third and eighth, respectively, cleared substantial profits and Brooklyn made a small one; otherwise it was another year of general losses in the National League.

That winter the baseball press was full of rumors about franchise reductions. The question seemed to be not whether the League would cut back, but how many cities would be dropped—and when. It wasn't until early March 1900, little more than a month before the new season started, that the League owners voted officially to operate with only eight franchises. Baltimore, Washington, Louisville, and Cleveland were left out.

John McGraw, resigned to the loss of Baltimore's franchise and at first unwilling to play anywhere else, threw himself into an abortive effort to revive the American Association. Others involved in the project included Cap Anson, Alfred H. Spink of the *Sporting News*, and Francis C. Richter, editor of *Sporting Life*. Formally organized in Chicago, the new Association sought financial backing in Boston, Milwaukee, Louisville, Providence, Detroit, and Philadelphia, besides Chicago and Baltimore. Philadelphia's participation was crucial; in mid-February, when the local backers in that city ran into trouble securing playing grounds, the whole enterprise fell apart.

Sold to St. Louis for $15,000 (along with Wilbert Robinson and infielder Billy Keister), McGraw remained in Baltimore until May, when he signed with the Robison brothers for $10,000, the biggest amount any player had ever been paid. The contracts both he and Wilbert Robinson signed, moreover, specifically omitted the reserve clause, so that both would become free agents at season's end.

Although he batted .344 over the remainder of the schedule, McGraw's presence at St. Louis did nothing to pump life into a ball club with lots of talent but little inspiration or direction from Patsy Tebeau, now affected by a mysterious lassitude on and off the field. The Cardinals, as local writers had started calling them (because of their red-trimmed uniforms), finished in sixth place. Brooklyn, again sparked by former Orioles and now including Joe "Iron Man" McGinnity, McGraw's ace at Baltimore the previous year, had little difficulty repeating as champions.

The eight-team National League was a trimmer organization with fewer also-rans, but it still suffered from the inability of the

Chicago and New York franchises to field contenders. The Chicago club (now called the Cubs, after its youthful players) had done no better than fourth place since 1891; the Giants, having finished ahead of only the doomed Washington and Cleveland clubs in 1899, settled on the bottom in 1900. The Polo Grounds—as the Players League park under Coogan's Bluff was renamed after the Giants occupied it in 1891—could accommodate about eighteen thousand people, more than any baseball facility in the country, but in the Freedman regime it had rarely been half-filled.

The National League's problems, as frequently rehashed in the baseball press, stemmed from inadequate capitalization for several of its clubs, lordly owners who wouldn't stand for a stronger central administration, and a long-standing willingness to tolerate rowdy players and bad umpires. Maybe a rival major league was needed. All of that accorded closely with the views of Byron Bancroft Johnson, the thirty-six-year-old president of the minor circuit that had operated in middle-sized midwestern cities as the Western League until 1900, when it took the name American League.

Ban Johnson was a Cincinnati native who'd attended Marietta College and the University of Cincinnati law school (although he received a degree from neither), before serving about ten years on the staff of the *Cincinnati Commercial-Gazette*, becoming its sports editor. Among the close baseball acquaintances he made was player-manager Charles Comiskey of the Cincinnati Reds. While professional baseball at all levels went through sharp ups and downs in the 1890s, under Johnson's presidency the Western League not only held together but prospered—mainly, it was agreed, because Johnson ran things with authority and resolution, paying his umpires well and wielding tough discipline over the players. Jowly and rotund but possessed of seemingly inexhaustible energy, Johnson was brilliant in his way. If inclined to be high-handed and bombastic, he also proved a shrewd judge of men and decisive moments.

Ban Johnson's horizons extended far beyond the Western League; once the Nationals dropped four franchises, he began to move. At that juncture his chief lieutenant was Comiskey, who'd given up playing in 1894, bought the Sioux City Western League team, and moved it to St.

Paul. At Johnson's behest, Comiskey now moved from St. Paul into Chicago's South Side, where he revived the old nickname White Stockings for his team. In 1900, renamed the American League, Johnson's organization still operated as a minor league in conformance with the National Agreement; but that winter, when the Nationals refused to accord the American League equal status, Johnson announced that his organization would no longer abide by the pact.

In the meantime many minor-league players and a number of prominent big-leaguers had formed the Ball Players Protective Association. Their main demand, an increase in the salary ceiling from $2,400 to $3,000, got nowhere with the National League owners. Clark Griffith, an outstanding pitcher for the Chicago National League club and the driving force behind the Protective Association, secured pledges from its members not to sign National League contracts without the Protective Association's approval.

Griffith himself then signed to manage and pitch for Comiskey's Chicago White Stockings and, in close consultation with Johnson, began urging players to come over to the new league. John McGraw, having turned down a chance to manage at Cincinnati, also joined with Johnson, in exchange for the chance to return to Baltimore as a manager and part-owner in the American League. And Connie Mack, manager of the Western-American League's Milwaukee club the past four years, sold his stock there and carried the new circuit's banner into Philadelphia.

Another man close to Johnson was Charles Somers, a Lake Erie millionaire who loaned money to lift various franchises off the ground and was majority stockholder in the Cleveland club. Washington was the remaining territory abandoned by the Nationals and now occupied by the American League; the AL's three other charter members would be Boston, Detroit, and Milwaukee. Thus in its first season as a self-proclaimed major league, the AL would go head-to-head with the Nationals only in Boston, Philadelphia, and Chicago.

From November to March, Griffith, Mack, and McGraw rode the trains across the country, selling the American League to players. Johnson declared that nobody in his league would sign any player currently under contract to another club, which of course encouraged

National Leaguers to delay signing their 1901 contracts until they'd met with Johnson's agents. In all, the American Leaguers signed 111 men who'd played in the National League at one time or another.

The catches included some of baseball's biggest stars. The Boston American Leaguers, for example, grabbed Cy Young from St. Louis and, from the rival Beaneaters, Chick Stahl, Ted Lewis, and Jimmy Collins, the last becoming player-manager of the AL entry. In Chicago, Griffith signed outfielder Fielder Jones of the 1899–1900 Brooklyn pennant winners, who also lost Joe McGinnity to John McGraw's entreaties from Baltimore. Hugh Duffy became player-manager at Milwaukee. Johnson even went after the Nationals' umpires, offering them a few hundred additional dollars and recruiting veterans Tom Connally, Tim Hurst, and Jack Sheridan, half the NL's staff.

Apart from Cy Young, the AL's biggest prize was Napoleon Lajoie, the Philadelphia Phillies' brilliant second baseman, who went over to Connie Mack's new Philadelphia Athletics. A Woonsocket, Rhode Island, native of French-Canadian ancestry, Lajoie was twenty-five years old at the end of the 1900 season. Since entering the National League in 1896, he'd hit for an accumulative .362 average. At 6-1 and nearly two hundred pounds, Lajoie was a far-ranging, graceful fielder, one of the finest all-around players the game had seen. Joining Lajoie in deserting the Phillies for the Athletics were Charles "Chick" Fraser and Bill Bernhard, two first-rate pitchers.

It didn't take a lot of money above the National League's salary limit to lure players into the new league; Lajoie signed for about $3,500, Cy Young for the same amount. As he bid good-bye to St. Louis and the National League, Young told Frank Robison, "Your treatment of your players has been so inconsiderate that no self-respecting man would want to work for you if he could do anything else in the world."

The American League's first major-league season was generally successful. A good pennant race kept attendance up in most ballparks, and at the end a total of 1,683,584 people had paid to see AL games, only about 236,000 fewer than National League teams drew. Comiskey's Chicago club, with manager Griffith pitching twenty-four wins, overcame Boston and Cy Young, who won thirty-three times.

Lajoie won the batting title with a majestic .422, highest for the twentieth century in the American League, and also hit an extraordinary fourteen home runs and scored 145 times.

American League batting averages and scoring were higher than in the National League. Although the Americans had also installed the new seventeen-inch-wide, five-sided home plate adopted by the Nationals following the 1900 season, Johnson's circuit didn't go along with the Nationals' new foul-strike rule, and wouldn't until 1903. Batters had always been able to foul off an unlimited number of balls without accumulating strikes, as long as they actually swung at the ball (foul bunts were ruled strikes in 1894). Under the NL's new rule, the first two foul balls counted as strikes. Lajoie and other American Leaguers could still foul off pitch after pitch without penalty.

But the level of competition remained tough in the older league. The Pittsburgh Pirates—benefiting from the addition of several quality players who'd been at Louisville before the NL dropped that franchise and Louisville owner Barney Dreyfuss bought the Pirates—gained the "city of smoke" its first major-league championship. John "Honus" Wagner, twenty-seven in 1901, a broad-shouldered, bow-legged shortstop with huge hands and a powerful throwing arm, was the Pirates' top player—and maybe the biggest prize that got away from the American League. The NL's batting leader in 1900, Wagner hit .353 in 1901 but still trailed St. Louis's Jesse Burkett, Philadelphia's Ed Delahanty, and Brooklyn's Willie Keeler.

That winter the National League owners, unwilling to reelect Nick Young as league president and unable to agree on a successor, also wrangled protractedly over Andrew Freedman's self-serving plan for making the National League in effect a holding company. Freedman proposed that the NL reorganize itself as the National Baseball Trust and then issue common stock in its different franchises; New York would get thirty percent of the stock, more than twice as much as any other club. With his own stock plurality and the twelve percent to be awarded to Cincinnati owner John T. Brush, Freedman's close ally, the New Yorker hoped to dominate the whole league. Thanks mainly to A. G. Spalding's impassioned opposition, Freedman's scheme was eventually voted down, but the National League lacked a president at the start of the 1902 season.

While the National Leaguers fought among themselves, Ban Johnson and associates worked in concert to further their American League enterprise. Milwaukee, the weakest link in the new league, lost its franchise to St. Louis, where owner Robert Lee Hedges coaxed Jesse Burkett and shortstop Bobby Wallace to desert that city's National League club. At Baltimore, John McGraw talked his old Oriole teammate Joe Kelley into jumping from Brooklyn. Washington landed its first outstanding National Leaguer when the Philadelphia Phillies' Ed Delahanty, one of the top hitters in the National League for a decade, signed to play in the nation's capital.

After the season began, amid much confusion, Connie Mack finally persuaded George Edward "Rube" Waddell, a big fastballing left-hander who'd pitched for Pittsburgh and Chicago in 1901, then jumped to Los Angeles in the "outlaw" California League, to play for him in Philadelphia. Joining the Athletics in June, the fun-loving, beer-guzzling, hugely talented Waddell won twenty-three games, struck out 210 batters, and was the main reason Mack's team finished in first place.

Waddell had come to Philadelphia just in time. Five days into the season, during Baltimore's home opener against the Athletics, an officer of the Pennsylvania supreme court served injunctions on Napoleon Lajoie, Chick Fraser, and Bill Bernhard, permanently forbidding them to play for any Philadelphia baseball club except the Phillies. The outcome of a suit brought by the Phillies against the Athletics a year earlier, the injunctions might have proved a crippling blow to the American League if not for Ban Johnson's ingenuity.

Acting with the kind of authority no National League president had ever possessed, Johnson simply reassigned the contracts of the three players to Cleveland. Fraser decided to jump back to the Phillies, but Lajoie and Bernhard helped transform a weak Cleveland team into a strong fourth-place finisher. Whenever Cleveland had playing dates in Philadelphia, however, Lajoie and Bernhard, legally barred from the Athletics' grounds, spent their time on the beaches at Atlantic City.

Johnson might finesse the Philadelphia Phillies and the Pennsylvania supreme court, but there was no handling John McGraw— through finesse or any other means. Drawn together by burning ambition and mutual need, McGraw and Johnson were always improbable collaborators in the American League venture. During the 1901 season a number of disruptive on-the-field incidents involving the Baltimore manager and his players had corroded relations with the American League's president.

McGraw insisted on using the same bullying tactics on Johnson's umpires that he had in the National League; Johnson was determined to have disciplined behavior from players and managers. McGraw thought he was being singled out for fines and suspensions; Johnson became convinced that McGraw was an unregenerate National Leaguer of the old-time "anarchistic" school. Moreover, it was generally understood that for 1903 Johnson would transfer the Baltimore franchise to New York City, where the American League would have to establish itself to remain viable. McGraw became convinced (no doubt correctly) that Johnson intended to close him out of the New York operation altogether.

In June 1902, McGraw and Andrew Freedman hatched a plot that would not only bring McGraw to New York to manage the somnolent Giants, but that would sabotage the American League as well. McGraw got the Baltimore directors to release him from his contract in exchange for turning back his $6,500 worth of stock; through a succession of complicated transfers, Freedman obtained that stock and other holdings, enough to gain control of the Baltimore franchise.

On July 8 McGraw signed a four-year contract to manage the Giants, at a record salary of $11,000 per year. The American League, he told the New York press, was controlled by "Czar Johnson" and his Chicago-Philadelphia-Boston combine. The Baltimore operation hadn't made a penny in the American League, and "the big white elephant" in Philadelphia was no better.

Freedman now directed the releases of ace pitcher Joe McGinnity and four other Baltimore players, all of whom went immediately to New York to sign Giants contracts. Joe Kelley, also released on Freedman's order, signed to manage the Cincinnati Reds and brought along Orioles outfielder Cy Seymour. Thus Freedman assisted his ally, Cincinnati owner John T. Brush, who in turn was preparing to buy control of the New York franchise from Freedman.

Facing his worst trouble so far, Ban Johnson again proved equal to the test: He declared the Baltimore franchise vacant and took control in the name of the American League. Left with only five players, the Orioles forfeited one game, then received enough men—reassigned by Johnson from other teams—to resume play and complete the season, albeit in last place. Johnson never forgave McGraw, nor did McGraw ever express any regrets about jumping the American League. "If [Johnson] planned to ditch me," McGraw said many years later, "I ditched him first." The two never spoke again.

Like the advent of the American and Union associations and the Players League, the rise of the American League disrupted a tightly restrained salary structure and cost everybody a lot of money. Not only had National Leaguers jumped to the new circuit at healthy increases, but a number of players had also jumped back to the NL for still bigger salaries. The campaign to persuade some players to jump and others not to jump promised to heat up again in the winter of 1902–1903.

By then just about all parties concerned were ready to talk peace, with the notable exception of John T. Brush, who hated Johnson from Western League days (when Brush had owned the Indianapolis franchise) and who'd formally taken control of the New York Giants the past September. The National League had experienced an attendance decline of more than three hundred thousand the past season—mainly because Pittsburgh finished 27½ games ahead of the nearest competitor—and could ill afford to continue the struggle. After all, the Americans had outbid them for players in most instances, had outdrawn them by more than half a million the past season without a New York franchise, and would undoubtedly have a franchise in Manhattan next season.

In December 1902 the National League owners elected Henry Clay "Harry" Pulliam, the thirty-three-year-old secretary of the Pittsburgh club, as their new president. Over Brush's bitter opposition, they then agreed to approach Johnson with a peace overture. The American League president was equally ready to bring labor costs under control, and he, Comiskey, Charles Somers, and Henry Killilea of the Boston AL club began talks with Pulliam, St. Louis's Frank Robison, Chicago's Jim Hart, and August "Garry" Herrmann, president of the Cincinnati club and a friend of both Johnson and Comiskey. On January 10, 1903, hostilities officially came to an end with the signing of an agreement in Cincinnati.

The National League affirmed the American League's status as a separate and equal entity; the two leagues mutually recognized each other's player contracts and reserve lists; and existing operating territories (including the AL's new New York franchise) were recognized. The two leagues would play under a common set of rules, which meant that the AL adopted the NL's foul-strike rule, and they agreed to avoid scheduling conflicts as far as was possible.

The fifth baseball "war" in twenty years had ended in a restored dual-league structure, one that would last. The American League had achieved its goals largely because its enterprise enlisted men such as Charles Comiskey, Connie Mack, Clark Griffith, and (for a time) John McGraw—well-known, experienced baseball figures who were able to recruit playing talent much more effectively than the American or Union associations had been able to do. Thus from the outset the AL exhibited a brand of baseball that was very close to, if not the equal of, that in the older circuit. Promoted in generally prosperous times, the well-run new league also offered an attractive alternative to the NL's characteristically discordant, disorderly way of operating.

Most of all, the American League had the dynamic talents of Ban Johnson, the strongest, most resourceful baseball executive since William Hulbert. Johnson's success in putting over the American League inaugurated a new era in baseball's history. "Modern baseball" had begun.

5.
The
Dead-Ball
Era

It was ironic that, for all the bad feeling they managed to engender, Ban Johnson and John McGraw each got exactly what he wanted. In April 1903 an American League club opened in New York City (sans McGraw), in a place that had been hurriedly transformed from hills and boulders into a barely serviceable playing field in a barely occupiable ballpark seating about fifteen thousand. The diamond was located at Broadway and 168th Street, on the highest spot on Manhattan Island. The "Highlanders," as the New York American Leaguers were quickly nicknamed, proved surprisingly strong that year, finishing in fourth place under the managership of Clark Griffith, who came over from Chicago at Johnson's direction.

Meanwhile John McGraw, making a larger salary than any manager or player before him, began reconstituting the New York Giants even as they struggled to one more last-place finish. In 1903 McGraw's Giants won eighty-four games and gave Pittsburgh plenty to worry about until the Pirates clinched their third straight pennant in mid-September. Joe McGinnity and twenty-three-year-old Christy Mathewson accounted for sixty-one of the Giants' wins. (Almost lost in the hoopla over the Giants' resurgence was the fact that the astute Frank Selee, now managing the Chicago Cubs, had kept his young team in contention almost as long as McGraw's.)

Ostensibly, peace reigned in major-league baseball. In fact, the peace agreement of January 1903 left a number of matters unsettled, including the disposition of various players who'd changed leagues in the period just before the NL and AL came to terms. Willie Keeler, for example, crossed the East River to join the newly established American League club in New York, while Jack Chesbro, winner of forty-nine games in 1901–1902 at Pittsburgh, had also signed with the Highlanders before peace was made. Sam Crawford, slugging Cincinnati outfielder, had recently jumped to the AL's Detroit Tigers.

Although the peace delegates at Cincinnati confirmed those and most interleague switches made before their agreement, disputes continued to arise in particular cases. When Johnson transferred the contract of infielder Norman "Kid" Elberfeld from Detroit to the New York Americans, Giants president John T. Brush and manager McGraw put up a great howl—to no effect. At the same time, George Davis, a former Giant who'd jumped to the Chicago American League club in 1902 and then signed to play with the Giants for 1903, had to return to the American League.

When he heard that Davis had (temporarily) returned to the Giants, Ed Delahanty—also paid a bonus by McGraw to jump back to the NL, then subsequently reassigned to Washington—left his teammates in Detroit and took a train for New York. Apparently Delahanty celebrated too much en route, because near Niagara Falls, Canada, a conductor ordered him off the train. Trying to walk across the railroad bridge over the river, Delahanty fell into the raging waters below the falls; his body surfaced several days later, not far from the bridge. At his death, Delahanty's career batting average of .346 was the highest in baseball history.

Intense hostility between Johnson on one hand and Brush and McGraw on the other hampered relations between the two major leagues throughout the 1903 season. It was a rocky transitional period that would persist through the next season, at least as far as the New York Giants were concerned. In 1903 things weren't yet amicable enough for the two league presidents to get together on a postseason championship series. Instead the immediately interested parties, the Pittsburgh Pirates and the Boston American Leaguers, arranged their own meeting—the first "modern" World Series—without official sanction.

The American League's prestige, already pretty lofty, soared still higher when its champion took only eight games (in a scheduled five-of-nine series) to dispose of the proud Pittsburghers. Cy Young won two games for Boston; Bill Dineen, another former Boston National Leaguer, won three. The great Honus Wagner was held to a .222 batting average and committed six errors. Lacking official status, the revived World Series received little press coverage outside of the two cities involved, but the eight games drew something over one hundred thousand and delivered total receipts of about $50,000.

In September 1903 Organized Baseball finally ratified a system of universal governance, in the form of still another National Agreement. Hammered out by Ban Johnson and Harry Pulliam, the pact created a three-member National Commission—consisting of the league presidents plus a chairman to be elected by the owners—that would rule baseball as a whole. The two-year-old National Association of Professional Baseball Leagues—formed by thirteen "A" to "C" minor organizations to protect themselves after both major leagues scrapped the old National Agreement—became a party to the new pact. Having little choice in the matter, the minors agreed that major-league franchises could draft an unlimited number of players after each season, except that no more than two could be taken from any Class A club.

Garry Herrmann, president of the Cincinnati franchise, was the choice for National Commission chairman. The "magnates" decided to return to a schedule of 154 games after three years at 140 in both leagues. Except for 1918 and 1919, the 154-game season would remain the major-league standard for the next fifty-eight years. And for the next fifty seasons, the major-league map would remain the same: New York, Brooklyn, Boston, Philadelphia, Pittsburgh, Cincinnati, Chicago, and St. Louis in the National League; New York, Boston, Philadelphia, Washington, Cleveland, Detroit, Chicago, and St. Louis in the American League.

The two potentially richest franchises in baseball were now both located on Manhattan Island. It would be a long time before the American League team fulfilled that promise, but with the arrival of John McGraw and, a couple of months later, John T. Brush, the New York Giants awakened.

By 1904 McGraw had assembled a club that was good enough to

win a record 106 games, which left the Giants thirteen ahead of runner-up Chicago. McGraw's team was built on speed (a league-leading 283 stolen bases), strong defense, and the pitching exploits of McGinnity (thirty-five wins) and Mathewson (thirty-three).

It was also built on McGraw's mastery of what, within a few years, would be called "inside baseball." Mainly because of McGraw's success with the Giants, inside baseball became the hottest topic of discussion in the sporting press and among followers of the game everywhere. Accurately defined by one commentator as "merely the outguessing of one team by another," inside baseball featured the manager's signaling from the bench or the coaching box for particular plays: base-stealing attempts, pitchouts to keep opponents from stealing, sacrifice bunts, squeeze and hit-and-run plays, even what one's pitcher should throw or whether one's batter should swing.

Other managers before McGraw—notably Frank Selee and Ned Hanlon—had done all that, but not to the same extent and, given the fact that McGraw managed in the national media capital, not with nearly so much publicity and praise. Because his 1904 team included so many players who were new to each other, McGraw later disclosed, he stayed on the bench and called every play; his favorite signal was to blow his nose.

McGraw had little use for the sacrifice bunt or the squeeze play. As an old Oriole, he based his offensive strategy on base-stealing and the hit-and-run, and he put the latter in motion as often as he could— too much, a few critics in later years would argue. A 1915 study of seventy-two attempted hit-and-run plays in major-league games showed that only eleven percent worked with complete success, with the batter making a safe hit and the runner advancing more than one base. Forty percent of the time, either the batter struck out or the runner was caught by the catcher's throw at second base, doubled up on a line drive, or forced at second on an infield grounder. At least until the 1920s, though, McGraw's faith in the hit-and-run never wavered.

Nor did his belief in the efficacy of umpire-baiting. The efforts of McGraw and his players to intimidate the umpires were systematic, ruthless, relentless, and generally unchecked by Harry Pulliam, even though the league president did penalize McGraw with various fines and suspensions. One in 1905, prompted by an ugly spat with Pittsburgh owner Barney Dreyfuss, lasted fifteen days; another the next season, when McGraw wouldn't admit umpire Jimmy Johnstone to the Polo Grounds, was for twenty.

Yet given John T. Brush's influence in NL affairs, the Giants' manager had no reason to fear for his job or career. Brush functioned as the most powerful club owner in the sport, despite suffering from a progressive paralytic illness that kept him in a wheelchair or bedridden. The McGraw-Brush combine not only produced pennants for New York City and transformed the penurious Giants into baseball's most prosperous operation; but, as the biggest draw wherever they played, the New York club made money for everybody else, so that most NL owners were reluctant to rally around their embattled young president.

Pulliam's complaint that the owners were "a lot of poltroons and dogs [who] eke out their existence through the receipts on the New York grounds" was to no avail. Robust neither physically nor emotionally, Pulliam would eventually break under the strain of his job and, in the summer of 1909, take his own life.

The only way to deal with the Giants, Ned Hanlon was convinced, was "to regard them as bitter enemies and treat them as such." At the end of the 1904 season, Brush and McGraw made even more enemies when they wouldn't renew the World Series with the American League winners, again the Boston club. "There is nothing in the constitution or playing rules of the National League," said Brush with supreme disdain, "which requires its victorious club to submit its championship honors to a contest with a victorious club in a minor league." Added McGraw, "I know the American League and its methods. I ought to, for I paid for my knowledge. . . . They still have my money." There'd be no "haphazard box-office game with Ban Johnson & Company."

In the face of widespread accusations of cowardice and bad sportsmanship, as well as complaints from their own players about missing out on the extra money, the Giants' leaders were unyielding; and so 1904 would go down as the only hiatus in the twentieth-century history of the World Series.

By the end of the 1905 campaign, though, Brush and his manager were no longer disposed to pass up the substantial additional profits to be gained in postseason competition. McGraw always said that his 1905 Giants were his greatest team. Starting to show the wear and tear of several seasons of 400-plus innings, McGinnity slumped to a 21–15 record, but young Leon "Red" Ames won twenty-two games and Mathewson, allowing about 1.25 earned runs per nine innings, led both leagues with thirty-one victories.

The main changes McGraw made in the previous year's champions were installing Mike Donlin, who batted .356, in center field, and shifting the versatile Roger Bresnahan from the outfield to catcher. Besides being one of the big reasons for the Giants' success, Bresnahan would make a lasting contribution to baseball history by inventing catchers' shinguards a couple of years later. With a record of 104–48, the 1905 Giants won by nine games over Pittsburgh.

In the AL, Connie Mack's Philadelphia club, getting twenty-six wins from Rube Waddell and twenty-five from left-hander Eddie Plank, edged out Chicago. Both teams had ninety-two victories, but the Athletics lost four fewer times.

That year's World Series, the first officially sanctioned by the league presidents, was unique in that all five games (in what was scheduled as a four-of-seven set) were shutouts. Mathewson held the Athletics scoreless three times and McGinnity blanked them once. Philadelphia's only victory was a 3–0 pitching gem in game two by Charles "Chief" Bender, Mack's American Indian right-hander out of Carlisle Institute, who wouldn't even have been in Mack's rotation if Waddell hadn't hurt his pitching shoulder playfully wrestling with a teammate aboard a train near the end of the season. (At least that was the official explanation for the big left-hander's absence; rumors circulated during the Series that gamblers had gotten to Mack's pitching ace, although nothing ever came to light.) The five games drew some one hundred thousand people and gave winners' shares of $1,142 to each Giant (based on receipts only from the first four games).

The all-shutout World Series was symptomatic of a pronounced shift in the game's offense-defense balance. Not only had pitchers fully adjusted to the sixty-foot-six-inch pitching distance instituted before the 1893 season, but they'd developed additional skills and techniques that now gave them the upper hand in their confrontations with hitters. The National League's overall batting average in 1899 was

.282; by 1908 it had fallen to .239, and NL teams were scoring about fifty-eight percent fewer runs than nine years earlier. That year 163 shutouts were pitched in the NL, as opposed to ninety in 1899. The American League didn't experience quite such a massive falloff in scoring (5,866 runs in 1901 to 4,284 in 1908), but batting averages dipped almost as much and shutouts increased even more.

In the popular understanding of baseball history, the first two decades of this century have come to be known as the "dead-ball era." Actually, the ball hadn't changed at all—it was still the same cork-centered, yarn-wrapped, stitched-horsehide-covered sphere in use since about 1870, the same object that had been pounded so heartily in the mid- and late-nineties—but some other things had changed.

The foul-strike rule instituted in the major leagues (and throughout Organized Baseball) between 1901 and 1903 was a major boon to the pitcher's craft. The new five-sided home plate was an easier target for pitchers than the old diamond-shaped, foot-square plate, and umpires could judge strikes more effectively. Although ground balls remained as unpredictable as ever in some parks, playing fields in other places received better maintenance. Fielders' gloves, still tiny and flimsy by later standards, improved somewhat with the addition of a leather strap between thumb and forefinger and increased padding in the heel, making for a deeper pocket. Average fielding percentages increased by nineteen points in the National League from 1899 to 1908, by twenty points in the American League from 1901 to 1908. The 1906 Chicago Cubs became the first team in baseball history to commit fewer than two hundred errors in a full season.

Mainly, though, batting averages declined because pitchers had found new ways to get hitters out. After 1900 a variety of "trick pitches" came into use, led by the spitball. That pitch, thrown with moisture applied to the fingers or directly to the ball itself to reduce friction and spin, dipped and swerved in mysterious ways as it reached the plate. Not restricted by anything in the official rules, pitchers "loaded up" by using sweat, moisture from damp grass, or (in most cases) saliva enhanced by chewing tobacco or slippery elm. If saliva was the moistening agent, they might lick the ends of their fingers, nestle the ball in a soaked glove pocket, or spit right on the ball.

Outright mutilation of the ball *was* supposed to be against the rules, but umpires usually did nothing when pitchers scuffed and cut it, using their belt buckles or bits of an emery board or a razor blade tucked into their gloves. Clark Griffith was even known to step off the mound and blithely pound the ball against his spikes!

The first pitcher to have great success with the spitball was Jack Chesbro, who in 1904 piled up forty-one victories for the New York Highlanders (the most in the majors since 1890) before his wild pitch let in the deciding run and gave Boston the American League pennant on the last day of the season. Four years later, spitball master Ed Walsh won forty games for the Chicago American Leaguers. Like Chesbro, Walsh lost the pennant-deciding game on the last day.

Throwing spitballs, cut balls, and later knuckleballs, pitchers generally predominated in the period from roughly 1902 through 1919. Cy Young, who'd come out of the hard-hitting nineties with 285 wins, went on to add 216 more after his thirty-fourth birthday. Walter Johnson, a lanky, long-armed Kansan who joined Washington in 1907, won 296 of his 416 career victories before 1920, despite pitching for poor teams nearly all those years. Grover Cleveland Alexander won twenty-eight games in 1912, his rookie season with the Philadelphia Phillies, and 373 over a twenty-year career, of which 208 came before 1920. Christy Mathewson also totaled 373 wins in a career that ran from 1900 to 1916. Left-hander Eddie Plank came to the Philadelphia Athletics in 1901, directly from Gettysburg College, and went on to win 305 times before he quit sixteen years later.

The baseball of those years may not have offered as much hitting, base-running, and scoring (or as many errors, either), but it attracted customers in unprecedented numbers. Once peace returned in 1903, major-league attendance increased almost every year until 1914. In 1908 blazing pennant races in both leagues pushed total attendance in the majors past seven million, and it stayed between seven and eight million most of the next six seasons.

The minor leagues shared in the flush times, multiplying to about forty circuits by 1910 and drawing more than twenty million people a year. In 1911, for example, paid attendance in the American Association, a strong Class A league mostly formed out of the old Western League, totaled 1,433,477, more than the National League had drawn for most of the nineties.

Prosperity brought significant changes. One indication of the new affluence was that by 1912 dressing rooms were furnished for visiting teams in all major-league ballparks, and in place of open benches, covered "dugouts" now sheltered players from debris-throwing spectators. Umpiring improved noticeably beginning in 1909, when both leagues hired enough additional men to provide two umpires for each regular-season game, and team roster sizes, which had ranged from around twelve to fifteen throughout the nineties, had grown to between twenty and twenty-three by 1910. Most important, nearly all the wooden ballparks gave way to new facilities erected partly or wholly in steel and concrete.

The first of the modern parks was that of the Philadelphia Phillies, constructed of iron and brick and opened in 1895; but the original steel-and-concrete showplaces of the post-1902 baseball boom were the Athletics' Shibe Park, occupied at the start of 1909 season, and Forbes Field in Pittsburgh, opened that July. Over the next six years, every club in the majors except the Phillies, the Chicago Cubs, and the perennially indigent St. Louis Cardinals either built a wholly new fireproof facility, rebuilt its previously wooden ball grounds, or (in the case of the New York American Leaguers) rented from the owners of a new park.

Ironically, the wealthy New York Giants didn't build in steel and concrete until the wooden Polo Grounds burned at the start of the 1911 season. The new Polo Grounds, raised on the same site under Coogan's Bluff, was the biggest yet—a double-decked horseshoe that seated about thirty-five thousand when it was finished late that same season. Meanwhile the Cubs, baseball's second-most-prosperous franchise, continued to operate out of wooden West Side Park.

Drawing record numbers of "fans" (as spectators were called starting around 1907–1908, presumably from "fanatics"), the club owners could afford to eliminate official salary limits. Despite the end of competitive bidding for players, the trend in salaries continued upward. Honus Wagner's salary by 1909 was about $12,000, tops in the majors; and among other first-rank players, Nap Lajoie was making about $7,500, Christy Mathewson $6,000, Ed Walsh $5,000. In 1911, according to the most informed estimates, club payrolls ranged from $55,000 to $75,000, the highest being the Chicago Cubs'.

Players' salaries made up about thirty-eight percent of franchise operating costs.

The league and club presidents often pointed to the steady rise in players' salaries when somebody in the press impugned the reserve clause, but their favorite rebuttal was to insist that a free market in ballplayers would quickly concentrate most of the talent on the richest clubs. Thus the reserve clause was essential to maintain competitive balance, which in turn was essential for the sport to survive.

The trouble with that argument was that competitive balance had never characterized major-league baseball at any time since the invention of the reserve clause in 1879. In the 1880s, Chicago, New York, and Boston won every National League championship except one, while the St. Louis Browns won four straight times in the American Association. In the nineties only Boston, Baltimore, and Brooklyn took NL pennants. From 1901 to 1914 nobody won in the NL besides Pittsburgh, New York, and Chicago, and every American League championship in the years 1901–1919 went either to Chicago, Philadelphia, Detroit, or Boston.

Basically baseball was a sports trust. Yet in a time when trust-busting was a popular political issue and Standard Oil and other corporate behemoths were prosecuted and actually broken up, baseball won general acceptance for the proposition that it was a different kind of business, one that shouldn't be brought under legal scrutiny. Irving F. Sanborn of the *Chicago Tribune*, one of the more astute sportswriters of the period, observed that "organized baseball to-day is apparently . . . impregnable."

Still unrivaled as a mass-appeal sport, baseball was more than ever the National Pastime. The early-century periodical press was full of encomiums to what John Montgomery Ward, now a successful New York attorney, hailed as "the inspired expression of our national character. . . ." "We may have failed to develop a national art or music or literature," bubbled the weekly magazine *Independent*, "but we have developed a national game and we are proud of it." The World Series, a writer in the popular monthly *Everybody's* decided in 1911, was "the very quintessence and consummation of the Most Perfect Thing in America." The next year, justices of the U.S. Supreme Court received bulletins on the decisive Series game during their early-afternoon lunch recess, and then, when the Court resumed, passed inning-by-inning reports from justice to justice.

In the final stages of the 1908 pennant races, crowds besieged newspaper offices in faraway Salt Lake City. Wrote one western observer, "In the most remote country towns there is a demand for long-distance service on the results. . . ." For Allen Sangree, a New York journalist writing in 1907, baseball functioned as "a national safety-valve. . . . It serves the same purpose as a revolution in Central America or a thunderstorm on a hot day." Editorialized the respected *Scribner's Magazine*, "Base-ball unites all classes and conditions of men, from the White House through every layer of our cosmopolite population. . . ."

If baseball was truly the National Pastime, then surely its origins must be uniquely national as well. The venerable Henry Chadwick had always maintained that the American game of baseball, however distinctive it may have become, derived from the English game of rounders, and over the years that had seemed to satisfy most people. Not A. G. Spalding. Generally regarded as baseball's elder statesman, Spalding had become so convinced that the game embodied American values and virtues that he set out to prove its indigenous origins as well.

In 1905, at Spalding's behest, Organized Baseball's ruling National Commission sanctioned the creation of a special seven-man panel to inquire into the matter. Although Spalding wasn't an official member of the group, his wishes determined its makeup. It included such luminaries as George Wright, U.S. Senator Arthur P. Gorman, and former NL presidents Morgan G. Bulkeley, Abraham G. Mills, and Nick Young. Mills served as its chairman.

For two years the Mills commission received "evidence," most of it fanciful, mailed in from all over the country. Spalding urged Mills especially to consider a letter from Abner Graves, an aged former mining engineer living in Denver. Graves claimed that in 1839, in Cooperstown, New York, his schoolmate Abner Doubleday had shown him and other boys a diagram for a game of "base ball" and explained its rules.

That was enough for Mills, who liked the idea of connecting baseball with an admired Civil War military figure. He drafted a report, agreeably signed by the others, affirming that "according to the best evidence obtainable to date, [baseball] was invented by Abner Doubleday at Cooperstown, N.Y., in 1839." Spalding was delighted, and the report found ready acceptance with everyone except Chadwick and a few other holdouts. For one skeptic, the acerbic journalist Rollin L. Hartt, the Mills commission's report was like "the infallibility of the Pope, which, as a Catholic savant once remarked to me, is 'a dogma we unfortunately have to believe.'" The Doubleday myth quickly became a staple of American folklore, as well as what most people took for authenticated history.

Of course, few fans worried about where or when baseball had originated. It was enough that the game agitated them mightily—and especially at World Series time. The 1906 Series was a unique all-Chicago event and the first postseason clash to receive truly national attention. Midway through the previous year, Frank Selee had turned his carefully rebuilt Cubs over to first baseman Frank Chance, and then moved to Colorado in a futile effort to fight off tuberculosis. With a fine infield that included, besides Chance, Johnny Evers at second base, Joe Tinker at shortstop, and Harry Steinfeldt at third; capable if undistinguished outfielders; the brilliant Johnny Kling behind the plate; and an outstanding group of pitchers, the 1906 Cubs won a staggering 116 games and finished twenty ahead of McGraw's Giants.

The White Sox (as local writers had modernized their nickname) beat out New York and Cleveland for the American League title. Player-manager Fielder Jones's "Hitless Wonders" batted .230 as a team and could wrangle only 570 runs (including a grand total of *six* home runs), but then nobody was scoring much anymore. The White Sox pitchers allowed slightly more than two earned runs per nine innings, the Cubs' pitchers a microscopic 1.76.

The outcome was one of the biggest surprises in Series history: The underdog White Sox needed only six games to dispose of their mighty West Side rivals. Ed Walsh, Nick Altrock, and G. Harris "Doc" White of the White Sox kept Cubs batters under control, while the Hitless Wonders exploded for twenty-two runs, including eight in the fifth game and eight more in the clincher. Nearly one hundred thousand people crowded into the two little wooden ballparks, bringing in receipts of $106,550.

In 1907 the Cubs were nearly as overpowering again in the

National League—their 107 victories left Pittsburgh seventeen games behind—and following a tie in the World Series opener, Chicago took four straight games from the upstart Detroit Tigers, managed by old Oriole Hugh Jennings. Orval Overall, Ed Reulbach, Mordecai Brown, and Jake Pfiester each beat the Tigers once and held Ty Cobb, the American League's young sensation, to only four hits over the five games.

Although that encounter with Cobb left the Cubs and National League fans unimpressed, the youngster was on the verge of becoming the brightest star baseball had yet seen, as well as its most explosively controversial figure both on and off the field. Not incidentally, he was also the main reason the Detroit franchise, hitherto one of the AL's weakest, was about to emerge as one of its most profitable.

Born near the end of 1886 in a rural community in Banks County in northern Georgia and raised a little south of there in the town of Royston, Tyrus Raymond Cobb came from circumstances several cuts above that of most professional ballplayers. His mother was from a well-fixed farming family; his father, a college graduate, served a term in the state senate as well as being the local school principal and editor of the town newspaper. One of the area's leading citizens, the senior Cobb was an imperious, demanding man who set standards young Cobb thought unreachable, at the same time that he stoutly resisted the boy's yearning for a career in baseball.

The youth left home anyway, determined to become a professional, and by August 1905, as an outfielder for Augusta, he was leading the Class C South Atlantic League in batting. At that point he was called home, where he learned the ghastly news that his mother had killed his father with two shotgun blasts because, she maintained, she mistook him for a nighttime intruder. Following the funeral and his mother's indictment on a manslaughter charge, Cobb managed to collect his wits in time to report to the Detroit Tigers, who'd just purchased his contract for $700 and specified immediate delivery.

The bizarre circumstances surrounding his father's death partly explain why Cobb turned from being "a mild-mannered Sunday School boy" into a self-described "snarling wildcat." The other reason had to do with the rough treatment he received at the hands of his Detroit teammates during spring training 1906 in Augusta.

Seeking a place on the team following a generally unimpressive showing in forty-one American League games, Cobb encountered the usual petty cruelties and humiliations to which "regulars" subjected rookies in those days. But Cobb, a sensitive, high-strung youngster to begin with, a Southern Baptist among men who were largely Irish-Catholics and all Yankees, reacted violently to the hazing and became estranged from the rest of the players. Although his mother was acquitted that spring, the messy affair still left a cloud of scandal hanging over the family name. Cobb began his first full major-league season determined to vindicate his family's honor and especially his father's memory, besides showing his tormenting teammates that he was good enough to play with anybody.

During the 1906 season Cobb battled opponents, members of his own team, and himself. Not naturally gifted like Wagner or Lajoie, he made himself into a great ballplayer through intelligence, tenacity, and a competitive drive that was always ruthless and frequently vicious. After batting .316 in ninety-eight games, the "Georgia Peach" (as a Detroit writer dubbed him) endured another strife-filled spring in 1907 that culminated in a sound thrashing at the hands of a brawny Detroit catcher, just before an exhibition game in Meridian, Mississippi.

Cobb never made any real friends on the teams he played for during his twenty-four-year career—at the end of which he held forty-three different offensive records. Suspicious, quick to take offense, unable to understand men less driven to achieve excellence, Cobb went his own way to fame and, ultimately, a sizable fortune. A left-handed batter (and right-handed thrower), slightly over six feet tall, 170 to 180 pounds in his prime, Cobb was unexcelled in his ability to drag bunts and push, slap, and drive the ball to all fields. He was also a fast, recklessly aggressive base runner who took no mercy on anybody in his path. "The base runner has the right of way," he insisted, "and the man who blocks it does it at his own peril."

"I have observed," Cobb remarked on another occasion, "that baseball is not unlike a war." It was, he said, "a struggle for supremacy, a survival of the fittest," with the objective being the "general demoralization of the opposition." The sport of baseball had never seen such a combination of carefully nurtured talents and competitive fire. Raymond "Rube" Bressler, a ballplaying contemporary, said of Cobb, "His determination was fantastic. I never saw anybody like him. It was *his* base. It was *his* game. *Everything* was his."

Unlike Babe Ruth later on, Cobb didn't actually change the way baseball was played, but he did bring the closely played style of the "dead-ball" years to its highest level of expertise and refinement. In 1907 Cobb batted .350 to lead the American League—which he also topped in runs batted in, total bases, and stolen bases—and for the next twelve seasons nobody else was the league's official batting titlist except Boston's Tris Speaker, who managed to beat him out in 1916. From 1907 to 1919 Cobb *averaged* .378, with his top marks being .420 in 1911 and .410 the next year. He stole eighty-three bases in 1911, ninety-six in 1915. By then his salary had climbed to $20,000, which made him the highest-paid player in the game, by about $2,500 over Speaker.

Cobb's big-league years were marked by a succession of fracases with people inside and outside ballparks, frequently with black people who didn't accord him the automatic deference a southern-born white man had grown up to expect; and his numerous run-ins with teammates and opponents made him the most hated man in the league. (So hated that in 1910 the St. Louis team undertook to deny Cobb his fourth batting title by letting Napoleon Lajoie reach base safely on seven bunts in a season-closing doubleheader. The ploy failed when Ban Johnson certified Cobb the winner anyway.)

Cobb's .324 batting average in 1908, the lowest he ever won with, was still eighty-five points above the league average. It was a year for magnificent pitching and epic pennant struggles. Cobb's Tigers won again in a down-to-the-wire battle with both Chicago and Cleveland. In the season's final game, they caught Ed Walsh without his best spitter and smashed Chicago's chances for a tie. Cleveland had been eliminated the previous day, but by winning its season finale, player-manager Lajoie's club finished only half a game behind Detroit. The White Sox ended up third, two games out.

The National League race did end in a tie, the result of a legendary blunder by rookie Fred Merkle of the Giants two weeks earlier in a game at the Polo Grounds with the Cubs. Following the custom of the period, Merkle had veered toward the clubhouse instead of running from first to second base while what should have been the winning run scored with two out in the ninth inning. Johnny Evers retrieved the ball and stepped on second, thereby executing a force play and nullifying the Giants' run.

When the two umpires, neither of whom had seen what happened, ruled it too dark to continue, John McGraw demanded that Harry Pulliam overrule them and declare for the Giants. Pulliam upheld his umpires—a decision that necessitated a replay of the disputed contest after Chicago eliminated Pittsburgh in its final regularly scheduled game, while New York swept its last three from the lowly Boston club.

The Chicago–New York tie-breaker—played in the newly enlarged Polo Grounds on October 8, 1908, before a howling mob of more than thirty thousand inside and thousands more watching the game from vantage points on Coogan's Bluff and elsewhere—was probably the most notable sports event in the nation's history up to then. Despite a brazen effort by the Giants' team physician to bribe umpires Bill Klem and Bob Emslie, things proceeded fairly smoothly once the game got under way.

Mordecai Brown, called "Three Finger" because a boyhood farm accident had mangled his pitching hand, came on in relief to shut down the Giants after they'd scored two first-inning runs, while Christy Mathewson, who'd pitched his team to victory thirty-seven times that season, subsequently yielded four runs. The Cubs left New York as National League champions for the third year in a row.

After all that, the World Series was something of an anticlimax. Detroit finally won a game from the Cubs—but only one out of five. The Tigers, a collection of ordinary players except for Cobb and hard-hitting outfielder Sam Crawford, did better in 1909 but still lost a third straight Series, in a hard-fought seven games to Wagner and the Pittsburgh Pirates. Charles "Babe" Adams, only a twelve-game winner in the regular season, was the difference in the World Series, beating the Tigers three times. It was to be the last World Series for thirty-five-year-old Wagner, and the last as well for twenty-two-year-old Cobb.

Beginning in 1910, the Philadelphia Athletics were the dominant team in baseball. After missing by only three games in 1909, they won the 1910 AL title by fourteen and a half. Connie Mack, now forty-eight, managed from the bench in dark suit, high starched collar, and derby (or straw boater in hot weather). Fond of giving anti-liquor lectures and exacting abstinence pledges from his charges, the "Tall Tactician," as Philadelphia writers called him, had already directed teams to American League pennants in 1902 and 1905. In 1910 Mack's Athletics knocked off the Cubs in five games, with the only close one being Chicago's lone win in game four. Conquerors of the National League in four of the past five years, the Cubs had brought in little new blood.

Meanwhile John McGraw had kept only Mathewson and a couple of others in a rebuilding program that produced three consecutive NL titles, starting in 1911. It was in those years that the New York writers anointed McGraw the "Little Napoleon." The contrast between Mack and McGraw accounted for much of the appeal in their three World Series confrontations. Both were Irish-Catholics, but whereas Mack always projected an image of dignity and rectitude, McGraw was always "Muggsy"—hothead, tough guy, umpire-bullier.

Unlike McGraw, moreover, Mack was content to teach his players beforehand and then trust them to do the correct thing once a game started. He could manage that way, he explained, because he sought smart ballplayers, often college men. Mack's 1910–1914 teams featured an unusual number of ex-collegians, including pitchers Eddie Plank (Gettysburg), Chief Bender (Carlisle), and Jack Coombs (Colby); shortstop Jack Barry (Holy Cross); and second baseman Eddie Collins, who joined Mack in 1906 directly out of Columbia University and quickly came to rival Lajoie as the game's foremost second baseman.

In 1911 the World Series truly came into its own as a national and even international sports spectacle. Reported as far away as Tokyo by trans-Pacific cable, it was the first played on both home sites in new steel-and-concrete ballparks. Mack's club triumphed four games to two, mainly because Frank Baker, the Athletics' third baseman, hit home runs in the second and third games (thereby forever becoming Home Run Baker) and Philadelphia's catchers held Giants runners, who'd stolen 347 times that season, to only four successfully executed thefts. Record receipts from the record attendance of some 180,000 made for record players' shares: $3,655 for each Athletic, $2,436 for each Giant.

McGraw's Giants lost again in 1912, and yet again in 1913. In 1912 they battled the Boston American Leaguers, now known as the Red Sox, to three wins apiece plus a tie. In the bottom of the tenth inning in game eight, Giants center fielder Fred Snodgrass dropped an easy fly ball, opening the door for a two-run rally that beat Mathewson. It was possibly the toughest loss in the great pitcher's glittering career.

The next year's Series was far less dramatic. Mack's Athletics were just too good, dispatching the Giants in five games. Mathewson lost the clincher to Eddie Plank, who allowed New York two hits and faced only twenty-nine batters. Thus McGraw equaled the record of his old Oriole teammate Hugh Jennings in managing three consecutive World Series losers. That, suggested Christy Mathewson in 1914, was largely because the Giants, "a team of puppets worked from the bench by a string," had made mistakes at critical moments. By contrast, Mack's men, able to think for themselves and "stand alone no matter how big the crisis," had played heady and steady baseball.

Whatever one thought about the managing style of the "Little Napoleon," it didn't produce a fourth straight pennant. In 1914 the long-downtrodden Boston club, known as the Braves since being acquired by New Yorker George Grant (a Brave of Tammany Hall), amazed the sports world by rising from last place in July to win everything. In breaking the fourteen-season New York–Chicago–Pittsburgh pennant axis, the Braves won sixty-eight of their last eighty-seven games, shot past the Giants, and ended up ten and one-half games ahead of McGraw's team.

Like Mack, Braves manager George Stallings directed his men from the bench in street clothes. Unlike Mack, Stallings was a firebrand whose curses often turned the air blue in the vicinity of the Braves' dugout. Hailed as the "Miracle Man," Stallings relied on the field leadership of ex-Cub Johnny Evers and the sturdy pitching of Bill James, George Tyler, and Dick Rudolph, while masterfully maneuvering a miscellany of journeymen, most of whom never played so well again. An early convert to the belief that left-handed batters hit best against right-handed pitchers (and vice versa), Stallings alternated players at five positions in his day-to-day lineups.

In the American League, meanwhile, Mack's great team easily

did it again. Huge favorites going into the World Series, the Athletics succumbed to the "Miracle Braves" in four games, one of the greatest upsets in American sports history. After allowing the American Leaguers only one run in the first two meetings in Philadelphia, Stallings's club won a twelve-inning thriller at Fenway Park (where the Boston games were played because of the inadequacy of the Braves' rickety South End Grounds). Rudolph shut down the Athletics to conclude the sweep, with Hank Gowdy, a tall catcher who'd batted only .243 in the regular season, pushing his average to .545 over the four games.

Given the drama of the onrushing Braves, 1914 should have been a big money-making season, at least in the National League. In fact, most clubs in both leagues ended with deficits that year. Partly this was a result of a national economic slowdown, but the main reason why attendance fell by approximately half a million in each league was the presence in Brooklyn, Pittsburgh, Chicago, and St. Louis of still another self-proclaimed major-league organization. In those cities, clubs affiliated with the new Federal League went head-to-head with the Americans and Nationals, while in four other cities—Kansas City, Indianapolis, Baltimore, and Buffalo—the Federals operated against top-level minor-league franchises.

In 1913 the Federal League had surfaced as an independent or "outlaw" organization, keeping hands off players under contract or reserve to AL and NL clubs, and recruiting exclusively outside Organized Baseball from the vast talent pool in (white) semipro ball. Over the winter president James Gilmore sought to bring his circuit under the National Agreement but was rebuffed by Ban Johnson; having once engineered a second major league, Johnson now told Gilmore and associates there wasn't room for a third. Declaring the reserve clause illegal and the National Agreement monopolistic, the Federals then started wooing National and American League players with contracts that not only paid more money but left out the reserve clause.

Hal Chase, an outstanding first baseman, jumped from the Chicago White Sox to the Buffalo Federals in midseason 1914, but the Federal League failed to sign any other top major-leaguers still in their primes. Joe Tinker, player-manager at Cincinnati in 1913, had already seen his best days when he signed to manage the new Chicago Whales, as had Chief Bender and Eddie Plank when they left the Philadelphia Athletics after the disastrous 1914 World Series to join the Baltimore Terrapins and St. Louis Terriers, respectively.

Although numerous former major-leaguers appeared in the Federal League—eighty-one in all in 1914–1915—and such notables as Fielder Jones, Three Finger Brown, and George Stovall (former first baseman and manager at Cleveland and St. Louis in the AL) managed Federal League teams, only eighteen men actually under contract jumped to the new circuit. Baseball's reigning stars—Cobb, Mathewson, Eddie Collins, Tris Speaker, Grover Cleveland Alexander, Cleveland's Joe Jackson—signed new contracts at substantial pay increases and stayed in the two established leagues. Walter Johnson, a thirty-six-game winner in 1913, did sign a Federal League contract, but then jumped back to Washington for a $5,500 pay boost.

Oilman Harry Sinclair, the Federals' biggest financial backer, sought John McGraw's services for a reported $100,000. But McGraw, working under the five-year contract at $30,000 per year he'd signed with Giants president Harry Hempstead after Brush's death in 1912, remained unconvinced that the putative third major league had any future.

McGraw made the right decision, but the struggle with what partisan sportswriters labeled the "invaders" proved a costly one. A report on the salaries of seventeen AL and NL players, prepared for National Commission chairman Garry Herrmann, revealed that the differences between their 1913 and 1915 pay varied from $8,000 for Cobb to $1,800 for Owen "Donie" Bush, Detroit's veteran shortstop. President Charles Comiskey of the Chicago White Sox signed George "Buck" Weaver, a young infielder making $2,500, to a three-year contract at $6,000 per year; Ivy Wingo, a run-of-the-mill catcher for the St. Louis Cardinals, saw his salary jump from $2,600 to $6,500.

The Federal League also badly hurt the upper minors; 115 players jumped minor-league reserve lists to join the Federals. Of the forty minor leagues operating in 1913, only twenty-three finished the season two years later. A particularly hard-hit franchise was Baltimore in the International League. Among the promising players owner Jack Dunn was forced to sell during his struggle with the Baltimore Fed-

erals was a nineteen-year-old left-handed pitcher named George Herman Ruth, already called "Babe" by the time he was sold to the Boston
Red Sox in midsummer 1914.

AL and NL clubs filed several suits in state courts seeking injunctions to restrain the execution of contracts signed with Federal League
teams. Early in January 1915 the Federals retaliated by suing Organized Baseball in the U.S. district court for northern Illinois under
the Sherman Antitrust Act, which prohibited monopolies operating in
interstate commerce. The Federals asked the court to declare the
existing National Agreement and all contracts and other actions taken
under it illegal, to dissolve Organized Baseball, and to dismiss all
injunction suits against Federal League contractees. Testimony and
arguments before Judge Kenesaw Mountain Landis ended on January
22, but Landis, an ardent baseball fan, wouldn't render a decision.
The longer he held off, Landis believed, the more likely it was that the
disputants would reach some kind of agreement.

That was what happened. As in 1882 and 1902, baseball's businessmen were ready to settle their differences and cut their losses.
Despite two down-to-the-wire pennant races (won by Indianapolis in
1914, Chicago in 1915), the Federals had lost hugely—about $2.5
million by the end of 1915—and that December representatives of the
twenty-four National, American, and Federal league clubs came to
terms in Cincinnati.

In effect the two older leagues bought out the Federals, who
dissolved their organization in return for a $600,000 payment to be
distributed among their eight groups of financial backers. The agreement also permitted Charles Weeghman, owner of the Chicago
Whales, to purchase the Chicago Cubs, and Phil Ball, who'd operated
the St. Louis Terriers, to buy control of the St. Louis Browns. The
validity of the Federals' contracts was implicitly recognized in a provision that the remaining clubs could sell any players the AL and NL
wanted to buy. The subsequent sale of seventeen players netted
$129,150, of which $50,000 went to Harry Sinclair for rights to Benny
Kauff, the league's batting and stolen-base titlist in 1914–1915, and
four other players purchased by the New York Giants.

On the whole, matters seemed to have worked out cordially and
successfully. Ball's money strengthened a weak American League fran-

chise in St. Louis, while Weeghman's purchase of the Cubs meant that they could vacate wooden West Side Park for the steel-and-concrete facility he'd built for his Whales on Chicago's near north side. The Federal League had also developed a number of young players who would go on to have successful careers in the NL and AL.

Everybody was happy with the settlement but the Baltimore Federal League investors, who insisted that they be allowed to buy the impoverished St. Louis Cardinals franchise and move it to Baltimore. Rebuffed by the NL club owners, the Baltimoreans first filed a complaint with the Antitrust Division of the U.S. Justice Department, then, denied again, brought their own antitrust suit against Organized Baseball. In September 1917, in U.S. district court in the District of Columbia, the suit began its five-year progress through the federal judiciary.

On the field, the level of play in 1914–1915 undoubtedly suffered from the diversion of talent to the Federal League. Irving F. Sanborn, the Chicago sportswriter, hadn't seen so much "rotten baseball" since the Brotherhood war. Too many players, thought Sanborn, were "afflicted by the strabismus that makes the figures on the bi-monthly paycheck loom larger than those on the score-board."

Connie Mack grimly agreed. Disgusted by his players' buzzings about the new league and then their collapse in the 1914 World Series, Mack watched Bender and Plank desert to the Federals and decided to tear his club apart and start over. Eddie Collins, who'd batted .344 in 1914, went to the Chicago White Sox for $50,000, and Mack sold Jack Barry to Boston in midseason 1915. Frank Baker wouldn't sign his contract, held out all that season, and was sold to the New York Yankees (as they were now called) for $35,000 early in 1916. Winners of four American League and three world's championships in five years, the Athletics won only forty-three games in 1915 to start a run of seven straight last-place finishes.

As the Athletics plummeted, the Boston Red Sox regained the top in the American League, beating out Ty Cobb and Detroit in a close race. Besides a superbly balanced pitching staff that included Babe Ruth, an eighteen-game winner in his first full season in the majors, the Red Sox relied on the all-around abilities of Tris Speaker. Generally conceded to be the finest center fielder baseball had seen, the

Texas-born Speaker also had been among the league's top batsmen since coming up in 1909 at the age of twenty-one.

In the 1915 World Series the Red Sox met the Philadelphia Phillies, who'd overcome the defending champion Boston Braves to win their first pennant—mainly on the strength of Grover Cleveland Alexander's thirty-one victories. Alexander handled the Red Sox easily in the Series opener in Philadelphia, but then Boston took four straight behind right-handers George Foster and Ernie Shore and lefty Hubert "Dutch" Leonard. Games three and four, Boston's home dates, were played in the Braves' brand-new Braves Field, which seated some ten thousand more than Fenway Park.

Major-league attendance recovered somewhat in 1916, even though the crowds were still smaller than they'd been in 1913. Seeking to recoup their losses from the Federal League affair, the league presidents and the club owners made retrenchment the watchword. Tris Speaker's two-year contract, which had paid him an aggregate $35,000 for not going to the Federals, expired after the 1915 season. When Boston president Joseph Lannin sent Speaker a one-year contract for $9,000, the Texan refused to sign, whereupon Lannin shipped him to Cleveland for $50,000 and a couple of young players. It would turn out to be the best deal in the history of the Cleveland franchise.

Speaker proceeded to end Ty Cobb's nine-year reign as American League batting champion, registering 211 hits and a .386 average to Cobb's .371. Yet the Red Sox obviously didn't have to have Speaker, because they still edged the increasingly tough Chicago White Sox by two games. Babe Ruth, at twenty-one, became the AL's premier left-hander, winning twenty-three games with an earned run average of 1.75. In Ruth, Shore, Leonard, Foster, and a young right-hander named Carl Mays, the Red Sox boasted the greatest concentration of pitching talent in baseball.

Ruth pitched one of Boston's victories in the World Series, and for the second Series in a row, the National League champion could win only once. Nicknamed after manager Wilbert Robinson, another old Oriole, the Brooklyn Robins, who brought that historic baseball hotbed its first pennant since 1900, were a very ordinary ball club. Held to a .200 batting average by Red Sox pitchers, Robinson's team scored its only victory in game three at Ebbets Field, the modern park completed under president Charles Ebbets's direction in 1912.

The 1916 World Series took place with the United States still at peace with the other nations of the world, some three weeks before incumbent President Woodrow Wilson won reelection on the slogan "He kept us out of war." For more than two years the peoples of Europe had been slaughtering each other in the bloodiest conflict in human history, while much of the American public had been preoccupied with such matters as the pennant races, the controversy surrounding the Federal League, Ty Cobb's battles on and off the ballfield, and the pitching feats of "the Ruth kid" at Boston. Despite successive disputes with Imperial Germany over the threat its submarines posed to the rights of neutral shipping and the safety of U.S. citizens traveling on British and French vessels, the war in Europe, for most Americans, had remained Europe's quarrel.

Then, in January 1917, the Imperial German high command announced a campaign of unrestricted submarine warfare in the northern Atlantic region—a step that prompted the Wilson administration to break diplomatic relations. Sinkings of U.S. ships and American deaths inevitably followed. On April 2 President Wilson, the man who'd been reelected to keep the country out of war, told a joint session of the Congress that the United States must enter the conflict to uphold its neutral rights, as well as defend the values of Western Civilization and "make the world safe for democracy." Four days later the Congress voted its declaration of war on Imperial Germany.

The "Great War," as Europeans were already calling it, would kill only about fifty-five thousand Americans, an almost insignificant number alongside the millions of Europeans who died between 1914 and 1918, but it would change everybody's circumstances in some degree. The sport and business of baseball, after making its way through one wartime season generally intact, would have its next season totally disrupted. Then, with the return of peace, baseball would enter its most prosperous years thus far, at the same time as it passed through its severest crisis and witnessed the emergence of its most dazzling performer.

6.
War,
Scandal,
and Babe Ruth

Americans had never been prepared for the wars they'd fought. For a year after the United States entered the Great War, it was able to contribute little to the desperate manpower needs of Great Britain and France, its unofficial allies in the struggle against Imperial Germany. Volunteers crowded military recruiting offices across the country, and on May 18, 1917, the Congress enacted a conscription law that affected all able-bodied American males between twenty-one and thirty years old. June 5 was set aside as National Registration Day, yet it wouldn't be until early the next year that the Wilson administration's program for mobilizing manpower and resources really started to take effect.

On April 11, 1917, for the first time, the professional baseball season opened with the nation at war. Bands played "The Star-Spangled Banner" and other patriotic airs; flags were much in evidence. President Wilson, continuing the custom established by William Howard Taft, his predecessor, threw out the first ball at the Washington Senators' park.

Some American League spectators might have been led to believe that the ballplayers were all about to enlist, because following pregame practice, they saw them shoulder their bats and go through military drills. The drills had been the brainstorm of T. L. Huston, a former army engineer who'd co-owned the New York Yankees since 1914, and were heartily endorsed by Ban Johnson. Starting in the southern spring-training camps, instructors assigned from nearby military posts put the players through their paces. John Tener, former governor of Pennsylvania and the National League's president since 1914, decided not to urge such quasi-military activity on the club owners in his circuit, but at least Johnson's league could boast of giving an example in "preparedness" for the rest of the country.

In most respects major-league baseball was little affected during the 1917 season by American entry into the war. By late summer the minor leagues were starting to lose players to military service, and attendance in the minors fell off badly as people worked longer hours and moved around to take advantage of high-paying war-related jobs. Yet big-league rosters held together and the crowds continued to turn out. Total attendance in the majors remained at around the five-million mark, little different from 1916. Hank Gowdy of the Boston Braves earned a great deal of acclaim by being the first major-leaguer to volunteer, but few ballplayers followed his lead. For the most part, it was business as usual in the first season of wartime baseball.

Charles Comiskey and John McGraw, two of baseball's biggest names, each made comebacks of sorts in 1917. Comiskey's teams had drawn well in the new ballpark he'd opened in 1910, but not since 1906 had they brought home a pennant. Then in 1917, under manager Clarence "Pants" Rowland, the White Sox won one hundred games and left the world's champion Boston Red Sox ten games back.

The keys to Chicago's success were the brilliant Eddie Collins, purchased from the Philadelphia Athletics late in 1914, and Joe Jackson, obtained from Cleveland in August 1915 for $15,000 and three second-rate players. Luckily for the future of the Cleveland franchise, Boston put Tris Speaker on the market the next spring, so that while the Indians (their nickname after Nap Lajoie's departure) virtually gave away one of the most gifted players of all time in Jackson, they subsequently acquired another one just as good in Speaker.

Collins and Jackson could hardly have been more unalike. Compact, combative, and a Columbia University graduate, Collins was so self-confident on and off the playing field that his teammates called him "Cocky." (Asked by the 1907 Columbia yearbook editors to name his favorite historical character, Collins had unhesitatingly replied, "Cap Anson.")

Jackson, known as "Shoeless Joe" because once in the Carolina Association he'd removed his tight-fitting shoes and played in his stocking feet, was lanky, diffident, illiterate—a product of southern textile-mill baseball. Ty Cobb always named Jackson as the greatest natural hitter he ever saw, and in 1911, his first full season in the majors, the South Carolinian had batted .408 (and still trailed Cobb by twelve points). The next year he hit .395 to Cobb's .410. A left-handed batter who held his "Black Betsy" at the very end and stood with his feet close together, Jackson took a long stride and a full swing. In a later time he would undoubtedly have been a prolific home-run hitter. As it was, he became known as an exceptionally "hard hitter," which meant that instead of punching and placing his base hits as Cobb usually did, Jackson slammed "blue darters" for numerous doubles and triples.

The White Sox also had a deft third baseman and timely batsman in switch-hitting Buck Weaver, the American League's best catcher in scrappy little Ray Schalk, and solid performers in center field and at first base in Oscar "Happy" Felsch and Charles "Chick" Gandil, respectively. Their deep pitching staff was headed by veteran right-hander Eddie Cicotte, master of the spitball, knuckleball, and an assortment of other pitches, and winner of twenty-eight games in 1917.

Meanwhile John McGraw and the New York Giants regained the top in the National League. Following a plunge all the way to last place in 1915, McGraw's club had finished fourth in 1916, despite winning streaks of fourteen and twenty-six games. The 1917 Giants weren't as strong as some of McGraw's earlier outfits, but with good defense and well-balanced pitching, they had a fairly easy time winning New York's sixth NL title under the Little Napoleon.

It was a tempestuous season for the Giants nonetheless, starting with a spring exhibition series with Detroit. In Dallas, Ty Cobb and Giants infielder Charles "Buck" Herzog first scuffled on the field and then staged a bloody after-dinner brawl in Cobb's hotel room. When Cobb and McGraw almost came to blows in the lobby the next morning, Cobb denounced McGraw as a "mucker" and refused to take the field against the Giants again. Marked by much throwing at batters' heads and several more melees, the exhibition series finally ended in Kansas City.

Then in June, in Cincinnati, McGraw repeatedly quarreled with umpire Bill Byron and ended up punching him under the stands after a game. After league president Tener hit McGraw with a $500 fine and sixteen-day suspension, several New York newspapers quoted the manager to the effect that everybody was out to get the Giants, and that "the Pennsylvania league" was headed by a politician who neglected his duties except to favor the Philadelphia Phillies. At that, the NL club owners met in New York, listened to McGraw deny making any such statements, and declared the matter officially closed—only to have the New York chapter of the Base Ball Writers Association pressure the owners into meeting again. At the second inquiry, several people testified that they'd heard McGraw say just what the papers had printed. Eventually McGraw's fine was upped to $1,000, which he paid cheerfully enough at the end of the season—and why not, since his Giants had again made it into the World Series.

It wasn't a memorable Series except for one strange, critical situation. Chicago won the first two games, at Comiskey Park; then the Giants won twice at the Polo Grounds. Back in Chicago, the White Sox battered Giants pitchers for fourteen hits and eight runs to go up three games to two. In game six, at the Polo Grounds, Chicago scored three times in the fourth inning, the key play being the failure of anybody to cover the plate while Giants third baseman Henry "Heinie" Zimmerman chased Eddie Collins home with the go-ahead run. The game ended 4–2 Chicago, wrapping up McGraw's fourth Series defeat in four tries since 1911.

That winter the National Commission and the club owners acted as if semi-wartime conditions would last for at least another full season. They should have known better, because by early 1918 the country was very much on a war footing, and the 1918 season would be the worst for professional baseball since the Brotherhood war. Of nine minor leagues that started the year, only the International League managed to complete its schedule. As the season progressed, a number of major-leaguers enlisted, many others were drafted, and others went to work in shipyards, steel mills, and munitions plants, where they were nominally employed in draft-exempt "essential occupations" but actually paid mainly to play for company baseball teams.

By July managers were scrambling to fill holes in their rosters with available minor-leaguers. McGraw, for example, had only three regulars and one starting pitcher from the previous year's team at the end of the 1918 season. The Giants came in a distant second to the Chicago Cubs and attracted only about 250,000 into the Polo Grounds. At that, they did better than most. Overall major-league attendance plunged below two million.

The season ended after the traditional doubleheaders on Labor Day. Faced with the War Department's "work or fight" directive, which threatened to shut down all "nonessential" activities and employments, the National Commission secured permission to continue through the holiday weekend and then hold the World Series directly thereafter. Thus on September 5, 1918, the earliest Series in history got under way, with the Boston Red Sox taking on a mediocre Chicago Cubs team.

Both clubs had gotten as far as they had because they'd been able to hold on to their mainstays while other clubs had been steadily depleted. Yet both Cubs manager Fred Mitchell and Ed Barrow, in his first year directing the Red Sox, had found it necessary to improvise. Inasmuch as Babe Ruth was an extraordinarily good-hitting pitcher, Barrow had played the big left-hander in the outfield when he wasn't taking his turn on the mound. Besides pitching thirteen wins, Ruth had batted .300 and hit eleven home runs, most in the majors.

Poor crowds at Fenway Park in Boston and at Comiskey Park (where the Chicago home games were held during the Series, rather than at the smaller Cubs facility) dimmed the players' expectations of substantial championship money. Besides that, the National Commission had inopportunely directed that part of the proceeds would go to wartime charities, and that the second- , third- , and fourth-place teams in each league would share in receipts from the first four games.

Ruth ran his World Series streak of scoreless innings to $29\frac{2}{3}$ by shutting out the Cubs in the opener in Chicago, then holding them without a run for seven more innings in game four, which the Red Sox won 3-2. Carl Mays, a right-hander with an old-fashioned three-quarter-underhand delivery, pitched Boston's other two victories, while the Cubs could win only the second and fifth games. The sixth and final contest almost wasn't played, because players on both teams, disgruntled by the small receipts and having to share what largesse there was, at first refused to take the field. After an impassioned appeal to their sportsmanship and patriotism by Ban Johnson, the game proceeded and the trouble-filled season sputtered to an end.

Within another month, much sooner than most military analysts had expected, German resistance began to crumble before the U.S.-British-French offensive. Kaiser Wilhelm II fled to Holland, a German republic was proclaimed, and on November 11, 1918, after fifty-two months of carnage, an armistice finally stopped the Great War.

In baseball, meanwhile, various circumstances had combined to create a climate of resentment and distrust at the highest levels. Pittsburgh owner Barney Dreyfuss, for example, continued to fume over the loss to the AL's St. Louis Browns of George Sisler, a superb player out of the University of Michigan, on whom Pittsburgh had insisted it had first claim. Dreyfuss could never forgive National Commission chairman Garry Herrmann, a nominal National Leaguer, for ruling Sisler a free agent, whereupon in 1916 Sisler had signed with Browns business and field manager Branch Rickey, his former coach at the University of Michigan.

NL president John Tener was able to swallow what happened in the Sisler matter, but he couldn't abide an injunction secured in federal court by the Philadelphia Athletics to prevent a pitcher named Scott Perry from joining the Boston Braves, even though the National Commission, the secretary of the minor leagues' National Association, and the Atlanta Southern League franchise (which owned reserve rights to Perry) all agreed that he should go to the National League club. Tener first resigned from the National Commission, then, late in 1918, resigned as NL president. John Heydler, former umpire and longtime NL secretary, assumed Tener's duties.

Apart from Tener's resignation, the major off-season baseball news had to do with the purchase of majority interest in the New York Giants by Charles H. Stoneham. A multimillionaire whose fortune rested mainly on questionably legal securities operations, Stoneham paid a record price—somewhat more than a million dollars—for baseball's most valuable property. As part of the deal, John McGraw, who'd

acted as broker between Stoneham and the Hempstead-Brush interests, became part-owner and vice president.

In planning the 1919 schedule, the presidents of the sixteen big-
league franchises again demonstrated that, whatever savvy they may
have exhibited in other lines, when it came to baseball, they usually
did the wrong thing. Seeking to avoid additional losses on top of what
they'd lost in 1918, the "magnates" departed from the 154-game schedule for the first time since 1903. The 1919 season was set for 140
games. At the end of the year, all they could do was commiserate over
the extra money they might have made in a season that produced record
major-league attendance, as well as a general minor-league recovery.

In the American League, much of the attendance surge was
attributable to Babe Ruth. Pitching only seventeen times (winning
nine, losing five) and playing the outfield nearly every day, Ruth batted
.322, drove in 112 runs, and became a national sensation by hitting
twenty-nine home runs—two more than Ed Williamson had hit back
in 1884. Despite Ruth's exploits, the champion Red Sox sagged to
sixth place.

Meanwhile baseball's governing structure took another jolt in
July after Ruth's temperamental teammate Carl Mays pitched two
innings of a game in Chicago, then walked off the field and deserted
the team. Ten days later Harry Frazee, president of the Boston club,
sold Mays to the New York Yankees for $40,000 and two players. Ban
Johnson, who'd ordered that Mays must be disciplined before any deal
involving the pitcher could be made, was furious with Frazee and with
T. L. Huston and Jacob Ruppert, owners of the Yankees. Johnson
declared Mays under suspension, but Huston and Ruppert activated
him anyway. In what remained of the season, Mays started thirteen
games for manager Miller Huggins, won nine of them, and helped the
Yankees to a third-place finish—their best showing in nine years.

The Mays affair presented a direct challenge to the league president's authority, the first time that had ever happened in Ban Johnson's
circuit. An ensuing legal battle ended late in October in Supreme
(district) Court in New York City, where the Yankees won a ruling that
permanently enjoined Johnson from trying to keep Mays from playing
for New York. Hitherto the most powerful figure in baseball, Johnson
had suffered a blow from which he would never fully recover.

In 1919 the Cincinnati Reds, always an also-ran since joining the National League in 1890, finally captured their first pennant, pulling away from the New York Giants in September. The Reds were a good ball club, with five reliable starting pitchers, an outstanding performer in center fielder and two-time league batting champion Edd Roush, a solid player at third in little Henry "Heinie" Groh, and a capable if unspectacular supporting cast.

Yet the Reds were heavy underdogs to the Chicago White Sox, now managed by Charles "Kid" Gleason (still another old Oriole who'd achieved managerial success). Stripped of its best players the previous wartime season and reduced to sixth place, the Chicago club regrouped in 1919 with almost the same people who'd won the World Series two years earlier. White Sox ace Eddie Cicotte won a career-high twenty-nine games; Claude "Lefty" Williams added twenty-three. It surprised some observers that Chicago finished only three and one-half games in front of the Cleveland Indians, who made a strong run in the last part of the season under new manager Tris Speaker.

The 1919 World Series, the first since 1903 played in a five-of-nine format, produced a Cincinnati victory in eight games and left a trail of doubts about its honesty. On the eve of the first game, a sudden shift in betting odds in Cincinnati's favor prompted buzzings about a possible fix, and Chicago's shoddy play in that and the next game fueled suspicions in various quarters. Cincinnati won four of the first six games, beating Cicotte and Williams twice each. Chicago's two victories were both pitched by Dickie Kerr, a diminutive rookie left-hander, and while Cicotte held the Reds to seven hits and one run to win game seven, Williams retired only one man in yielding three runs at the start of game eight. It ended 10–5, Cincinnati, Williams's third Series loss.

Among those who came away shaking their heads were Hugh Fullerton, the noted Chicago baseball writer, and Christy Mathewson, who covered the games for a press syndicate. Comparing notes, Fullerton and Mathewson marked seven plays by the White Sox as highly suspect. In several articles over the winter, Fullerton not only questioned the honesty of the Series but discussed specific plays by specific players that had convinced him something was amiss.

Though harboring his own suspicions, manager Kid Gleason kept silent, as did the other White Sox. But as early as mid-October, owner Charles Comiskey was in possession of the essential story—given to him by a gambler named Harry Redmond—of how several of his players had thrown the Series. Unwilling to go public with what he knew and thereby wreck his powerful team, Comiskey flamboyantly offered a $10,000 reward to anybody who had information that the Series hadn't been on the up-and-up, at the same time that he delayed sending his players their losing Series shares.

Meanwhile the *Sporting News* (baseball's exclusive trade paper since the disappearance of *Sporting Life* a couple of years earlier) dismissed rumors of a fix as the work of "a lot of dirty, long-nosed, thick-lipped and strong-smelling gamblers." Comiskey's reward would get no takers, predicted the *Sporting News*, "because there is no evidence except in the mucky minds of the stinkers. . . ."

John B. Sheridan of St. Louis, usually a perceptive observer of the baseball scene, was one of a number of supposed experts who that winter repeatedly insisted that baseball was just too hard to fix—a consensus in the sporting press since the 1877 Louisville scandal. The usual comparisons were to horse racing or prizefighting, sports that were notorious for their chicanery. The very structure of the game of baseball, John Montgomery Ward had written in 1910, was such that "no player would dare to be dishonest, no matter how willing he might be." Two years before that, Rollin Hartt had maintained that "save in sporadic and insignificant cases of individual betting," baseball hadn't been affected by gambling. It just wasn't possible, Hartt believed, to fix all the players, not to mention managers and umpires. "Indeed, it is the very certainty that no such roguery can be practiced that makes a ball game so popular."

Yet as Fullerton noted, baseball games could be fixed easily enough, provided honest players didn't squeal on their corrupt teammates. All anybody had to do was dig back through the past fifteen years or so to find a string of questionable episodes, starting with the rumor after the 1905 Series that gamblers had reached Rube Waddell.

Frequently in such episodes, the New York Giants and John McGraw had come under suspicion. For example, before the famous Giants-Cubs tie-breaker game in 1908, Joseph M. Creamer, M.D.,

Boston Red Stockings, 1874 National Association champs. *Seated center:* Harry Wright; *seated on floor, left:* George Wright; *middle row, second from left and second from right:* Andy Leonard, Ross Barnes; *standing, left to right:* Cal McVey, Albert G. Spalding, Deacon White.

Congress Street Grounds, home of the Chicago White Stockings, 1885–1891, as drawn by W. P. Snyder.

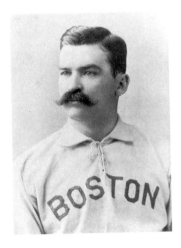

Mike Kelley in 1887, his first year with Boston, National League.

Boston Beaneaters, 1897–1898 National League champions. *Bottom row, left to right:* Bobby Lowe, Chick Stahl; *middle row, left to right:* Fred Tenney, Jimmy Collins, Jim Stafford, manager Frank Selee, Hugh Duffy, Billy Hamilton, Herman Long; *standing, left to right:* Kid Nichols, Bill Clarke, Frank Killen, Vic Willis, Marty Bergen, Ted Lewis, Charlie Hickman.

Ban Johnson, 1905.

Napoleon Lajoie, ca. 1905.

Christy Mathewson warming up at the Polo Grounds, 1908.

Cy Young in 1906.

Honus Wagner standing in at the Polo Grounds, New York, in 1908. The catcher is Roger Bresnahan, wearing the shinguards he invented.

Ty Cobb, ca. 1910.

Walter Johnson, 1913.

The 1919 Chicago White Sox, American League champs, including the eight "Black Sox." *Standing left to right:* Joe Jackson, Chick Gandil, Fred McMullin; *middle row, third from left and extreme right:* Hap Felsch, Buck Weaver; *bottom row, second, sixth, and seventh from left:* Swede Risberg, Lefty Williams, Eddie Cicotte. Also included, *middle row, extreme left and fourth and fifth from left:* Ray Schalk, manager Kid Gleason, Eddie Collins; *bottom row, third from left:* Dickie Kerr.

John McGraw, early 1920s.

Babe Ruth in 1922.

Connie Mack, 1923.

Cap Anson and Rube Foster, ca. 1925.

Rogers Hornsby, 1929.

Lou Gehrig, early 1930s.

Joe McCarthy in 1936.

Kenesaw Mountain Landis, 1936.

Babe Ruth hitting the game-winning home run in the first All-Star Game, Comiskey Park, Chicago, July 6, 1933.

Lefty Grove (*left*) and Dizzy Dean,
starting pitchers for the 1936 All-Star
Game, Braves Field, Boston.

Jimmie Foxx homering at Fenway Park,
Boston, 1941.

Grover Cleveland Alexander (*left*) and Tris Speaker
pose for Johnny Vander Meer before the 1938 All-Star
Game, Crosley Field, Cincinnati.

Satchel Paige as a Kansas City Monarch, ca. 1942.

Josh Gibson crossing home plate after homering against the Baltimore Elite Giants, Griffith Stadium, Washington, 1942.

Hank Greenberg batting at Briggs Stadium, Detroit, shortly after returning from military service in 1945. The catcher is Boston's Bob Garbark.

Branch Rickey, ca. 1943.

Bill Veeck as president of the Cleveland Indians, 1948.

Before Spud Chandler's opening pitch in the 1943 World Series, a B-17 bomber roars over Yankee Stadium. Note the wartime admonition printed on the second-deck railing: "SEE SCORE CARD FOR ALERT INSTRUCTIONS." (*AP*)

the Giants' team physician, offered umpires Bill Klem and Jimmy Johnstone $2,500 each to make sure the Giants won. Later, after hearing the umpires' report on the bribe attempt, all the National Commission would do was permanently bar Creamer from ballparks within Organized Baseball.

Chicago writers argued that the Cubs wouldn't have had to travel to New York for that game in the first place if the Boston team (which included four 1907 Giants) hadn't deliberately let down in the three-game sweep at the Polo Grounds that enabled the Giants to pull even with the Cubs. And sixteen years after the fact, Charles "Red" Dooin, the Philadelphia Phillies' regular catcher in 1908, disclosed that he and other Phillies were offered a total of $40,000 to throw five games with the Giants late that season. "In fact," said Dooin, "the money was placed in my lap by a noted catcher of the New York Giants while I was in a railroad station."

During the 1912 season, which brought a second straight pennant for the Giants, first president Charles Murphy of the Cubs intimated, then president Horace Fogel of the Phillies openly said, that the St. Louis Cardinals, now managed by ex-Giant Roger Bresnahan, didn't play their best in games with the New York club. Fogel also accused umpire Bill Brennan of favoring New York; during the Giants' last series at the Philadelphia ballpark, he pronounced the pennant race fixed. When the National League owners subsequently looked into the charges, they decided Fogel was the real villain. Judged to have slandered the National League and its umpires, Fogel found himself barred from the league for life.

Four years later, in the sixth inning of a Giants loss at Brooklyn that clinched a National League title for the Robins, McGraw left the dugout and afterward accused his players of "indifferent playing" and ignoring his instructions. "I lost my patience," he told reporters. "Such baseball disgusted me. . . . I refused to be connected with it." The Giants players to a man denied letting down, but several writers agreed with McGraw that they'd played listless and sloppy baseball, effectively if not intentionally handing Brooklyn the pennant. Although Phillies manager Pat Moran, whose club had barely lost out to Brooklyn, demanded an investigation, league president Tener and the NL owners were willing to let the matter drop.

In the 1917 World Series, rumors circulated in New York and Chicago that gamblers had reached some of the participants. Afterward McGraw confided to sportswriter Fred Lieb that he was convinced Buck Herzog, his second baseman, had deliberately positioned himself in the wrong spot a number of times, with the result that balls he should have stopped went through for base hits. McGraw wouldn't let Lieb print anything about what he suspected, but in the off-season he traded Herzog to the Boston Braves.

And then there was the notorious Hal Chase, whose many skullduggeries climaxed during his stay with McGraw's club. A masterful first baseman and solid batter, Chase had entered the majors in 1906 with the New York American League club. In 1910 George Stallings, then Chase's manager, accused him of throwing games. Backed by club president Frank Farrell (himself known for his involvement with organized gambling and Tammany Hall graft), Chase not only stayed in New York but replaced Stallings as manager. After the Yankees fell from second place under Stallings to sixth under Chase, Frank Chance was hired to manage the club. In 1913, having also come to distrust Chase's ballplaying, Chance traded him to the Chicago White Sox. From there Chase jumped to Buffalo in the Federal League, then joined the Cincinnati Reds for the 1916 season.

In July 1916, McGraw traded Christy Mathewson to Cincinnati so the great pitcher could become the Reds' new manager. Eventually Mathewson also began to suspect Chase's honesty. On July 25, 1918 (so it later became known), Chase and outfielder Lee Magee each placed $500 bets against their Reds teammates before a game with the Boston Braves. (The Reds won anyway when Edd Roush's inside-the-park homer chased home a reluctant Magee.)

On that eastern swing, opposing players frequently yelled at Chase, "Well, Hal, what are the odds today?" Chase went so far as to try to bribe Giants pitcher Bill Perritt before a game at the Polo Grounds, and the next day Mathewson finally suspended his first baseman for "indifferent play and insubordination," whereupon Chase filed suit against the Cincinnati club for the balance on that season's salary.

That winter John Heydler, who'd just stepped into the National League presidency following John Tener's angry resignation, conducted an inquiry into Chase's suspension. Chase had the advantage because Mathewson was still in France, having joined the army's Chemical Warfare Service near the end of the 1918 season. After reading Mathewson's affidavit and another from Perritt, then taking testimony from Chase (accompanied by three lawyers), other Reds players, and John McGraw, Heydler officially exonerated Chase. A few days later McGraw, who'd just testified about Chase's trying to bribe his pitcher, incredibly signed the suspect player to a Giants contract.

During the 1919 season, McGraw found out for himself what a succession of managers before him had known: Hal Chase was incorrigibly crooked. As McGraw later disclosed, Chase and Heinie Zimmerman tried to bribe various Giants players into throwing games, which was why McGraw suspended Zimmerman in mid-September. McGraw never explained why Chase remained with the team until the next-to-last day of the season, ostensibly in good standing with the club. But when Chase and Zimmerman received their 1920 contracts, the salary figures were so low that, as McGraw and Giants president Stoneham had intended, neither would report in the spring.

If Chase's reputation was smelly everywhere, so, in lesser degrees, were the reputations of various other players. Of course some of the rumors about game-fixing and bribery had been farfetched, but others were sufficiently credible to have prompted vigorous, thoroughgoing probes and swift punishment for those found culpable—if a willingness to take such action had ever existed within Organized Baseball.

Basically, the men who ran baseball—the members of the National Commission, the major-league club owners, the minor-league presidents and owners—had been prepared to put up with a certain amount of dishonesty, as long as it didn't go too far. Unquestionably the readiness of Chicago White Sox players to collude with gamblers in the 1919 World Series had much to do with official baseball's longtime toleration of Chase and others of his ilk. Soon, though, the lid would blow off.

In the winter of 1919–1920, the general news of the day—arrests and deportations of Bolsheviks and other political radicals, the worst succession of strikes in the country's history, the advent of a nationwide ban on alcoholic beverages—was enough for most people to worry about without their also having to fret over the honesty of the recent World Series.

In January the sale of Babe Ruth to the New York Yankees dominated the sporting news. Seeking additional funds to invest in Broadway musical productions (always his first love), Red Sox owner Harry Frazee took $125,000 in cash for Ruth and also, as Yankees co-owner Jacob Ruppert later revealed, received a $300,000 loan from Ruppert, secured by a mortgage on Fenway Park, the home of the Red Sox. Even without the loan, it was far and away the highest price ever paid for a baseball player.

Ruth came to the Yankees at the perfect moment. The Polo Grounds, which the Yankees still rented from the Giants, seated more people than any baseball facility in the majors. In 1920, with the 154-game format restored, Ruth's home fans would get to see him in seventy-seven games. The balls Ruth swung at in 1920 were supposed to be cleaner, drier, and smoother, because the AL-NL joint rules committee had just outlawed the spitter and other "trick pitches" throughout Organized Baseball. Exceptions were made for seventeen veteran spitballers in the majors, but for nobody pitching in the minors.

Once the season got under way, pitchers, fielders, writers, and fans would also start talking about the ball's being a lot "livelier" than in previous seasons. Run-scoring and especially home-run hitting suddenly jumped throughout baseball. American and National League batsmen hit 634 homers in 1920, as compared to 338 in 1917 (the last previous 154-game season); total runs scored increased by seventeen percent over the same period.

A. G. Spalding and Brothers, still exclusive supplier to leagues throughout Organized Baseball, affirmed that the ball's design hadn't changed since 1910, when, late that season, a new type with a cork center enclosed in rubber had replaced the all-rubber-centered ball in use up to then. Batting had improved substantially in 1911 and 1912 (when, for example, Ty Cobb recorded .420 and .408 marks), but over the next few years pitchers had generally regained the upper hand.

In 1920, though, hits rained as they hadn't since the 1890s; balls disappeared over fences as never before in the game's history. If Ruth had been a sensation the previous season, he was an absolute phenomenon in 1920, belting homers with astonishing frequency and distance at the Polo Grounds and everywhere else he played—fifty-four homers in all, to which Ruth added 158 runs scored, 137 driven in, a .376 batting average, and an incredible .847 slugging average.

Thanks to Ruth, the Yankees became baseball's most popular team, the first to surpass one million in home attendance as well as the top draw around the American League. Charles Stoneham and John McGraw disgustedly watched the Yankees outdraw the Giants by some four hundred thousand in their own ballpark and decided that sooner or later the tenants had to go.

Plenty of others contributed to the batting boom. The St. Louis Browns' George Sisler, for example, batted .407, the highest average in either major league since 1911, and knocked nineteen homers, more than any American Leaguer besides Ruth had ever hit. Lacking a Ruth, the National League experienced more modest improvements in batting statistics. Even at that, Rogers Hornsby's .370 average was the NL's best mark in eight years.

Injured a good portion of the time and having one of his poorest seasons, Ty Cobb found himself no longer baseball's top gate attraction or topic of conversation. "Ruth has stolen all of Cobb's thunder," announced a *New York Times* reporter in May 1920. Later that season, Detroit fans welcomed Ruth as a "conquering hero," according to H. G. Salsinger of the *Detroit Free Press*. "He got the applause, the shrieking adoration of the multitude, in Cobb's own city. Cobb, standing aside, could feel deeply how fickle the adoration of the sport-loving public is. He saw before him a new king acclaimed. . . ." While real students of baseball still appreciated Cobb's finesse, remarked Yankees manager Huggins, "Nowadays the American public likes the fellow who carries the wallop."

Cobb quickly came to despise the Yankees' big slugger, not only for Ruth's eclipsing fame but for the Babe's brute-force playing style and wastrel life-style. Spartan, intense, a perfectionist who took care of himself year-round, Cobb simply couldn't understand how Ruth could do what he did night after night in speakeasies and whorehouses, and then do what he did day after day on the ballfield. Of course, neither could anybody else understand the apparent ease with which Ruth combined wenching, boozing, and gluttonous eating with the greatest offensive production in major-league history. For Cobb, though, it was more than a puzzlement; it was a source of irritation and resentment that grew as the seasons passed.

Ruth's unprecedented feats at the plate, together with Carl Mays's twenty-six wins, kept the Yankees in contention with Chicago and Cleveland nearly the entire 1920 season. Pitching the best ball of his career, Mays also remained a source of acrimony and discord. On August 16, at the Polo Grounds, one of Mays's "submarine" pitches hit Ray Chapman, Cleveland's popular shortstop, squarely in the left temple. His skull shattered, Chapman died early the next morning.

Known as a surly, hard-bitten man who liked to throw close to batters, Mays convinced few people with his insistence that he'd thrown a curveball that apparently "froze" Chapman. From around the league came demands for Mays's permanent banishment. Ban Johnson, whom Mays had infuriated by jumping to the Yankees in 1919, nevertheless calmly and carefully investigated the Chapman incident and then absolved the pitcher of any wrongful intent. Mays was back on the mound after only a week's layoff.

Despite playing under a cloud of doubt that had never entirely gone away, the Chicago White Sox remained an outstanding baseball team. In 1920 Cicotte, Williams, Kerr, and the veteran Urban "Red" Faber all won at least twenty games; Eddie Collins, Joe Jackson, and Hap Felsch enjoyed outstanding years; and most observers kept expecting Chicago to pull away. But Cleveland and New York wouldn't fade. Tris Speaker, in his first full season managing the Indians, batted .388, played his usual sparkling center field, and kept his club rolling despite the upsetting effect of Ray Chapman's death.

Still, it should have been apparent to anybody who followed the off-the-field baseball news that things weren't right in the National Pastime. Early in 1920 opposition to Garry Herrmann in both leagues had forced his resignation, leaving the National Commission without a chairman and seemingly with little future as a governing body.

Meanwhile Lee Magee, traded by Cincinnati to the Cubs before the 1919 season and then released the following winter, sued for the remaining salary he claimed the Cubs owed him under a two-year contract. During the trial on Magee's suit (which he lost) in March 1920, the details of his and Hal Chase's game-fixing activities at

Cincinnati were laid bare—the first public disclosure of such player dishonesty since the Louisville scandal forty-three years earlier. Moreover, suspicions persisted not only about the last World Series but even about occasional White Sox losses during the course of the 1920 race.

Then, at the end of August, president William H. Veeck, Sr., of the Cubs received a tip that pitcher Claude Hendrix had been bribed to throw that afternoon's game versus the Phillies. Veeck instructed manager Fred Mitchell to hold out Hendrix and instead start Grover Cleveland Alexander (now the ace of the Cubs' staff). Eight days later, after Chicago newspapers publicized what had happened, the Cook County district attorney announced that he intended to convene a special grand jury to investigate gambling in baseball.

Beginning in Chicago on September 22, 1920, the hearings prompted a parade of baseball luminaries, including NL president Heydler, John McGraw, and a number of past and present Giants players. McGraw explained why he'd discarded Hal Chase and Heinie Zimmerman. Acknowledging that "Chase deliberately threw us down," he went on to lament that he'd "never been more deceived by a player than by Chase." Yet neither then nor later did the Giants manager account for why he'd suspended Zimmerman but kept Chase on the club for the balance of the 1919 season.

Perhaps McGraw might have explained that matter if the grand jury had kept its attentions on NL affairs. By the end of September, though, the *North American*, a Philadelphia daily, had not only declared the 1919 Series fixed but published much of the story of the conspiracy, as provided by a small-time gambler named Billy Maharg. Largely at the insistence of Ban Johnson (who for years had been on the outs with his onetime chum Comiskey), the grand jury quickly turned its attentions to a possible Series fix.

On the morning of September 28, Eddie Cicotte and Joe Jackson confessed to the district attorney in Chicago that they'd thrown the Series, and named six teammates as coconspirators. Chick Gandil had dropped out of Organized Baseball, but Hap Felsch, Lefty Williams, Buck Weaver, shortstop Charles "Swede" Risberg, and substitute infielder Fred McMullin were still with the club.

With a week still to play, the White Sox trailed first-place Cleveland by only six percentage points, but White Sox owner Comiskey, who'd known for nearly a year that some of his men had played dishonestly, now had no choice but to act. All seven players were suspended as of that day. While Kid Gleason took advantage of two open dates to try to reorganize his team, Cleveland won two games at St. Louis. On October 1 a patched-together White Sox lineup lost to St. Louis 10–1, and Cleveland split a doubleheader at Detroit. Although the gutted Chicago ball club beat the Browns the next day, another Indians victory over Detroit clinched Cleveland's first major-league championship. At 98–56, Speaker and his men finished two games ahead of the White Sox, three ahead of the Yankees.

The surprisingly easy winner in the National League was Wilbert Robinson's Brooklyn club, which ended the season seven games in front of the New York Giants. Except for Zack Wheat, a stellar outfielder, and right-hander Burleigh Grimes, a tough spitballer (one of the seventeen veteran pitchers so designated), the 1920 Robins probably weren't as strong as the club that had lost to the Boston Red Sox four years earlier. In the second straight Series in a five-of-nine format, Brooklyn took two of the first three games, all played in Ebbets Field, then dropped four in a row in Cleveland. Game five featured three Series firsts, all by Indians: outfielder Elmer Smith's grand-slam homer, pitcher Jim Bagby's homer, and second baseman Bill Wambsganss's unassisted triple play.

Hardly anybody questioned the honesty of that World Series, given the extraordinary number of fine plays and the fact that the winners committed twice as many errors as the losers. But by mid-October the "Black Sox scandal," as the press quickly labeled the rapidly unfolding tale of the 1919 Series, had become a daily front-page item in newspapers across the country.

As ballplayers, gamblers, managers, and owners took their turns talking to the grand jury and, in some cases, to the press as well, it became apparent that the conspiracy had been a remarkably open secret. Besides the eight White Sox players and two different if overlapping groups of gamblers with whom they dealt, a number of other gamblers and past and present major-leaguers had known about the fix before the Series started. Hal Chase, for example, bet on Cincinnati and may have won as much as $40,000. Joe Gedeon, an infielder with the Browns, learned about the fix from St. Louis gambling acquaintances; Giants pitcher Jean Dubuc got the word from Bill Burns, one of the gamblers behind the plot and a former teammate at Detroit; and Giants pitcher John "Rube" Benton won several thousand dollars betting on the Reds after ex-Giant Buck Herzog passed along what he'd heard.

At the end of October the Cook County grand jury indicted the eight White Sox players plus Hal Chase, Bill Burns, and seven other gamblers for conspiracy to defraud the public. Subsequently five more gamblers were also indicted.

Notably missing from the list was Arnold Rothstein, probably the most powerful single figure in the New York City underworld. Besides being a hugely successful gambler, Rothstein was known for bankrolling drug and liquor smugglers as well as a variety of ostensibly legal activities, including Charles Stoneham's securities operations. Rothstein was also a good friend of John McGraw, with whom he'd once been a partner in a New York poolhall venture. "AR" was probably the key man in the fix, either as the actual financier for those who dealt with the players or as the fabled big-timer who manipulated lesser-time fixers into believing he was behind them. In any case, Rothstein handled himself so adroitly in his appearance during the Chicago inquiry that he wasn't charged with anything.

In the meantime the major-league owners had finally taken decisive steps to restructure the way the sport was governed. In the wake of the Black Sox revelations, a majority of the owners quickly approved a proposal by Albert D. Lasker, a wealthy Chicagoan and stockholder in the Cubs, for a reconstituted National Commission, to be made up of three nonpartisan members chosen from outside baseball.

An arcane power struggle followed, with the NL owners plus Ruppert and Huston of the Yankees, Frazee of the Red Sox, and Comiskey of the White Sox not only favoring the Lasker plan but also moving to dump Ban Johnson and reorganize as a single twelve-team major league. Johnson fought back with his "Loyal Five" American League supporters and substantial backing from the minor leagues. If he had to accept the Lasker plan, then Johnson wanted his own man, Charles MacDonald, presiding judge in the Chicago grand jury hearings, to be the commission's chairman.

The National Leaguers and the AL "insurrectos," on the other hand, had already decided to offer the job to Kenesaw Mountain Landis, who'd presided over the Federal League's suit against Organized Baseball in 1915 and had then agreeably done nothing until the disputants worked out a settlement on their own.

By early November, Ban Johnson had lost. The Loyal Five deserted in the interest of getting on with the business of reform, which by then had come to mean not a new National Commission but a single Commissioner of Baseball, vested with supreme authority to rule the sport. On November 12 fifteen club presidents (minus Phil Ball of the Browns, an unregenerate Johnsonite) trooped to the federal building in Chicago to tender the commissionership to Landis. After exacting a pledge that his authority would be absolute and unchallenged, Landis accepted the appointment and the $50,000 annual salary that went with it. At the same time, he made it clear that he intended to keep his federal judgeship.

The events of 1919–1920 were, in many ways, the most momentous in baseball's long history as a sport and business enterprise. Accomplished under varieties of duress, the creation of the office of Commissioner of Baseball signaled the beginning of a new, authoritarian, tough-minded era in baseball governance. Kenesaw Mountain Landis was hired for the express purpose of cleaning up a mess, or actually two messes—the most obvious having to do with gambling and bribery; the other, less understood by the sports public, involving the failure of the baseball businessmen to police themselves and their employees.

That winter the Black Sox scandal hung over baseball and, insofar as baseball still held its position as the National Pastime, over the whole country. For some pessimists, the future of the sport seemed in grave doubt. The future was especially doubtful for the Chicago White Sox, as ravaged as any team had ever been from one season to the next. One of Landis's first pronouncements upon accepting the commissionership sealed the doom of the indicted but as-yet-untried Chicago players: "There is absolutely no chance for any of them to creep back into Organized Baseball. They are and will remain outlaws." A seventh-place finish awaited White Sox fans in 1921, and not until 1936 would Chicago's American League entry climb as high as third.

A shadowy, impossibly tangled set of circumstances, the Black

Sox affair bewildered contemporaries looking for any kind of logical consistency, as it would continue to baffle historians over succeeding decades. Although many key questions would always remain unanswered, what was conclusively established—in players' confessions and other evidence—was that, contrary to the popular image of innocent players duped by sinister underworld figures, Gandil and Cicotte, well before the 1919 season ended, thought up the whole idea of fixing the Series and then sought out various gamblers.

Promised at least $100,000, the Chicago first baseman and star pitcher then enlisted Swede Risberg, Hap Felsch, and Lefty Williams; apparently Fred McMullin, who wasn't important to the success of the plot, insisted on being taken in. Nobody ever accused Buck Weaver of dishonest play or taking anything from gamblers—for the eight games of the 1919 Series, Weaver batted .324 and made no errors—but Weaver's offense was knowing about the fix and remaining silent, out of perverse loyalty to his teammates.

Joe Jackson's role is the most perplexing. Although Jackson's participation was considered vital and he undoubtedly had prior knowledge that a fix was in, before the Series opened he asked Comiskey to be benched. When the White Sox president wouldn't consider it, Jackson went ahead and played every inning of all eight games. Besides fielding flawlessly, he made twelve base hits (a new Series record), including a homer and three doubles, batted in six runs, and scored five times. His .375 average led both teams. Obviously Jackson played to win, yet after the last game he accepted $5,000 from Lefty Williams and took the money home to Savannah, Georgia.

Gandil collected $30,000 (evidently enough to secure his retirement) and Cicotte $10,000; Felsch and Williams supposedly got $5,000 each, as did Jackson. It's not clear whether Risberg or McMullin got paid at all, although Risberg contributed notably to the Reds' victory with four errors and a .080 batting average. Gandil made seven hits, including a double that drove in two runs in Dickie Kerr's third-game shutout, as well as a tenth-inning single to win game six for Kerr. Cicotte pitched superbly to defeat the Reds in game seven.

How to account for such anomalies? One might posit three plausible hypotheses (for a situation where, to be sure, little appears plausible): (1) Not every game was fixed, so that all the White Sox played to win some of the time. (2) The gamblers with whom the corrupt players were dealing bet on Chicago in some games, on Cincinnati in others (which would presuppose that the White Sox were so good they could win or lose as they pleased). (3) At least in games six and seven, Gandil, Cicotte, and associates, angry with the gamblers for holding back on what they'd agreed to pay, did their best to win. According to various sources, Lefty Williams received a death threat before taking the mound for game eight. That would presumably account for his lasting only one-third of an inning and putting his team at a deficit from which it never recovered.

As to why certain White Sox would have decided to throw the Series in the first place, plenty of people then and long afterward put the blame on Charles Comiskey, whose well-known stinginess had supposedly alienated his men, destroyed their professional integrity, and made them willing tools of gambling interests. That Comiskey was cheap about some things can't be doubted—he was, for example, the only owner who charged his players for having their uniforms laundered—yet the idea that the White Sox were grossly underpaid doesn't really stand close scrutiny.

In 1919 Ty Cobb was still the highest-salaried player in baseball, making the same $20,000 per season he'd drawn since 1915. Eddie Collins was among the three or four top money-makers, having exacted a five-year contract at $15,000 per year when he came to Comiskey's club in the midst of the Federal League war. Ray Schalk made about $7,500, a handsome salary for that day, as was Buck Weaver's $6,500. At $6,000 for 1919, Joe Jackson was certainly making less than he was worth, but his salary was comparable to that of such leading American Leaguers as Frank Baker and George Sisler, or Edd Roush, Zack Wheat, and Hal Chase in the National League. Chick Gandil's $4,000 was good pay for somebody who was basically a journeyman, while plenty of young players of the caliber of Hap Felsch were making no more than his $3,750. Cicotte, who'd taken a long time to reach stardom, drew a base salary of $5,000 but received a $2,000 bonus in 1918 and probably another in 1919. Lefty Williams made about $3,500 in the Black Sox year, Risberg maybe a thousand less.

In 1919, in fact, salaries in both major leagues remained fairly modest, little changed over the past three seasons. The record profits recorded by a number of franchises that year (despite the officially shortened season) had much to do with the fact that the general level of salaries remained low, at least relative to those later in the booming postwar period. In the first postwar year the prevailing attitude among major-league owners—coming off the Federal League troubles and the generally disastrous 1918 season—was that payrolls ought to be held down.

Indeed, despite the anxieties and uncertainties surrounding baseball in the winter of 1920–1921, the sport's most prosperous years were just ahead. Public confidence in the competitive integrity of what was still almost universally considered the National Pastime would prove a lot tougher to shake than many had supposed. The golden age of American baseball—its Ruthian age—was about to dawn.

7.
The
Golden
Twenties

The disposition of the Black Sox affair showed the American system of criminal justice at neither its most efficient nor its most just. The legal proceedings followed a course that was bizarre even for Chicago, where people had learned to expect the unexpected. The nearly two dozen players and gamblers who'd been indicted in September 1920 weren't even arraigned until the following February. By then a new district attorney for Cook County was in office and three assistant district attorneys on his predecessor's staff were working as defense lawyers—at Charles Comiskey's expense, rumor had it.

While that was suspicious enough, William Crowe, the new district attorney, then revealed to the court that the signed copies of Eddie Cicotte's and Joe Jackson's confessions had mysteriously disappeared during the transition from one district attorney to another. The loss was probably the work of William Fallon, Arnold Rothstein's buccaneering attorney, although Arnold Austrian, Comiskey's lawyer, may also have had a hand in what Crowe termed "a peculiar conspiracy." After Cicotte and Jackson filed affidavits repudiating their confessions, William Dever, the new judge in the case, ruled that all the indictments were faulty.

Crowe persuaded Dever to delay rather than dismiss the proceedings. Meanwhile baseball commissioner Kenesaw Mountain Landis ordered the accused players placed on the official ineligible list within

Organized Baseball. At that, Comiskey had no alternative but to terminate their contracts and formally notify them of their releases.

Ban Johnson, determined to see justice done and to embarrass Comiskey in the process, set out on his own for Texas to offer Bill Burns, one of the gamblers involved in the World Series fix, $700 to agree to tell everything he knew, in exchange for a promise of immunity from prosecution. More than anything else, it was Johnson's efforts that enabled the Cook County authorities to secure new indictments—this time of seven White Sox (Fred McMullin was unnamed because of insufficient evidence) and ten gamblers, including Hal Chase.

By the time the trial finally began, on June 27, 1921, several of the gamblers had simply disappeared. Hal Chase was arrested under the new indictment in San Jose, California, but then released on a technicality. Chase remained in the San Francisco Bay area, where he busied himself arranging bribes and fixes in the Pacific Coast League. He never came to trial for anything.

Inasmuch as their attorneys wouldn't let any of the accused White Sox take the stand, the state's efforts to prove a conspiracy to commit fraud rested mainly on the testimony of Bill Burns and Billy Maharg (also granted immunity and also, as Maharg acknowledged, paid by Johnson). That just wasn't enough, especially when Judge Hugo Friend instructed the jury that to find the players guilty, it must decide that they not only willingly lost games but also *wanted* to commit fraud. Friend added that the prosecution's case was so inadequate where Buck Weaver and Hap Felsch were concerned that he wouldn't accept a guilty verdict on either of them.

On the evening of August 2 the jury brought in an acquittal for all seven players, as well as for the only two gamblers against whom the prosecution hadn't already dropped its charges. The packed courtroom exploded in cheering; several jurors joined spectators in hoisting the players to their shoulders. Then, joined by the jurors, the players spent the rest of the night at a local Italian restaurant, celebrating not only their acquittal but what they may have reckoned was their rejuvenation in Organized Baseball.

If so, they reckoned without any real understanding of baseball's new "czar," as the press had tagged Landis. The very day after the

Chicago trial ended, Landis announced that "regardless of the verdict of juries," no player who threw ballgames, or had knowledge that others had thrown games and wouldn't inform on his teammates, "will ever play professional baseball." Wholly extralegal, Landis's ukase was nonetheless absolute as "baseball law."

It was an especially harsh judgment for Weaver and Felsch, whom even Judge Friend had evidently thought guiltless. Some were also prepared to make extenuations for Joe Jackson, who unarguably had played a terrific World Series in 1919.

In the years that followed, the banned Black Sox all were able to pick up money playing here and there in the far-flung, complex landscape of "outlaw baseball." It was frequently hard for them, though, because as much as possible, Landis, Ban Johnson, and others in positions of influence blocked the banished players' use of ballparks and their appearances in games with "eligible" players. Felsch eventually received $1,100 in a breach-of-contract suit against Comiskey (Buck Weaver lost a similar action), and in 1924 Jackson sued Comiskey for the remaining two years (and one week) of salary on a three-year contract he'd signed before the 1920 season—at a time when Comiskey already suspected Jackson of being in on the Series fix.

At that civil trial, in Milwaukee, attorneys from Arnold Austrian's firm, representing Comiskey, submitted as evidence the original copy of the confession Jackson had signed in September 1919—the same document that had disappeared from the district attorney's office! Almost as amazing, the presiding judge allowed Comiskey's lawyers to read excerpts from the supposedly confidential testimony Jackson had given before the Cook County grand jury. Despite all that, the jury found for Jackson in the amount of nearly $17,000—only to have the judge overturn the verdict. Shoeless Joe went home to his laundry business and his career as a baseball "outlaw," plying his trade with whoever would risk exhibiting his talents.

Landis's banishment of the never-convicted White Sox players won plaudits in nearly every quarter, as did the campaign of official ostracism that followed. The sentiments of the New York *Evening World* were typical: "There are no two sides to the case. If the crooks who were acquitted try to show their faces in decent sporting circles they should be boycotted and blackballed." Meanwhile Eddie Collins emerged as the foremost of the "Clean Sox," a lonely hero who, as the liberal weekly *New Republic* said in 1922, "is still out there playing as near perfect ball as is permitted mortal man in a universe where error seems to be the order of the day."

Charles Comiskey would die in 1931, never having seen another winning White Sox team. With one of the major leagues' smallest payrolls, Comiskey continued to make money through that last decade, though never as much as the half-million dollars he cleared in 1920 with his tainted ball club.

Landis proceeded zealously if erratically in his drive to "clean up baseball." Among his earliest official actions was ordering Charles Stoneham and John McGraw to dispose of their holdings in the Oriental Park racetrack and casino, located just outside Havana, Cuba. They did so in July 1921, but neither Stoneham nor McGraw was ready to change old friends or old habits, and Arnold Rothstein continued to enjoy the use of Stoneham's personal box at the Polo Grounds. Although Landis reprimanded Stoneham on that score, he couldn't or wouldn't force him to break his various ties to Rothstein.

Nor was Landis prepared to move against the Giants' president when, in 1923–1924, Stoneham was indicted by two federal grand juries for perjury and mail fraud in connection with the collapse of two New York securities firms. In the face of the widely expressed feeling that the Giants were run by a bunch of crooks, Stoneham continued to preside comfortably over one of baseball's most profitable enterprises. In 1925, following a complicated seven-week trial, he was cleared in the mail-fraud case, after which federal prosecutors dropped the perjury indictment.

In dealing with allegedly miscreant players, Landis was maddeningly inconsistent. Some fourteen major-leaguers implicated in gambling matters during the early twenties were barred by the commissioner, including, besides the eight tainted White Sox, Joe Gedeon, Lee Magee, and Heinie Zimmerman. Landis also banished several Pacific Coast League players, most of whom had connections to the ubiquitous Hal Chase; but for reasons known only to himself, Landis never took any official action against Chase, who continued to play "outlaw" ball in the West and Southwest for more than a decade longer—no doubt sometimes honestly.

While Chase inexplicably escaped the commissioner's wrath, Benny Kauff bore its full force. The outstanding player in the Federal League and a capable performer for McGraw's Giants, Kauff had always conducted himself honestly and in 1919, in fact, promptly reported to his manager Chase's and Zimmerman's efforts to bribe him. The next year, though, Kauff was indicted in New York in an auto-theft case involving his brother. Though acquitted in Bronx County court, Kauff found himself forever barred from Organized Baseball because, said Landis, the verdict "smell[ed] to the high heaven, and was one of the worst miscarriages of justice ever to come to my attention."

Yet at the same time that he ousted Kauff, Landis permitted former Giants pitcher Rube Benton, who'd admitted winning bets on the 1919 Series because he knew beforehand it was fixed, to remain in Organized Baseball. In 1922, moreover, the commissioner sanctioned Benton's return to the National League when Cincinnati purchased his contract from Minneapolis of the American Association.

If sometimes self-contradictory, frequently despotic, and nearly always arrogant and bombastic, Landis was also probably indispensable under the circumstances. Fifty-four years old when he assumed his duties as commissioner, wiry and hatchet-faced, with a headful of unfashionably shaggy white hair, Landis had the look and bearing of an Old Testament prophet. Born in southwestern Ohio and raised in southern Indiana, the son of a Union army veteran who named him after the site of a Civil War battle (and misspelled "Kennesaw"), Landis had parlayed a scanty legal education and a few political connections into appointment to a U.S. judgeship.

Although he'd been a generally poor magistrate, handing down harsh verdicts and sentences (such as a $29 million fine for Standard Oil) that were frequently reversed on appeal, many people admired his rough justice. During the recent war he'd crusaded from the bench against political radicals, draft-resisters, and anybody else who seemed a less-than-zealous patriot. His lack of concern for constitutional safeguards appalled civil libertarians but won him popular acclaim.

Far more than he did the law, Landis revered baseball. A longtime Chicago Cubs fan, he truly believed that baseball embodied the finest elements in American life and that nothing should ever be allowed to jeopardize its sacred place. The operators of National and American

League franchises never forgot the favor he'd done them in sitting on the Federal League case until they reached a settlement outside the law, one that Landis eagerly approved.

Within a year and a half after Landis took over as commissioner, the U.S. Supreme Court indirectly confirmed his power as the sport's "czar" by sanctioning Organized Baseball's monopolistic character. In 1922 the antitrust suit brought five years earlier by the Baltimore group shut out of the Federal League settlement finally reached the Supreme Court. In July, with Associate Justice Oliver Wendell Holmes, Jr., giving the majority opinion, the Court agreed with attorneys for Organized Baseball that, while the sport was obviously a form of business, it wasn't "trade or commerce in the commonly accepted use of those words." Based on "personal effort" and not the production of goods, and involving interstate activity only "incidental" to its main business of staging exhibitions for profit, Organized Baseball therefore wasn't subject to antitrust prosecution. It was a momentous decision, one that gave baseball a favored legal status that would become unique in professional sports.

The biggest loser in the restructuring that made Landis baseball's top man was Ban Johnson. Having once been the most powerful figure in the sport, Johnson never became reconciled to his distinctly subordinate status—president of the American League and nothing else. So far, the two principal objects of hatred in Ban Johnson's life had been John McGraw, whom he never forgave for deserting and trying to destroy the American League, and Charles Comiskey, with whom Johnson's quarrel, if obscure in origin, was ceaseless and bitter. Now Kenesaw Mountain Landis became Johnson's foremost nemesis, and for six years Johnson and Landis continually sought to undermine each other. Their rivalry would finally end in the fall of 1927, when Johnson, in ill health and deserted by even his oldest supporters, finally resigned.

If Landis was one indispensable man in the aftermath of the Black Sox affair, then Babe Ruth was another. The greatest drawing card in the history of sports, Ruth also had the greatest impact on the way his particular sport was played. Having turned twenty-six just before the start of spring training in 1921, Ruth was at the height of his physical powers. Standing 6-2½ and weighing a rock-hard two hundred pounds, the Babe was still flat-stomached and powerfully torsoed, still several years from the potbellied, spindly-legged figure forever fixed in popular consciousness by late-twenties and early-thirties newsreels.

Ruth hadn't really grown up—some would say he never did. Not an orphan, he'd been, by his own admission, "a bad kid," a youth who spent most of the time between his eighth and nineteenth birthdays in St. Mary's Industrial School in Baltimore, a home run by the Xaverian Brothers for both orphans and "incorrigibles." Poorly educated and socially backward, Ruth came into professional baseball with an insatiable physical hunger for just about everything life held. Especially after he joined the New York Yankees in 1920, Ruth's dissipations became as heroic as his deeds on the diamond. Yet for all the damage he did to his chances for a long life, George Herman Ruth was probably the most marvelously talented athlete in the game's history.

Ruth freely acknowledged that he'd modeled his hitting style on Joe Jackson's. Taking his stance about two-thirds back in the left-hand batter's box with his feet close together, Ruth peered over his shoulder at the pitcher, then wound up and swung his forty-eight-ounce bat with all the power he could muster. Characteristically, he spun 360 degrees when he missed the ball. (In 1920 an Ohio physicist calculated that Ruth's swing generated 24,000 foot-pounds per second— about forty-four horsepower.) But he made plenty of contact, enough to produce 2,146 other base hits (including more than 1,500 singles) besides 714 regular-season home runs. The Babe's lifetime batting average of .344 testified to his being an inordinately skilled batsman, as well as the most prolific distance hitter over the first century of professional baseball.

Fast enough to leg out as many as sixteen triples one season, Ruth also knew what he was doing on the basepaths, as he did anywhere on the playing field. After he recorded twenty-one assists in 1920, base runners rarely tried to take an extra base on his powerful throwing arm. "He played by instinct, sheer instinct," said his ballplaying contemporary Rube Bressler. "He was like a damn animal. He had that instinct. [Animals] know when it's going to rain, things like that. Nature, that was Ruth!"

Ruth changed baseball in many ways—its playing style, competitive structure, pay scales, and entertainment value, among others. No doubt home-run hitting and scoring would have increased substantially in the 1920s even without the presence of the "Sultan of Swat," as one New York scribe exuberantly christened Ruth, but it was the Babe who first demonstrated that home runs translated directly into bigger paychecks. In 1920 Ruth made $20,000 and clouted fifty-four home runs. The next year he was paid $41,000 and pushed his own record to fifty-nine homers, and after that he signed a five-year contract for $52,000 a season. By 1930, under a two-year pact, he was making $80,000 a year.

The lesson wasn't lost on Ruth's contemporaries. "He has not only slugged his way to fame," announced F. C. Lane in *Baseball Magazine,* "but he has got everybody else doing it. The home run fever is in the air. It is infectious."

By 1925 the sixteen major-league teams combined for 1,167 homers, as opposed to 338 in 1917. Overall scoring in the majors grew by nearly forty percent in that period, even though, with continuing improvements in fielders' gloves (especially the use of the preformed pocket model patented by pitcher Bill Doak in 1920), total errors declined by nearly nine percent. Base-stealing and the use of such other "inside baseball" stratagems as the bunt, the squeeze play, and the hit-and-run fell off sharply.

One sign of the new offense-oriented style was the initial appearance in 1920—in the *Sporting News,* the annual baseball guides, and other statistical sources—of the runs-batted-in category. From the 1920s on, "rbi's" would be an increasingly valued measure of offensive effectiveness—as well as an increasingly serviceable argument at contract time, whether used by players to bolster their negotiating positions or by club officials to devalue last season's performance.

John McGraw, with whom "inside baseball" had been virtually synonymous in the prewar years, admitted in 1923 that he no longer managed the old way. Now, "with the . . . ball being hit all about the lot the necessity of taking chances on the bases has decreased. . . . A manager would look foolish not to play the game as it is. . . . There is no use in sending men down on a long chance of stealing a bag when there is a better chance of the batter hitting one for two bases, or, maybe, out of the lot." McGraw's 1911 pennant winners had stolen 347 times; by 1925 the Giants registered only seventy-nine thefts.

Whereas McGraw merely regretted the passing of the tightly

played game of the prewar years, Ty Cobb took it as a personal offense. The baseball of that day—*his* baseball—was the way the game *ought* to be played, he felt. Yet despite his contempt for the new "power game," Cobb, as player-manager of the Detroit Tigers from 1921 to 1926, found himself managing basically according to its dictates, just as McGraw did. Cobb's Detroit teams were hard hitters, but were also generally slow-footed and unskilled in the intricacies of "Cobbian" ball. The third-place 1922 Tigers, for example, batted .305 as a team and scored 828 runs, but stole only seventy-eight bases, eighteen fewer than Cobb had stolen by himself seven years earlier.

Although he won no more batting titles after 1919, Cobb continued to be one of the American League's premier hitters. In 1921 he batted .389 (to teammate Harry Heilmann's league-leading .394); and in 1922, for the third time, he topped .400 (while George Sisler soared to .420). With home runs flying out of ballparks in unprecedented numbers, Cobb continued to drop bunts, coax pitchers for walks, and slap and punch the ball to all fields, just as he always had.

Had he sought homers, Cobb undoubtedly could have collected twenty to twenty-five per year. Before a game in St. Louis in May 1925, he told a Detroit writer that he was tired of reading how Ruth knocked 'em over fences while he got his hits on grounders and bunts. "I'll show you something today," he promised. "I'm going for home runs for the first time in my career." He proceeded to clout three in that game (as well as two singles and a double) and two more the next day. At that time nobody except Cap Anson, back in 1884, had ever homered five times in two games. Following the St. Louis outburst, Cobb returned to his normal playing style; he hit only seven more homers in 1925, and just seventeen more before he retired three years later with a career total of only 113.

Ruth, of course, was the culprit in changing baseball for the worse, as far as Cobb was concerned. Later on, after both men had retired, even the distrustful, abrasive Cobb succumbed to the Babe's garrulous, unaffected charm and became his friend, but for nearly all of their playing days Cobb despised Ruth and what he'd done to baseball. The Tigers' manager and his players bombarded the Babe with extraordinarily vile epithets whenever the two clubs met, and Yankees-Tigers games often produced brawls.

Cobb and Ruth never actually traded blows (although they came very close during one memorable melee in Detroit in 1924), but the Georgian rarely eased up in a campaign of verbal abuse that invariably included slurs on the racial ancestry of the swarthy, full-lipped, and flat-nosed Ruth. While the Babe was hardly a saint, in verbal exchanges he usually came off second best, whereas Cobb's harassment of Ruth showed him at his meanest.

Although Ruth did more to bring about the new-style baseball than anybody else, a number of other factors were also at work. Regardless of what the Spalding company said, the ball seemed livelier—by at least twenty-five percent, the venerable John B. Sheridan estimated in 1925. That year National League owners commissioned a Columbia University scientist to study the present ball versus that supplied by Spalding in 1914. The conclusion was that while the ball was the same in design and composition, the materials in the 1925 ball, particularly the woolen yarn, were of higher quality. That much the Spalding company would acknowledge, but nothing more.

Part of the explanation for the batting boom's starting in 1920, granted some observers, might be the livelier ball or the banning of the spitter, but mainly it was a matter of the passing of the previous decade's "forearm hitters" in favor of players who held their weapons at the end and swung freely. Wrote F. C. Lane in 1923, "Almost any batter that has it in him to wallop the ball is swinging from the handle of the bat with every ounce of strength that nature placed in his wrists and shoulders."

In the twenties most players started using thinner-handled bats that had more weight concentrated in the barrel, or "fat" part, and featured big knobs offering a firmer grip at the end. With such bats, hitters could take full, whiplike swings and try to drive the ball, as opposed to slapping, punching, or pushing it in the characteristic batting style of the "dead-ball" years.

Then, too, batters increasingly enjoyed the luxury of swinging at clean, new baseballs. Per instructions, umpires now removed scuffed and smudged balls from play, at the same time that most club owners, now making bigger profits, no longer compelled their customers to return balls knocked into the stands.

Thus the 1920s was a decade of potent offensive baseball, featuring far more home runs than ever before in the game's history. More people paid more money than ever to watch the new-style baseball, making the twenties the sport's golden age as a "live" spectator attraction. For most of the decade the New York Yankees drew at least two million in combined home-road attendance, and for the decade as a whole, the Yankees franchise netted a $3.5 million profit. The prosperity was fairly well distributed, though; by 1930 total admissions in the major leagues topped ten million.

The attendance boom prompted newspapers to increase their baseball coverage; most of the bigger dailies now featured wholly separate sporting-news sections. With such writers as John Kieran, Hugh Fullerton, Grantland Rice, and Heywood Broun on the job, American sports journalism may well have reached its peak in the twenties, the last period clearly dominated by print media.

By the close of the decade, however, something like a third of American families owned radios, from which listeners could learn baseball scores more quickly than from newspapers, besides receiving on-the-spot broadcasts of World Series games every October. President William H. Veeck, Sr., and chief stockholder William K. Wrigley of the Chicago Cubs had discovered that by permitting local stations to broadcast their team's regular-season games, they could win new fans, particularly housewives, and generally stimulate interest in the Cubs' fortunes. That notion was still too avant-garde for other major-league club owners, but the wedding of baseball and electronic communication was well under way.

The New York Yankees—based in the nation's largest city and its media capital, winners of six pennants and three world's championships in eight seasons, and exhibitors of Babe Ruth's talents—became the most successful operation in baseball history, both on the playing field and at the ticket windows. Their first pennant came in 1921— with Ruth topping his own homer record by five, driving in 171 runs, scoring 177, and batting .378—but they lost to McGraw's Giants in the all–Polo Grounds World Series, five games to three, dropping the final two games with Ruth disabled.

In 1922 the Yankees had to struggle to overcome the best team St. Louis ever fielded in the American League, while the Giants had little trouble with their NL opposition. With the Series restored to seven games (at Landis's direction), the Yankees won only once, largely because McGraw's pitchers held Ruth to only two hits and a .118 average.

Evicted from the Polo Grounds by the Giants after the 1922 season, the Yankees' ownership built the greatest baseball facility thus far, promptly and properly dubbed "The House That Ruth Built." Yankee Stadium—located in the extreme South Bronx, directly across the Harlem River bridge from the Polo Grounds—could seat close to seventy thousand people and, in keeping with massive changes under way in personal transportation preferences, even offered parking spaces for a couple of thousand automobiles. It opened on April 18, 1923, with the Yankees beating the Boston Red Sox. Ruth, of course, christened the big stadium with a homer.

Apart from Ruth's prowess with the bat and field manager Miller Huggins's shrewdness in handling his men, the principal reason for the Yankees' success was their season-by-season procurement of talent from Boston. Beginning with Carl Mays and then Ruth, Yankees business manager Ed Barrow made deal after deal with Harry Frazee. Barrow succeeded in stocking the New York roster with first-rate players who, had they stayed with the Red Sox, would likely have restored Boston's 1912–1918 hegemony. Except in the case of Ruth, Frazee unloaded his mainstays for neither a lot of money nor players of comparable worth.

The "rape of the Red Sox," as hometown fans called the departure of their favorites, reduced the Boston club to one of the American League's weakest. From sixth place in 1920–1921, the Red Sox fell to last in 1922 and, except for a seventh-place finish in 1924, stayed on the bottom the rest of the decade. Between the pillaged Red Sox and the impotent Braves, Boston fans had to watch some of the worst baseball ever offered in big-league guise.

In 1923, in winning a third straight AL title by fifteen games over Cobb's Detroit club, the Yankees featured former Red Sox as their regular catcher (Wally Schang), shortstop (Everett Scott), third baseman (Joe Dugan), and right fielder (Ruth), as well as four of the five pitchers in their starting rotation (Waite Hoyt, Sam Jones, Joe Bush, and Herb Pennock). (Former Red Sox pitcher Carl Mays, used mainly in relief, was sold to Cincinnati after the season.)

By four games to two, the Yankees finally triumphed over the Giants in that year's World Series, and Ruth finally played up to his standard, hitting three homers and batting .368. The New York Yankees, it seemed, had finally arrived as baseball's foremost team, supplanting the Giants in the allegiance of the fans and the attentions of the press and baseball-followers across the country.

Now gray and rotund, managing exclusively from the bench in street clothes, the fifty-four-year-old John McGraw had watched his men lose a World Series for the fifth time in eight tries. Yet his Giants were on their way to doing something that hadn't been accomplished since Charles Comiskey led the old St. Louis Browns to American Association titles from 1885 through 1888. In 1924 the Giants narrowly beat out Brooklyn and Pittsburgh for their fourth consecutive league championship, before losing still another Series, this time an exciting seven-game set to the Washington Senators. Washington won in the bottom of the twelfth inning on a bad-hop base hit, as McGraw and the Giants continued their history of victimization by freakish plays.

For all their pennants, though, the New York Giants couldn't entirely escape the suspicious odor that had hung over the franchise for most of McGraw's tenure. Besides Charles Stoneham's connections to securities scams and big-time criminals, and McGraw's penchant for embarrassing off-the-field brawls, players of questionable honesty continued to show up on the Giants' roster.

In the middle of the 1922 season Phil Douglas, a hulking, alcoholic, gifted spitballer who'd come to hate McGraw, wrote Les Mann, a former teammate on the St. Louis Cardinals, that he would go home to Tennessee if the Cardinals made it worth his while. When news of Douglas's offer to desert his team reached the commissioner's office, Landis immediately banished the pitcher for life.

The Douglas incident was relatively cut-and-dried. Not so the circumstances surrounding an effort on the part of Giants reserve outfielder Jimmy O'Connell to bribe a Philadelphia Phillies shortstop near the end of the 1924 season. Besides naming coach Alvin "Cozy" Dolan as the one who'd put him up to the attempt, O'Connell insisted that second baseman Frank Frisch, right fielder Ross Youngs, and first baseman George Kelly, the Giants' three top players, all knew about it and encouraged him to go ahead.

On the eve of the World Series opener, in Washington, Landis hastily interviewed various players involved, as well as McGraw and Stoneham. While clearing Frisch, Youngs, and Kelly, the commissioner suspended O'Connell and Dolan—permanently, as it turned out. Readily admitting his guilt at the same time that he implicated others, O'Connell seemed bewildered. "They're making a goat out of me," he told a reporter. "I've been a damned fool. They were all in on it and they deserted me. . . ." Six months later, obviously finished in Organized Baseball, O'Connell still hadn't changed his story: "I was working for the Giants and I thought the management wanted me to do it."

Like the Black Sox episode, the O'Connell-Dolan affair left a string of questions that weren't answered then and never would be. Plenty of people were as bewildered as Jimmy O'Connell by Landis's almost perfunctory handling of the case. Ban Johnson, always ready to cause Landis whatever discomfort he could, wanted the 1924 World Series canceled in light of the bribery revelation. Pittsburgh Pirates owner Barney Dreyfuss, an ancient enemy of McGraw, termed the notion that O'Connell and Dolan were the sole culprits "an insult to the intelligence of the public." John B. Sheridan found it "almost incredible . . . that [a] man could manage a baseball club, be about his players when crooked dealing was in the air and not 'feel' it, not know it."

Americans might still "expect their national game to be considerably further beyond suspicion than Caesar's wife," as W. O. McGeehan of the *New York Times* put it, yet the baseball-loving public again exhibited a short memory; by spring training 1925, the foggy O'Connell-Dolan business was almost forgotten. Apparently people still kept their belief in the sport's fundamental integrity. Impatient to get back to the action on the playing field, they remained willing to take baseball officialdom at its word.

While nobody was more eager than Kenesaw Mountain Landis for the ghosts of baseball past to vanish for good, unfinished business continued to surface. Following the 1926 season, both Ty Cobb and Tris Speaker resigned their managerial posts. Although Cobb, unable to get his club close to a pennant in six seasons, had been under fire in Detroit for some time, Speaker's resignation was baffling, inasmuch as he'd just led Cleveland to a strong second-place finish.

The explanation in both instances, it was later revealed, was that Ban Johnson had come into possession of letters supplied by Dutch Leonard, former Red Sox and Tigers left-hander, implicating Cobb and Speaker in a scheme to rig a Detroit victory over Cleveland at the end of the 1919 season. Cobb, Speaker, Cleveland outfielder Joe Wood, and he, claimed Leonard, had all placed bets on Detroit. Johnson had confronted the two player-managers with Leonard's evidence and, in one of his last significant actions, bluffed them into resigning without protest.

In his ongoing, intricate power game with Johnson, Landis then decided to make public Leonard's accusations and evidence, which he did on December 21. While much of the country gasped at the notion that two of the greatest and most respected players in history could have been part of a fix, Cobb and Speaker, now free to speak, denounced Leonard as a liar, hired lawyers, and demanded exoneration by the commissioner. Landis bided his time, waiting, as it turned out, for Johnson to make a bad move.

When Johnson did publicly declare that the American League had additional evidence it hadn't given Landis, the commissioner summoned the AL owners to an emergency meeting to hear whatever Johnson had held back. Forced to admit that Landis had already seen everything bearing on the case, Johnson was humiliated. The AL owners voted to send him on a leave of absence, and although he was back in time for the 1927 season, he'd become little more than a figurehead.

Having again one-upped his adversary, Landis could now exonerate Cobb and Speaker, at the same time that he moved to ensure that both would remain in the AL, contrary to what Johnson had announced. Cobb ultimately signed for 1927 with Connie Mack's Philadelphia Athletics, Speaker with Washington.

While the Cobb-Speaker matter was making headlines across the nation, Landis also had to hold a much-publicized inquiry into another reported fix from the pre-Landis years. This one had to do with claims by Swede Risberg, backed by Chick Gandil, that they and their Chicago White Sox teammates had paid the Detroit team to throw consecutive doubleheaders in Chicago early in September 1917.

In a public hearing in his little Chicago office, Landis listened to the two barred players' stories, then heard from thirty-four others who'd been with either the White Sox or Tigers in 1917, including Ty Cobb. All contradicted Risberg and Gandil, explaining that the White Sox had made up a $1,100 pot to reward the Detroit pitchers for their strong work against Boston, Chicago's closest competitor for the pennant that year.

On January 12, 1927, Landis ruled that no fix had taken place, that in fact the incident involved nothing more than a "bonus" payment to the Detroit pitchers—a common gesture on the part of contending clubs at that time. It was, said Landis, "an impropriety, reprehensible and censurable, but not corrupt." Having disposed of that matter and, two weeks later, the Cobb-Speaker allegations, Landis wearily proclaimed a statute of limitations on things that had happened before he took office.

Landis had undoubtedly made baseball a more honest profession; no more bribery attempts would come to light in the major leagues in that or succeeding decades. Which is not to say that anybody had given up gambling. A large proportion of players had always liked to make bets, on anything from cards to dice to prizefights to horse races—and sometimes baseball games as well. T. L. Huston, co-owner of the Yankees until he sold out to Jacob Ruppert in the fall of 1922, later revealed that fines had been levied on various New York players that season for betting on horse races. Asked why the Yankees' management presumed to tell players what they could do off the field, Huston snapped, " 'Off the field' is just it. They bring it onto the field. We found them running out between innings to get horse-race returns."

The biggest horseplayer in baseball was probably the St. Louis Cardinals' Rogers Hornsby, who was also the outstanding ballplayer in the National League. In 1920, at the age of twenty-four, the right-handed Hornsby hit .370 to win the NL batting title, the first of six straight league-leading seasons. Over those years he *averaged* .397 and topped .400 three times; his .424 mark in 1924 established what is likely to remain the major-league standard for the twentieth century. Only the second native Texan (after Tris Speaker) to excel in baseball's fastest company, Hornsby also hit for power. Until 1930 no National Leaguer topped his forty-two homers in 1922 or thirty-nine in 1925 and 1929. Never an outstanding defensive player, Hornsby nonetheless did a creditable job at second base after settling there in 1922.

As a horseplayer, Hornsby was a heavy wagerer and consistent loser—a situation that increasingly annoyed Cardinals owner Sam Breadon and Branch Rickey, who served as both business and field manager of the St. Louis club. Besides that, the Texan was a man of generally unpleasant disposition—insufferably blunt-spoken, caustic, and "as cold as tempered steel," in the estimate of one acquaintance.

Whatever else one might say about him, there was no denying Hornsby's greatness with the bat. Far and away the most valuable property of a financially weak franchise, Hornsby was the center of trade rumors nearly every winter. John McGraw repeatedly tried to work out some kind of deal for Hornsby, but the wily Rickey always asked too much in return.

So the Texan remained in St. Louis as the nucleus of a team that finally became good enough to put the franchise in the black. In 1922 the Cardinals abandoned their dilapidated wooden ballpark and became the Browns' tenants in modernized Sportsman's Park. That year, with a fourth-place team, they set a franchise record by drawing half a million. At $30,000, Hornsby became the NL's top-salaried performer.

Rickey knew, though, that the Cardinals, operating in a city that wasn't really big enough for two major-league franchises, couldn't build a pennant winner by spending money and making trades, as the Giants had done under McGraw and the Yankees were now doing as well. Affordable minor-league talent had become scarce under a new agreement signed early in 1921 with the major leagues, whereby any minor league could exempt itself from the annual player draft. The three top-level minors (the International League, American Association, and Pacific Coast League) had all opted for the draft exemption, as had the Western and Three-I leagues. Thus a minor-league franchise could hold on to a quality player indefinitely—or until an owner finally got his price. In the International League, for example, owner-manager Jack Dunn kept his Baltimore Orioles mostly intact through seven consecutive championships.

So Rickey undertook to develop talent for the Cardinals from the bottom up—on "farm clubs" in a "chain" or "farm system." He wasn't the first to have the idea; in the past, major-league clubs had frequently made agreements with minor-league owners to assign a player or two in exchange for the pick of those controlled by the minor club. Billy Evans, a longtime American League umpire and subsequently general manager at Cleveland, credited Charles W. Somers with inventing chain-system operations before the Great War, when Cleveland owned Waterbury in the Eastern League, New Orleans in the Southern League, and Toledo in the American Association. But after the financially strapped Somers sold the Indians in 1916, his successors dismantled what he'd built up in the minors. Rickey, said Evans, had only "expanded the Somers idea."

Whether or not Rickey was the father of farm-system baseball, he carried it to its ultimate effectiveness. Early in 1921 he persuaded Breadon to purchase controlling interest in the Syracuse International League franchise; later that same year, they gained control of the Houston club in the Texas League. By 1926 they'd added Sioux City (Western League), Fort Smith (Cotton States League), and Danville (Three-I League). The Syracuse franchise was sold in 1928; Rochester, also in the International League, became the Cardinals' highest-level farm. A few years later, having already put about a million dollars into the system, the Cardinals added Columbus (American Association).

Rickey's idea was to sign raw young players for little or nothing, assign them to the Cardinals' farms in the low minors, and carefully scout, grade, and advance them. It proved a remarkably successful way to develop a growing surplus of major-league-caliber players. In 1919 Rickey had paid $10,000 for minor-league pitcher Jess Haines; that was the last player the Cardinals purchased for twenty-seven years. Meanwhile Rickey sold $2 million worth of talent to other major-league teams. Taking a healthy commission on those sales, he became by far the richest salaried executive in baseball.

Rickey's grand design finally paid off in 1926 in the first pennant in St. Louis's National League history—one of nine (along with six world's championships) that would come to the franchise over the next two decades. A quarter of the way through the 1925 season, with the Cardinals languishing at the bottom of the league, Rickey quit as field manager in favor of Hornsby, who guided the team to a fourth-place finish. Then in 1926, despite Hornsby's own slump (to .317), the Cardinals put on a late-season drive to beat out Cincinnati and Pittsburgh. Two-thirds of Hornsby's players had come up through Rickey's farm system.

Meanwhile the 1925 Yankees had plummeted to seventh place, largely because Ruth slumped and stayed in trouble with Miller Huggins much of the time, ultimately suffering suspension and an unprecedented $5,000 fine. In 1926, with Ruth behaving himself and hitting with his customary authority and young Lou Gehrig and Tony Lazzeri adding punch to the lineup, the Yankees climbed back to the top.

The 1926 World Series featured the biggest (legitimate) upset since the Miracle Braves swept the Athletics in 1914. Overcoming Ruth's four homers, Hornsby's team defeated the Yankees in seven games, winning the deciding contest 4–3 in a cold drizzle at Yankee Stadium. In the seventh inning of that game, thirty-nine-year-old Grover Cleveland Alexander, a midseason pickup from the Cubs who'd already pitched two victories in the Series, trudged in from the bullpen to kill a Yankees rally by striking out Tony Lazzeri with the bases loaded. "Old Pete" held the hard-hitting New Yorkers scoreless the rest of the way, with Ruth's ill-advised attempt to steal second base ending the Series.

After 1924 the New York Giants never won another pennant under John McGraw, although they usually were strong contenders. In poor health much of the time, McGraw had to rely on assistants to run the team in his frequent absences; in 1927, for example, Rogers Hornsby filled in for McGraw most of the second half of the season. In the aftermath of the Cardinals' brilliant Series triumph, Sam Breadon and Branch Rickey turned down Hornsby's demand for a big pay raise and a multiyear contract, and dealt the NL's top player to New York for Frank Frisch, plus a journeyman pitcher and lots of cash. Hornsby had a big year at bat in '27, but in the process he alienated Giants president Stoneham. That fall he was on the move again. In 1928, with the seventh-place Boston Braves, Hornsby won his seventh batting title, besides managing the club after May.

Meanwhile the Pittsburgh Pirates continued to seek winning combinations in the traditional manner, with judicious purchases from the minors plus a few trades. In 1925 the Pirates outdistanced the rest of the National League, then beat Washington in the World

Series. Following the Cardinals' spectacular 1926 season, Pittsburgh regained the NL title under Donie Bush.

In the American League the Washington Senators, based in one of the majors' smallest markets, were able to break the Yankees' domination in 1924–1925. Led by second baseman Stanley "Bucky" Harris, youngest manager in the majors, the Senators defeated the Giants in their first World Series, one of the most exciting ever. In 1925, though, Washington lost in seven games to Pittsburgh, which pounded the great Walter Johnson in a rain-soaked finale at Forbes Field.

After their upset at the hands of St. Louis in the '26 Series, the Yankees came back to win 110 games and run away with the AL title, fielding a team that many would always regard as the finest of all time. Ruth reached the summit of his career in 1927, walloping sixty home runs to surpass his own record; young Lou Gehrig, playing only his second full season as the Yankees' first baseman, hit forty-seven (the highest total for anybody except the Babe up to then) and drove in a record 175 runs. The Yankees batted .307 as a team and scored nearly a thousand times, while their pitching staff showed the lowest earned run average in the majors. In the World Series they won four straight from a good Pittsburgh team.

The next season the Yankees withstood numerous injuries and the death of pitcher Urban Shocker from heart disease to beat out the resurgent Philadelphia Athletics. They made it eight straight Series wins by sweeping the Cardinals, Gehrig homering four times and Ruth three.

Between 1927 and 1930, the World Series should have convinced even the most die-hard National League fans that the AL had become the stronger circuit. In 1929 Ruth and Gehrig continued to hammer the ball, but various other regulars, as well as the whole New York pitching staff, started to sag. Meanwhile Connie Mack, still handicapped by Pennsylvania's statewide ban on Sunday baseball, had carefully spent his franchise's modest profits to turn the once-proud but long-downtrodden Athletics into champions once again.

Mack's runner-up 1927–1928 Athletics mixed eminent veterans (Ty Cobb, Eddie Collins, Tris Speaker, and Zack Wheat) with outstanding youngsters such as catcher Gordon "Mickey" Cochrane, outfielder Al Simmons, catcher-infielder Jimmie Foxx, shortstop Joe Boley, second baseman Max Bishop, and pitcher Robert "Lefty" Grove. The last three players Mack had bought from the great Baltimore International League club, with Grove carrying a record $105,000 price tag.

By 1929 the graybeards were gone, having served their purpose in hyping attendance, and Mack's club was finally better than the Yankees—by seventeen games at the end. In the World Series the Athletics met the Chicago Cubs, pennant winners for the first time in the postwar period under Joe McCarthy, a career minor-leaguer until he came to Chicago in 1925.

In the 1928–1929 off-season William K. Wrigley had spent about $400,000 to strengthen his ball club; half of that cash, as well as five players, went to Boston for Rogers Hornsby. Joining his fourth team in four seasons, the tactless Texan enjoyed what would prove to be his last big year, batting .380 with thirty-nine homers and 149 runs batted in—a performance that brought him his second Most Valuable Player Award. Hornsby was part of a potent offense that included Hazen "Kiki" Cuyler, Riggs Stephenson, and Lewis "Hack" Wilson. A powerfully built, 5-6 outfielder the Giants had let get away, Wilson assaulted opposing pitchers almost as robustly as he downed the bootleg liquor that was abundantly available in Chicago.

The Athletics disposed of the Cubs in five games. The turning point came in game five, when Philadelphia, down 8–0, scored ten times in the seventh inning, with help from Hack Wilson's two misplays on fly balls. The Series clincher in Philadelphia two days later was almost anticlimactic.

In 1930 the Athletics cruised to another pennant, then knocked off the St. Louis Cardinals in six games. National League entries had now managed to win only three games in the past four World Series. Yet missing in all the talk about American League domination was any real appreciation of the Cardinals' achievement—three pennants and a world's championship in five years, all done with a modest payroll and attendance, but with a sophisticated, largely self-supporting means of producing players.

Of course, at any time in the 1920s, any big-league club could have easily and inexpensively obtained some of the finest baseball players in the world, simply by breaching the unofficial racial barriers in place since the 1890s throughout Organized Baseball. After 1900 black baseball developed as a world of its own, with numerous professional and semiprofessional clubs forming, disbanding, and re-forming, not only throughout the United States, where racial distinctions were firmly fixed, but in the new Republic of Cuba and other Hispanic-American countries, where they weren't.

Sol White, captain of the strong Philadelphia Giants and the foremost chronicler of early black baseball, was undoubtedly accurate when he wrote in 1907: "Of the players of to-day, with the same prospects for a future as the white players [,] there would be a score or more colored ball players cavorting around the National or American League diamonds at the present time."

Lacking those "same prospects for a future," black players made their own way. Before 1920 they operated independently, playing other black clubs, white semipro clubs, occasionally even white big-league clubs on open dates in their schedules or in postseason matchups. Such outfits as the Brooklyn Royal Giants, Cuban Giants (New York), Philadelphia Giants, Leland Giants (Chicago), and Chicago American Giants gained notoriety in the black press, which by the early 1900s was flourishing in the major northern cities. (Black teams showed a remarkable affinity for the nickname "Giants," probably because the New York Giants were riding high in those years and commanding more publicity than anybody else.)

Yet the exploits of John Henry Lloyd (sometimes called the "black Honus Wagner"), Spotswood Poles (frequently compared to Ty Cobb), or "Smoky Joe" Williams, probably the equal of Walter Johnson or any other pitcher, were little known to the white sports public. As for baseball in Cuba, where the game had taken hold as early as the 1870s, about the only news *los norteamericanos* were exposed to consisted of word-of-mouth reports from visits to the island by white U.S. professional and semipro outfits—one of the earliest of which, in 1890, had included seventeen-year-old John McGraw.

That all began to change in 1908, when the Cincinnati Reds, fifth-place finishers in the National League that season, journeyed to Cuba for what they thought would be a postseason frolic organized around games with the Havana Reds and Almendares, the two leading Cuban professional clubs. Dismayingly, Cincinnati lost the majority of its games against competition that was surprisingly tough. Then, in 1909, without Ty Cobb, the three-time AL champion Detroit Tigers won only four of twelve games against the two Cuban clubs. Playing that year for the Havana Reds were John Henry Lloyd and three other standouts from the Chicago-based Leland Giants.

In succeeding years, big-leaguers from the U.S. continued to struggle against Cuban outfits that often included North American black professionals. As a rule, such players were found on the Havana club, whereas Almendares was usually all-Cuban. With or without U.S. players, the Cuban teams were always racially mixed.

Jose Méndez, a slender, very black right-hander, was the great hero of Cuban baseball in that period. In 1910 the Detroit Tigers returned to Cuba, and this time Cobb joined them for the final four games of a series won by the Tigers, 7–4–1. But in one contest catcher Bruce Petway from the Leland Giants threw out the daredevil Cobb on a steal attempt, and in another Méndez added to his status as a national idol by holding Cobb to a single and striking him out.

The next year the Philadelphia Phillies won five and lost three against the Cuban teams; then John McGraw brought in his National League champions and scored the first decisive victory over the local baseballers, who played all-Cuban that year. Vowing "I didn't come down here to let a lot of coffee-colored Cubans show me up," McGraw drove his team to eight wins in eleven tries against Havana and Almendares. Afterward Christy Mathewson called Méndez "a great pitcher"; McGraw said he'd pay $50,000 for him if he were white. W. A. Phelon, a Cincinnati baseball writer, mused on "what a sensation Méndez would be if it was not for his color. But, alas, that is a handicap he can't outgrow."

Several acceptably Caucasian Cubans did sign with big-league clubs. Armando Marsans, for example, had an eight-year career (1911–1918) as an infielder in the National, Federal, and American leagues, while left-hander Adolfo Luque, who defeated the Giants in Havana in 1911, won 194 games over twenty years in the National League. In 1923 Luque posted twenty-seven wins for the Cincinnati

Reds, exceeded in the majors that season only by Brooklyn's fireballing Arthur "Dazzy" Vance's twenty-eight.

But black men, from the U.S., Cuba, or anywhere else, continued to be shut out of Organized Baseball. As a consequence, a steady stream of outstanding black Hispanic-Americans—Méndez and Christobel Torrienti in the 1920s, Martin Dihigo and Luis Tiant, Sr., in the thirties and forties, to name only a few—came north to ply their trade with black teams in the summer months, then returned home for the warm winter season. Teams of Cuban all-stars also regularly visited the U.S.

While the door to Organized Baseball and a chance for good money would remain closed for another generation, as of 1920 black players, whether native U.S. or Caribbean, had an alternative. That year the efforts of Rube Foster brought into being the Negro National League (NNL).

"If the talents of Christy Mathewson, John McGraw, Ban Johnson, and Kenesaw Mountain Landis were combined in a single body, and that body were enveloped in a black skin, the result would have to be named Andrew (Rube) Foster." So Robert Peterson, in his pathblazing history of black baseball, has summed up Foster.

Born in 1879 in the all-black town of Calvert, Texas, Foster made a regional reputation as a pitcher before coming to Chicago to join the local Union Giants. Over the next ten years Foster, like most black professionals, jumped from club to club, making a tremendous name among black fans—admiration that carried over among white players and managers who occasionally saw him pitch. An aging Honus Wagner would remember him as "the smartest pitcher I have ever seen in all my years of baseball." (Foster's nickname, according to legend, resulted from his having once outpitched Rube Waddell.)

In 1911 Foster joined with a white tavern-keeper named John Schorling to form the Chicago American Giants, and as its manager and (until 1915) star pitcher, Foster built that club into the strongest and most popular in black baseball, taking it as far south as Florida, as far west as California. He also came to control booking arrangements for black teams in most of the Midwest; his rivalry with Nat Strong, a white promoter whose booking agency dominated the East, was one factor behind Foster's determination to bring some order to black baseball by creating a well-organized league. Yet Foster also seems to have envisioned a day when his organization might be accepted as a full partner by the National and American leagues, separate but equal in a tripartite major-league setup.

Foster expected that under a stable, competitive league structure, everybody would make more money. He wasn't a demographer, but then one didn't have to be to see the huge growth in the black population of the urban, industrial North that began shortly after 1900, greatly accelerated during the wartime boom, and continued through the twenties. The northern cities now teemed with black people who could afford a variety of black-oriented entertainments, including baseball.

Whatever Foster's motives, he was able to organize an eight-team circuit that, for 1920, consisted of his American Giants plus the Chicago Giants (a separate ball club), Cuban Stars (Cincinnati), Kansas City Monarchs, Detroit Stars, Indianapolis ABC's, St. Louis Giants, and Dayton Marcos. Teams came and went in the Negro National League, but Foster's American Giants and the Kansas City Monarchs, owned by a white man named J. L. Wilkinson, were its bellwether franchises.

Playing a schedule of sixty to eighty games, the NNL clubs also crammed in that many or more games on open dates against independents, usually white semiprofessional outfits. In the middle and late twenties, in the midst of generally prosperous economic conditions that affected all elements of the population to some degree, the American Giants, the Monarchs, and other black clubs made enough money to travel in their own Pullman cars, in the style of the white big-league teams.

Times were so good that in 1923 Nat Strong and other Easterners organized a second all-black circuit called the Eastern Colored League (ECL), made up of six clubs based in and around New York City, Philadelphia, and Baltimore. The next year Foster and Strong arranged for the NNL and ECL winners to meet in the first black World Series. In the manner of the early white World Series in the 1880s, the games took place in several cities: Philadelphia, Baltimore, Kansas City, and Chicago. The Monarchs bested the Hilldale Club (out of Darby, Pennsylvania) five games to four, with one tie.

The NNL-ECL World Series continued only three more years, until 1927. Lacking Foster's strong rule and organizational skill, the ECL had been a tenuous, loosely run operation from the start, and it folded in the spring of 1929. By that time the NNL was also on the skids. Three years earlier, after suffering a complete nervous collapse, Foster had been institutionalized. He died in the state mental hospital at Kankakee, Illinois, late in 1930.

Another black organization called the American Negro League, taking in most of the former ECL teams, struggled through the 1929 season before disbanding. The NNL survived in increasingly straitened circumstances into the early 1930s, as the economic slowdown that followed the stock market collapse of October 1929 turned into the worst economic crisis in the nation's history. By 1932 the Negro National League—Rube Foster's dream for a viable organization that would function as a counterweight to all-white professional baseball— had gone out of business.

So, by that time, had many other leagues and clubs, black and white. The years 1932–1933 were the bottom point of what economists came to call the Great Depression, and were the worst time baseball and professional sports in general had experienced in the twentieth century. The ten-million-plus customers who watched the sixteen American and National League teams in action during the 1930 season wouldn't be equaled for another sixteen years.

Nor would the individual-franchise attendance mark of 1,485,166, set by the Chicago Cubs in 1929 in the facility originally built for the Federal League, then subsequently expanded and renamed Wrigley Field. (The Cubs topped the one-million mark for five straight years, from 1927 to 1931.) In 1930, despite finishing a distant third, sixteen games behind the Philadelphia Athletics, the Yankees still were able to draw more than a million fans into their cavernous stadium.

After that, though, the fat years were in the past. The 1930s would bring some remarkable baseball, maybe the best ever played in the Jim Crow era, but it would be a bleak period for baseball entrepreneurs or anybody else trying to make money in professional sports.

8.
The
Gray
Thirties

As the American economy tailed off in 1930, baseball batting averages and other indices of offensive production continued to climb, especially in the National League. That year NL hitters averaged .303, led by the New York Giants' .319, the highest team mark since the 1897 Baltimore Orioles'. Nearly nine hundred home runs cleared the fences in NL ballparks. In narrowly losing the pennant to the St. Louis Cardinals, the Chicago Cubs pounded 171 homers to break the Yankees' 1927 record, even though Rogers Hornsby, plagued by a bone spur and a broken ankle, missed three-fourths of the season. But the Cubs' Hack Wilson, with fifty-six homers, far surpassed Hornsby's league mark in that category, while the squat Wilson's 190 runs batted in set a standard still unequaled in either league more than sixty years later. Giants first baseman Bill Terry (at .401) became the first major-leaguer to reach the .400 level since Hornsby in 1925.

The Philadelphia Phillies, with such heavy hitters as Chuck Klein (.386) and Frank "Lefty" O'Doul (.383) bouncing drives off the short, high right-field fence in their home ballpark, batted .315 as a team and scored 944 runs, yet managed to win only fifty-two games and finished dead last. Phillies pitchers, no doubt suffering from a peacetime version of shell shock, allowed earned runs at the rate of nearly seven per nine innings—but then, the earned run average for the whole National League was close to five. Everybody agreed that Spalding's 1930 ball was the liveliest yet, although neither the owners, the league presidents, Commissioner Landis, nor the Spalding company ever admitted as much.

American League pitchers had things a bit more in hand. They held batters to an overall .288 average and some 220 fewer home runs than were hit in the NL, although the third-place Yankees, batting .309 as a team, led the majors with 1,062 runs. Babe Ruth, now making $80,000 a year, batted .359 and knocked forty-nine homers; teammate Lou Gehrig, paid about a quarter that much, hit forty-one and drove home 174, besides batting .379. The Philadelphia Athletics, AL and World Series champions for the second year in a row, featured such formidable batsmen as Al Simmons (.381, thirty-six homers, 165 rbi's), Jimmie Foxx (.335, thirty-seven homers, 156 rbi's), and Mickey Cochrane (.357, ten homers, eighty-three rbi's).

In 1931 the ball was less lively—its horsehide covering was slightly loose and its stitching was higher. Thus the ball was easier to grip, especially to throw curveballs; more effective curves, in turn, meant fewer home runs. Lefty O'Doul and Floyd "Babe" Herman (a .393 hitter with Brooklyn in 1930) were among those who also complained that balls were being left in play longer and getting discolored and misshapen. Another thing that took several points off averages was the elimination of the "sacrifice fly" rule adopted back in 1908. Henceforth a run-scoring fly ball would be charged as an official time at bat.

By mid-May National League president John Heydler was satisfied that he and his associates had "brought about . . . the very result at which we aimed when we adopted the new ball in February." Thus while in 1930 nobody would admit officially that there was anything wrong with the ball, now National Leaguers, at least, were ready to congratulate themselves on having reduced its "rabbit" content. William Harridge, the American League's new president, kept silent on the subject of the baseball, showing the official cautiousness that would feature his twenty-seven-year tenure.

In any case, NL averages dropped by thirty-two points, home-run totals by forty-five percent, and scoring by nearly a third. In the AL, where batting statistics had been less spectacular in 1930, the effects of the deadened ball were less dramatic: a decline of ten points in overall batting averages, fifteen percent in homers, only eight percent in scoring. Again, though, the Yankees topped a thousand runs; again Ruth and Gehrig, with forty-six homers apiece, plus 163 and 184 rbi's, respectively, continued to intimidate AL pitching staffs.

Not every pitching staff, though. Connie Mack's champion Athletics, besides batting nearly .300 as a team (with Al Simmons's .390 leading the majors), again boasted baseball's best mound corps. Coming off a 28–5 season in 1930, Lefty Grove became only the second pitcher since the war to reach the thirty-win mark—thirty-one, to be exact, against only four losses. Grove also led the majors with 175 strikeouts and a dazzling 2.06 earned run average.

On form, Mack's ball club should have beaten the St. Louis Cardinals again and claimed a third-straight world's championship, but St. Louis, led by outfielder John "Pepper" Martin's twelve hits and five stolen bases (of eight steals the Cardinals made on the strong-armed Cochrane), won in seven games. Burleigh Grimes, one of two designated spitballers still in the majors, outpitched George Earnshaw in the finale at Sportsman's Park.

Earlier that 1931 season, amid general grumbling by batters about the deadened ball, Harold "Pie" Traynor, Pittsburgh's star third baseman, predicted that lower averages would give club owners an excuse for general salary cuts. By 1929 the average salary of a big-leaguer had climbed to approximately $7,500. While Babe Ruth, at $70,000 that year and $80,000 for 1930–1931, was in a class by himself, the Cubs paid Rogers Hornsby $40,000 a year between 1929 and 1931, and a number of other topflight players had also made it into the $20,000–$30,000 range.

Actually, all the magnates had to do to justify a new austerity program was point to plummeting attendance and profits. In 1930 the sixteen major-league franchises collectively had cleared nearly $1.5 million; for 1931 that dropped to $217,000, with eleven clubs running a deficit. Players across the U.S. cursed and groaned when they received their 1932 contracts. In the absence of anything resembling a players' union, club officials were free to attack their mounting deficits according to the classic formula: Slash labor costs first, then look for other ways to economize.

Hack Wilson, injured part of the 1931 season and drunk much of the rest of it, had slumped terribly for the Cubs. Traded first to the Cardinals (for Burleigh Grimes), then sold to Brooklyn, Wilson ended up signing for $7,500, which represented a cut of close to seventy-five percent. (Within another two years Wilson would have drunk himself out of the majors.) Bill Terry's average had tailed off to .349 in 1931, but he'd still come within a fraction of a point of winning another batting title. Cut twenty percent from his 1931 salary of $22,500, Terry threatened a season-long holdout, then finally gave in to John McGraw's pleas that he swallow his medicine as manfully as his teammates had.

The weekly magazine *Outlook* no doubt spoke for most fans in calling Terry "an unconvincing martyr." In the face of widespread business failures, factory shutdowns, breadlines and masses of unemployed in the cities, and a collapsing agricultural economy, *Outlook* had no sympathy for Terry or any other "well-fed, bankroll-padded baseball holdout." Even Babe Ruth had to settle for a $10,000 cut, despite estimates that he generated at least three times as much revenue as what the Yankees paid him.

By 1932 the Great Depression had left approximately twelve million Americans without jobs—at least a quarter of the national work force. In the early part of the economic slump, as attendance climbed to all-time highs, some commentators supposed that people out of work were more likely to take in baseball games. Such thinking no longer made any sense (if it ever had) in the midst of the harsh circumstances Americans confronted in the summer of '32.

That baseball season, attendance at major-league games totaled about three and a half million, a drop of nearly seventy percent in two years. The combined losses of major-league franchises amounted to $1,201,000—an average loss margin of fifteen percent. Only four clubs made any kind of profit, led by the Yankees and Cubs, who returned to the top in their respective leagues. But the St. Louis Cardinals lost heavily in falling all the way to seventh place, and so did the Philadelphia Athletics, whose second-place finish still left them thirteen games behind the Yankees.

The New York Giants' home attendance, less than 250,000, was their smallest since the pre-McGraw era. It was a bad year all around for the Giants. In ill health, seeming older than his fifty-nine years, and going nowhere with a last-place team, John McGraw resigned in June in favor of Bill Terry. Under player-manager Terry, the Giants improved but still couldn't rise above sixth place, their worst showing since 1915.

The 1932 Yankees, now managed by Joe McCarthy, weren't as strong overall as New York's 1927–1928 teams. At thirty-seven, Ruth had settled down considerably, in large part because his second marriage, a few months after the death of his long-estranged first wife in 1929, proved a happy one. The Babe was slow, prone to injury, and chronically overweight, but he could still connect frequently and with power—as demonstrated by a .341 average, forty-one homers, and 137 rbi's that year. Besides Ruth and Gehrig, the Yankees still had such veterans from the 1927–1928 champions as Tony Lazzeri and Earle Combs, and recent additions included Bill Dickey, a lanky, hard-hitting catcher, and Vernon "Lefty" Gomez, a wisecracking Californian who posted twenty-four wins.

The Cubs put on a late-season drive after manager Rogers Hornsby (who'd succeeded Joe McCarthy less than twelve months earlier) was fired in favor of first baseman Charley Grimm, but in the World Series the Cubs finally ran out of luck. Scoring thirty-seven runs, including a Series-record eight homers, the Yankees won four straight, taking the first two games at home, then battering Grimm's pitchers at Wrigley Field, with Lazzeri homering twice and Combs once in the 13–6 finale.

A day earlier Ruth and Gehrig had each homered twice, including back-to-back blows in the fifth inning to put the Yankees ahead for good. On his second homer, according to baseball legend, the Babe pointed to far center field before hitting Charlie Root's pitch over the wire fence at the flagpole, right where he'd apparently indicated he would. What Ruth actually did was take two strikes (maybe holding up a finger after each), then wave at his hecklers in the Chicago dugout to shut up, and then, on the next pitch, drive the ball to the flagpole. Yet despite decades of denials from Root and others at the scene, the "called shot" quickly became the centerpiece in a vast Ruthian folklore—and a fable Ruth himself would come to believe and revel in telling. (Typically, Gehrig's second homer of the game, which immediately followed Ruth's, would be all but forgotten.)

The worst of the Depression came in the first half of 1933. Early in March, newly inaugurated President Franklin D. Roosevelt ordered all banks temporarily closed so that federal examiners could audit their books, certify which banks were sound, and thereby restore depositors' confidence and avert a complete collapse of the nation's banking structure.

The "bank holiday" left Rud Rennie of the *New York Herald Tribune*, covering the Yankees' training camp in Florida, with $8.75 in his pocket. That spring, Rennie later wrote, "We came home . . . through Southern cities which looked as tho [sic] they had been ravaged by an invisible enemy. People seemed to be hiding. They even would not come out to see Babe Ruth and Lou Gehrig. They simply did not have the money to waste on baseball games or amusements." Once the season began, traveling from city to city in the majors was almost equally dispiriting. Everywhere, Rennie remembered, "one saw stores for rent, silent shops, idle factories, half-empty hotels, and slim crowds in the ball-parks."

If the situation for the major leagues was bad, for the minors it was close to disastrous. One innovation intended to shore up attendance in the minors was in effect a postseason tournament for the top four finishers in each league—called the "Shaughnessy playoffs," after International League president Frank Shaughnessy, who originated the plan. Another was the trend toward extra-baseball offerings such as raffles and giveaways, touring clown acts, as well as home-run-hitting, long-distance-throwing, and even cow-milking contests. All added to minor-league baseball's distinctive identity, but didn't reverse the attendance slide.

At the end of 1930 the delegates to the minors' annual National Association meeting did away with the provision by which a league could opt to remain outside the majors' draft. In exchange, the major leagues pledged to limit their draft to players in the higher minors with at least four years of professional experience, and to draft no more than one player per minor-league club.

Although that made it easier for many minor-leaguers to reach the majors, the circumstances of those who didn't steadily worsened. By 1933 salaries for minor-league players had fallen about forty percent in four years, which meant that in Class D, at the bottom of the minors, players were averaging about $50 per month. Even for that kind of pay, the chances of finding a place within Organized Baseball were slim. Only fourteen minor leagues opened the 1933 season, a third of the number that had operated three years earlier. Of the surviving circuits, probably no more than two or three would have made it without a massive shift to nighttime baseball throughout the minor leagues—a development with far-reaching implications for baseball's future.

Various minor-league towns would later claim to have been the site of the first night game in professional baseball—by which, of course, was meant Organized Baseball. Actually, as early as 1929 the Kansas City Monarchs had begun traveling with several long flatbed trucks, from which hinged light towers could be raised once the trucks were positioned around a ballfield. Sometimes the Monarchs also used their portable lighting system at Muehlebach Field, which they shared with the Kansas City American Association team. On July 25, 1930, the Monarchs brought their lights into Forbes Field in Pittsburgh and staged the first nighttime game in a major-league ballpark, against the local Homestead Grays.

But because the exploits of the Monarchs were little known except to black fans, the game that received the most recognition as the first in organized competition under lights was a Western League contest that took place in May 1930 at Des Moines, Iowa. There a meeting between the local Demons and the Wichita Aviators was illuminated by banks of lights mounted on six permanently set, ninety-foot towers. Irving Vaughan of the *Chicago Tribune*, who saw the game, thought the lighting was generally adequate except for fielding fly balls. He also thought hitting would probably suffer somewhat.

So many more people came out for the earliest night games in the minors that within a matter of weeks scores of ballparks had been equipped with lights, and by the close of the 1931 season night baseball was the norm throughout the minors. Although it didn't stop some leagues from folding, it definitely saved others.

The other development that carried the minor leagues in the Depression era, according to a widely held view then and later, was the rapid growth of major-league farm systems. By affiliating with a big-league club, a minor-league operator could unburden himself of all or most of his players' salaries, which represented the bulk of his costs. If the minors were to survive, argued the *New York World-Telegram's* Dan Daniel in mid-1932, then "the majors will have to go into the chain store business on a large scale." That was precisely what happened.

At their December 1931 meetings, the major-league owners authorized unlimited "working agreements" with minor-league franchises. Within a short time, most big-league clubs had moved into farm-system development; for Branch Rickey and the St. Louis Cardinals, the door was open wider than ever.

Twenty years later Rickey would claim before a congressional investigating committee that "the farm system was the savior of baseball, and without it today, it is a problematical question whether you would have minor-league baseball in the smaller minors at all." However that may be, in the Depression years farm systems became the dominant element in minor-league operations. By the late thirties the Cardinals either owned or had agreements with thirty-three franchises and controlled some six hundred players. At one point, sixty-five players in the two major leagues—about sixteen percent of the total—had come up through the Cardinals' organization.

Meanwhile the New York Yankees, with more money to spend than any other organization, also got into farm clubs in a big way. Starting in 1932 with the purchase of the Newark International League franchise, the Yankees steadily expanded their minor-league connections, in accordance with the careful planning of George Weiss, whom Jacob Ruppert hired as baseball's first farm-system director.

In October 1938, only a few months before his death, a bedridden Ruppert had the satisfaction of listening to a radio broadcast of the deciding game in the "Little World Series" between the Yankees' top farm clubs—the Newark Bears and the American Association Kansas City Blues. Although the Yankees would continue to pluck needed veteran players from other big-league clubs, by the early forties—when they controlled thirteen minor-league teams—nearly all of their young talent had ripened on their farms.

But not everybody shared in the enthusiasm for farm-system baseball. The Chicago Cubs fielded contenders throughout the thirties using older methods—buying top minor-leaguers and buying and trading for what they needed from other clubs in the majors. Eventually, though, the Cubs' traditionalism would catch up with them. Philip K. Wrigley, who became president of the franchise in 1934 following the deaths of his father and William H. Veeck, would admit in 1951 that "the sad plight of the Cubs at the present time is probably due one hundred percent to the fact that we resisted the farm system so long that we dropped way behind in the competitive field."

And commissioner Kenesaw Mountain Landis was openly antagonistic to the trend toward "chain-store" baseball. With some justification, Landis was convinced that farm systems kept many players from making it into the big leagues as quickly as they should. He noted, for example, that a player in a particular "chain" remained draft-exempt for four years; then, once placed on the roster of the "parent club," he could be "optioned out" for three more seasons before he could be claimed on waivers by another major-league club. Landis was especially irked by sub-rosa agreements whereby major-league outfits controlled more than one franchise in the same minor league, making it possible to "cover up" draft-liable players. In March 1938 the commissioner, ruling that the Cardinals had violated the majors-minors prohibition on intraleague working agreements, made free agents of ninety-one St. Louis–controlled players. Two years later, Landis came down on the Detroit Tigers, in whose minor-league operation he "emancipated" an even one hundred players.

Building a farm system involved a commitment to long-range player development and presumably long-range hopes of success. Yet in the Depression era the immediate goal for many operators of baseball franchises was just to stay in business for another season. Despite being located in one of the nation's three biggest baseball markets, the Philadelphia Athletics, now wholly owned by Connie Mack and his sons, had never made a lot of money. In large part that was because, until 1934, the state of Pennsylvania refused to repeal a ban on Sabbath commerce dating back to the Colonial period. Although between 1929 and 1931 Mack had fielded some of the strongest teams in baseball history, attendance at Shibe Park had never approached what, in a comparably sized ballpark, the Chicago Cubs had been able to attract.

In 1932, with the Yankees way out front in the pennant race most of the time, the Philadelphia franchise ran a big deficit. As he'd done seventeen years earlier, Mack decided that his ball club was too expensive, that it wouldn't get any better, and that the time had come to sell off his best players while their market value was still high. Over the next three years he unloaded $590,000 worth of talent, the cream of his three-time AL and twice World Series champions. At the end of the 1932 season Al Simmons, along with third baseman Jimmie Dykes and outfielder George "Mule" Haas, went to the Chicago White Sox for $150,000; George Earnshaw joined them at Chicago the next year. In 1933 Mickey Cochrane was sold to Detroit for $100,000 to become the Tigers' player-manager. For another $125,000 and various third-rate players, Mack sent Lefty Grove, Max Bishop, and veteran pitcher George "Rube" Walberg to Boston, where young Thomas Yawkey, the new, multimillionaire Red Sox owner, was determined to buy a winner.

The last of Mack's stars to go was Jimmie Foxx, who in 1932 came within two home runs of Ruth's single-season record of sixty. That year and the next, Foxx won the AL's Most Valuable Player Award, but late in 1935 Mack took Yawkey's $150,000 for the slugging Foxx, still only twenty-eight. The Mack family remained solvent, but the Athletics finished last that season and the next; they wouldn't rise above sixth place until 1947.

By 1933 the dismantling of the Athletics and the decline of Ruth and other Yankees had created an opening for the Washington Senators. Walter Johnson was finally gone from the national capital, having retired as an active player in 1927 and then having served four also-ran seasons (1929–1932) as Washington's manager. For the second time, Clark Griffith, president of the Senators since 1920, gave the job to a "boy manager"—Joe Cronin, his twenty-seven-year-old shortstop. In 1933, besides batting .309 and driving in 118 runs, Cronin directed a group of mostly older players to ninety-nine wins, eight more than the Yankees.

In the National League Bill Terry led the New York Giants, a sixth-place entry in 1932, to victory in a tough fight with Pittsburgh and Chicago, and John McGraw, with only five months to live, took part in the Giants' thirteenth pennant celebration. Although the 1933 Giants weren't in a class with some of McGraw's outfits, they did include stocky Mel Ott, the NL's leading power hitter, and scrawny

Carl Hubbell, a left-hander from Oklahoma whose reverse-breaking "screwball" had made him one of the game's top pitchers. Terry's team had a surprisingly easy time of it in the World Series, defeating Washington four games to one.

The 1933 Senators and Giants were good baseball teams, but, so veteran commentators thought, they lacked the color and fire of many earlier champions. A common theme in baseball discussions from the late 1920s on was that ballplayers had started acting like bland businessmen—that they just didn't have the competitive spirit of the old-timers.

Ty Cobb, for one, became a chronic gripe on the subject of both home-run-dominated baseball and what he insisted was a lack of drive and dedication on the part of contemporary players. In 1932, his last full season as Giants manager, John McGraw also complained that "the men don't get out and fight for the games like they used to—that's what is wrong with baseball." That year a Philadelphia writer recalled that in the old days, when McGraw's men came into town, "everybody knew there'd be plenty of excitement to stir the blood." Now the Giants had become "just another ball club."

In the midst of that kind of talk, the St. Louis Cardinals won a pennant and World Series in 1934 with a team that evoked memories of colorful, rollicking outfits of the past. Nicknamed the "Gas House Gang," the Cardinals were managed by the combative Frank Frisch. A onetime protégé of McGraw, Frisch was the finest switch-hitter the game had seen thus far, still a good second baseman, and an umpire-baiter of the old school. Frisch, scrappy Pepper Martin, pitcher "Wild Bill" Hallahan, and a few others were carryovers from the 1931 champions; but the strength of the '34 Cardinals was in younger players such as outfielder Joe Medwick, first baseman James "Ripper" Collins, and the Dean brothers on the mound.

Older brother Jerome Herman Dean, whose zany antics in the minors had won him the nickname "Dizzy," was a lean, long-armed sharecropper's son from Lucas, Arkansas (although he claimed several other birthplaces). Minimally schooled, the twenty-three-year-old right-hander possessed an abundance of native shrewdness and a remarkable aptitude for self-promotion, plus vast ability. "If you can do it, it ain't braggin'," was one of his many bits of folk wisdom.

Coming off eighteen and twenty wins in his first two seasons, Dizzy was nearly unbeatable in 1934. In winning thirty games and losing only seven, he pitched seven shutouts, struck out 195, and held opponents to an average of 2.65 earned runs per nine innings. Paul Dean, two years younger, turned in nineteen victories in his rookie season, including a no-hit game. In the spring Dizzy had predicted that "me and Paul" would win forty—one of the few occasions when he would be guilty of understatement.

In that year's World Series, the Gas House Gang overcame the favored Detroit Tigers four games to three, with the Dean brothers accounting for all of St. Louis's wins. Knocked unconscious in game five when hit by a throw on the basepaths ("X-Rays of Dean's Head Show Nothing," headlined a Detroit newspaper), Dizzy came back to shut out the Tigers 11–0 in the deciding game, at Detroit.

In the sixth inning of that finale Joe Medwick slid hard into third base, scuffled with Detroit's Marvin Owen, and then met a shower of debris from the packed bleachers when he resumed his position in left field. With the Cardinals already ahead 7–0 and Dizzy Dean in command, commissioner Landis ordered manager Frisch to remove Medwick, both to protect the player and to get the game resumed. Although Medwick's seventeen-year career in the majors produced an excellent set of offensive statistics, he would usually be remembered as the only player ever taken out of a World Series game by the commissioner.

The 1934 Tigers, Detroit's first pennant winners in a quarter-century, generally fitted the profile of thirties major-league baseball. They batted .300 as a team, scored close to a thousand runs while running the bases cautiously, and won with a pitching staff that showed a four-plus earned run average. Besides manager Mickey Cochrane, who caught 121 games and batted .320, the Tigers' top players were second baseman Charlie Gehringer, a quiet perfectionist who batted .356 that year and would average .320 over nineteen seasons, and Hank Greenberg, their big first baseman.

In his second big-league season, the Manhattan-born Greenberg, the son of Romanian immigrants, emerged as a full-fledged star, batting .339 with twenty-six home runs and 139 rbi's. Although he was still erratic afield and would always be painfully slow, Greenberg had already established himself as the most important Jewish player up to that time—the kind of player both the Yankees and Giants had vainly sought to attract New York City's big Jewish population.

By 1935 general economic conditions had improved significantly, in large part because of federal money pumped into the economy under the multifarious programs that made up the Roosevelt administration's New Deal. Full-scale recovery—usually taken to mean prosperity of 1920s proportions—was still a distant goal, but industrial output had largely revived, millions of people had gone back to work (albeit on government work-relief projects in many instances), agricultural prices had recovered from the 1933 nadir, the rate of farm and home mortgage foreclosures had slowed drastically—and people were coming back to ballparks. Major-league attendance in 1935 was the best since 1930.

That happened despite the departure of Babe Ruth, the greatest individual attraction in American sports history. In 1933 and 1934 the Babe's offensive performance fell off badly (though not as badly as his salary, cut from $70,000 to $35,000). Released by the Yankees, Ruth signed with the Boston Braves, who expected to capitalize on his name if not his fading ability. On May 25, 1935, the Babe enjoyed his last big day at bat. In Pittsburgh he clouted three homers, the last his 714th in regular-season play and the first ever to clear the right-field stands at Forbes Field. A week later, batting .181 after twenty-eight games, he finally quit for good as a player (although he would serve as a coach for Brooklyn in 1938).

For the Cincinnati Reds, a last-place finisher the past four years and only a sixth-place team in 1935, improved home attendance was largely a consequence of several night games. The brainchild of Leland Stanford "Larry" MacPhail, Cincinnati's flamboyant general manager, the inaugural major-league game under lights was played at Crosley Field on May 24, 1935, before 20,442 people, the biggest home crowd in years. For MacPhail, a few night games provided a way to turn regular losses into small profits; for the majors as a whole, they represented a halting, tentative step in the direction the minors had taken five years earlier.

In 1938, when MacPhail became executive vice president of the debt-ridden Brooklyn franchise, he quickly boosted attendance by having lights installed. In the first night game at Ebbets Field, on June 15, Johnny Vander Meer, a young Cincinnati left-hander, pitched the second of his back-to-back no-hit games—a feat that is still unique in baseball's long history.

By 1940 all the big-league clubs except the Yankees, Cubs, Detroit, and the Boston Red Sox had equipped their home ballparks with lights. Seventy night dates were scheduled that season, double the number in 1939, when such games had averaged twenty-four thousand paid admissions. Except for two perennial contenders—the New York Giants, seeking to counter the Yankees' drawing power, and the St. Louis Cardinals, located in one of the majors' smallest markets—night ball appealed most to the clubs that were weakest financially, and usually weakest on the field as well.

In 1935 the Detroit Tigers drew a million people in repeating as AL champs after a tough battle with the Ruthless Yankees. Hank Greenberg's 170 runs batted in probably made the difference. Still managed by Charlie Grimm, the Chicago Cubs went on a twenty-one-game winning streak to beat out the Cardinals, despite the Dean brothers' combined forty-seven wins. The Cubs fell four games to two in the Series, as Tommy Bridges, Detroit's smallish, curveballing right-hander, pitched two complete-game victories.

For the next six years, despite a sharp downturn in the economy in 1937–1938 (the so-called Roosevelt Recession), the overall attendance trend throughout Organized Baseball continued upward. By 1940, forty-four minor-league circuits were in operation, drawing approximately eighteen and a half million fans to games that were now played under lights at least ninety percent of the time.

The major leagues drew about eight million customers in 1937, and as was usually the case, some clubs made out handsomely while others lost badly. For the decade, the New York Yankees topped the majors with a total attendance of about 8,900,000, followed by Detroit (7,803,000), the Chicago Cubs (7,700,000), and the New York Giants (7,400,000).

But the St. Louis Browns, never better than a sixth-place team after 1931, drew only 1,271,579 fans in the thirties. The Browns' 1933 attendance, about seventy-nine thousand, was the lowest for a full schedule since the 1890s; and in 1936, a year in which ten of the sixteen major-league franchises showed a profit, the Browns could persuade only ninety-three thousand to come to Sportsman's Park.

The Philadelphia Phillies, who finished sixth or lower every year in the decade except one, showed the next-lowest attendance, out-drawing the Browns by some nine hundred thousand. Until 1938, when they leased the Athletics' Shibe Park for their home games, the "Phutile Phillies" continued to play in the oldest, smallest, and most ramshackle ballpark in the majors.

Like its American League counterpart, the Philadelphia NL franchise stayed afloat by selling off its best players. "All you have to do with the Phillies is hustle," remarked Jimmy Wilson, their manager from 1934 through 1938, "and you stand out like a lighthouse with the Phils. . . . If you hustle, you'll look so much better than the bums around you that the other clubs will think you're a great player. First thing you know, the Phils have a bundle of cash and you're out from behind the eight ball."

The years 1936–1939 brought renewed domination of the American League and the World Series by Joe McCarthy's New York club. By 1936, thirty-three-year-old Lou Gehrig was the Yankees' bellwether, each year ending at or near the top of the AL in batting, homers, runs, and rbi's. Powerfully muscled, a man of abstemious personal habits, Gehrig hadn't been out of the lineup since taking over first base in mid-1925. Baseball's highest-paid player at $36,000, he was probably its most respected as well.

The son of German immigrants, Gehrig was a native New Yorker who'd been an all-around athletic star at Columbia University before dropping out to sign with the Yankees. Though a considerably more complex man than he was rendered by his sportswriting contemporaries, Gehrig truly was a modest, unprepossessing celebrity—"a quiet hero," in the phrase of one of his biographers.

Gehrig had always played in Ruth's shadow; for what remained of his career he would have to share the spotlight with Joe DiMaggio, the tall, surpassingly graceful San Franciscan who took over center field in 1936. Although the Yankees were rapidly building their farm system, they were still willing to pay $60,000 for DiMaggio, who'd put in three outstanding years with the hometown Seals, an independent club in the Pacific Coast League. At twenty-one, DiMaggio was an instant success, batting .323 in his first major-league season. Gehrig, meanwhile, had one of his finest years—a .354 average, forty-nine homers, 152 rbi's—and Bill Dickey emerged as a major offensive force, batting .362 with twenty-two homers.

It was the same old Yankees combination of power and reliable pitching, especially from Lefty Gomez, Charles "Red" Ruffing, and Monte Pearson; New York finished nineteen and a half games ahead of Detroit. The 1936 World Series brought another AL triumph, with the Giants, still managed by Bill Terry and still relying heavily on Carl Hubbell's pitching and Mel Ott's hitting, falling in six games.

The next three seasons saw an unprecedented run: three more pennants and World Series triumphs for the Yankees. It was all pretty easy for the "Bronx Bombers"—one of many nicknames writers had hung on the New York powerhouse. In 1937 and 1938 DiMaggio, Gehrig, and Dickey again headed a tremendous attack, and as Gomez faded, Ruffing became one of the league's top pitchers, while Johnny Murphy worked effectively as one of the few relief specialists of that period. The Giants succumbed in five games in the 1937 Series, the Cubs in four straight the next year.

Game two of the 1938 Series was a heartbreaking loss for Dizzy Dean, who'd ruined his arm when he altered his natural pitching motion after suffering a broken toe in the '37 All-Star Game. Purchased from the Cardinals for $185,000 plus three players, Dean pitched in only thirteen games in 1938 (winning seven). Yet in the Series he battled the Yankees into the eighth inning, when Frank Crosetti, their light-hitting shortstop, barely lifted a two-run homer into the left-field seats to put the Yankees ahead for good. It was the last big moment in Dean's brief but brilliant career. (Brother Paul Dean never recovered from an arm injury of his own sustained in 1936.)

In 1939 the Yankees won again, sweeping the Cincinnati Reds, winners of that city's first pennant in twenty years and only its second in the National League. First baseman Frank McCormick and catcher Ernie Lombardi were the Reds' main offensive weapons, but it was pitchers William "Bucky" Walters and Paul Derringer, with twenty-seven and twenty-five wins, respectively, who accounted for their team's presence in the World Series—where to many observers they seemed little more than sacrificial lambs. From 1936 through 1939 the Yankees' Series record was an awe-inspiring 16–3.

Lou Gehrig was no longer with the Yankees when they claimed that fourth straight world's championship in '39. Suffering from what was subsequently diagnosed as amyotrophic lateral sclerosis (a degenerative condition in the central nervous system), Gehrig had slumped in 1938, although he still put in a good season by most players' standards. The next spring he couldn't get his bat around or field his position, and on May 1, 1939, after nearly fourteen years and a total of 2,130 consecutive games, the Iron Horse took himself out of the lineup.

That July 4, Gehrig was honored at Yankee Stadium by a host of dignitaries, past and present teammates (Babe Ruth, with whom Gehrig had feuded in the Babe's last year with the Yankees, was on hand to embrace his onetime slugging partner), and close to seventy thousand somber fans. Unable to straighten his back, the fatally ill Gehrig hobbled to the microphone at home plate to say that he considered himself "the luckiest man on the face of the earth." Less than two years later, two weeks shy of his thirty-eighth birthday, he died of the disease that would thereafter be known by his name.

Gehrig's death was the most widely mourned of any baseball figure's since Christy Mathewson, who had succumbed to tuberculosis while the 1925 World Series was in progress. Like Mathewson, Gehrig became something of a sports paragon, universally regarded as representing the best in professional athletics. His apotheosis became complete with the release early in 1942 of *The Pride of the Yankees*, a Hollywood motion picture based loosely on his life. Despite (or because of) the miscasting of Gary Cooper in the lead, the movie was a huge success with both critics and the public.

One measure of the esteem in which Gehrig was held was the willingness of the Baseball Writers Association, late in 1939, to elect him to the newly established National Baseball Hall of Fame, waiving the rule that specified a five-year waiting period following a player's retirement. Opened in ceremonies the previous June at Cooperstown, New York—where, in baseball's official mythology, Abner Doubleday had invented the game one hundred years earlier—the Hall of Fame began with an inaugural class of nineteen. Living inductees Ty Cobb,

Babe Ruth, Cy Young, Honus Wagner, Napoleon Lajoie, Tris Speaker, Walter Johnson, George Sisler, Grover Cleveland Alexander, Eddie Collins, and Connie Mack were all on hand.

Difficult to reach by automobile, the Hall of Fame nonetheless quickly proved a mecca for baseball-lovers. They came from everywhere to view the growing collection of artifacts in the National Baseball Museum, stand reverently before the plaques in the gallery of "immortals," take in the annual summertime induction of new Hall of Famers, and watch two major-league teams play an exhibition game at Doubleday Field, the little ballpark built on the very spot where young Abner was said to have thought up baseball.

The post-Gehrig (and post-Ruth) 1939 New York Yankees were arguably the best ball club the city's AL franchise had fielded in its thirty-six-year history. DiMaggio, already being compared with the finest players ever, led both leagues in batting at .381 and continued to exhibit the *sprezzazura* (Italian for making what's difficult look easy) that would always be his trademark. Bill Dickey didn't have any real rivals as the game's top catcher after an errant pitch almost killed Mickey Cochrane and ended his playing career. By 1939, excellent products of the Yankees' farm system—second baseman Joe Gordon, outfielders Charlie Keller and Tommy Henrich (an earlier Cleveland farmhand freed by Landis)—had fused with veteran infielders Frank Crosetti and Robert "Red" Rolfe and outfielder George Selkirk, while Red Ruffing, with another twenty-one wins, headed up a deep pitching staff. Joe McCarthy, often belittled as a "push-button manager" because of the unequaled talent at his disposal, was nonetheless an extraordinarily shrewd man in the dugout.

How shrewd was apparent in 1940. The previous winter Washington president Clark Griffith persuaded six of his seven AL peers (everybody except the Yankees' Ed Barrow) to agree to a rule banning trades with the previous season's pennant winner. Yet with nearly everybody except DiMaggio (who won a second straight batting title) struggling through an off year, McCarthy still kept his club in contention all season long. At the end Detroit was one game better than the Cleveland Indians, two better than the Yankees. A lesser aggregation than the 1934–1935 Tigers, Detroit won on the batting prowess of Greenberg, Gehringer, and newcomers Rudy York and Barney Mc-

Cosky, plus the fine pitching of the much-traveled Louis "Bobo" Newsom.

Now playing on Sundays, holidays, and at night in huge Municipal Stadium, a multipurpose facility opened in 1932 (although most home dates were still in little League Park), the Cleveland club was the city's best since 1920. Its stars were slugging first baseman Hal Trosky, young shortstop Lou Boudreau, and Bob Feller, a fireballing Iowa farm boy. Already a five-year veteran at twenty-one, Feller led the majors in wins (twenty-seven), complete games (thirty-one), innings pitched (320), and strikeouts (261).

Late in the 1940 season, with the franchise's first pennant in twenty years within reach, most of the Cleveland players rebelled against manager Oscar Vitt, a onetime teammate of Ty Cobb and an old-time martinet. The rebellion fizzled when the front office backed the manager, and the widely publicized troubles of the "crybaby Indians," as they were derided around the league, probably cost them just enough of an edge to make the difference at the end.

The Cincinnati Reds, despite being shaken by the suicide of catcher Willard Hershberger early in August, were easy repeaters in the National League, and they then beat the Tigers in seven games— the NL's first Series victory since 1934. Bucky Walters and Paul Derringer held hard-hitting Detroit to only six runs in pitching two complete-game victories apiece.

In 1941 the Yankees returned to their accustomed place atop the AL. Feller's twenty-five wins couldn't stop Cleveland's slide to fourth, while Detroit dropped to fifth without Hank Greenberg. Baseball's highest-paid player at $55,000, Greenberg, a bachelor with no dependents, became one of the earliest major-leaguers inducted into the U.S. Army under the peacetime military draft enacted by the Congress the previous September. He started basic training two weeks into the '41 season.

Still unable to find an adequate replacement for Gehrig, the Yankees were solid otherwise, with Keller and Henrich flanking DiMaggio in the outfield, Dickey behind the plate, Gordon at second, Rolfe at third, and a sparkling rookie at shortstop in little Phil Rizzuto. More than ever, though, DiMaggio was the heart of the ball club. Besides batting .357, knocking thirty homers, and leading both majors with 125 rbi's, the "Yankee Clipper" hit safely in fifty-six consecutive games, until stopped on July 17 in a night contest before more than fifty thousand at Cleveland's Municipal Stadium. DiMaggio's streak broke Wee Willie Keeler's 1897 mark by twelve.

Despite that magnificent run—decades later, still frequently identified as the greatest individual achievement in American sports history—DiMaggio didn't win a third batting title. That crown went to Ted Williams, Boston's stringbean, twenty-three-year-old left fielder, who on the season's final day made six hits in a doubleheader to push his average to .406.

A temperamental perfectionist (at least where hitting was concerned), the San Diegan had come up to the Red Sox from Minneapolis in 1939 and quickly established himself as one of the AL's top players. Like most of the high-average hitters of that period, the lefty-swinging Williams also hit with plenty of power—thirty-one and twenty-three homers in his first two seasons, thirty-seven in 1941. Quick to anger and given to periods of moody withdrawal, Williams was already on bad terms with most of the Boston press corps, but nobody in Boston or anywhere else would deny that the prickly young man was one of the finest natural hitters ever to come along.

Williams and his teammates finished second in 1941, thirteen games behind the Yankees, Boston's lot three of the last four years—as it would be again in 1942. Content with only a rudimentary farm system, Tom Yawkey had spent millions buying major-league stars and top prospects from minor-league independents, as well as expanding and improving cozy Fenway Park. Eddie Collins, who became the Red Sox front-office chief in 1933, generally got good value for Yawkey's money. Lefty Grove, for example, continued for several years to be the best left-hander in the American League, and Jimmie Foxx hit prodigiously, winning his second batting title and third Most Valuable Player Award in 1938 (besides totaling 207 homers as a Red Sox from 1936 through 1941). Player-manager Joe Cronin, who came to Boston in 1935 in exchange for $250,000 paid to Washington, continued to be the game's hardest-hitting shortstop. Besides Williams, the team's prize minor-league purchases included second baseman Bobby Doerr and center fielder Dominic DiMaggio, Joe's bespectacled younger brother.

All that restored the Boston team to respectability and produced the biggest crowds in the franchise's history—but nothing close to a pennant. Like the Chicago Cubs, the prosperous Red Sox would eventually learn that spending lots of money without a strategy for the long run usually produced limited results.

The 1941 National League championship went to Brooklyn, a club brought back to contention beginning in 1939 under the dynamic, often clashing leadership of Larry MacPhail in the front office and Leo Durocher on the ballfield. Thirty-six years old and still an occasional player, Durocher had been a light-hitting shortstop with the Yankees, Reds, and the Cardinals' Gas House Gang before coming to the Dodgers (as they were again known) in 1938. Pugnacious and profane, a bench-jockey and umpire-baiter par excellence (as well as a gambler and night-lifer who wasn't particular about his friends), Durocher often reminded veteran reporters of the late John McGraw. In '41 Durocher's team beat out the Cardinals by two and one-half games and drew more than a million people into Ebbets Field, by far the biggest attendance in Brooklyn baseball history.

MacPhail and Durocher put over several shrewd deals, obtaining first baseman Dolph Camilli and third baseman Harry "Cookie" Lavagetto from the Phillies, second baseman Billy Herman from the Cubs, shortstop Harold "Pee Wee" Reese from the Louisville farm club of the Red Sox, and outfielders Joe Medwick from the Cardinals and Fred "Dixie" Walker (on waivers) from Detroit. Among the Cardinals' minor-leaguers who'd been "emancipated" by commissioner Landis in 1938 was Harold "Pete" Reiser; in 1941, at twenty-two, Reiser led the league with a .343 batting average and played a recklessly brilliant center field.

Having made Brooklyn more than ever a baseball hotbed, "dem Bums," as they were affectionately known at Ebbets Field, lost the World Series in six games. The critical moment came in the top of the ninth inning in game five, when, with two men out and the Dodgers ahead 4–3, catcher Mickey Owen let a third-strike pitch get past him, enabling Tommy Henrich to reach first safely. That opened the door for one of the Yankees' patented late-inning rallies, enough to put the game—and the Series—out of reach.

The teams in the 1941 World Series, probably the most ethnically mixed pennant winners up to that time, exemplified the changing backgrounds of players within Organized Baseball. Although the German influence on the two teams remained strong (Keller, Henrich, Sturm, Breuer, Rosar, Reiser, Herman), players of Irish descent were much less in evidence than in earlier decades. Yankees pitcher Johnny Murphy was the only identifiably Irish-American on either roster.

Most striking was the presence of several Italo-Americans (DiMaggio, Rizzuto, Camilli, Lavagetto, Russo). Although Ed Abbaticchio had put in nine years as a National Leaguer beginning in 1897, only a few other men of Italian ancestry had made it to the majors before the 1930s, with Tony Lazzeri being the outstanding example until Joe DiMaggio's appearance. In the thirties, though, names such as Lombardi, Cavaretta, Cuccinello, Crosetti, Bonura, Mancuso, and Chiozza showed up regularly in major-league lineups.

Similarly, aside from the brothers Stanley and Harry Coveleski, winners of 296 major-league games between them in the period 1907–1928, and the slugging Al Simmons (né Aloys Szymanski), players of eastern European background hadn't made much of a mark before the thirties. That decade saw Hal Trosky (né Troyavesky), Joe Medwick, Wally Berger, and Joe Vosmik reach stardom, while Adam Comorosky, Hank Majeski, Ambrose "Brusie" Ogrodowski, Mike Kreevich, and Alex Kampouris, among others, played lesser roles. (Like Simmons and Trosky, some players continued to Anglicize their names, such as John Paveskovich, who in 1942, as Johnny Pesky, would begin a distinguished career at shortstop for the Red Sox.) By the late 1930s, besides Hank Greenberg, front-line Jewish major-leaguers included Morrie Arnovich, Harry Danning, and Goodwin "Goody" Rosen.

Of course, old prejudices were still very much alive in thirties America. Players from what had earlier been called the "new immigration"—eastern and southern European, non-Protestant arrivals—had to put up with ethnic and religious slurs that were sometimes casual (as when the popular magazine *Life* noted that rookie Joe DiMaggio "speaks English without an accent" and "never reeks of garlic") and sometimes quite nasty, such as the anti-Semitic taunts from opposing dugouts that became routine to Hank Greenberg. Yet if one scanned the names in major-league lineups around 1941, it was hard to argue that anybody who was good enough couldn't become a big-leaguer.

Anybody, that is, who wasn't black. Despite frequent speculations in the black press that this or that white team might be willing to sign a black player, Organized Baseball continued to be lily-white. If anything, "Jim Crow" (an old euphemism for racial discrimination) hardened under the regime of Kenesaw Mountain Landis. While publicly denying the existence of racial barriers, in closed meetings with owners and other baseball officials Landis wouldn't even discuss taking blacks into Organized Baseball.

Then, too, the fact that by the 1930s as many as a third of all major-leaguers were white Southerners gave added credence to the long-held belief that, even if club owners were willing to hire blacks, their players wouldn't go along. Coming from the region where racial feeling was most intense, "southern boys," so the argument went, would quit en masse rather than accept "colored boys" on their teams. A remark in a 1938 radio interview by Jake Powell, a Maryland-born Yankees outfielder—that in the off-season, as a policeman in Dayton, Ohio, he kept in condition "by cracking Niggers over the head"— supposedly typified racial attitudes among southern ballplayers.

So black baseball remained a world apart. Throughout the 1930s, despite basketball's growing popularity, baseball held its place among black Americans as the favored team sport for both participants and spectators—as it did among whites. Yet in the early Depression years, while the Kansas City Monarchs and a number of other black clubs managed to stay in business, organized professional league competition among blacks nearly died out.

In 1933 the Negro National League reappeared, mainly because of the efforts of Gus Greenlee, a rich and powerful black man who'd made himself king of the numbers racket in Pittsburgh. After the Great War, as tens of thousands of black people migrated northward to the Pittsburgh area in search of jobs in the booming steel mills, that city and its industrial environs became a major center for black baseball. Persistently high unemployment rates among black workers throughout the 1930s didn't keep them from spending part of whatever they had on baseball—and on the numbers game as well.

A substantial portion of the income from Greenlee's numbers operation went into building up his own baseball club, called the Pittsburgh Crawfords. Besides hiring the best players he could find,

Greenlee spent $100,000 to construct a modern ballpark and sent his team on the road in a new bus equipped with bunk beds. The Crawfords—and Greenlee's money—became the nucleus for a revived Negro National League that, unlike Rube Foster's mostly midwestern creation, was based in the northeastern cities.

From 1933 through 1936 the NNL, varying from six to eight members, was the only black professional league in operation. The Homestead Grays—a second Pittsburgh club named for one of the city's heavily black industrial suburbs and operated by Cumberland "Cum" Posey, a Pennsylvania State College graduate long prominent in black Pittsburgh's athletics—were expelled in the NNL's inaugural season for raiding other league affiliates, although the Grays regained admission two years later. By 1937 the NNL was exclusively eastern, consisting of the Crawfords and Grays, the Newark Eagles, the Philadelphia Stars, the New York Black Yankees, and the Baltimore-Washington Elite Giants.

In 1936 a second black organization called the Negro American League—instigated mainly by H. G. Hall, who owned what had once been Rube Foster's Chicago American Giants—formed with teams in eight midwestern and southern cities. Besides the Chicago American Giants, the NAL's stronger entries were the Kansas City Monarchs, Birmingham Black Barons, and Memphis Red Sox.

Not until 1939 did either the NNL or NAL schedule as many official league games as had been played in the twenties, in the heyday of the original NNL and the Eastern Colored League. Typically, NNL-NAL teams listed only about forty league contests, because more than ever, black professionals needed plenty of free dates for special engagements with white semipro teams—games that usually drew better than ordinary league contests.

Playing nearly every day—and frequently two and sometimes three games in a single day (and night)—black teams traveled by bus or in automobile caravans; posh Pullman-car trips were in the distant, pre-Depression past. They slept as best they could (usually en route to still another game) and snatched their meals at cheap cafes. It was a gruelling, unrelenting life, sometimes also an outright dangerous one, especially on the road in the Deep South.

Yet the life of a professional baseball player was irresistible for

young black males everywhere—as it still was for white youths. Apart
from the glamor and excitement associated with being a professional
and the sheer joy of playing the game, black ballplayers made relatively
good money. The typical NNL-NAL player earned $2,000 to $3,000 a
year, about half as much as his counterpart in the white majors but
still far more than most black people could hope to earn in the Depression years.

Although they wouldn't hire black players, white major- and
minor-league club owners were happy to rent their ballparks to black
teams when the home team was away—usually for ten percent of the
per-game receipts. In Chicago, for example, the American Giants
leased Comiskey Park, while in Cleveland the local Buckeyes played at
League Park and in Pittsburgh the Homestead Grays used Forbes
Field. The Baltimore-Washington Elite Giants played in Griffith Stadium in Washington, as did the Homestead Grays on Sundays beginning in 1940. The Monarchs were a popular attraction for both black
and white fans in the Kansas City American Association park; the
Birmingham Black Barons rented Rickwood Field from the Southern
Association white Barons; and the Yankees' organization, which owned
Ruppert Stadium in Newark, had the NNL Eagles as tenants. Ulti-
mately (in 1946) the lordly Yankees would even be willing to rent
Yankee Stadium to the Black Yankees—for a $100,000 yearly fee.

An average crowd at a NNL or NAL game would be about four or
five thousand—half what most white major-league teams were drawing by the end of the thirties—but on special days the turnouts might
be as big as any in the majors. A crowd of at least thirty to thirty-five
thousand could always be expected for the East-West All-Star Game,
played every year beginning in 1933 at Comiskey Park. For the first
three years of the game's history, opposing teams consisted of players
from the eastern and western clubs in the NNL, but starting in 1936
the All-Star Game matched the best from the NNL against the best
from the NAL. A showcase for the finest talent in black baseball, the
All-Star Game became the Negro leagues' foremost annual attraction,
an event that brought trainloads of black fans to Chicago from as far
away as Memphis. (The black World Series, never a major source of
profit in old NNL-ECL days, wouldn't be resumed until 1942.)

Special days also included any meeting in Pittsburgh between the

Crawfords and the Grays, always hot rivals, as well as any pitching appearance—almost anywhere—by Satchel Paige, who was an attendance magnet for black fans comparable to what Babe Ruth had been for whites.

Although the matter of his age would become central to a seemingly endless Paigian folklore, Leroy Robert Paige was actually born in Mobile, Alabama, on July 7, 1906. Like fellow Southerner Dizzy Dean (born five years later), Paige was tall, lean, long-armed, able to throw a blazing fastball with excellent control, poorly educated, and a natural showman. At the age of seven, young Paige began work as a railway baggage-handler (whence his nickname "Satchel"), and at twelve, convicted of petty theft, he entered a black reform school. Five years later, having developed his baseball skills, Paige emerged to begin his career in black professional baseball, pitching for teams first in Mobile, then Chattanooga, Birmingham, Nashville, and Cleveland.

In 1932 Paige came to Pittsburgh to pitch for Gus Greenlee's Crawfords (then still an independent club), at the same time that he hired out on a per-game basis to various other black teams. The next season, in pitching the Crawfords to a disputed championship in the revived NNL's inaugural season, Paige compiled a record in league games thought to be 31–4. (Record-keeping in the Negro leagues had always been less than reliable, and always would be.) That fall Paige and Dizzy Dean formed two teams—all-black and all-white—and barnstormed across the country to California. Thirty years later Bill Veeck, Jr., would remember Paige's twelve-inning victory over Dean in Los Angeles as the greatest baseball game he ever saw.

Late in the 1934 season, when Greenlee wouldn't give him a raise, Paige deserted the Crawfords and joined the famous House of David team, a group of long-haired, bearded ballplayers who toured to advertise the religious colony located at Benton Harbor, Michigan. The only nonwhite on the team, Paige pitched the House of David to the championship in the prestigious semipro tournament sponsored annually by the *Denver Post*, beating the Kansas City Monarchs in the title game. The next year, again operating with no fixed address, Paige led a racially integrated club based in Bismarck, North Dakota, to the championship of the National Baseball Congress tournament, played at Wichita, Kansas.

The Pittsburgh Crawfords ball club that Paige rejoined in 1936 was among the strongest ever assembled—black or white. Even without Paige, the Crawfords had taken the '35 NNL pennant in a playoff series with the New York Cubans, first-half winners in the split-season schedule usually favored in the Negro leagues. Oscar Charleston, the Crawfords' manager and first baseman, had once been a marvelous outfielder whose feats prompted comparisons with Tris Speaker (and vice versa), and the Crawfords also had James "Cool Papa" Bell, an astonishingly fast, spray-hitting center fielder; Ted Page and Jimmy Crutchfield, two other first-rate outfielders; and William "Judy" Johnson, a slick-fielding third baseman.

The Crawfords' catcher was Josh Gibson, who turned twenty-four years old during the 1936 season and was already one of the greatest players in the history of black baseball. For his career, including league and nonleague games, the Georgia-born, Pittsburgh-reared Gibson may have hit more home runs than Babe Ruth; and like Ruth, with whom he was often compared, Gibson made plenty of contact otherwise, regularly posting .400-plus averages against the strong pitching he faced in the NNL. An inch over six feet tall and a heavily muscled 215 pounds, he was also a capable man behind the plate, agile and rugged, with a fine arm. Walter Johnson once put a $200,000 price tag on a white Gibson.

For all their talent, the 1936 Crawfords finished behind the Elite Giants over the first half of the schedule. They did easily win the second half, but inasmuch as no playoff series to determine the pennant winner ever took place, the Crawfords' finest team—maybe the best ever in black baseball—missed taking a clear-cut championship. That fall, though, Paige, Gibson, Bell, and other NNL standouts, playing as the Negro All-Stars, swept through the *Denver Post* tournament and split about $7,500 in prize money.

One of the characteristic features of black professional baseball had always been high personnel turnover from year to year. Nothing like the reserve clause existed in black baseball; club owners and players often didn't even go to the trouble of signing contracts. Thus Gus Greenlee had no legal hold on Satchel Paige when he jumped the Crawfords to play in the Dominican Republic for a team sponsored by the dictator Rafael Trujillo, who sought to popularize his hard-handed regime with a championship baseball team. When Paige persuaded Gibson, Bell, and other black professionals to join him, what was left of the Crawfords finished the 1937 NNL season far down in the standings. In growing financial difficulty, Greenlee could keep his team going only one more season after that.

Paige and his colleagues stayed in the politically volatile Dominican Republic only long enough to win a championship for Trujillo and collect their hefty wages ($30,000, in Paige's case). Fearful that Trujillo's foes might shoot them, they hustled back to Miami aboard a Pan-American Airways Clipper, returning in time to enter the annual *Denver Post* tournament, which, as the "Ciudad Trujillo Team," they again won.

While Paige pitched in Mexico and elsewhere and struggled with a sore arm, Gibson and later Bell signed on with Cum Posey's Homestead Grays, where they teamed with Walter "Buck" Leonard, a power-hitting first baseman likened to Lou Gehrig in the inevitable racial comparisons of the time. Beginning in 1938, the Grays completely dominated the NNL, winning eight consecutive undisputed league titles.

Meanwhile Paige recovered from his arm troubles and more or less settled with the Kansas City Monarchs. With Paige, Chet Brewer, and Hilton Smith, the Monarchs (still operating under J. L. Wilkinson, their white owner) had unequaled pitching strength, as well as enough talent otherwise to make them the strongest club in the Negro American League for most of the late thirties and early forties.

For many black players, summertimes on ballfields in the U.S. made up only part of their professional lives. As an elderly Judy Johnson would remember, "There was always sun shining somewhere." Although Cuba continued to attract the largest number of U.S. players (black as well as white) for winter-league play, by the 1930s the sport had also put down deep roots in Mexico, Panama, Venezuela, the Dominican Republic, and Puerto Rico. Not accidentally, those were the Western Hemisphere countries where the U.S.'s presence—economic, military, and sociocultural—had been most pronounced.

In the less color-conscious societies of the Caribbean and Central American region, black players experienced an acceptance they'd never known up north. In a season that usually lasted from early November into January, they played with and against both local heroes who appeared in the North American Negro leagues and players from the white majors and minors. Although intact white major-league teams had ceased coming to Cuba after 1920, the interracial baseball now carried on there and elsewhere (as well as barnstorming trips back home against teams that frequently included white stars) gave black players plenty of opportunity to test their skills against the best on the other side of Organized Baseball's color line. Their experiences convinced them that, given the chance, they could hold their own in any company. "I just knew I was good enough to play in the big leagues," Judy Johnson said long afterward. "I just knew it."

Johnson would never get that chance, nor would most of the other top black performers of the Depression era—men born "twenty years too soon," in the poignant phrase of Quincy Trouppe, a fine catcher with many black teams. Given baseball's still-dominant position in American sports and the limited job opportunities for both blacks and whites during the 1930s, it may well be that more good baseball was played then—albeit in a segregated framework—than at any other time in the game's history.

Of course, any late-twentieth-century baseball fan miraculously projected backward to, say, the Polo Grounds in New York in, say, the summer of 1941 would immediately be struck by the absence of black men on the playing field. When the teams changed sides, moreover, the time-traveling fan would probably notice that players left their gloves on the field—as they'd always done and would continue to do until 1954, when bigger gloves (and a desire to reduce on-field clutter) would prompt a rule requiring everybody to bring his equipment into the dugout.

Otherwise, though, not a great deal would jar one's sense of time. The players' light flannel uniforms had now reached maximum roominess (or bagginess), consistent with the notion that baseball clothing ought to allow for maximum movement within the garment. But the loose-fitting shirts would all have numbers on their backs, as had been the case since the early thirties. Those numbers would be announced along with players' names (and a plethora of other information) through an amplified "public-address system," another innovation at the beginning of the thirties.

Three umpires would take their positions at the start of the game, because since 1933 both major leagues had mandated that number for regular-season contests. One might hear an old-time fan lamenting the absence of Bill Klem, who'd retired in 1940 after thirty-five seasons of colorful service as a National League arbiter. Never again would an umpire insist on working behind the plate most of the time, as had the imperious (and tireless) Klem.

This particular 1941 game might be a nighttime event, played under the lighting system the Giants had installed the previous year; in the National League, only the Chicago Cubs didn't have lights (and wouldn't until 1988). Giants fans at home might be able to hear the game on radio, an appliance with which something like three-fourths of all American households were now furnished. Having failed to persuade Brooklyn's Larry MacPhail to go along with an earlier three-way ban on regular-season broadcasts, the Giants and Yankees now permitted a limited amount of such play-by-play coverage themselves. Across the rest of the United States that night, broadcasts of major- and minor-league games filled the airwaves.

If the game had taken place before mid-July, fans at the Polo Grounds or anywhere else might discuss selections for the upcoming All-Star Game. Since 1933, when the efforts of Arch Ward of the *Chicago Tribune* brought together the best from the National and American leagues in Comiskey Park, the All-Star Game had remained a well-attended and closely followed midsummer extravaganza. Already the All-Star Game had contributed memorable moments to baseball history, such as Babe Ruth's homer that won the first game or Carl Hubbell's 1934 feat of striking out Ruth, Gehrig, Foxx, Simmons, and Cronin in succession at the Polo Grounds. In 1941, at Detroit, young Ted Williams's ninth-inning, two-out, three-run homer would put the AL up five games to four.

That summer night in 1941 the players may have seemed more cautious, less fiercely motivated than players of earlier generations, but, given the economic history of the past decade, most of the men trying to make it in professional baseball must have been hungrier than ever—more determined to succeed at something promising greater rewards than whatever else they might aspire to. In many cases, what might have looked like a lower-keyed, more businesslike approach to the game may actually have been a wariness grounded in a heightened fear of failure. Such an attitude suited the period, one of hard times and worry about the future—a gray, anxious decade.

Times were about to get better—in fact already had under the Roosevelt administration's new war-production campaign, which was putting millions of previously unemployed men and women to work. For the 1941 baseball season, despite another Yankees runaway in the American League, total major-league attendance climbed slightly above the ten-million mark, only a couple of hundred thousand short of the 1930 record.

Two months after Yankees pitcher Ernie Bonham retired the last Brooklyn batter in the World Series, Japanese carrier-based aircraft attacked and crippled the U.S. Pacific fleet based at Pearl Harbor in the Hawaiian Islands. The next day the Congress voted a declaration of war against Imperial Japan, and a few days after that voted a similar declaration against Nazi Germany and Fascist Italy, which had declared war on the United States under their 1940 treaty with Japan. Far more than the Great War (now, of course, renamed World War I), this conflict would permanently alter American society and, in the process, profoundly affect the business and sport of baseball.

9.

War, Plenty, and the End of Jim Crow

Hank Greenberg was the first baseball star drafted, but not the first big-leaguer. That distinction belonged to Hugh Mulcahy, a right-hander with the Philadelphia Phillies called to army service late in 1940, some three months after President Roosevelt signed the Selective Service Act. Possibly draftee Mulcahy, who'd been charged with so many losses he'd acquired the nickname "Losing Pitcher," surmised that actual combat couldn't be any worse than pitching for the Phillies.

Within a matter of days following the Japanese bombing of Pearl Harbor, Bob Feller enlisted in the U.S. Navy. A number of other major-leaguers volunteered for military service following official U.S. entry into the European and Asian-Pacific conflicts, but most players proved no more anxious to get into anything besides a baseball uniform than their counterparts in previous American wars had. As in 1917–1918, they bided their time in hopes that through some kind of deferment, they would still be able to continue their professional careers.

Meanwhile baseball's officialdom fretted over how to proceed—and what the government in Washington might do. The picture clarified considerably on January 15, 1942, when President Roosevelt, in an official reply to commissioner Landis's inquiry about baseball's status, gave the sport what was widely hailed as a "green light."

Although ballplayers would be under the same military obligation as everybody else and baseball would have to cope with wartime restrictions on travel and materials, the sport was such an important element in national morale, said Roosevelt, that it ought to be allowed to carry on. A year later Paul V. McNutt, head of the War Manpower Commission, announced that ballplayers could leave off-season jobs in "essential occupations" and report for spring training, although they would thereby lose their draft-exempt status.

Thus while World War II would be a much more protracted, demanding, and intrusive experience for the American people than World War I, at no time did professional baseball face the total shutdown it had in 1918. Aided by full employment, high wartime wages, and gasoline rationing that kept people close to home, attendance would hold up well throughout the war years. More night games were played than ever before, as well as occasional contests scheduled in the morning for the convenience of workers coming off the "graveyard shift" in war-production plants. Sooner or later nearly all the majors' highest-salaried players were in the armed forces, so that payrolls— about a quarter of operating costs—tended to shrink as the war progressed.

In other respects, though, the war presented baseball—all organized sports, for that matter—with an even more difficult set of circumstances than had been the case under the infirm economy of the thirties. By the spring of 1942 the military draft had hit the minor leagues hard; several circuits, including the strong Texas League, decided to suspend operations "for the duration," in the parlance of the war years. The toll of suspended minor leagues increased year by year, until only ten remained in operation at the end of the 1944 season. Somehow the Southern Association, the Texas League's counterpart, managed to stay in business, as did the American Association and the International and Pacific Coast leagues, the three top-level minors. In those circuits, as in the majors, nondraftable players became increasingly scarce, the play increasingly substandard.

Through the 1942 season, most of the top major-leaguers still hadn't been called up, so that the overall level of play changed little. The Yankees won again—their sixth American League pennant in seven seasons—with basically their 1941 team. Although Tommy

Henrich departed for military service late in the season, Joe DiMaggio, Joe Gordon, Charlie Keller, and Phil Rizzuto were still on hand at World Series time. Bill Dickey had started to fade; first base was still a problem; and now, with the decline of Red Rolfe, so was third. But the pitching staff—headed by Ernie Bonham (21–6), Spurgeon "Spud" Chandler (16–5), rookie Hank Borowy (15–4), and aging Red Ruffing (14–7)—was still a deep one.

Leo Durocher's Brooklyn Dodgers won 104 games, four more than in 1941, and might have repeated as National League champions if, in August, Pete Reiser hadn't crashed into a concrete outfield wall (none were padded as yet) and incapacitated himself for the rest of the race. Winning two games more than the Dodgers, Billy Southworth's St. Louis Cardinals took the franchise's sixth NL pennant with a team consisting almost entirely of men who'd matured in the Cardinals' minor-league empire.

Young and fast, they were maybe the best group of Cardinals so far. Terry Moore, Enos Slaughter, and rookie Stan Musial were a superb outfield; George "Whitey" Kurowski was a solid third baseman; Marty Marion was a tall, far-ranging shortstop; and Walker Cooper provided sturdy catching. Brother Mort Cooper won twenty-two games, one more than rookie Johnny Beazley. After dropping the World Series opener, at Sportsman's Park, the Cardinals surprised everybody by sweeping four straight, winning twice on complete games by Beazley.

Both the Yankees and Cardinals easily repeated in 1943, the Yankees by thirteen and one-half games over Washington, the Cardinals by a whopping eighteen over Cincinnati. The Yankees won without DiMaggio or any of their other '42 regulars except Keller, Gordon, and an overage Dickey. Johnny Murphy, who got credit for twelve victories in relief and saved eight others, and Spud Chandler, with twenty wins and the lowest earned run average (1.64) in the majors in nearly a quarter-century, were big reasons why the patched-together Yankees found themselves in still another World Series.

Meanwhile the Cardinals had lost Slaughter, Moore, and Beazley (who would never recover from a bad arm he developed pitching in the military). But the twenty-one-year-old Musial, with a .357 average, captured the first of his seven NL batting titles; Walker Cooper also had a strong year at bat; Mort Cooper again led the league in wins (twenty-one); and lefty Max Lanier (15–7) became the number two man on the staff.

Unaccustomed to going into a World Series as underdogs, the Yankees drubbed the defending champions in five games. Chandler, too old to be drafted, yielded two runs to the Cardinals in beating them in game one, then pitched a 2–0 shutout to end the Series. The Cardinals made ten errors and scored only nine runs off Chandler and the rest of the New York staff.

The caliber of baseball in the American and National leagues from 1943 through 1945, while perhaps not as bad as later depicted, was undoubtedly lower than at any time since 1918. Besides various Cardinals and Yankees, the list of first-rank major-leaguers who'd entered the armed forces before spring training 1943 included Ted Williams (AL batting, home-run, and rbi leader in 1942), Williams's Red Sox teammates Dom DiMaggio and Johnny Pesky, Brooklyn's Pee Wee Reese and Pete Reiser, and the Giants' hard-hitting Johnny Mize. By the next season the Yankees' Joe Gordon and Charlie Keller, Washington's first baseman James "Mickey" Vernon, and Dodgers infielders Billy Herman and Floyd "Arky" Vaughan and pitcher Kirby Higbe, among other headliners, had been called to the colors.

As military manpower demands steadily drained the available (white) North American talent pool, some of the major-league clubs sought out acceptable ballplayers from Cuba, Mexico, and other parts of Central America and the Caribbean. Probably the best of the wartime Hispanic Americans were the Puerto Rican Luis Olmo, who batted .313 with 110 rbi's for Brooklyn in 1945, and Roberto Estalella, a stocky Cuban who had a couple of good seasons at the plate for the Philadelphia Athletics.

Washington president Clark Griffith carried various Hispanic Americans on his payroll, all of whom, with the exception of Cuban infielder Gilberto Torres, had been with the Senators before Pearl Harbor. In the postwar decades the myth would grow that during the war Griffith had loaded his club with draft-proof (and cheap) Latinos. Actually, the maximum number of such players on the wartime Senators' twenty-five-man roster was seven (in 1944), and as to whether Griffith required them to sign affidavits affirming their racial purity, as was widely rumored, ¿quién sabe?

By the spring of 1943, big-league managers had come to cherish physically deferred "4-Fs"—players with some chronic condition (such as ulcers, allergies, color blindness, subpar hearing, or minor heart irregularities) that didn't seriously hamper their on-field performance. In that category were three outstanding American Leaguers: Cleveland shortstop Lou Boudreau, named to manage the Indians in 1942 at age twenty-four, who was bothered by heel spurs; Vernon "Junior" Stephens, the St. Louis Browns' young shortstop, an allergy sufferer; and Detroit left-hander Hal Newhouser, the top pitcher in the majors in 1944–1945, deferred because of a heart murmur.

Also much prized was the occasional star player such as Stan Musial, who could claim enough dependents that his local Selective Service board had spared him; but by late 1944, with upwards of twelve million Americans under arms, that kind of deferment was almost impossible to come by. Eventually reclassified by his board in Donora, Pennsylvania, Musial entered the navy early in 1945.

At the same time, overage veterans often discovered a new vigor (and inevitably an old weariness) in the midst of the worsening wartime talent shortage. In 1943, at age thirty-eight, Luke Appling of the White Sox won his second AL batting title. At thirty-seven and in his twelfth year in the AL, outfielder Bob Johnson batted .324 for the Red Sox. Paul Waner, three-time NL batting champion in the twenties and thirties, hung on through the war years to finish with 3,154 career base hits and a .333 lifetime average. Jimmie Foxx, released by the Red Sox, put in a couple of inglorious seasons with the Cubs and Philadelphia Phillies before quitting with 535 homers and a .325 career average. Even forty-two-year-old Babe Herman, who hadn't appeared in a big-league game since 1937, became a pinch hitter for the Dodgers.

A number of underage players also made their big-league debuts, although they usually departed for the armed services by the latter part of the war. The extreme example of a "kid big-leaguer" was Joe Nuxhall, a fifteen-year-old Hamilton, Ohio, high-schooler signed by the Cincinnati Reds. On June 10, 1944, the youth pitched two-thirds of an inning during a 19–0 slaughter by the Cardinals, yielding two hits, five walks, and two runs, which would be the extent of Nuxhall's big-league career until he rejoined the Reds in 1952, after several years in their farm system.

The extreme example of a 4-F big-leaguer was one-armed Pete Gray. Born Peter Wyshner in 1915 in Nanticoke, Pennsylvania, Gray lost his right arm in a childhood accident, but he was determined to make his future in baseball. Playing with semipro and "outlaw" professional teams in the U.S. and Canada, he developed amazing batting and outfielding dexterity, and in 1944, after hitting .333 and stealing sixty-eight bases for Memphis, he won Most Valuable Player honors in the Southern Association. Purchased by the St. Louis Browns (mainly to spark attendance, said cynics), Gray appeared in seventy-seven American League games in 1945, batting .218. Although he was released that fall, he would go on to play several more years in the minors.

Pete Gray's presence in a big-league uniform would always be cited to show just how bad things got before the war finally ended, about a month prior to the 1945 World Series. Of course, one might suggest that even playing with one arm in a talent-depleted American League, Gray still had to exhibit skills superior to those of the great majority of people who'd ever tried to master the game. Gray, moreover, wasn't even the first one-armed player in major-league history; in the 1880s Hugh Daily had compiled a 73–89 record pitching in the National League and Union and American associations. For that matter, during the same 1945 season that Gray was with the Browns, left-hander Bert Shepard, a former army pilot whose lower right leg had been amputated in a German prison camp, pitched in one regular-season and several exhibition games for Washington.

The willingness of American and National League clubs to employ one-armed and one-legged players and a fifteen-year-old schoolboy, while still refusing to tap the abundant talent in the Negro leagues, more than ever highlighted the absurdity and injustice of baseball's color barrier. That same persistent Jim Crowism, however, also made possible the most prosperous years in the history of the Negro leagues.

Although the basic features of American race relations remained unchanged, labor scarcities and consequent wage increases in the war years did relatively more for urban blacks than for whites. As Satchel

Paige later said, "Everybody had money and everybody was looking around for entertainment." Recalled Buck Leonard, "During the war when people couldn't get much gas, that's when our best crowds were." Then, too, for various reasons the military draft cut less deeply into the ranks of black ballplayers; the quality of play in the Negro leagues probably suffered less than in the white majors.

For the first time, most teams in the Negro leagues showed profits, with the Homestead-Washington Grays, Kansas City Monarchs, and Newark Eagles being the most consistent money-makers. The annual East-West All-Star Game was a bigger attraction than ever, and crowds in the war years filled Comiskey Park for contests that matched many of the finest baseball players in the United States—few of whose names were at all recognizable to white fans.

The Negro-league World Series finally resumed in 1942, with the Kansas City Monarchs, Negro American League champs, defeating the Homestead Grays, titlists in the Negro National League, in four straight official decisions (one disputed). Fine crowds watched the games in Griffith Stadium in Washington, Forbes Field in Pittsburgh, Yankee Stadium in New York, and Muehlebach Field in Kansas City, as Satchel Paige pitched the first and fourth victories for the Monarchs.

In 1943 the Grays won a seven-game series over Birmingham (played in Washington, Chicago, Columbus, Indianapolis, Birmingham, and Montgomery), and the next year they beat the Black Barons in five games in Birmingham, New Orleans, and Pittsburgh. Some of the biggest crowds in the history of the Negro leagues watched the 1945 World Series, played in Cleveland, Pittsburgh, Washington, and Philadelphia. In a major upset, Josh Gibson, Buck Leonard, and the rest of the powerful Grays fell in four straight to the NAL's Cleveland Buckeyes.

By the early forties, every honest baseball man recognized that the Negro leagues offered a cornucopia of gifted ballplayers, and a couple of white big-league clubs actually staged meaningless tryouts for selected black players. But when Leo Durocher remarked that he'd seen "a million good colored players" and would have them on his team "if they weren't barred by the owners," commissioner Landis privately warned Durocher to keep his mouth shut on that subject.

Publicly, Landis continued to insist that nothing kept National or American League owners from signing blacks.

Early in 1943 Bill Veeck, Jr., twenty-nine-year-old president of the profitable Milwaukee American Association franchise and son of the late Cubs executive, was prepared to take the commissioner at his public word. Veeck naively informed Landis that, if allowed to buy the impoverished Philadelphia Phillies from Gerald Nugent, he intended to fill his roster with Negro-league stars and win the National League pennant. Soon Veeck learned that Nugent had pulled his franchise off the market and turned it back to the league, which then arranged its sale to a lumber dealer named William Cox. (Less than a year later, Landis kicked Cox out of baseball for betting on his team's games.)

Among the many anomalies of the war period was the fact that between 1943 and 1945, because of government restrictions on nonessential railroad travel, American and National League clubs conducted spring training either at home or in such unlikely places as Bear Mountain, New York; Asbury Park and Lakewood, New Jersey; Wallingford, Connecticut; and French Lick, Indiana. That meant, of course, that they spent much of their time performing calisthenics and throwing the ball around indoors in local gymnasiums before getting in a few chilly preseason exhibition games.

Starting in 1943, even the baseball itself was different. Available rubber supplies were diverted to war-production needs; choice Bolivian horsehides and high-grade Australian wool were no longer available. Thus the Spalding company secured its horsehides and woolen yarn at home, while it substituted a South American rubberlike gum called balata for the sheathing around the baseball's cork center. The result was a ball that was just as durable as the prewar model but, so hitters complained, quite a bit deader. If so, the "balata ball" produced no drastic changes in offensive output.

Team batting averages actually increased somewhat during the 1943–1945 period, while total scoring fluctuated. The American League's batting leaders did win with lower-than-normal averages: Appling's .328 in 1943; Boudreau's .327 in 1944; and the .309 with which Yankees infielder George "Snuffy" Stirnweiss (one of only three .300-plus hitters in the league) took the 1945 crown. With the American League's foremost power hitters in military service, its home-run output fell twenty percent; but the National League, the more pitching-oriented of the two circuits by the late thirties, produced some nine percent *more* homers in 1945 than in 1942.

Perhaps the most memorable baseball event of the World War II years was the St. Louis Browns' only American League pennant. Both on the field and at the gate, the Browns' AL history had been generally marked by futility. Their peak season's attendance, 713,000, had been registered in 1922, when George Sisler and a fine supporting cast almost wrested the AL title from the Yankees. While the 1942 Browns finished a distant third, their best showing in thirteen years, they dropped to fifth in 1943.

If not for the war, the Browns probably wouldn't have remained in St. Louis; in 1941 Donald Barnes, head of a group of stockholders who'd bought the franchise in the mid-thirties, planned to move it to Los Angeles. President Philip K. Wrigley of the Chicago Cubs, who also owned the Los Angeles Pacific Coast League franchise and ballpark, agreed to sell his California holdings to the St. Louis group for $1 million, and Los Angeles civic boosters promised to underwrite any losses the Browns might incur if seasonal attendance fell below five hundred thousand (about four times what they'd been drawing in Sportsman's Park). After conferences with the commercial airlines and AL schedule-makers, Barnes announced that relocating on the Coast was feasible. At the annual major-league meetings in Chicago, planned for December 8, 1941, he intended to seek the necessary unanimous consent of his AL peers and majority approval of NL owners. The Japanese attack at Pearl Harbor on the seventh threw the whole project into limbo.

So in 1944 the Browns were still in St. Louis, where they won with the oldest group of players in the majors, including a pitching staff made up entirely of overage and 4-F moundsmen. Their main competition came from Detroit and Washington, although Joe McCarthy's Yankees, now fielding a lineup virtually unrecognizable to prewar fans, didn't fall back until late in the season.

The Browns started with nine straight victories, three of which were shutouts by thirty-four-year-old Sig Jakucki, of late a semipro pitcher in Houston. Jakucki, Jack Kramer, Nelson Potter, and Bob Muncrief made up a steady rotation, while Vern Stephens, the only young player with the team at the end of the season, was the heart of the Browns' attack. Manager Luke Sewell juggled the rest of his men with sufficient savvy to produce a one-game victory margin over Detroit, which stayed in the race mainly by getting twenty-nine wins from lefty Hal Newhouser and twenty-seven from righty Paul "Dizzy" Trout. The Browns' 89–65 was the poorest pennant-winning record to date in the century.

With Musial, Kurowski, Marion, the Cooper brothers, Lanier, and Johnny Hopp (a .336 batter in center field) still available, the Cardinals won 105 times, far more than they needed for their third NL title in a row. In the only all–St. Louis (and of course all–Sportsman's Park) World Series ever played, they dropped two of the first three games, then took three straight to end whatever notions of a world's championship the Browns' long-suffering fans may have entertained. The unlikely Series batting star was rookie Emil Verban, the Cardinals' third regular second baseman in three seasons.

By the spring of 1945 some sixty percent of the men listed on big-league rosters four years earlier were in the armed forces, and baseball writers frequently quipped that various service teams actually made up a "third major league." Bob Feller was one of the few big-leaguers who saw combat; most spent the war in some kind of duty that left plenty of time for baseball. Although the rosters of service teams changed frequently, those representing Norfolk Naval Training Station (which in 1943 had *both* Phil Rizzuto and Pee Wee Reese to play shortstop and Dominic DiMaggio in center field), Great Lakes Naval Training Station (where, at different times, Bob Feller, Billy Herman, and Johnny Mize played), or Bainbridge Naval Training Center (where Stan Musial hit line drives in 1945) may have been the equal of most teams in the white majors.

During the war, baseball was played literally around the world. In 1944, in Hawaii, all-star teams represented the army and navy in an "Armed Forces World Series," with everybody in both starting lineups being either a present or future major-leaguer. The next year another all-star series, also played in Hawaii, pitted navy American Leaguers (including Marine aviator Ted Williams) against navy National Leaguers.

On the home front, baseball's officialdom decided against holding the 1945 All-Star Game. Difficulty in working out travel arrangements was the announced reason, but the consensus among officials, owners, and baseball writers was that the level of play had deteriorated so much that it was pointless to stage the game with the talent available.

It might not have been the best brand of baseball, but the American League's last wartime season offered an exciting four-way race between the Browns, Detroit, Washington, and New York. The Browns ended up in third place, a half-game ahead of the Yankees. Having rejoined Detroit in July, after four and one-half years in the army, Hank Greenberg hit a two-out, bases-loaded homer in the ninth inning of the season's final game, at St. Louis, to give the Tigers the pennant by a margin of a game and a half over Washington. Detroit's record was a game worse than the Browns' the previous year; Hal Newhouser was the winning pitcher in twenty-five of Detroit's eighty-eight victories.

The Chicago Cubs, following three desultory wartime seasons under hard-bitten Jimmie Wilson, again responded to "Jolly Cholly" Grimm's easygoing presence in the dugout. With Musial and Walker Cooper in military service, Cardinals president Sam Breadon refused to meet Mort Cooper's salary demands, traded him to Boston, and thereby possibly forfeited a fourth straight pennant. As it was, the Cardinals finished only three games behind the Cubs, who featured the NL's batting leader in first baseman Phil Cavarretta (.355), the league's leading pitcher in Hank Wyse (22–10), and critical late-season mound help from Hank Borowy, purchased from the Yankees.

When asked for his pick in the World Series, Chicago sportswriter Warren Brown replied, "Neither team is good enough to win it." Actually, it was an interesting if unevenly played seven-game Series, performed before capacity crowds in both cities. Behind Newhouser, who pitched his second complete-game victory after lasting less than three innings in the opener, Detroit took game seven, 9–3. Roger "Doc" Cramer, the Tigers' thirty-nine-year-old center fielder, made eleven hits over the seven games, while Greenberg, now thirty-four, belted two homers and drove in seven runs.

On hand to congratulate manager Steve O'Neill in the Tigers' locker room was Albert B. "Happy" Chandler, who'd succeeded the late Judge Landis as commissioner of baseball the previous March.

Touted mainly by Larry MacPhail (now with the War Department), Chandler was finishing a term as U.S. senator from Kentucky when he received the club owners' call. Affable and seemingly more tractable than the despotic Landis, Chandler nonetheless was given to plain speaking. Asked shortly after taking office whether he favored lowering the color bar, Chandler unhesitatingly replied, "If a black boy can make it on Okinawa and Guadalcanal, hell, he can make it in baseball."

Meanwhile Branch Rickey moved ahead with a plan that would ultimately achieve the integration of Organized Baseball, although the full particulars of that plan will probably never be understood. At the end of 1942 Rickey finally broke with Cardinals president Sam Breadon, who'd become increasingly irked by Rickey's practice of taking ten percent on all player sales, and signed as general manager of the Brooklyn Dodgers at a salary of $65,000. Sixty-one years old when he assumed his duties in Brooklyn, Rickey was already something of a baseball legend, not only for his genius in building a farm system and selling its products for big profits but also for his long-winded homilies—a legacy, perhaps, of his pious Methodist upbringing in southern Ohio.

After coming to Brooklyn, Rickey promoted a venture in black baseball called the "United States League," although it's uncertain what the crafty and conniving Rickey really intended. He may have wanted to create a new, viable black baseball organization that would be free of what he regarded as the "racketeer influence" and, not incidentally, bring the Dodgers revenue on the rental of Ebbets Field. Or he may have been thinking of such a league as basically a farm organization, within which the Dodgers would prepare players for the coming integration of the majors. Or it may all have been a cover behind which Dodgers scouts could look over talent in the existing Negro leagues. Whatever Rickey was up to, the United States League never existed anywhere but on paper.

Eventually, though, Rickey did move to erase baseball's color line. Late in August 1945 he met in his Ebbets Field office with Jack Roosevelt Robinson, who'd just arrived from Chicago in the company of Dodgers scout Clyde Sukeforth. Rickey offered the twenty-six-year-old Robinson the opportunity to become the first black person to play within Organized Baseball in the twentieth century. (At the time, of course, almost no one realized that Robinson wouldn't be the first-*ever* such player.)

Jackie Robinson, a native of Georgia who'd grown up in racially integrated circumstances in Pasadena, California, had been a multi-sport star at the University of California at Los Angeles. Commissioned an army second lieutenant in 1942, he wouldn't go along with Jim Crow practices at Fort Hood, Texas, and was court-martialed. Though acquitted, he made a reputation as a troublemaker, which was the main reason he was discharged in the fall of 1944.

When summoned by Rickey, Robinson was playing shortstop for the Kansas City Monarchs; the previous month he'd appeared in the annual East-West Game at Comiskey Park. Handsome, very dark-skinned, slightly under six feet tall and a powerfully built two-hundred-pounder, Robinson was exceptionally fast and a good hitter.

Though by no means the top player in the Negro leagues, Robinson possessed other qualities Rickey found attractive. Better educated than most ballplayers of any color, an articulate man who spoke in clipped accents, Robinson was also a teetotaler, engaged to a refined young woman, and thus able to meet Rickey's standards of respectability. His experience as a student and athlete in a predominantly white environment was another factor in his favor. In Robinson, Rickey became convinced, he'd found the right man.

In their first meeting, Rickey subjected Robinson to a lengthy, agitated discourse on the hardships that awaited him as a lonely racial pioneer. Although the young man hardly needed to be reminded of American racial realities (or instructed in racial etiquette, either), he listened patiently and promised to turn the other cheek to tormentors. A proud, naturally excitable and combative person, Robinson nonetheless understood what he would have to do—and also what he couldn't afford to do.

Sworn to secrecy, Robinson endured two months of anxious waiting before Rickey had him fly to Montreal and there, on October 23, 1945, sign a contract to play the 1946 season for the Montreal Royals, the Dodgers' farm club in the International League, one notch below the majors. Basing Robinson in the relatively liberal racial climate of the French-speaking Canadian city was a key element in Rickey's meticulous strategy. In effect, Robinson would integrate baseball from outside the United States.

Inasmuch as Rickey had long regarded Negro-league baseball as a racket, he simply ignored the Kansas City Monarchs' financial interest in Robinson, thereby establishing a precedent for other major-league clubs. J. L. Wilkinson, the Monarchs' white owner, told the press that while he was entitled to some kind of compensation, he wouldn't protest to commissioner Chandler. "I am very glad to see Jackie get this chance," he said.

No minor-league player had ever been the object of such media coverage as focused on Robinson in the spring of 1946. Besides all the other pressures he faced, he had to learn to play second base, because, according to Brooklyn scouting reports, his arm wasn't strong enough for shortstop. On April 18, 1946, before more than twenty thousand people at Roosevelt Stadium in Jersey City, Robinson made his debut in Organized Baseball with a home run, three bunt singles, and a pair of stolen bases (one a theft of home) in the Royals' 14–1 victory over the Jersey City Giants.

From that spectacular beginning, he went on to lead the International League with a .349 batting average and tie for the leadership in runs scored. Although his forty stolen bases (second best in the league) weren't a large number by earlier (or later) standards, what most impressed observers was his intrepidness—his ability to beat out bunts, stretch singles into doubles, upset pitchers by dancing up and down the basepaths, and generally demoralize opponents' defenses in ways that reminded a few old-timers of Ty Cobb. Robinson gave International League fans a sample of the speed and dash that characterized Negro-league play, even as those qualities had largely disappeared from white baseball.

"I never had it made," Robinson would say years later, and almost everywhere the Royals went, he had to deal with hostile and often abusive white fans, pitchers who threw at his head, and base runners who came in with spikes high. Robinson took it and kept his temper under control, but teammate John Wright, a veteran Negro-league pitcher signed by Montreal following his navy discharge in February 1946, couldn't endure the stress. Optioned to Three Rivers, Quebec, in the lower minors in May and subsequently released, Wright returned to the Homestead Grays, his prewar club. Pitcher Roy Partlow, another Negro-leaguer, also spent part of 1946 with Montreal, but by late summer he had followed Wright to Three Rivers.

Rickey left no doubt about the Dodgers' commitment to integrating their organization. Catcher Roy Campanella of the Baltimore Elite Giants, already a nine-year professional at twenty-five, and Don Newcombe, a young pitcher with the Newark Eagles, were signed in the spring and sent to Nashua, New Hampshire, in the Class B New England League. Again the Dodgers made no gesture of compensation to the players' former employers.

Effa Manley, a beautiful, very light-skinned woman whose husband (the local numbers boss) owned the Newark Eagles, would always be bitter over the way Rickey simply dismissed the issue of prior claims to players he signed out of the Negro leagues, yet the feelings of the Manleys and most other black owners were ambivalent. Obviously they wanted to field the best clubs they could; they hoped to be paid for whatever talent they lost and feared that the passing of Jim Crow would doom black professional baseball; yet by and large they supported the sport's integration and rooted for Robinson and the others who broke the color line.

In 1946 times were still good for black baseball. Crowds for regularly scheduled league games were bigger than ever; the East-West Game in Chicago drew more than forty-five thousand. Satchel Paige was barnstorming with his own team, but Josh Gibson and Buck Leonard were still pounding the ball for the Homestead Grays and an abundance of younger stars—Monte Irvin and Larry Doby with Newark, Sam Jethroe with Cleveland, Artie Wilson with Birmingham—were back from military service. In that fall's Negro World Series, Irvin and Doby led Newark to victory over Kansas City in seven games, the first of which took place at the Polo Grounds in New York.

The following January, commissioner Chandler presided at a meeting in New York at which the major-league clubs voted 15–1 against adding black players to their rosters, with Rickey the only dissenter. Having arranged the purchase of the Yankees by Del Webb and Dan Topping and having himself gained the presidency of the franchise, Larry MacPhail was more influential than ever in baseball affairs. Professing pious concern over the welfare of the Negro leagues, MacPhail led the opposition to racial integration, with active support from Tom Yawkey of the Red Sox, Sam Breadon of the Cardinals, and Phil Wrigley of the Cubs. Chandler's stance was one of official neutrality, while he privately assured Rickey that he wouldn't interfere in whatever plans Brooklyn had for Robinson.

In 1947 both the Dodgers and Montreal trained in Havana, mainly to avoid the housing and other difficulties Robinson and his new wife had encountered in Florida a year earlier. Officially, Robinson remained with Montreal until April 10, when the Dodgers, as long expected, announced his addition to their roster. A half-dozen or so southern-born Brooklyn players immediately tried to persuade their teammates to refuse to play, but stern lectures by Rickey and a barrage of profane threats from manager Leo Durocher, along with the refusal of Kentuckian Pee Wee Reese and other team leaders to join the dissidents, quickly stifled the would-be mutiny.

That was Durocher's last significant action as Brooklyn manager for 1947. A few days later he received notification from Chandler that he was suspended for the season for "conduct detrimental to baseball." As Chandler saw things, Durocher's life-style—especially his friendship with the movie actor George Raft and other big-time gamblers and his gossip-enshrouded marriage to the lately divorced actress Laraine Day—damaged the sport's image. In retrospect, Durocher appears as considerably less a sinner than a number of others before and after him who escaped chastisement, but most people at the time seemed to share Chandler's conviction that Durocher's off-the-field activities diminished the National Pastime's moral stature.

So it wasn't "Leo the Lip" who would be Robinson's first big-league manager but sixty-year-old Burt Shotton, a Dodgers scout and Rickey's longtime associate and close friend, hurriedly elevated to the job. Moreover, when the Dodgers opened the season on April 15, at Ebbets Field against the Boston Braves, Robinson was at first base, not second, which was occupied by feisty Eddie Stanky. Struggling to master a third infield position in three years, Robinson also had to endure efforts at physical intimidation and torrents of racial invective from opposing players and fans that were beyond anything he'd experienced so far. The Philadelphia Phillies, exhorted by Ben Chapman, their Tennessee-born manager, proved especially vicious in their harassing tactics.

Ultimately Robinson won everybody's respect as a ballplayer, however grudgingly given. He batted only three points below .300, led the National League with twenty-nine stolen bases, and was second in runs scored. At the end of the season the *Sporting News*, which had never liked the idea of blacks in Organized Baseball, nonetheless chose Robinson for its first National League Rookie of the Year Award.

Mostly remembering the twin sensations of Durocher's suspension and Robinson's arrival, Walter "Red" Barber, the venerated radio announcer of the Dodgers' games, would later describe 1947 as "the year all hell broke loose." Actually, quite a lot of hell had already broken loose the previous year, when the return to peacetime baseball brought a succession of unanticipated problems.

Some players returned from military service with strong feelings about the need to change their relations with the owners. As had been true for decades, their grievances mostly concerned the reserve clause, the lack of a regular pension plan, and arbitrary salary cuts. Meanwhile American labor unions, spurred by protective New Deal legislation and wartime manpower shortages, were at the peak of their strength and ambitiousness. Robert Murray, an attorney for the Congress of Industrial Organizations, persuaded players on various clubs to form an American Baseball Guild, and in August 1946 the Pittsburgh Pirates went so far as to take a vote on whether to strike for better pay and collective-bargaining rights. Although the players rejected the strike, they succeeded in scaring the club owners into conceding on several issues.

Besides more meal money on road trips and $25 per week for spring-training expenses, the players gained a salary minimum of $5,000, a twenty-five-percent limit on cuts from one year to the next, an assured World Series pool of at least $250,000, and a pension plan. Funded mainly by contributions from World Series and All-Star Game receipts, the plan guaranteed a pension to players with five years of big-league service. With most of their immediate concerns taken care of, the players' militance quickly subsided.

Fully as upsetting to the owners' equilibrium was the Mexican League threat. In the winter of 1945–1946 Jorge Pasquel, a multimillionaire liquor distributor who controlled the Mexican baseball league, began luring major-leaguers with what for that time were lavish salaries and perquisites. Pasquel envisioned the Mexican League as a full-fledged rival to *las ligas grandes* up north, and all told, he corralled eighteen players, six from the New York Giants alone. His best-known acquisitions were Max Lanier, undefeated in six decisions when he left the Cardinals early in the 1946 season, and Mickey Owen, still the Dodgers' number one catcher.

The Browns' Vernon Stephens also accepted Pasquel's offer—in Stephens's case, $25,000 per year for five years—and played two games in Mexico before dropping out of sight. Surfacing in Brownsville, Texas, a few days later, Stephens was full of apologies for having ever left St. Louis.

That quick change of heart saved Stephens from the blacklist proclaimed by commissioner Chandler for the "Mexican jumping beans," as they were derided in the sporting press. Sooner or later and for a variety of reasons, they all became disenchanted with life south of the border. Some got tired of the food, the gruelling bus travel, and the rickety ballparks. Others resented league president Pasquel's rank partiality toward his own Vera Cruz Blues (who, despite their name, were based in Mexico City). Still others didn't like being teammates with black players from the U.S. and the Caribbean.

Ex-Giants pitcher Sal Maglie stuck it out longer than most, winning forty-one games for Puebla in 1946–1947. After that season, Jorge Pasquel's death and financial troubles for most clubs caused the Mexican League's temporary disbandment, and in 1948 Maglie pitched for a touring team put together by Max Lanier, who'd earlier played briefly in Cuba (as had several other jumpers after leaving Mexico).

By 1949, threatened by two antitrust suits—one brought by Danny Gardella, former Giants outfielder, the other by ex-Cardinals Lanier, Freddie Martin, and Lou Klein—the baseball owners decided to give in. They instructed Chandler to lift the blacklist, at the same time that they settled out of court with the plaintiffs. Of the players who'd gone to Mexico in 1946, only Maglie had a significant post-1949 big-league career.

Of course, for all the controversy over Jackie Robinson, players' unions, and Mexican raids, what captivated most baseball fans in the spring of 1946 was the prospect of the first "normal" season in five years. Nearly all the players who'd been in the armed forces sought to regain their jobs, and by midsummer only about one in five big-league regulars had been in the lineup a year earlier. With such stellar performers as Joe DiMaggio, Bob Feller, Ted Williams, Stan Musial, Hank Greenberg, and Pete Reiser back in action and mostly regaining prewar form, everybody agreed that baseball was about as good as ever.

Attendance climbed to an unheard-of (and rarely imagined) eighteen and a half million, with most franchises reaching new seasonal highs. Brooklyn, drawing more than a million and a half paying customers into Ebbets Field, broke the Cubs' eighteen-year-old National League record; the Yankees, having finally installed lights, set a new mark for both leagues, and Detroit, where owner Walter O. Briggs also joined the trend toward nighttime baseball entertainment, far exceeded its franchise record. At St. Louis, Cardinals owner Sam Breadon continued to make lots of money by selling players ($358,500 worth in 1946 alone), but for the first time he also sold more than a million tickets. So did the New York Giants, despite finishing dead last.

With the 1941–1943 frontliners all back, the Yankees were favored to regain their eminence in the American League. Although Spud Chandler, still in wartime form, posted twenty wins and Floyd "Bill" Bevens, a big right-hander who'd also remained a civilian, added sixteen, nearly every Yankees regular had a subpar year. Troubled all season by a bad foot, Joe DiMaggio batted under .300 for the first time in his life, and the Yankees struggled to a poor third-place finish without Joe McCarthy, whose inability to get along with the mercurial Larry MacPhail led to his resignation a quarter of the way into the season.

Second-place Detroit still relied on Hank Greenberg, the league's leader in homers and rbi's despite batting only .277, and Hal Newhouser, who proved he was no wartime fluke by winning twenty-six times and recording a sparkling 1.94 earned run average. Outfielder Dick Wakefield, paid a princely $55,000 in 1941 to sign with the Detroit organization out of high school, was the first of the "bonus babies" to fizzle in the majors.

Newhouser's performance was overshadowed by Bob Feller's heroics with a sixth-place Cleveland entry. Besides throwing his second no-hit game (on opening day) and matching Newhouser's twenty-six wins, Feller struck out 348 batters—a figure exceeded in major-league history only by Rube Waddell, who had fanned one more back in 1904. Feller's pitching was the main reason the Indians passed the magical one-million attendance figure, eclipsing their previous highest total by some 250,000 fans.

Besides Feller's pitching, the promotional stunts of Bill Veeck, head of a syndicate that purchased the Cleveland franchise in June, kept people coming to watch the Indians. Bringing to the big leagues the same freewheeling philosophy he'd practiced earlier at Milwaukee, Veeck offered his customers fireworks, giveaways, swimsuit pageants, clown acts, and an assortment of other "bonus attractions." To widespread protests that he was cheapening the National Pastime, the self-described "hustler" answered: "A baseball team is a commercial venture, operating for a profit. The idea that you don't have to . . . hustle your product the way General Motors hustles its products is baseball's most pernicious enemy."

Although he'd quit playing, Joe Cronin still led the Boston Red Sox, and Ted Williams picked up where he'd left off in 1942, batting .342 with thirty-eight home runs—while resuming his feud with the Boston press. Williams dominated the 1946 All-Star Game in Fenway Park, with two homers, two singles, and five rbi's in a 12–3 American League victory. With Dom DiMaggio, Johnny Pesky, Bobby Doerr, and Rudy York (acquired from Detroit early in 1946) also having outstanding seasons, Cronin's team built a big early lead and coasted to the franchise's first pennant in twenty-eight years. Two right-handers— Cecil "Tex" Hughson, ace of the '42 staff, and Dave "Boo" Ferriss, who'd matured in military baseball—combined for forty-five of Boston's 104 wins.

The National League offered a pennant battle that couldn't have been closer. At the end of the 154-game season, the Dodgers and Cardinals showed identical 96–58 records, a unique circumstance in major-league history up to that date. (The famous 1908 tie-breaking game between the Cubs and Giants had actually been a replay of a no-decision regular-season game.)

Although Stan Musial (NL batting champ at .365), Enos Slaughter (the majors' rbi leader with 130), Marty Marion, and Terry Moore were all service returnees, the Cardinals still had a young ball club, still a group of players developed almost entirely in the Rickey-built farm system. The Dodgers, on the other hand, were a veteran outfit, made up mostly of men Durocher and Larry MacPhail had bought and traded for before Pearl Harbor. Although for three years Rickey had been adding scouts, signing teenage prospects, and accumulating farm-club affiliations, as yet the Brooklyn team didn't fully bear his stamp.

The Cardinals swept what was scheduled as a two-of-three-game playoff and went into the World Series as pronounced underdogs against the powerful Red Sox. The teams alternated victories for six games; then, with the score tied 3–3 in the eighth inning of the finale at Sportsman's Park, Johnny Pesky hesitated in relaying the ball on Harry Walker's long single, and Country Slaughter scored all the way from first. Harry Brecheen, a slightly built left-hander who'd already pitched two complete-game victories, retired the Red Sox in his second inning of relief to get credit for his third Series win, bringing the Cardinals their third world's championship in five years.

Ted Williams, in what would turn out to be his only World Series, made five singles in the seven games. Throughout the Series, when Williams came to bat with the bases empty, Cardinals manager Eddie Dyer shifted everybody except his left fielder to the right of second base—a variation on the defense Cleveland's Lou Boudreau had employed that summer. In the opinion of writers covering the Red Sox, Williams's refusal to try to hit the ball toward left field had probably cost him the batting title to Washington's Mickey Vernon. Convinced that he was paid mainly to hit home runs, the stubborn Williams resisted Ty Cobb's and everybody else's advice, and wouldn't alter his magnificent swing until much later in his career.

The 1947 season brought a continuation of the postwar attendance boom. Cleveland, for example, drew a million and a half with a club that still did no better than fourth place, and the New York Giants, boasting Johnny Mize, Walker Cooper, and a power-packed lineup otherwise, also finished fourth and drew 1.6 million, despite setting a new major-league record with 221 homers. At Pittsburgh, a group of owners that included the singer Bing Crosby paid Detroit an undisclosed sum for a fast-fading Hank Greenberg. Greenberg closed out his career with twenty-five homers, but it was young Ralph Kiner, with fifty-one round-trippers to tie Mize, who was principally responsible for the big turnouts at Forbes Field. Despite finishing in a tie for last place, the Pirates played before 1,283,000, a half-million more than in 1946.

Although as yet relatively few black people lived in Brooklyn, throngs of them now came from Newark, Harlem, and elsewhere in the New York area to root for Jackie Robinson; and their presence at Ebbets Field more than compensated for whatever white customers the Dodgers may have lost. For the season, 1,807,526 people paid to see the Brooklyn club in its home ballpark, which could accommodate only about thirty-three thousand in the narrowest seats in the majors.

Another aspect of the Robinson phenomenon was that considerable numbers of politically conscious New Yorkers—people who hadn't paid much attention to baseball previously—now hailed the Dodgers for setting the pace in the drive against Jim Crow. They took Brooklyn for their team, despite Rickey's insistence that Robinson had become a Dodger not "to solve a sociological problem" but "for one reason: to win the pennant." Besides the *Amsterdam News* in Harlem and other major black newspapers, the Communist party's *Daily Worker*, which had pushed for the integration of baseball throughout the war years, fell in love with "dem Bums."

Under the gentle direction of Burt Shotton, the Dodgers finally overcame the Cardinals in a race that was close until mid-September. Young Ralph Branca, a twenty-one-game winner, and Hugh Casey, who won ten and saved eighteen, anchored the pitching staff. The aging Dixie Walker batted .306 and drove in ninety-four runs; Pete Reiser batted .308, although he missed much of the season because of still another collision with a wall and then a broken ankle. Robinson, Stanky, and Reese provided solid infield play and timely batting.

Under Bucky Harris, onetime boy manager at Washington, a revived Yankees club handily won the franchise's fourteenth pennant in twenty-six years. Charlie Keller, hurt much of the time, was all but finished at thirty; but Joe DiMaggio and Tommy Henrich led a strong attack and Allie Reynolds, obtained from Cleveland for Joe Gordon, won nineteen games. Lefty Joe Page, the AL's counterpart to Hugh

Casey, won fourteen for himself and saved seventeen for Reynolds and others.

Meanwhile Boston's pitching collapsed and the Red Sox faded to third, even though Ted Williams led the American League in batting, home runs, rbi's, runs, walks, total bases, and slugging average. (Several games under the newly installed lights at Fenway Park helped keep the turnstiles clicking despite the club's poor showing.)

In one of the best World Series, the Yankees prevailed in seven games, with the most memorable encounter being the fourth, at Ebbets Field. Bill Bevens, who'd struggled to a 7–13 record that season, had walked ten batters and given up a run but, with two outs in the ninth inning, still held the Dodgers hitless. At that point pinch hitter Cookie Lavagetto bounced a drive off the concave right-field wall to score two runs and give Brooklyn a 3–2 victory. After having come that close to the first World Series no-hitter, Bevens would never pitch in the majors again.

Jackie Robinson made seven hits in that Series and stole two bases, and pitcher Dan Bankhead, late of the Negro American League's Memphis Red Sox, became the second black man to appear in the World Series when he was used once as a pinch runner. Besides those two Dodgers, fourteen other blacks played somewhere within Organized Baseball in 1947, three of them in the majors.

In July, Cleveland president Bill Veeck broke the American League's color line—and also exhibited an uncommon regard for the situation of Negro-league owners—when he paid $10,000 for Larry Doby, the Newark Eagles' twenty-two-year-old second baseman. Used mostly as a pinch hitter, Doby endured much of the same abuse Robinson had met in the other league and batted a forlorn .156.

A month after Doby joined the Indians, the last-place St. Louis Browns plucked Henry Thompson, a young infielder, and Willard Brown, a veteran outfielder, from the Kansas City Monarchs. Signed hurriedly (and without compensation to the Monarchs), neither man had been scouted as well as Robinson or even Doby. Playing in a city that was still mostly Jim Crowed, the Browns' recruits did poorly; by the end of August both were back with the Monarchs. (Thompson would return to the majors in 1949 with the New York Giants.)

That 1947 season was also one in which long-standing predictions that the integration of Organized Baseball meant the end of the Negro leagues really started to materialize. Even if Josh Gibson hadn't died in Pittsburgh of a stroke early in the year, not much would have been different. Caught up in the drama of black professionals actually playing with and against whites in Organized Baseball, black fans deserted the Negro leagues en masse. The Newark Eagles, for example, saw their attendance drop from 120,000 in 1946 to 57,000 in 1947. Once Larry Doby joined the Cleveland Indians, blacks by the thousands stopped attending Buckeyes games at League Park and started going to Municipal Stadium, where Bill Veeck based his team full-time in mid-1947.

The story was basically the same throughout black baseball as, year by year, admired veterans retired and the best young players—among them Willie Mays, Henry Aaron, and Ernie Banks—entered Organized Baseball. The NNL disbanded following the 1948 season, and while the Baltimore Elite Giants, Philadelphia Stars, and New York Cubans joined the NAL, the once-mighty Homestead Grays simply ceased to exist. As black baseball's only league, the NAL managed to keep going for another decade. Reduced to the Kansas City Monarchs and three other franchises, the circuit finally disbanded following the 1960 season.

For a few more years the once-proud Monarchs would survive by staying on the road, appearing mostly in small towns in the Midwest. The Clowns, formerly a strong Indianapolis-based NAL entry, would become literal embodiments of their nickname, traversing the country with a species of baseball burlesque akin to that of basketball's vastly more successful Harlem Globetrotters.

While the black leagues withered, the white majors and the rest of Organized Baseball were in the midst of postwar plenty, with the 1948 season marking the pinnacle of baseball's popularity in the pre-television era. Some 20.8 million paying customers watched regular-season games in the major leagues. With their team in the thick of the pennant race and special trains bringing them in from Toledo, Youngstown, and Columbus, more than 2.6 million Indians fans paid their way into Cleveland's enormous stadium. Several regular-season crowds exceeded 70,000; a doubleheader in June and another in July each drew 80,000-plus. The Yankees attracted 2,373,000 at home; most other clubs broke their previous attendance records.

The Boston Braves far exceeded any previous season's attendance, drawing a million and a half at Braves Field, still one of baseball's best facilities. Under Billy Southworth, a three-time winner with the Cardinals, Boston's National Leaguers gained their first pennant since the Miracle Braves of 1914. Eddie Stanky, acquired from Brooklyn, teamed in the Braves' middle infield with former Louisiana State University football star Alvin Dark, who batted .322 to win Rookie of the Year honors. Veteran third baseman Bob Elliott enjoyed his best year, batting .317 with 22 home runs and 113 runs batted in; and center fielder Tommy Holmes, NL batting champ in 1945, hit .325. Johnny Sain, the National League's best right-hander in the early post-war period, won twenty-four games, while Warren Spahn, a young left-hander who'd registered twenty-one victories in 1947, added fifteen. (The Braves' pitching, went a saying of the day, was "Spahn and Sain and pray for rain.")

With much fanfare, Leo Durocher returned from his suspension to manage Brooklyn, then, in June, stunned the Ebbets Field faithful by resigning to succeed Mel Ott as manager of the hated Giants. Burt Shotton, the only manager in street clothes besides Connie Mack, again moved into the Brooklyn dugout. Without Alabamian Stanky and Georgians Dixie Walker and Hugh Casey, the Dodgers ended up third behind the Braves and Cardinals. Walker and Casey had been traded to Pittsburgh, where they joined South Carolinian Kirby Higbe, swapped early in the 1947 season. The commonly understood reason for all those changes was Branch Rickey's determination to clear the Brooklyn club of any Southerner who still resented Jackie Robinson's presence.

In June 1948 the Dodgers called up Roy Campanella from St. Paul and made him their number one catcher. With Campanella behind the plate and Robinson at second base (where he relocated after Stanky's departure), Brooklyn now had blacks at two of the critical "up-the-middle" positions. If, as some believed, Rickey's trades cost Brooklyn the 1948 pennant, he also gave the Dodgers a preferential position in the market for black players, at the same time that his twenty-five-team farm system became the most talent-rich in baseball.

The American League season produced a nerve-wracking three-way scramble between the Yankees, the Red Sox, and Cleveland. Joe DiMaggio batted .320 and led the AL with thirty-nine homers and the majors with 155 rbi's; Tommy Henrich enjoyed his best season; Lawrence "Yogi" Berra, a squat, powerfully built second-year man with an affinity for malapropisms and bad-ball base hits, emerged as the AL's foremost catcher; and Allie Reynolds, Vic Raschi, and left-hander Eddie Lopat were a steady pitching trio.

Now managed by Joe McCarthy, Boston combined lusty hitting with shaky pitching; while the Red Sox scored 907 times, their pitchers yielded earned runs at the rate of 4.20 per nine innings. Ted Williams batted a league-leading .369, and he, Bobby Doerr, and Vern "Junior" Stephens (obtained from the Browns with Jack Kramer the previous November) combined for eighty-one homers and 375 rbi's.

At Cleveland, Bob Feller slipped to a 19–15 record, but right-hander Bob Lemon, a converted infielder, won twenty, as did Gene Bearden, a tall rookie left-hander with matinee-idol looks and a highly effective knuckleball. Of the Indians' 155 homers, Larry Doby accounted for fourteen, besides batting .301 and adapting well to center field under Tris Speaker's coaching. Joe Gordon put in a strong offensive year, as did third baseman Ken Keltner, while player-manager Lou Boudreau batted .355 and earned Most Valuable Player recognition.

On July 19, 1948, Satchel Paige made his major-league debut, pitching two innings in relief for the Indians against the Browns at Municipal Stadium. Cleveland's signing of the aging pitcher (who'd again attached himself to the Kansas City Monarchs) was roundly criticized as just another of Bill Veeck's stunts, but Veeck had known Paige personally since the early thirties and kept close track of his peripatetic career, including the arm trouble that had diminished his once-overpowering speed. Satch could still pitch, as he'd demonstrated the previous fall before fifty thousand at Yankee Stadium, when, pitching for his touring black all-stars, he held a team of white major-leaguers scoreless and struck out sixteen in a postseason duel with Bob Feller.

While the jokes about Paige's age continued, he quickly proved a major asset in the Indians' pennant drive, as well as a tremendous gate attraction. Pitching seventy-three innings, he started seven times,

Joe DiMaggio sliding into third base under Washington's Eddie Yost in 1949, with the home-plate umpire covering the play. (AP)

Casey Stengel, 1950.

Jackie Robinson stealing home plate at Ebbets Field, Brooklyn, 1952. The catcher is Harry Chiti, the batter Preacher Roe. (*UPI*)

Stan Musial, 1952.

Mickey Mantle, late 1950s.

Ted Williams near the end of his playing career, ca. 1960.

Dodger Stadium, Los Angeles.

Roger Maris at spring training, St. Petersburg, Florida, 1961.

Sandy Koufax pitching in the ninth inning of his second no-hit game (versus San Francisco), May 11, 1963, at Dodger Stadium, Los Angeles.

Bob Gibson in the 1964 World Series. (AP)

Frank Robinson, 1966.

William D. Eckert and Charles O. Finley, 1967.
(*Rochester Times-Union*)

Cincinnati's Pete Rose turning a double play in the 1965 All-Star Game, Bloomington, Minnesota. Behind Rose is Dodgers' shortstop Maury Wills, sliding is Cleveland's Vic Davalillo. (*Rochester Times-Union*)

Denny McLain in 1968.

Roberto Clemente, 1971.

Johnny Bench and Joe Morgan after Cincinnati's victory in game six of the 1972 World Series. (AP)

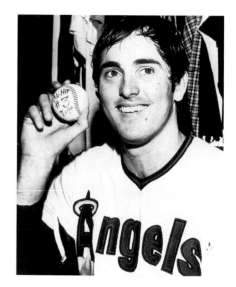

Nolan Ryan after his third no-hit game, September 28, 1974.

Clockwise from bottom: fingerless glove worn in the 1880s; George Sisler's first-baseman's mitt, 1920s; fielder's glove, 1970s–1980s; Warren "Buddy" Rosar's catcher's mitt, 1940s.

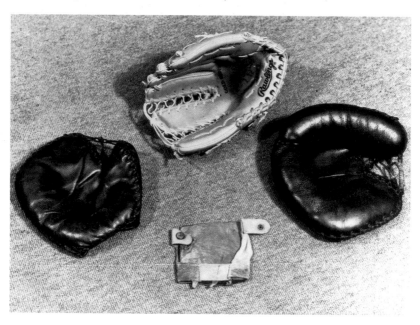

Henry Aaron, moments before
hitting homer number 715—
Atlanta, April 8, 1974.

Lou Brock scoring at Busch Stadium, St. Louis, in 1974. The sprawling catcher is the
Cubs' Steve Swisher.

Rollie Fingers pitching in the 1974 World Series. (*UPI*)

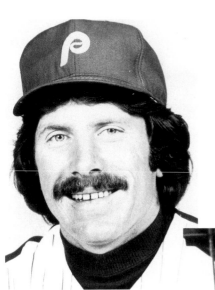

Mike Schmidt, ca. 1978.

Carl Yastrzemski, ca. 1979.

Rod Carew, early 1980s.

Marvin Miller, 1981.

George M. Steinbrenner.

Reggie Jackson and Gene Autry
following Jackson's signing with
the California Angels as a free
agent, 1982.

Rickey Henderson, 1980.

George Brett, 1980.

Left to right: Carmelo Martinez, Tony Gwynn, Kevin McReynolds—outfield of the San Diego Padres, 1984 National League champs.

Roger Clemens, ca. 1987.

relieved fourteen, received credit for six victories against a single loss, and threw two shutouts.

Exactly four weeks after baseball's most popular black performer finally made it into the majors, the most beloved figure in the sport's history died in New York. Babe Ruth's death, at fifty-three, was mourned by people in many countries, even by some in war-devastated Japan, where the Babe's 1934 tour with Lou Gehrig and other big-leaguers had created a national sensation. The Babe had struggled against throat cancer for nearly two years; baseball fans had become accustomed to the sight of the gaunt, white-haired home-run king hoarsely whispering his thanks on the several occasions when the Yankees publicly honored him.

While the Braves clinched and waited, the AL race ended in a dead heat between the Indians and Red Sox, with the Yankees finishing only a game behind them. Opting for a one-game playoff format, AL president Will Harridge determined by coin toss that the decisive meeting would be in Boston's Fenway Park. It was an easy 8–3 victory for Cleveland, Boudreau's two homers and Keltner's one providing all the runs rookie Bearden needed for his twentieth win.

The 1948 World Series was also relatively easy for the Indians, although Sain defeated Feller 1–0 in the opener. The winning run scored on Tommy Holmes's single, following umpire Bill Summers's hotly disputed safe call on a pickoff play at second. Cleveland then won three straight behind Lemon, Bearden, and Steve Gromek, Doby's homer winning Gromek's game. The Braves battered Feller in game five, only to have Bearden come on to save a 4–3 clincher in the sixth game at Braves Field. Game five, at Cleveland, was played before 86,200 customers, more people than had ever been in one place at one time for a game in Organized Baseball.

The 1949 season, at least for the minors, was absolutely the best of times. No fewer than fifty-nine minor leagues—now classified from Class AAA down to Class D—were in operation, and total paid admissions reached forty-two million. In hundreds of places across the United States and much of Canada—from cities as big as Los Angeles, Kansas City, Montreal, and Houston to little towns such as Houma in Louisiana, Johnson City in Tennessee, Yakima in Washington, and Three Rivers in Quebec—minor-league baseball was the baseball that mattered to most people most of the time. Although many minor-league operators still wouldn't allow radio broadcasts of home games, they generally agreed that play-by-play coverage of road games (usually done in local studios off teletyped reports from distant ballparks) encouraged interest in the local club.

In the majors, despite exciting races in both leagues, paid admissions mysteriously fell about six hundred thousand. In retrospect, it's evident that spreading home-television ownership in the eastern metropolitan areas had already started to affect attendance. The Yankees beat the Red Sox on the final day of the season to take the AL flag, while Cleveland slipped to third, largely because of Feller's continuing decline and Bearden's ineffectiveness. At the end of the 1949 season, Bill Veeck sold his holdings in the Cleveland franchise and Satchel Paige, released after winning four and losing seven, drifted back to the Kansas City Monarchs.

In the other league, Burt Shotton's Brooklyn club edged the Cardinals by one game, defending-champion Boston running a poor fourth behind the no-longer-Phutile Phillies. Still featuring Stan Musial, Enos Slaughter, and other farm-grown standouts, the Cardinals continued to travel on the momentum of the Rickey years, but the St. Louis organization no longer produced a steady stream of talent. The Brooklyn system, besides getting the jump on other clubs in signing blacks, was turning out promising youngsters by the bushel; in 1949, sixteen of the Dodgers' twenty-five farms finished in the top four in their leagues, and eight won pennants. As he did at St. Louis, Rickey sold his surplus players—for $250,000 following the 1949 season alone—and reinvested much of what he made in the farm system.

In 1949, no longer willing or needing to keep his competitive fires in check, Jackie Robinson ranted at umpires, wrangled with opposing players, and reached full stardom. His .342 batting average and thirty-seven stolen bases led the National League and the majors, respectively. Named the NL's Most Valuable Player, Robinson also clubbed sixteen homers, drove in 124 runs, and scored 122.

The oft-disabled Pete Reiser had been sent to Boston to play out his frustrating career, but Edwin "Duke" Snider, a cocky, power-hitting, far-ranging Californian, looked even better than Reiser in center field. Buddha-built Roy Campanella, solid behind the plate and at bat, gained general recognition as the NL's best catcher; slugging Gil Hodges, a converted catcher, finally solved the Dodgers' first-base problem; Pee Wee Reese still sparkled at shortstop; and Billy Cox, obtained from Pittsburgh, was a master gloveman at third. Ensconced in right field was hard-hitting Carl Furillo, a Pennsylvanian whose throwing arm had earned him the nickname "the Reading Rifle." Hulking Don Newcombe, the third black player to stick with the Dodgers, won seventeen games in his first season; left-hander Elwin "Preacher" Roe, a bony Arkansan acquired from Pittsburgh in the Dixie Walker trade, contributed fifteen.

The Yankees triumphed again (for the fifteenth time since 1921) under the unlikely leadership of Charles Dillon "Casey" Stengel. After guiding Oakland to a Pacific Coast League title, Stengel signed to manage the Yankees at a salary of $25,000. Although he'd been a respectable ballplayer in the NL during the teens and twenties, as a manager the fifty-nine-year-old Stengel carried a reputation for comedy more than baseball savvy. In nine years with Brooklyn and the Boston Braves, Stengel had provided plenty of laughs, but his teams never finished better than fifth; in Boston he became so unpopular that, when an automobile struck him on a downtown street and shattered one of his legs, many local fans publicly regretted it hadn't been his neck.

In the minors at Milwaukee, Kansas City, and Oakland, however, Stengel had managed successfully, and George Weiss, who became Yankees general manager in 1948, had long admired him. Still, it was hard to see Stengel—with his whimsical manner and long-winded, frequently unintelligible way of talking (called "Stengelese")—fitting into the dignified, pin-striped tradition of Miller Huggins, Lou Gehrig, Joe McCarthy, and of course Joe DiMaggio, still the strongest presence on the ball club.

The Red Sox again fell short, despite a batting attack that produced nearly nine hundred runs (of which Williams and Stephens drove in 318) and sterling pitching from lefty Mel Parnell (twenty-five wins) and righty Ellis Kinder (twenty-three). Raschi, Reynolds, Lopat, and Tommy Byrne, bolstered by Joe Page's matchless relief work, provided the deepest pitching the Yankees had enjoyed since before the war. Stengel adroitly used all of his mound staff, as he did his entire roster. Even if chronic foot trouble hadn't disabled DiMaggio for half the season, Stengel would still have juggled his personnel inveterately.

The left-handed Stengel had batted only against right-handed pitching when he played for John McGraw between 1921 and 1923; Stengel revered McGraw as a teacher, and his faith in what, by the 1940s, was called "platooning" far exceeded even McGraw's. At New York, Stengel found himself blessed with more than one good player at almost every position, so that he was able to platoon his men as only George Stallings had done with the 1914 "Miracle Braves." In 1949 Phil Rizzuto was the only Yankee to register as many as 450 official times at bat.

At the close of that year's World Series, it was hard to argue with Stengel's methods. After two 1–0 gems—the first won by Reynolds over Newcombe, the second by Roe over Raschi—the Yankees took three straight. In his third relief appearance, Page stifled a Brooklyn rally in the seventh inning to save Raschi's game and win the finale, 10–6, at Ebbets Field. With the onetime funny man of the National League at the helm, the Yankees had nailed down still another world's championship—and Brooklyn had failed for the fourth time in four Series.

Although hardly anyone would have guessed it at the time, the Yankees were starting a run of success such as no major-league team had ever accomplished. Over the next fifteen seasons, thirteen more pennants and eight more Series championships would come to the New York "dynasty"—to use a term the Yankees helped to popularize. Yet the Yankees' monotonous triumphs—a tribute to expert management both in the front office and on the field, to the value of a winning tradition, and of course to lots of money—would nevertheless be one of the principal ills besetting baseball in the 1950s. There would be plenty of others.

10.

Shrinking
Crowds and
Shifting
Franchises

On Sunday, October 1, 1950, in the tenth inning of the season's final game, George Sisler's oldest son Dick sliced a home run into the lower left-field stands at Ebbets Field to beat Don Newcombe and give the Philadelphia Phillies their first National League pennant in thirty-five years. Long a league doormat, the Phillies had undergone a renaissance in the postwar years under the ownership of Robert Carpenter, young heir to the Du Pont fortune. Clad in bright-red pinstripes and managed by avuncular Eddie Sawyer, Philadelphia's "Whiz Kids" were the youngest team ever to win a major-league title.

The Phillies' stars were swift center fielder Richie Ashburn (twenty-three), one of the few players still using a big, thick-handled bat and choke-hitting to all fields; Robin Roberts (twenty-four), a strong right-hander out of Michigan State University starting a run of six straight twenty-win seasons; and slugging left fielder Del Ennis (twenty-five), NL runs-batted-in leader. Left-hander Curt Simmons (twenty-one) won seventeen games before being inducted into the army a few weeks before the season was over—the first major-leaguer drafted as a result of the outbreak of war in Korea the previous June— and Jim Konstanty, the oldest Phillie at thirty-three, set a "modern" (twentieth-century) record by pitching in seventy-four games, all in relief. Besides saving twenty-two of those games, Konstanty was the winner in sixteen others. That performance brought Konstanty the NL's Most Valuable Player Award, the first given to a relief pitcher.

Six days later, at Yankee Stadium, the Phillies' fantasy ended for good when the Yankees' own Whiz Kid, a twenty-one-year-old lefty named Ed "Whitey" Ford, held the National Leaguers to two runs while Yogi Berra homered and four other Yankees scored. That completed a four-game sweep and gave Casey Stengel a second straight world's title. Berra had sparkled all season long, driving in 124 runs on twenty-eight homers and a .328 batting average. Joe DiMaggio (.301, thirty homers, 122 rbi's) stayed comparatively healthy that season, and little Phil Rizzuto, batting a career-high .324, gained Most Valuable Player honors. Vic Raschi, Allie Reynolds, Eddie Lopat, and Tommy Byrne pitched seventy of the Yankees' ninety-eight wins (three more than Detroit's ninety-five). Ford, a native New Yorker brought up in midseason from Kansas City, won nine of ten decisions, while aging Johnny Mize, purchased the previous year from the Giants, hit twenty-five homers and drove in seventy-two runs in only ninety games.

The Dodgers, not much older on average than the Phillies, had fielded a stronger team in almost every respect, and their failure cost Burt Shotton his job. His successor was Charlie Dressen, a hard-driving pepper pot and Shotton's temperamental opposite. Shotton's friend Branch Rickey, having lost a protracted power struggle to Walter O'Malley, also left Brooklyn. Since becoming the Dodgers' attorney in 1941, O'Malley had carefully built his holdings and influence in the organization at Rickey's expense. Following the disappointing 1950 season, he could finally pressure Rickey into giving up his twenty-five-percent ownership in the Dodgers, for $1,025,000. O'Malley then bought the remaining Dodgers stock from the Ebbets estate and gained absolute control of one of baseball's choicest enterprises.

Rickey, at age sixty-nine, signed as general manager of the Pittsburgh Pirates for $100,000 a year. The Pirates had climbed to fourth in 1948 with the help of several aging former Dodgers, had slipped to sixth in 1949, and then had finished last the past season, seven behind the seventh-place Chicago Cubs. The Pirates' principal asset was Ralph Kiner, whose forty-seven homers led the majors in 1950. Since his rookie year (1946), the Californian had totaled 215 round-trippers, to which he would add seventy-nine over the coming two seasons.

Rickey would keep Kiner until 1953, when, correctly judging that at thirty he was already slipping, he traded him to the Cubs. Meanwhile Rickey tried the same formula he had used with the Cardinals and Dodgers, hiring more scouts, laboring to put together a productive farm system, and building around young players. An added ingredient in Rickey's Pittsburgh program was that, given the advancing ills of the minor leagues, he sought to short-circuit the developmental process by offering big bonuses to boys just out of high school. The problem was that, until the early 1960s, major-league regulations stipulated that each "bonus baby" (anybody receiving more than $4,000 to sign) had to spend three years on a big-league roster before he could be farmed out and really start to hone his skills. Although most of the big-league clubs speculated in bonus babies, the Pirates signed more—and generally with less success. Rickey's ultimate bonus fiasco was Paul Pettit, a nineteen-year-old Los Angeles pitcher given a record $100,000 in 1951. Pettit pitched in a total of twelve major-league games, winning one, losing two.

Rickey spent five years as Pirates general manager and another four as chairman of the board of the corporation that owned the franchise. In the early and mid-1950s the city of Pittsburgh was represented by some of the worst ball clubs in major-league history; assuredly the 1951 aggregation, which finished 42–112, should be put somewhere in the all-time bottom ten. Yet for all the ineptitude suffered by the Pirates' remarkably faithful fandom, Rickey was building— uncertainly, even erratically, but building. By the late fifties—with such young stars as Roberto Clemente, Bill Mazeroski, Dick Groat, Bob Friend, and Vernon Law—the Pirates were again competitive.

After the Korean War ended in the summer of 1953, Americans generally continued to enjoy a high standard of living, in the midst of the longest sustained peacetime prosperity since the 1920s. The Pirates' foibles to the contrary notwithstanding, the caliber of 1950s baseball in the majors—in the minors as well, for that matter—may have been the highest yet, especially with the lowering of color barriers. Ostensibly the economic expansion of the fifties should have meant boom times for professional baseball, but in fact it was a decade of slump and barely concealed pessimism, from the majors down to the lowest minors.

In 1950 major-league ball park attendance dropped sharply—to 17,227,000—and two years later the sixteen teams could pull in only about fifteen million customers. Big-league baseball had lost more than a quarter of its paying fans since 1948. Something of a recovery took place for the remainder of the decade—to sixteen and a half million by 1955, seventeen and a half by 1958—but the flush times of the late forties seemed gone for good.

For the minor leagues the historic cycle of boom and bust turned into protracted bust. From an aggregate forty-two million in 1949, minor-league attendance fell sickeningly to fifteen and a half million by 1956. The fifty-nine officially recognized minor circuits operating in 1949 shrank to thirty-three in 1953, twenty-eight in 1957. Although the three AAA and two AA leagues survived, the lower minors (Classes B, C, and D) were devastated. Small-city professional baseball—a basic part of American life for some eighty years—largely disappeared.

Baseball's financial woes related to major changes in where and how Americans lived. The economic boom of the post–World War II years enabled millions of families to leave the cities and relocate in suburbs, where they developed distinctly suburban life-styles, largely independent of what was happening in the city—at least as far as entertainment and recreation were concerned. Meanwhile the areas around ballparks tended to decay and become crime-ridden, a particularly discouraging circumstance in light of estimates that about forty percent of baseball customers were now women and children.

With the majority of games now being played at night (about ninety percent of home dates in the case of Washington, Pittsburgh, Cincinnati, and the St. Louis Cardinals), suburban families faced the prospect of driving considerable distances to reach a ballpark, then searching for parking on poorly lighted streets and alleys, and often paying neighborhood urchins not to vandalize their autos. After making their way into a facility that was probably at least forty years old and not in good repair, customers had to pay steadily rising prices for cramped seats that might turn out to be located behind one of numerous steel girders. Returning in late-night semidarkness to their cars, they then faced traffic jams and trips home that might last until the early-morning hours.

Millions of people simply decided it wasn't worth the trouble and turned to other things—backyard barbecues and bridge clubs; drive-in movies and neighborhood swimming parties; tennis, golf, and softball for themselves and Little League baseball for their children. Postwar Americans also typically enjoyed two weeks or more of annual paid vacation time, commonly taken in the summer months and involving travel to other parts of the country. In 1948 baseball's share of the consumer recreation dollar was sixty-eight cents; within just two years, that had dropped to forty-nine cents.

But it was television that accounted for the single most significant change in leisure-time use. After 1950 the ownership of television sets became nearly universal, growing from about twenty-five percent of American households to some eighty-five percent within ten years.

Baseball's response to the new electronic medium was erratic and uncertain. As far back as 1939 a game at Ebbets Field between the Dodgers and Cincinnati had been experimentally telecast in the New York area; the first televised World Series was that of 1947, with the National Broadcasting Company, which had maintained Series radio rights for the past decade, adding video coverage that reached perhaps half a million people in the Northeast. Following the precedent established in selling radio rights, the Yankees, Dodgers, Giants, Cubs, and subsequently other franchises individually negotiated contracts granting regular-season TV rights to particular stations. The amounts paid by the broadcasters varied according to the size of the local market for televised advertising—according to population, in other words. Thus from the outset the New York and Chicago clubs realized substantial additional revenue from television, whereas for teams in smaller markets such as St. Louis, Cincinnati, Washington, and Cleveland, the new medium made little difference financially. By 1959, for example, the Yankees were already realizing $1 million from television rights alone, Washington only $150,000.

All big-league franchises did share equally in All-Star Game and World Series broadcast revenues. Under a contract negotiated by the commissioner's office late in 1950, NBC paid $6 million for radio-TV rights for the period 1951–1956; for 1957–1962, the fee jumped to $15 million.

Apart from the appeal of television as a stay-at-home, general-entertainment medium, televised major-league baseball directly undercut support for minor-league teams within range of the telecasts. In 1940, in the heyday of radio, the major-league owners had agreed to ban broadcasts of games beyond a fifty-mile radius of their ballparks. Had that rule remained in force, television's impact on the minors would have been less ruinous, although even then the Newark and Jersey City franchises, among many others, wouldn't have survived. (As early as 1950 those two cities had dropped out of the International League, unable to compete with Dodgers, Yankees, and Giants telecasts.)

In 1951 Organized Baseball found itself under investigation by the U.S. House of Representatives Subcommittee on the Study of Monopoly Power, as well as threatened by still another suit attacking the reserve clause. No legislation came out of that congressional inquiry; two years later, moreover, the U.S. Supreme Court would reaffirm baseball's privileged legal status. Yet the major-league club owners sought to avoid controversy by lifting restrictions on radio-television transmissions. The fate of the Newark Bears and Jersey City Giants now awaited numerous other minor-league clubs.

In June 1953 the American Broadcasting Company telecast a Saturday afternoon game from Comiskey Park, Chicago, between the White Sox and Indians. Blacked out around major-league cities, that initial "Game of the Week" offering reached far into the South and West, transmitted by hundreds of stations in what New York's literati liked to call the "hinterlands." Although people everywhere had become accustomed to All-Star Game and World Series telecasts and the Mutual Broadcasting System had been carrying a daily radio game for years, millions of Americans *watched* their first regular-season big-league contest that afternoon.

From that point on, the minors had little chance. In 1955 the Columbia Broadcasting System took over the TV Game of the Week, bringing in Dizzy Dean to do the play-by-play for Saturday and subsequently Sunday games. Fifteen years earlier, his pitching career cut short by arm trouble, Dean had moved into the broadcasting booth for the St. Louis Browns, and in 1950 he came to New York to work Yankees games on local radio and television. Dean's corn-pone humor, fractured grammar, rambling game narration, and tireless self-promotion had already endeared him to New Yorkers; now, thanks to CBS's Game of the Week, he became something of a national folk hero. Only a minority of viewers complained that the action on the field was often secondary to the ruminations of "Ol' Diz" on everything from quail-hunting to the Gas House Gang.

A final factor weakening the minors was the movement of major-league franchises into what had previously been minor-league territory. Milwaukee, Baltimore, Kansas City, San Francisco, and Los Angeles-Hollywood, all once strong upper-minors territories, went big-league in the fifties, as would Houston, Minneapolis-St. Paul, Atlanta, San Diego, Montreal, Oakland, and Seattle by the end of the next decade. Relatively little territory would remain that wasn't within the orbit of a major-league franchise. Older big-league clubs, moreover, became in effect regional franchises with the advent of high-speed freeways that tied Americans closer than ever to metropolitan centers. From June through August, a majority of customers for St. Louis Cardinals, Cincinnati Reds, or Boston Red Sox weekend games typically came from distances of fifty miles or more.

What happened to the Hopkinsville (Kentucky) Hoppers was fairly typical of the fate that befell teams in the lower minors. A member of the Kitty (Kentucky-Illinois-Tennessee) League, the nation's oldest Class D circuit, the Hoppers drew 56,569 in 1946. By 1952, needing thirty-five thousand fans to break even, they could attract only twenty-one thousand. Unable to compete with television, drive-in movies, and boating, fishing, and swimming at newly developed Kentucky Lake, Hoppers owner Bill Goff decided to give up and divide his ballpark property into building lots. The collapse of the Kitty League as a whole soon followed.

In the majors, crowds fell off more in the American League than in the National, mainly because of the Yankees' domination. New York pennants in every year but two from 1949 to 1964 discouraged attendance even at Yankee Stadium, particularly in those seasons (1956, 1958, and 1960) when the Yankees tucked the flag away early. Players came and went in Casey Stengel's scheme of things, but the usual result was another championship.

Unwilling to hang on simply to draw his $90,000 salary, Joe DiMaggio quit after a poor 1951 season, just short of his thirty-seventh birthday. His place was readily taken by twenty-year-old Mickey Mantle, the most powerful switch-hitter baseball had ever seen. Besides that, the young Oklahoman was a much faster base runner than DiMaggio and covered center field almost as well, if with considerably less grace.

With the departure of the great DiMaggio, the Yankees' machine never missed a click. Berra continued behind the plate season after season; Ford, following two years in military service, became one of baseball's top pitchers. Rizzuto, Henrich, Raschi, Lopat, and Reynolds gave way to the likes of Billy Martin, Tony Kubek, Elston Howard, and Bob Turley, but the Yankees kept on winning—nearly all the time. Except for Berra, Mantle, and a couple of others, Stengel continued to platoon faithfully and astutely, while George Weiss finagled whatever extra material the Yankees needed at critical times. The intangible "Yankees tradition" seemed to make a better player of almost anybody who donned New York pinstripes.

The NL was much more competitive, even though Brooklyn remained the class of the league. In 1951 Philadelphia's Whiz Kids, from whom great things had been expected for years to come, fizzled and fell to fourth place. Charlie Dressen's Dodgers built a lead of thirteen and one-half games, only to watch it fade as Leo Durocher's New York Giants went 37–7 in August and September. At the end the two teams were dead even—ninety-six wins and fifty-eight losses apiece.

The teams split the first two games of the tie-necessitated playoff. In the decisive matchup, at the Polo Grounds, the Giants trailed 4–2 and were down to their last out, but had put two runners on base. Dressen waived in Ralph Branca to relieve weary Don Newcombe. Branca's first pitch was a high, inside fastball that Giants outfielder Bobby Thomson lined into the short left-field seats to give the Giants the pennant. Because it was described to a national radio audience and seen regionally on television (and, of course, because it happened in New York, with its enormous media concentration), Thomson's blast became perhaps baseball's most vivid moment—the "shot heard 'round the world."

Like the Phillies the previous year, the 1951 Giants possessed some fine players but didn't really measure up to the Dodgers overall.

With three blacks in the lineup, though, they now equaled the trail-blazing Dodgers. Former Negro-league star Monte Irvin batted .312, hit twenty-four homers, and led the NL with 121 rbi's. Henry Thompson, given a short trial with the St. Louis Browns four years earlier, held down third base most of the time. Twenty-year-old Willie Mays, a Mobile native signed off the Birmingham Black Barons, came up in May following a torrid start with the Giants' Minneapolis American Association farm club. Although Mays struggled in his first weeks with the Giants, he ended the season with twenty homers, a respectable .274 average, and a reputation for making dazzling plays in the outfield.

The Giants were an obviously tired ball club going into the Series against the Yankees. After winning the opener behind the superb pitching of journeyman left-hander Dave Koslo, they lost four of five. Raschi, Reynolds, and Lopat accounted for all the Yankees' wins, while the Giants' tandem of twenty-three-game winners—Pacific Coast League veteran Larry Jansen and ex-Mexican Leaguer Sal Maglie—took three of the four defeats. Hitless in the first three games, DiMaggio broke out with a single and two-run homer in game four.

Mays's departure for the army early in the 1952 season, Irvin's broken leg, and Jansen's ineffectiveness killed the Giants' chances to repeat. Although Brooklyn also lost Newcombe to military service, the Dodgers were never really threatened by Durocher's club or the third-place Cardinals. Robin Roberts's 28–7 record was the best in the NL in eighteen years, but the still-youthful Phillies continued to flounder around the .500 mark.

The Yankees won again, although they managed only a two-game margin over Cleveland, which now fielded the most ethnically and racially mixed lineup in the majors. Besides Larry Doby (AL home-run leader that year), the Indians' black regulars included Harry Simpson, signed off the Philadelphia Stars, and big Luke Easter, formerly of the Homestead Grays. Third baseman Al Rosen, whose 105 rbi's led the league, was the foremost Jewish player since Hank Greenberg; Roberto Avila, a Mexican citizen, starred at second base; and Mike Garcia, a California Mexican-American, pitched twenty-two victories to go with a like number by Bob Lemon and Early Wynn's twenty-three.

The result of the fourth Yankees-Dodgers Series was the same as the others, even though it took seven games before the American Leaguers prevailed. Joe Black, former Baltimore Elite Giant, had been the major factor in the Dodgers' pennant drive, gaining all but one of his fifteen victories in relief and saving fifteen other games. A surprise starter, Black defeated the Yankees in the opener behind homers by Jackie Robinson, Duke Snider, and Pee Wee Reese. But at Ebbets Field six days later, with the Series tied at three games apiece, Black lost for the second time when Mickey Mantle and Gene Woodling homered and Bob Kuzava, an obscure right-hander, came in to retire the last eight Dodgers and save a 4–2 win.

Even though they still missed Newcombe, player-for-player the 1953 Brooklyn Dodgers were among the strongest teams ever to take the field. Amassing 208 homers, including Duke Snider's forty-two, Roy Campanella's forty-one, and Gil Hodges's thirty-one, the Dodgers batted .285 as a team, scored 955 runs, and won 105 games. Carl Furillo led the majors with a .344 batting average; Jackie Robinson, now thirty-four and spending half his time in left field while rookie Jim "Junior" Gilliam settled at second base, batted .329 and drove in ninety-five runs. Carl Erskine, an Indianian with a big overhand curve, won twenty games to lead an unsteady pitching staff.

For all their talent, the Dodgers succumbed yet again to superior Yankees pitching. Erskine had a fine outing to beat the New Yorkers in game three, and Billy Loes, an unpredictable young right-hander, held on to win the next day's game. But the Yankees flayed Brooklyn pitchers for twenty-eight runs and forty-one hits in winning on four other occasions. Second baseman Billy Martin, who went 12–24 with two homers and eight rbi's, led the Yankees' attack.

Nearly everybody had supposed that, given the overall attendance slump and the Browns' historic financial woes, the St. Louis AL franchise would be the first to move to another city. (The Browns had survived in the postwar years by selling players—for $1,290,000 from 1947 to 1951.) Bill Veeck headed a group that bought the Browns during the 1951 season, and for a while things got better at Sportsman's Park. Veeck pulled out all his old promotional ideas and even a few new ones, the most outrageous being to send a midget named Eddie Gaedel to the plate as a pinch hitter in a game with Detroit. (From a low crouch Gaedel took four high pitches, jogged to first, then proudly gave way to a pinch runner.) Veeck also brought back Satchel Paige, who in 1952 became the AL's top relief pitcher, working in forty-six games, winning twelve and saving ten.

In bringing back Rogers Hornsby, whom his father had fired at Chicago twenty years earlier, Veeck was less successful. Hornsby hadn't managed in the majors since being dismissed by the Browns in 1937, but he had directed pennant winners at Beaumont (Texas League) and Seattle (Pacific Coast League) in 1950 and 1951. Accompanied by a sizable publicity buildup, he signed to manage the Browns for 1952. He lasted exactly fifty games before Veeck, Jr., like Veeck, Sr., decided he couldn't abide Hornsby's scorn for anybody's opinion but his own. (Later that summer Hornsby succeeded Luke Sewell at Cincinnati, where he remained thirteen months in his last managing stint anywhere.)

Veeck wanted to move the Browns to Baltimore, but he'd made such enemies in AL councils—especially New York officialdom—that he couldn't get the unanimous consent he needed. While Veeck prepared to struggle through another losing season, Louis Perini, president of the Boston Braves, ended the majors' half-century of geographical stability by moving that franchise to Milwaukee.

The fortunes of the Braves had waned quickly following their 1948 pennant, and by 1952 they were a seventh-place team attracting only about 250,000 to Braves Field. Warren Spahn had become the game's top left-hander, but aside from Spahn and Eddie Mathews, a young third baseman who hit twenty-eight homers in his rookie season, the Braves had little to offer their fans. Even Sam Jethroe, former Cleveland Buckeye who batted well and led the NL in stolen bases his first two seasons, went into a deep slump in 1952 and, at thirty, was all but washed up in the majors.

The move to Milwaukee provided instant rejuvenation for the Braves, both on the field and at the ticket windows. Managed by Charlie Grimm (a popular figure in the area going back to his early-forties tenure with the local American Association club), the Milwaukee Braves attracted some 1.8 million customers, as people came from all over Wisconsin to enjoy themselves at new, publicly financed County Stadium. The Braves finished way behind Brooklyn but still in second place with a 92–62 record, twenty-eight games better than the previous year's Boston entry. Spahn led the majors with twenty-three wins; Mathews knocked forty-seven homers. The next year, with a third-place team, the Milwaukee franchise became the NL's first to surpass two million paid admissions; in each of the next four years, the Braves would continue to top the two-million mark.

It was one of the great success stories of the 1950s—and an utterly compelling example for owners of other ailing big-league franchises. A frustrated Bill Veeck sold out at the end of the 1953 season, during which the Browns lost an even one hundred games and played before 297,238 loyalists. As soon as Veeck was out of the way, Yankees owners Del Webb and Dan Topping gave their blessing to the Browns' relocation to Baltimore; the rest of the AL promptly approved. Sportsman's Park was sold to August A. Busch, new owner of the Cardinals and the nation's foremost beer baron, who renovated it and renamed it Busch Stadium.

The next April, with parades and other civic festivities, major-league ball returned to Baltimore for the first time since 1902. Some forty-six thousand fans turned out for the home opener, many of them having to climb over bricks, cement rubble, and boards to get to their seats in Memorial Stadium, which was still being revamped for base-ball. Although the locale, the manager (Jimmy Dykes), and the nickname (Orioles) were all different, it was still basically the old Browns on the field—a seventh-place team that again lost one hundred games. Yet the novelty of being able to watch the Yankees and other practitioners of authentically big-league baseball produced a season's attendance of about 850,000, far more than the Browns had ever drawn in St. Louis.

A third franchise shift in three years took place before the 1955 season when the Athletics deserted Philadelphia for Kansas City. If St. Louis had never been big enough to support two major-league clubs, then Philadelphia, still the nation's fourth-largest city, had always seemed to be. Yet besides being unable to play Sunday home dates until 1934, the two Philadelphia teams had frequently offered wretched baseball, all too often in the same season.

In the post–World War II years the Phillies won a pennant and finally started making money consistently, while the Athletics, despite improving to four fourth-place showings, ended up in the red most of the time. Connie Mack finally quit managing in 1950, at the age of eighty-eight—after 7,878 games, nine pennants, five world's championships, and seventeen finishes in the league cellar. He and his sons continued to operate the franchise for three years before selling out to Arnold Johnson, who happened to own the ballpark in Kansas City where the Yankees' American Association farm club played, and who only recently had sold his controlling interest in Yankee Stadium.

After a decent interval of one season, Johnson received approval to set up shop in Kansas City. In the winter of 1954–1955, historic Muehlebach Field was razed and, on its foundations, new double-decked Municipal Stadium was erected, with a capacity of about thirty-five thousand. Managed by Lou Boudreau, the Athletics in their Kansas City incarnation rose to sixth place and drew 1,330,000, second in the AL only to the Yankees' million and a half.

Attendance in Kansas City peaked that first year; it didn't take long for mid-continent fans to sour on a franchise that seemed somehow still tied to the Yankees. Season by season, the Athletics' best players went to New York in exchange for "promising youngsters" who usually settled into mediocrity. Kansas City was officially a big-league city, but plenty of people there and elsewhere wondered whether the ball club wasn't still effectively a Yankees farm.

As attendance and profits fell and long-anchored franchises headed elsewhere, one element of normality did return once a cease-fire was negotiated in Korea in mid-1953—a couple of dozen players who'd been drafted at the height of the Asian conflict were again in big-league uniforms. The most illustrious was Ted Williams, who, because of a shortage of experienced pilots, had been reactivated as a Marine aviator early in the 1952 season, at age thirty-three. After flying thirty-nine combat missions in Korea (and narrowly escaping death in a crash landing), Williams returned in August 1953, in time to bat .407 and hit thirteen homers in thirty-seven games.

Willie Mays, Whitey Ford, Don Newcombe, and Curt Simmons were among other notables who'd rejoined their teams by the spring of 1954. The Korean War had moderately affected baseball's personnel situation but had barely touched general operations. U.S.-Soviet and U.S.-Chinese hostility remained intense, but for baseball, about the only evidence of the continuing Cold War would be an interval in the mid-fifties when the Cincinnati Reds deemed it politic to become "Redlegs."

In 1954, at twenty-three, Willie Mays established himself as one of baseball's best—a multitalented, effervescent young man who was a pleasure to watch and, as Leo Durocher never tired of saying, a pleasure to manage. For all-around excellence, Mays's center-field play drew comparisons to Joe DiMaggio's, although nobody ever claimed that Mays, making catches at his belt buckle and losing his cap on every other outfield chance, did it as elegantly as had the Yankee Clipper.

Mays led the majors with a .345 batting average, hit forty-one homers, drove in 110 runs, and scored 119. His performance and that of twenty-one-game winner Johnny Antonelli, onetime Boston Braves bonus baby, keyed the Giants' pennant drive. They finished a fairly comfortable five games ahead of Brooklyn, where taciturn Walter Alston, after many years of managing Dodgers farm clubs, had succeeded the loquacious Dressen. Neither Newcombe nor anybody else pitched well for the Dodgers, who made it something of a race mainly because Gil Hodges and Duke Snider had big years at bat.

After five world's championships in five years, the Yankees finally didn't win a pennant. With Yogi Berra and Mickey Mantle having fine seasons, they did win 103 games (the most for a Yankees club since 1942); but Cleveland won 111, one more than even the fabled '27 Yankees.

Indians manager Al Lopez, a soft-spoken Floridian who held the major-league record for games caught, was blessed with the best pitching in baseball. The Cleveland staff's 2.78 earned run average was the lowest in either league in a decade; Early Wynn and Bob Lemon pitched twenty-three victories apiece, Mike Garcia won nineteen, Art Houtteman fifteen, and Bob Feller thirteen in only nineteen outings. Roberto Avila, at .341, was the AL's top batter; Larry Doby led in homers and rbi's; and Al Rosen provided most of the rest of the Indians' offense.

Durocher's Giants confounded the odds-makers by sweeping the Indians in four straight. Held to a .190 batting average, the Indians could score only nine runs to New York's twenty-one. In the opener at the Polo Grounds, Mays throttled an Indians rally with a spectacular back-to-home-plate catch on Vic Wertz's 440-foot drive, and little-known James "Dusty" Rhodes pinch-hit a game-winning three-run homer. Rhodes tied game two with a pinch single, later put it out of reach with another homer, and then drove in two runs with a pinch single in game three.

Although the two games at the Polo Grounds were fifty-two-thousand-plus sellouts, about four hundred thousand fewer people had paid to see the Giants during the regular season than had watched a fourth-place team seven years earlier. Cleveland's 1954 attendance was a million less than in 1948, when, to be sure, the pennant race had been far more suspenseful. Going to either the Polo Grounds or Municipal Stadium—with their numerous bad seats, run-down environs, and (in the case of the Polo Grounds) scarce parking—was something many people who still considered themselves Giants or Indians fans were no longer willing to do, at least not on a regular basis.

With major-league attendance way down and the minors falling apart, the times seemed to demand imaginative, visionary leadership. "Baseball needs another Judge Landis," went a common plaint of the period, but after Landis died the club owners had been determined never to have another "czar." Even Happy Chandler didn't prove sufficiently pliant; in 1951 the owners dismissed him and gave the commissioner's job to Ford Frick, a former sportswriter, onetime ghostwriter for Babe Ruth, and NL president since 1934. Perhaps Frick's most notable achievement had been to push for the creation of the National Baseball Hall of Fame; as commissioner, he would generally follow the owners' wishes. Frick, wrote a critic in 1962, "walks softly and carries no stick at all."

Except for the Yankees' owners, Walter O'Malley was the strongest force with which Frick had to contend. As early as 1955, O'Malley wrote off Ebbets Field as a hopelessly small, outdated home for the Dodgers; either he got a new physical plant in Brooklyn within the next few years, he said, or he might move his ball club. In the meantime, even though Dodgers attendance fell to about 1.2 million, O'Malley made money from television rights. (For the benefit of viewers of experimental color telecasts, he even had red numbers put on the front of the Dodgers' uniforms.) Seeking to hype attendance by a change of scenery, O'Malley got the rest of the NL owners to agree to his scheduling a few games in otherwise-unused Roosevelt Stadium in Jersey City.

Whatever O'Malley intended to do, the Dodgers still could field more talent than anybody else in the NL. In 1955, while the defending-champion Giants barely finished above .500, Brooklyn outdistanced Milwaukee by thirteen and one-half games. Newcombe returned to form with twenty wins, and Snider, Campanella, Hodges, and Furillo headed up baseball's most potent attack. Meanwhile the Yankees regained their accustomed eminence, winning a tight AL race over Cleveland and Chicago.

In the World Series the Dodgers finally triumphed, although it took them seven hard-fought games to do it. The Series hero was Johnny Podres, a young left-hander who came off a 9–10 regular-season record to beat the Yankees in two complete games—the latter a shutout to win it for Brooklyn. Walter Alston, whose big-league playing career had consisted of one time at bat (he struck out), had steered "dem Bums" to the world's title that had eluded all his Ebbets Field predecessors.

In 1956 Newcombe ran up a 27–7 record as Brooklyn won again. The Dodgers built a big lead, then had to fight off both Milwaukee, where Fred Haney succeeded Charlie Grimm a third of the way into the season, and the Cincinnati Reds (or Redlegs), who tied the Giants' 1947 record with 221 home runs while becoming the final franchise to reach a million in home attendance. By a margin of one game over the Braves and two over Cincinnati, Brooklyn gained its sixth pennant in ten years.

The Yankees coasted in by nine games over Cleveland, and Mickey Mantle was the top player in the majors that year. Usually troubled by bad knees, Mantle stayed healthy in 1956 and, at twenty-four, enjoyed one of the best seasons anybody ever had. Besides hammering fifty-six homers from both sides of the plate, Mantle batted .353, drove in 130 and scored 132 runs, and had a .705 slugging average—all majors-leading totals and more than enough to bring him AL Most Valuable Player honors.

For various reasons, the 1956 World Series would prove exceptionally memorable. It was the seventh and last Dodgers-Yankees "subway series" and also the last for Jackie Robinson. It capped a comeback by thirty-nine-year-old Sal Maglie, picked up by Brooklyn in time to win thirteen games plus the Series opener, at Ebbets Field. It was a Series that produced three shutouts but also twelve homers by the Yankees—two by Billy Martin and three each by Mantle and Berra. And in game five, at Yankee Stadium, big Don Larsen, a bibulous, run-of-the-mill right-hander, threw only ninety-seven pitches in accomplishing the first hitless game in Series history and the first *perfect* game in the majors since 1922. Mantle's homer off Maglie was all the offense Larsen needed. Two days later, in game seven, the Yankees pounded Newcombe and four other Brooklyn moundsmen for nine runs. Johnny Kucks threw a shutout and the Yankees were world's champions for the seventeenth time.

In the post–World War II period the Yankees had beaten National League winners six times in seven tries, yet in the current decade, argued many close observers of year-by-year major-league competition, the NL had become stronger overall, with more outstanding young players and a more interesting style of play. From 1933 through 1949 the AL won twelve of sixteen All-Star games, but in 1950, at Comiskey Park, a fourteenth-inning homer by the Cardinals' Al "Red" Schoendienst gave the National Leaguers their first victory since 1944. Of the twelve games played over the remainder of the decade, the Nationals won eight. (Between 1959 and 1962, to fatten the players' pension fund, two games were played each summer.)

Part of the explanation for the NL's supposed superiority was that—with the notable exception of Cleveland—NL clubs showed a greater willingness to scout, sign, and promote black players. Starting the 1957 season, the NL featured such black standouts as the Giants' Willie Mays, Milwaukee's Henry Aaron and Bill Bruton, the Cubs' Ernie Banks, and Cincinnati's Frank Robinson and Brooks Lawrence. All told, some eighteen blacks held positions on NL rosters in 1957.

That season American League teams fielded only eight black players. Larry Doby, now with the White Sox, had started to fade, although teammate Orestes "Minnie" Minoso, a black Cuban originally signed out of the Negro leagues by Cleveland, continued to be one of the AL's top performers. In 1955, after Vic Power, a black Puerto Rican judged too flamboyant for the dignified Yankees, was dealt to the Athletics, Elston Howard, a quiet, hard-hitting catcher-outfielder, became New York's first black player. At Baltimore, Clifford "Connie" Johnson, onetime Kansas City Monarch, pitched fourteen victories in 1957 to help the Orioles rise to fifth place.

By 1956–1957 Roy Campanella was on the downside of a career that had brought three Most Valuable Player awards; Don Newcombe, plagued by alcoholism, had also seen his best days. Jackie Robinson, unceremoniously traded to the Giants late in 1956 for a second-rate pitcher and $30,000, retired to pursue a variety of lucrative business ventures and to become a civil-rights spokesman. Yet already the National League had moved into a second generation of black players, including Mays (twenty-six), Banks (twenty-six), Aaron (twenty-three), Frank Robinson (twenty-one), and Pittsburgh's Roberto Clemente, a twenty-two-year-old Puerto Rican who hit line drives everywhere and showed a powerful arm from right field.

The presence of such men as Clemente, Minoso, and Power pointed up an infrequently noted consequence of the passing of Jim Crow baseball: Jackie Robinson had also opened the doors for black and racially mixed Caribbean-area players, who otherwise would have spent their careers in the Negro leagues, Cuba, Puerto Rico, Venezuela, the Dominican Republic, or Mexico.

To be sure, racial discrimination was still very much part of the lives of blacks throughout Organized Baseball—in Florida during spring training, in southern minor-league towns, often in northern cities as well. If Jackie Robinson never had it made, neither did any of his successors; and the road to *las ligas grandes* was especially hard for black Hispanic Americans, forced to struggle with problems of language and culture as well as race.

Big-league organizations recruited black players with varying degrees of enthusiasm, sometimes with no enthusiasm at all. After they traded pitcher Brooks Lawrence to Cincinnati early in 1956, the St. Louis Cardinals didn't have a black regular until Curt Flood occupied center field two years later. Also in 1958, substitute infielder Osvaldo "Ozzie" Virgil, from the Dominican Republic, became Detroit's first nonwhite player. Infielder John Kennedy came up for five games with the Phillies at the end of the 1957 season, but not until 1959, when former Giant Ruben Gomez (a Puerto Rican) joined their pitching staff, did the Phillies have a player of black ancestry for a full season. It was still another year before two blacks, infielders Juan "Pancho" Herrera and Tony Taylor, both native Cubans, broke into the Phillies' everyday lineup.

The Boston Red Sox held out longest; Tom Yawkey's club remained an all-white team until July 21, 1959. On that date, twelve years and three months after Jackie Robinson had taken the field for the Dodgers, Elijah "Pumpsie" Green debuted at shortstop for the Red Sox. Once asked why Boston had been the last to add a black man to its roster, Yawkey explained that blacks were "clannish," so that when they somehow got the idea the Red Sox didn't want black players, "they all decided to sign with some other club." In any case, "we didn't want one because he was a Negro. We wanted a ballplayer."

If, in the manner of the Negro leagues, blacks tended to play with greater style and verve than whites, in personal terms they tended to be equally undemonstrative. Of whatever color, contemporary players seemed to lack both the personality and the competitive temperament of the old-timers. While that line of argument stretched back irregularly over thirty years, such allegations took on a new sharpness in the 1950s, in the midst of baseball's obvious need to reawaken people's interest in coming to the ballparks.

In 1952, in a widely discussed two-part piece in the weekly magazine *Life*, Ty Cobb brought into focus his long-standing discontents with baseball and ballplayers in the post-Cobb era. Cobb gave high praise to Phil Rizzuto and Stan Musial, but most present-day players, he charged, "limped along on one cylinder." Obsessed with trying to hit home runs, they failed to master the intricacies of the game; they were "a fragile lot" that gave in too much to injuries; in general they were unwilling to pay the price to reach the top. The men of his time, on the other hand, had been "a strange, hard-bitten and ambitious crew—up from the small towns and by no means eager to go back, trained at nothing but that one profession and battling to hang on to it to their last breath."

Others were inclined to agree with Cobb that contemporary big-leaguers just weren't as tough as the old-timers. Players now stayed in the best hotels and received generous meal allowances, traveled on air-conditioned trains (and, increasingly, airplanes), played most of their games in cooler night air, received the attentions of team physicians and professional trainers—in short, enjoyed the best of everything.

Moreover, by the late fifties (about ten years too late for Pete Reiser) most concrete outfield walls were padded, and dirt "warning tracks" helped fielders get their bearings as they chased deep fly balls. As required by league regulations, batters now wore either plastic batting helmets (mandated by Branch Rickey for the Pirates as early as 1952) or rigid liners inside their cloth caps. If all that made players' lives easier and safer, then surely, so the argument went, they must have become less ruggedly competitive.

"Where are the drunks of yesteryear?" Bill Veeck plaintively asked. Veeck wanted to know what had happened to the breed of roistering, rollicking, tobacco-spitting, hard-drinking men who'd loved the game and, in turn, been loved by the fans. "What we have [today]," said Veeck, "are good gray ballplayers, playing a good gray game." According to Roger Angell (in one of his earliest reflections on baseball), both the colorful eccentrics and players with "that aura of distinction and excitement that distinguishes a true star" had pretty much passed from the scene. Angell perceived "a flattening out of differences," so that "off the field most ballplayers now look and act like suburban householders instead of like giants."

Articles in popular magazines by two of the leading players of the day added to doubts about the dedication of contemporary professionals. In 1956, in the biweekly Collier's, Duke Snider admitted that he played baseball "for money, not fun," and complained about the amount of time away from his family taken up in long road trips, about abusive fans, unfair sportswriters, and martinet managers (namely the deposed Charlie Dressen). All in all, Snider said, "I feel that I'd be just as happy if I never played another baseball game again."

Three years later Jackie Jensen, slugging Red Sox outfielder, offended many Saturday Evening Post readers when he said that the honor of being named AL Most Valuable Player for 1958 was less important than the big pay raise it entitled him to. "The more money I get," announced Jensen, "the sooner I can quit." Like Snider, Jensen hated protracted absences from his wife and children; most of all, he hated (and feared) flying, which by 1960 would account for eighty-five percent of major-league travel. Admitting that he wasn't "consumed by a passion for the game, as many men are," Jensen looked forward to retiring early. (Which he would do in 1961, at thirty-four.)

Of course, such attitudes—a determination to make as much as possible as quickly as possible, a growing weariness with the travels and travails of a ballplayer's life—had been common to plenty of Snider's and Jensen's predecessors. The only difference was that those two players were prepared to air their feelings in mass-circulation magazine pieces. As for the tendency on the part of people such as Veeck to pine for the hard-living old-timers, two points might be made: The "drunks of yesteryear" had frequently ended up with blighted careers and broken families; and in the 1950s baseball still had plenty of rogues and reprobates, even if sportswriters still were usually as reluctant to report off-the-field misconduct—at least that of stars—as they'd been in Babe Ruth's time.

In the midst of widespread grumbling about the current state of the game and the men who played it, Bucky Harris sagely remarked, "I can't remember a period when old-timers didn't bemoan the quality of the players following them." Whether because it had a longer history as an organized sport, because its athletes generally achieved longer careers and perspectives, or because the unique versatility and refinement of skills it required seemed to allow for relatively little change in players' abilities, baseball had always generated arguments about the relative merits of past and present players and teams—much more so than other team sports. Such arguments couldn't be proven one way or another, but the fact that they still went on was proof of baseball's persistent appeal in the troubled fifties.

For all of baseball's power to perpetuate a strong sense of its own history (often a preference for past over present), any fair-minded person would have to acknowledge that the caliber of play in the 1957 World Series could hardly have been better. The Milwaukee Braves broke their own NL attendance record in giving that baseball-and-beer-loving city its first major-league title. Henry Aaron, who'd led the league in batting in 1956, turned on the power in '57, with forty-four homers and 132 rbi's to go with a .322 average. The Braves won by eight games over the St. Louis Cardinals, for whom Stan Musial batted .351 to lead the NL for the seventh (and last) time. Brooklyn faded to third, eleven games out; the best thing about the Dodgers' season was young Don Drysdale, a towering, sidearm right-hander who posted a 17–9 record.

Although Mickey Mantle and other Yankees spent much of the summer disabled, Casey Stengel again demonstrated how to win by constantly mixing regulars and substitutes, veterans and youngsters. None of Stengel's pitchers won more than sixteen games, but six won at least ten. Bob Grim, a twenty-game winner and Rookie of the Year in 1954, worked out of the bullpen in '57 with great effectiveness, compiling a 12–8 record with nineteen saves.

The 1957 Cleveland Indians dropped all the way to sixth place and drew fewer than 750,000 people—a falloff of nearly three-fourths from the glorious 1948 season. Boston finished third, thirteen games behind the Yankees, but Ted Williams made the season a memorable one for Red Sox fans by batting .388 and, at thirty-nine, becoming the oldest man ever to win a major-league batting title. Although he accumulated only 420 official at bats, Williams hit thirty-eight homers and drove in eighty-eight runs. At $100,000, Williams and Stan Musial drew the top salaries in baseball.

The World Series sent Yankee-haters—of whom there were tens of millions by now—into ecstasy. Although twenty-one-game-winner Warren Spahn received credit for one of the Braves' victories, the Series pitching star was right-hander Lew Burdette, a fidgety, thirty-year-old West Virginian who'd pitched seventeen wins during the season. Reputed to possess the majors' best illegal spitball, Burdette beat the Yankees 4–2 in game two, then shut them out 1–0 in game five. At Yankee Stadium, with the Series tied at three games, Burdette came back to throw another shutout, 5–0. Aaron was the batting star with five homers and a .393 average; Eddie Mathews contributed four solo homers.

The baseball map was about to change again. In August 1957, Horace Stoneham announced that at the end of the season he would move his New York Giants to San Francisco. Willie Mays's brilliant all-around play hadn't been enough to keep the Giants from going into sharp decline following their stunning victory in the 1954 Series, and Leo Durocher was fired after a poor third-place showing in 1955. Under Bill Rigney the Giants fell to sixth the next season and stayed there in '57. Meanwhile attendance sank to Depression-era levels and the Polo Grounds continued to deteriorate.

Given Stoneham's known plans and Walter O'Malley's long-held dissatisfaction with his situation in Brooklyn, nobody should have been shocked when, in October 1957, O'Malley announced that he was transplanting the Dodgers to Los Angeles. For two years he'd sought a new baseball stadium in Brooklyn, and while he intended to build the facility with his own money, he wanted the Greater New York planning officials to grant him a building site in the heart of the borough, one that would be sufficiently spacious to allow for ample parking. Frustrated by seemingly endless political wrangling and bureaucratic entanglement, O'Malley gave up and decided to leave Brooklyn altogether. For Brooklyn fans—a dwindling number of whom had found their way to Ebbets Field in the past decade—it was an absolutely crushing loss, arguably the greatest treachery by an American since Benedict Arnold.

Despite what Donald Barnes had assumed on the eve of Pearl Harbor as he sought to relocate his St. Louis Browns, airline service to the Pacific Coast probably wouldn't have been adequate for baseball scheduling needs back in 1941, and would have remained problematical at any time up to 1957. That year the commercial airlines put into service the Boeing 707 jet transport—an aircraft that could traverse the continent in about six hours and enable a ball club to leave Los Angeles or San Francisco in the morning and be in St. Louis in plenty of time for that night's game. Not coincidentally, Stoneham's and O'Malley's decisions to relocate their franchises on the other side of the continent followed shortly upon the 707's introduction.

The arrival of the Giants and Dodgers shattered the stability of the Pacific Coast League. In the late forties and early fifties, before the bottom fell out of minor-league attendance, the PCL had entertained strong hopes of developing into a legitimate third major league. Some Coast League players had even signed multiyear contracts in anticipation of becoming, in effect, back-door big-leaguers. Instead the Dodgers and Giants occupied the PCL's two most-prosperous cities and forced out *three* PCL franchises: the San Francisco Seals, Los Angeles Angels, and Hollywood Stars.

Major-league-quality physical plants were available for neither the Dodgers nor Giants, but at least the Giants had a baseball park. While the Giants occupied Seals Stadium, built in 1931 and seating about twenty-four thousand, the Dodgers moved into the Los Angeles Coliseum, an enormous oval originally constructed for the 1932 Olympic Games. With uncovered, bleacher-type seating for nearly one hundred thousand, the Coliseum was totally unsuited to baseball. As laid out for the 1958 season, its outfield distances were 390 feet down the right-field line, 435 to dead center, and a bare 250 down the left-field line, where a forty-foot screen was raised in an effort to keep home runs at an acceptable figure. Even at that, 183 of the 193 homers hit at the Coliseum in 1958 went to left field.

The San Francisco Giants drew well over a million into their little park and, with a power-hitting Puerto Rican named Orlando Cepeda joining Mays in the batting order, jumped to third place. For the Los Angeles Dodgers, it was a season of tribulation. Paralyzed from the neck down in an auto accident the previous winter, Roy Campanella would never play in Los Angeles or anywhere else. Obviously bothered by the strange Coliseum environment, veterans Gil Hodges, Duke Snider, Carl Furillo, and Johnny Podres all had bad years. Thus while 1,845,556 Southern Californians thronged to watch big-league ball in the flesh, the new local favorites finished only two games out of last place—the worst showing by a Dodgers team since the World War II years.

Getting twenty-three victories from Warren Spahn and twenty from Lew Burdette, another fine season from Henry Aaron, and heavy hitting from Wes Covington (whom Fred Haney platooned against right-handers), Milwaukee had an easy time repeating as NL champs. Pittsburgh finished second, the first time that had happened since 1944, largely because of right-hander Bob Friend's twenty-two wins. At long last, it appeared, Branch Rickey's efforts were about to pay off.

The Yankees' tenth AL pennant since World War II was even easier than the Braves' encore; at season's end the second-place Chicago White Sox trailed by ten full games. Mickey Mantle slammed forty-two home runs; portly Bob Turley won twenty-one games using the no-windup delivery that Don Larsen had adopted (and that many pitchers would subsequently copy); and Ryne Duren, a wild-throwing, fireballing reliever afflicted with severe myopia and (he would later acknowledge) alcoholism, saved twenty games. With the huge New York market all to themselves, the Yankees drew 1,416,000 people—some sixty thousand *fewer* than in 1957.

At Boston, meanwhile, Ted Williams batted sixty points below his 1957 mark but, at age forty, again led the AL—and again spent a good deal of his time spatting with local scribes. Although some Red Sox fans continued to boo him, most worshiped the no-longer-stringbean Californian, forgiving his temperamental interludes.

The 1958 World Series was a thorough disappointment for those who assumed the Yankees were only the class of an inferior league. After winning three of the first four games, the Braves looked unbeatable. But as Yogi Berra liked to say, "It ain't over 'til it's over." In game five, the New Yorkers knocked out Burdette to win 7–0 behind Turley, and after pushing across two tenth-inning runs to defeat Spahn, they assaulted Burdette again in a four-run eighth to take the Series before a disconsolate Milwaukee crowd. It was the first time since the Pirates did it in 1925 that a team had come back from such a disadvantage.

In 1959, finally getting their bearings at home, the Los Angeles Dodgers surpassed two million in paid admissions at the Coliseum and won California's first major-league pennant. Hodges and Podres had solid years, Don Drysdale won seventeen games, and Duke Snider, helped by the erection of an interior fence that cut the distances in right and right-center by some sixty feet, did plenty of damage in only 370 at bats. Outfielder Wally Moon, obtained from the Cardinals, became a master at slicing balls against or over the "Chinese wall" in left field.

It took a lot to dethrone the Braves, as Aaron enjoyed what may have been the best of his twenty-three big-league seasons: thirty-nine homers, 123 rbi's, and a majors-leading .355 batting average. Eddie Mathews, with a .306 average, forty-six homers, and 114 rbi's, also had one of his best years. Spahn and Burdette won twenty-one games apiece. Despite Elroy Face's remarkable 18–1 record, compiled entirely in relief, Pittsburgh finished a disappointing fourth behind San Francisco, which stayed in the race most of the season on Mays's and Cepeda's hitting and the pitching of Johnny Antonelli and Sam "Toothpick" Jones.

After the 154th game, the Dodgers and Braves both had 88–68 records, the fourth time in the postwar period that a pennant race had ended in a tie. Los Angeles swept two games in the playoff and headed into the World Series to meet the Chicago White Sox.

With nearly everybody slumping, the 1959 Yankees finished third, only four games above .500. Cleveland, sparked by Minnie Minoso (regained from Chicago the previous year) and tall, handsome Rocco Colavito, who cracked forty-two homers, made it a close race into mid-September, when the White Sox pulled away by five games.

Now headed up by Bill Veeck, with Hank Greenberg (who'd first moved into front-office work under Veeck at Cleveland) as part-owner and general manager, Chicago won its first AL pennant since the unhappy events of 1919. Al Lopez's club got strong pitching from Early Wynn, Bob Shaw, and Billy Pierce and timely hitting from an assortment of generally forgettable players. Both at bat and afield, Chicago's key men were second baseman Nelson Fox, a throwback to the punch-and-slap batsmen of earlier decades, and Luis Aparicio, a slightly built Venezuelan shortstop who stole fifty-six bases—the most in the major leagues since 1943 and the second-highest total since 1920.

The 1959 World Series was notable principally for the crowds that witnessed games three, four, and five in the Coliseum. After splitting the first two meetings in Chicago, the Dodgers won the next two at home on the splendid relief pitching of Larry Sherry. Game five, played before 92,706, was a 1–0 win for Chicago, with Shaw, Pierce, and Dick Donovan combining on the shutout and former bonus baby Sanford "Sandy" Koufax, an 8–6 pitcher that season, taking the loss. It ended in game six, at Comiskey Park, where Sherry came on to relieve Podres in the fourth inning and hold the White Sox scoreless. Final score: Los Angeles 9, Chicago 3.

Despite big profits in the Coliseum, Walter O'Malley remained determined to have his own ballpark. Originally assured that he could build in Chavez Ravine, near downtown, O'Malley ran into various kinds of opposition, especially from people who disliked the idea of giving away three hundred acres of valuable public land, not to mention evicting poor Angelenos living at the site. Local authorities finally submitted the issue to the public in the form of a referendum. The narrow victory for O'Malley and his backers probably wouldn't have happened without heavy support from Los Angeles's black voters, who, like blacks everywhere, would always remember the Dodgers as the organization that broke the color line. By 1961 construction was under way on what O'Malley intended to be the finest for-baseball-only facility in the world.

In San Francisco matters went much more smoothly, with the voters approving a bond issue to finance a multipurpose stadium for both the Giants and the National Football League 49ers. Built south of the city on Candlestick Point, a hill overlooking San Francisco Bay, the stadium was the first constructed entirely of reinforced concrete, which made it the first without a single obstructed seat. With a capacity of about forty-five thousand, Candlestick Park was ready for the Giants' home opener on April 12, 1960.

Although it was the latest thing in sports facilities, Candlestick Park stood on a site that was battered by strong, chilling winds most of the time. For Mays, Cepeda, and other right-handed Giants hitters, the prevailing currents from left to right field would be a source of persistent frustration.

That first year at Candlestick Park, the Giants set a new franchise home-attendance record—1,795,386—yet they descended to fifth place, three games behind the Dodgers, whose Brooklyn-era stars had about reached the end of the line. Milwaukee and St. Louis were two games apart in second and third place, and at the top, for the first time in thirty-five years, were the Pittsburgh Pirates, seven games ahead of Milwaukee.

Managed by Danny Murtaugh, the Pirates were a relatively young team that featured no more than three top-notch regulars: the brilliant Roberto Clemente in right field; former basketball All-American Dick Groat, a solid shortstop and the NL's batting leader at .325; and second baseman Bill Mazeroski, a defensive wizard with occasional power. Bob Friend (eighteen wins) and Vernon Law (twenty) were the frontline pitchers, with Elroy Face coming in to save twenty-four of the Pirates' ninety-five victories.

Not a great team by any means, the Pirates were apparently overmatched against a powerful Yankees club that finished eight games ahead of Paul Richards's fast-rising Baltimore Orioles. The Yankees hit 193 home runs, including forty by Mantle and twenty-six by first baseman Bill "Moose" Skowron. Roger Maris, a twenty-five-year-old outfielder obtained in one of the Yankees' numerous deals with Kansas City, struck thirty-seven homers, led the AL with 112 rbi's, and gained Most Valuable Player recognition. New York's spotty pitching depended heavily on bullpen support from thickly bespectacled Ryne Duren and lefty Luis Arroyo, a paunchy NL castoff.

The 1960 World Series was one of the strangest ever played. The Yankees pummeled Pittsburgh's pitching for ten homers, fifty-five runs, and a .338 team batting average; their three victories were by scores of 16–3, 10–0, and 12–0. The Pirates scored only twenty-seven runs, hit only four homers, and batted .256, yet at the end of six games the teams were even up. Game seven, at Forbes Field, was a slugging match in which the Pirates took a 9–7 lead on catcher Hal Smith's two-run homer, only to see Yogi Berra tie it in the top of the ninth with a two-run shot of his own. Then Bill Mazeroski, leading off the bottom of the inning, lined Ralph Terry's pitch over the left-field fence to send the long-denied Pittsburgh fans into rapture.

Capped by that unforgettable Series, the 1960 season was something of a turning point in major-league history—for a number of reasons. For one, it was the final season for Ted Williams; the last of the pre–World War II stars, Williams closed out his glittering career in high style with a home run (his twenty-ninth of the season) in his last time at bat in his last game at Fenway Park. He departed with a .344 career average, 521 homers, 1,839 rbi's, 1,798 runs scored, and endless speculation about what kind of numbers he might have piled up if not for four seasons spent in military service.

Casey Stengel also wouldn't be around for 1961; losing the '60 Series cost him his job. After ten pennants and seven world's titles, the seventy-one-year-old Stengel was too old to continue—or so it appeared to Yankees officialdom. Ralph Houk, a little-used catcher and then a coach under Stengel, moved into the top job. Besides getting rid of Stengel, Yankees owners Webb and Topping also eased out George Weiss, who'd been responsible for Stengel's readily available supply of quality ballplayers.

And after 1960, big-league scouts would no longer be able to mine the rich lode of Cuban baseball talent. At the end of 1958, Marxist-Leninist revolutionaries led by Fidel Castro overthrew the military dictatorship of Fulgencio Batista. Government takeovers of U.S.-owned businesses and trade pacts with Soviet-bloc countries followed, accompanied by increasingly hostile rhetoric emanating from Havana and Washington. In January 1961 the Eisenhower administration broke off diplomatic relations with Castro's government in an effort to isolate Cuba in the Western Hemisphere. Among other things, that brought an abrupt halt to the outward flow of Cuban ballplayers. In the decades to come, baseball would remain at the center of Cuban life as a basic element in a nominally amateur national sports program, one effectively sealed off from the decadent professionalism to the north.

Finally, the 1960 season also closed out a fifty-six-year period in which the National and American leagues consisted of eight teams each and (except for 1919) *scheduled* 154-game seasons. That schema held up despite the migration of five franchises after 1952, but by the end of the decade still another effort to float a third major league had forced Ford Frick and associates to accept the inevitability of expansion. The 1960s would bring not only more changes in baseball's map but eventually a radical restructuring of the competitive framework in the two major leagues.

11.
The
Expansion
Era

The Continental League was Branch Rickey's final moment in the baseball sun. In 1959, at the age of seventy-eight, Rickey threw himself into the promotion of a third major league, one that would establish itself in the huge New York market as well as in Toronto, Buffalo, Minneapolis-St. Paul, and in such booming southern and western cities as Atlanta, Houston, Dallas, and Denver. Given the financial history of the past decade, most wise investors might have written off professional baseball, but Rickey and associates were confident that a new circuit could command enough live spectator interest plus radio-television revenues to produce profits. Hiring scouts and signing a few young players, the Continental Leaguers announced that they intended to have their inaugural season in 1961.

The American and National League owners had to move quickly. In return for agreeing to the NL's reentry into New York, the American Leaguers gained access to the rich Los Angeles territory, hitherto the exclusive domain of Walter O'Malley. Meanwhile Calvin Griffith, who'd inherited the ailing Washington operation from his adoptive father in 1955, secured the rest of the owners' consent to move his franchise to Minneapolis-St. Paul, where, five years earlier, a publicly financed stadium had been built in suburban Bloomington. That left Washington open as the site for a second AL expansion team.

While the National Leaguers projected 1962 for moving back into New York and adding Houston, the AL owners decided to operate with franchises in Los Angeles and Washington in 1961.

Blocked by the movement of the existing major leagues into three of its intended territories, the Continental League died aborning. Like Rickey's almost-forgotten United States League project, it had never gotten beyond the blueprint stage, and Rickey subsequently returned to the St. Louis Cardinals as a paid adviser with little to do. Often described as baseball's most profoundly imaginative and innovative figure, he would die in December 1965, a little short of his eighty-fourth birthday.

So for 1961 the NL remained at eight clubs and a 154-game schedule, while the AL, with ten members, scheduled 162 games, which meant that its teams would meet each other eighteen times. Called the Angels after the old Pacific Coast League entry, the Los Angeles outfit was owned by Gene Autry, onetime star of numerous low-budget Hollywood musical westerns. Autry's team would play its first season in cramped Wrigley Field, the old PCL ballpark now owned by the city.

The new Washington club, still called the Senators, moved into Griffith Stadium, recently vacated by Calvin Griffith's organization. At Minneapolis-St. Paul, Griffith hit upon the idea of calling his team the Minnesota Twins, which made his the first professional sports enterprise named after an entire state.

Baseball fans had to keep reminding themselves that the Minnesota Twins of 1961 were really last year's Washington Senators, whereas this year's Senators were a wholly new team. Like the Los Angeles Angels, the Washington entry was put together almost entirely by drafting from a pool of second- and third-string players designated by the other eight clubs from their reserve lists. Receiving a fixed $75,000 apiece for their pooled reservists, the AL owners realized a nice windfall and gave up little they really needed.

Now managed by Ralph Houk, the 1961 New York Yankees swept to another pennant and a nineteenth world's championship with one of the truly great teams in baseball's history. The Yankees won 109 games, hammered a record-breaking 240 home runs, yielded the second-lowest number of runs in the majors, and made the second-fewest errors. Roger Maris and Mickey Mantle accounted for 115 homers and 270 runs batted in between them. Elston Howard, catching full-time, batted .348, with Yogi Berra taking over left field. (Battling the afternoon shadows at Yankee Stadium, Yogi complained, "It gets late early out there.") Whitey Ford posted a 25–4 record; Luis Arroyo won fifteen games in relief besides saving twenty-nine for Ford and New York's other starters.

In almost any other year the Detroit Tigers, who won 101 times, would have finished first. Using illegal corked bats (as he would admit many years later), Detroit's Norman Cash led the majors with a .361 average, socked forty-one homers, and drove in 132 runs—by far his best production in a seventeen-year career. Teammate Rocky Colavito (acquired from Cleveland two years earlier in an even-up swap for batting champion Harvey Kuenn) contributed forty-five homers and batted in 140 runs.

For most of that 1961 season it seemed that both Mantle and Maris might surpass Babe Ruth's season record of sixty home runs. In the thirty-four years since Ruth had accomplished it, that feat had taken on an almost sacrosanct quality, not only for the Babe's contemporaries but for younger followers of the sport as well. In the intensifying news-media coverage of Mantle's and Maris's home-run parade, the prevailing attitude seemed to be that if anybody were to beat Ruth's record, it ought to be Mantle, a multitalented player in the tradition of DiMaggio, Gehrig, and the Babe himself.

It was, of course, Maris who succeeded where Mantle, Hank Greenberg, Jimmie Foxx, Hack Wilson, and other fifty-homer-plus sluggers had fallen short. His sore-legged teammate dropped out in mid-September with fifty-four, but Maris stayed in the lineup every day, even with the pennant safely won. At Yankee Stadium on October 1, in the final game of the season, he pulled a pitch from Boston's Tracy Stallard into the lower right-field stands for number sixty-one. By then the crew-cut North Dakotan, a naturally shy, introverted young man, had been physically worn down as well as emotionally damaged by a media assault such as neither Ruth nor any other athlete had ever been subjected to.

Roger Maris was a good player—not a great one. A fine outfielder with a superior arm, he would never bat higher than .283 or, except for

1961, total more than thirty-nine home runs. Whereas Ruth had batted .356 when he hit sixty and .342 for his career, Maris could manage only a .269 average in 1961 and a career .258. Worst of all for Ruthian loyalists, Maris broke the Babe's hallowed mark in an expansion year when, as most people realized, AL pitching as a whole was diluted and two staffs consisted mostly of hurlers who would have been in the minors the previous year. Finally, Maris needed all of the new 162-game schedule to surpass Ruth.

As Ruth's ghostwriter and friend, baseball commissioner Ford Frick simply couldn't let Maris's achievement stand unqualified. While he apparently had no problem with the team homer mark set by the Yankees, Frick decreed that in baseball's official records, Maris's sixty-one homers would be accompanied by an asterisk denoting the 162-game season. Presumably, as far as Frick was concerned, Ruth's sixty would remain the "real" home-run record.

It wasn't a good year for taking on the Yankees in the World Series, as the Cincinnati Reds quickly discovered. With Pittsburgh plunging to sixth place and nobody else able to get consistent pitching, the Reds gained their first pennant since 1940, outdistancing Los Angeles by four games. Jim O'Toole, Joey Jay, and Bob Purkey combined for fifty-six wins, while bespectacled Jim Brosnan, author of *The Long Season* (1960), a controversial, unprecedentedly honest book about day-to-day life in the majors, won ten and saved sixteen games. The Reds' attack centered on outfielders Vada Pinson, a .343 hitter, and Frank Robinson, who batted .323, hit thirty-seven homers, drove home 124 runs, and won NL Most Valuable Player honors.

Obviously affected by his summer-long pursuit by swarming newspaper, magazine, television, and radio people, Maris endured a poor Series, making only four hits (one a home run) and batting .105. Mantle, barely able to walk, got into only two games. But the Yankees were so strong otherwise that the "M&M Boys" weren't really needed, and the Reds won only game two, behind Joey Jay. Second baseman Bobby Richardson, first baseman Bill Skowron, and reserve catcher Johnny Blanchard (who totaled twenty homers in only 243 at bats during the season) were the Yankees' batting stars. Whitey Ford blanked the Reds in the opener, then pitched five shutout innings before an ankle injury forced him out of game five. In reaching thirty-two scoreless innings in Series play, Ford eclipsed still another of Ruth's records—by two and one-third innings.

The previous summer, at seventy-four, Ty Cobb had died, still disparaging the past forty years of baseball. (His posthumously published autobiography echoed his complaints even beyond the grave.) Yet for all that was patently unfair in many of Cobb's opinions, he was obviously right in saying that expansion had spread the existing number of big-league-caliber players over too many rosters and too many chronically weak teams.

The Los Angeles Angels, for example, enticed slightly more than six hundred thousand people into their little ballpark to watch a team that finished twenty-one games under .500, yet still did better than both the new Washington entry and Kansas City, tied for tenth with 61–100 records. In the AL's new ten-team setup, six teams lost more than they won, including the Minnesota Twins, who in their new guise edged the Angels for seventh place by half a game.

Undeterred by the obvious, the NL formed its own $75,000-per-player draft pool, fashioned teams for its new Houston and New York franchises, adopted a 162-game schedule, and headed into its first expansion season. The Houston Colt 45's (as the team was called until 1965, when a company producing a malt liquor under that label forced a name change) moved into a hurriedly built, completely uncovered ballpark seating about thirty-two thousand. Colt Stadium, with its staggering heat and swarming mosquitoes, would become the dread of everybody in the NL. Taking over the freshened-up Polo Grounds, the New York NL franchise revived the elegant nickname Metropolitans (after the city's 1880s American Association entry)—again promptly shortened to Mets. Seventy-three-year-old Casey Stengel and sixty-six-year-old George Weiss, both dumped by the Yankees in 1960, signed with the Mets as field manager and general manager, respectively.

With an eye to the future, Houston drafted mostly younger players, whereas the Mets, in competition with the mighty Yankees for the local baseball dollar, not only hired Stengel but drafted Gil Hodges, Richie Ashburn, and several other dimming NL stars. Houston fielded a drab team that drew about 940,000 and finished eighth, five games better than the Chicago Cubs, who'd operated at or near the bottom of the league most of the past fifteen years.

The 1962 New York Mets—a mix of aging veterans and younger men of little ability—were an absolutely awful aggregation that won only forty games and committed more errors (204) than any major-league team in twenty-four years. Yet even in the decrepit Polo Grounds, they drew close to a million people, who found their hapless play somehow endearing.

The fans' favorite was Marvin Throneberry, once a leading light in the Yankees' farm system. A player who hit with power (but rarely) and played an inept first base, "Marvelous Marv" nonetheless became a kind of antihero hero in New York. "No other city," remarked a bemused Bill Veeck, "is so confident of its own preeminence that it could afford to take such an open delight in its own bad taste."

Meanwhile the Washington Senators and Los Angeles Angels started their second seasons in new playing sites—a circumstance that apparently benefited the Angels more than their expansion counterparts. Occupying the just-completed, multipurpose District of Columbia Stadium, the Senators ended up dead last at 60–101. The Angels became Walter O'Malley's tenants in his new Dodger Stadium in Chavez Ravine. There they surprised the 1,330,000 who paid to see them by winning eighty-six games and finishing third—the franchise's best showing over its first nine seasons.

Built for $18 million of O'Malley's money and designed solely for baseball, Dodger Stadium was state-of-the-art in every respect. Seating fifty-two thousand, it provided parking spaces for twenty-four thousand automobiles and offered customers a uniquely attractive, comfortable ballpark environment. It was what Yankee Stadium had been forty years earlier—the ultimate place to watch and play baseball.

The Dodgers' baseball palace was the best thing to come out of a postwar boom in stadium-building that had begun in the early 1950s with the construction of Milwaukee's County Stadium. New or rebuilt plants at Baltimore, Kansas City, Minneapolis-St. Paul, San Francisco, and Washington had preceded Dodger Stadium; and by 1971 New York, Houston, St. Louis, Oakland, San Diego, Cincinnati,

Philadelphia, and Pittsburgh would also have built new sports facilities, as would Anaheim, where in 1966 the Los Angeles AL team relocated as the California Angels.

Dodger Stadium was the only one financed with private capital—and the only one reserved exclusively for baseball. The rest were funded by public bond issues and intended as well for football, concerts, auto shows, and a variety of other public events. For all their increased comforts and conveniences, the multipurpose stadia all looked pretty much alike, prompting a longing for the idiosyncratic, genuinely baseball parks that had already been razed—and a new protectiveness toward the few that survived.

In 1962, the inaugural year for Dodger Stadium, more than two and a half million customers paid to watch a team that—in its Los Angeles as in its Brooklyn incarnation—showed a remarkable affinity for pennant standoffs. This time the Dodgers lost ten of their last thirteen games, enabling the San Francisco Giants, now managed by Alvin Dark, to pull even with a 101–61 record. Led by Willie Mays with forty-nine and Orlando Cepeda with thirty-four, the Giants pounded 204 home runs. All that power backed up a strong pitching corps that included Juan Marichal, a high-kicking Dominican right-hander with a classic overhand curveball.

Walter Alston's Los Angeles club would probably have walked away with the 1962 pennant if Sandy Koufax hadn't been hindered by the arm troubles that prematurely ended his career four years later. Finally mastering the wildness that had plagued him for six seasons, the Brooklyn-born Jewish left-hander had arrived as a big-leaguer in 1961, at the age of twenty-five, by winning eighteen games and striking out 269 batters. In 1962, limited to twenty-eight outings, he won fourteen, including the first of four no-hitters he pitched in four consecutive seasons. Don Drysdale, with a 25–9 record, was the bulwark of that year's Dodgers staff. Offensively, the Dodgers' leading producers were Tommy Davis, a muscular left fielder who led the majors with a .346 batting average and 153 rbi's; Frank Howard, a 6-7, 250-pound right fielder (thirty-one homers, 113 rbi's); and Maury Wills, a slightly built, switch-hitting shortstop. Batting .299, Wills shattered Ty Cobb's supposedly untouchable record of ninety-six stolen bases for a season, which had stood since 1915. In 165 games (including three in the NL playoff), Wills piled up 104 steals, an achievement that by itself did much to revitalize baseball's long-lethargic running attack.

The three-game playoff was decided in the top of the ninth inning of game three, at Los Angeles. Leading 4–2, the Dodgers yielded four runs despite Alston's frantic pitching changes and lost the pennant in a manner that, especially to East Coast fans, was strikingly reminiscent of 1951.

So, to some extent, was the World Series. The Yankees were there again, having overcome power-hitting Minnesota by five games. It was still an excellent Yankees team, although Mantle had been hobbled much of the year and almost everybody hit less than in 1961. Ralph Terry won twenty-three games to compensate for Whitey Ford's drop to seventeen, and again the Yankees came up with effective relief pitching—this time from Marshall "Sheriff" Bridges, a previously (and subsequently) run-of-the-mill left-hander.

Because of a three-day rain delay in San Francisco, it took nearly two weeks to complete the seven-game World Series. Terry capped a Series marked by good pitching with a four-hit, 1–0 shutout at Candlestick Park, as second baseman Bobby Richardson leaped to grab Willie McCovey's scorching line drive for the final out, leaving two Giants base runners stranded and giving the Yankees their twentieth world's championship. It would be their last for fifteen years.

The Yankees still were good enough to capture two more pennants—an easy one in 1963 and then, the next year, a hairsbreadth victory over the Chicago White Sox and Baltimore Orioles. Both times, though, the New Yorkers fell to their NL adversaries in the World Series.

In 1963 the Yankees suffered the most humiliating defeat in the franchise's lustrous history, when they lost the Series to Los Angeles in four straight games. In the opener, at Yankee Stadium, a healthy Koufax—25–5 with a splendid 1.88 earned run average and 306 strikeouts that season—threw third strikes past fifteen Yankees to establish a new Series record, and in game four he held the New Yorkers to a single run while his teammates scrounged two. In the intervening two games, Johnny Podres, hero of the Brooklyn Dodgers' 1955 victory, and sidearming, fastballing Drysdale limited the Yankees to one run and seven hits. For the Series as a whole, the two teams could score only sixteen times.

Although they continued to pack in the fans at home, the Dodgers tailed off to sixth place in 1964. Koufax could make only twenty-nine starts (winning nineteen), and Drysdale's 18–16 record belied a 2.18 earned run average; the Dodgers were sixteenth in the majors in runs scored.

For the first time, the St. Louis Cardinals won with players who weren't mostly farm-system products, although Stan Musial wasn't part of that championship. The congenial, modest "Stan the Man" retired in 1963 after twenty-three seasons in a Cardinals uniform, a .331 career batting average, 3,630 base hits (second only to Cobb at the time), and nearly two thousand rbi's and runs scored.

Managed by longtime organization man Johnny Keane, the 1964 Cardinals survived a gruelling fight with Cincinnati, San Francisco, and Philadelphia. The Phillies, leading by six games with ten to play, stumbled through ten losses in a row to end up tied for second with the Reds, pennant losers by only one game, while the Giants finished only two games out of first.

With Ralph Houk now in the front office, the job of managing the Yankees had fallen to Yogi Berra. Berra inherited a team in decline, even though Mickey Mantle and Elston Howard enjoyed what turned out to be their last good years; Whitey Ford, at thirty-seven, posted seventeen wins; and Jim Bouton, a brassy young right-hander who'd won twenty-one times in 1963, came back to win eighteen.

The 1964 World Series—the fifth Yankees-Cardinals matchup— was a battle all the way. In game seven Bob Gibson, a scowling, fiercely intense right-hander, struck out nine Yankees (for a total of thirty-one in three Series games) and survived three home runs (two by Mantle) in struggling to a 7–5 clinching victory at St. Louis.

As had happened to all baseball dynasties sooner or later, the Yankees fell victim to age, infirmity, and a lack of sufficient new blood. The extraordinarily productive farm system George Weiss had created—twenty-three clubs and some six hundred players in 1949— had dwindled to seven clubs and about one hundred and fifty players by the mid-sixties. Mantle, the heart of the Yankees for more than a decade, was simply no longer capable of holding up for a full season;

Roger Maris would never completely recover from a succession of injuries sustained in 1965, nor would Bouton from severe arm trouble. Howard, Ford, Bobby Richardson, and Tony Kubek all had their best baseball behind them. Yankee Stadium, for all the glamor and legend that attached to it, was showing its age; the South Bronx, where it was situated, had become a high-crime, badly run-down area.

In August 1964, amid protests that a communications conglomerate threatened to take over the American League, the Columbia Broadcasting System purchased the Yankees from the Webb-Topping interests for a record $11.2 million. That season, in winning a fifth straight pennant after a torrid race, the Yankees drew four hundred thousand fewer people than the Mets, who lost 109 games operating in new Shea Stadium, near Flushing, Long Island. (The facility was named for the late William Shea, who was instrumental in influencing the NL to move back into New York.)

The acquisition of the Yankees turned out to be a generally bad deal for CBS. Although the corporation profited from its control of Yankees telecasts, its product did worse and worse, and it didn't help CBS's image when Berra was fired and Johnny Keane hired away from the Cardinals right after the World Series. Yogi's legion of admirers took satisfaction in the Yankees' dive to sixth in 1965, then all the way to the bottom the next year—the first time the team had finished last since 1912.

Early in the 1966 season Ralph Houk succeeded Keane as field manager, giving up his general manager's office to quiet-spoken Lee MacPhail, son of the colorful Larry. While MacPhail and associates studied the Mets' operation to gain pointers on attracting customers, the Yankees struggled through a succession of so-so seasons.

Among various factors that undermined the Yankees' domination were interleague trading and the free-agent draft. Beginning in 1957, it was no longer necessary for a team in one league to obtain waivers on a player before trading him to the other league. That made for greatly increased traffic between the two circuits and also made it easier for teams to trade for what they needed. If fewer players now spent their whole careers in one league, where they had plenty of time to learn opposing pitchers, ballparks, and the like, fewer also found themselves stuck for the duration of their baseball lives on bad teams. And with players moving around more than ever, it became harder for anybody to sustain the success the Yankees and, to a lesser extent, the Dodgers had enjoyed in the post–World War II years.

Late in 1964, nearly three decades behind professional football, the major-league owners finally agreed to a universal draft for ballplayers not already under contract within Organized Baseball, with the last-place teams the previous season automatically entitled to pick first. In the first draft, held in June 1965 at the Commodore Hotel in New York, the Kansas City club, the worst in 1964, started things off by selecting Rick Monday, an Arizona State University outfielder.

Under the provisions of the draft, Kansas City held exclusive negotiating rights to Monday for six months. If the player refused to sign, then his name went back into the pool for the next draft. Monday did sign—for a $100,000 bonus—but Tom Seaver, a pitcher at the University of Southern California drafted by the Dodgers, decided to remain in college. (The Braves subsequently drafted Seaver but lost him when his signing, done before the college season ended, was invalidated. Placed in the pool for a third time, Seaver was drafted and signed by the New York Mets.)

Over time the free-agent draft, by funneling choice talent to the tail-enders each year, exercised a moderately equalizing influence. Farm systems would still be necessary for nurturing and appraising skills, but given the fact that the best amateur players in the country would nearly always show up in the free-agent draft, elaborate scouting became less important. By the early 1970s most big-league teams relied primarily on the Major League Scouting Bureau, which centralized information on players throughout the United States, Canada, and Hispanic America. The far-ranging "bird dog" of baseball lore was no longer basic to the business.

It was no coincidence that the first pick in the first free-agent draft was a college player. By the mid-1960s, baseball in the nation's colleges and universities had undergone something of a renaissance; the major leagues were increasingly looking to the campuses to provide a steady supply of semifinished ballplayers. As early as 1952 *Newsweek* magazine had estimated that about one hundred and fifty current big-leaguers were former college players, although only thirty-one, by

Newsweek's count, had completed their college baseball eligibility before signing professional contracts.

Professional baseball's leaders had never considered the colleges to be a primary training ground, as the owners of professional football and basketball franchises always had. Instead of developing close ties to the colleges (as happened in Japanese baseball), the major leagues plowed huge sums into minor-league farm systems and occasionally raided college campuses for prize prospects. But as the minors continued to diminish and youngsters increasingly opted to attend college on athletic scholarships rather than start at the bottom in Organized Baseball, the collegiate game looked increasingly attractive as a source of talent.

Having benefited from good coaching and 50-to-75-game seasons, ex-collegians tended to spend less time in the minors than noncollegians; by 1968 there were only 130 minor-league teams in operation anyway. In 1967 the NL's top rookies—Cincinnati's Gary Nolan and the Mets' Tom Seaver—had pitched in only twelve and thirty-four games, respectively, in the minors. Minnesota's Rod Carew, the 1967 AL Rookie of the Year, had appeared in only 274 minor-league games.

Not only was the route to the majors usually quicker than in earlier decades, but the doors were now absolutely wide open to everybody. In 1961, for the first time, every team in the majors started the season with at least one black player, and a year later the black-oriented monthly *Ebony* could report that ten black players were earning at least $50,000—with Willie Mays, at $90,000, now reportedly the sport's highest-paid player. Making up nineteen percent of big-league rosters, blacks accounted for twenty-one percent of salary values.

Meanwhile large numbers of black and racially mixed Hispanic Americans entered Organized Baseball, even a few from the U.S.-owned Virgin Islands. The 1964 batting champions in the majors were the Puerto Rican Roberto Clemente (Pittsburgh) and Rookie of the Year Tony Oliva (Minnesota), who was one of the last Cubans to reach the majors. The next year forty-eight players from the Caribbean region appeared on major-league rosters; eight participated in the All-Star Game; and Zoilo Versalles, Minnesota's Cuban-born shortstop, became the first Hispanic American to win Most Valuable Player honors.

More than any other country, the Dominican Republic took up the slack created by the Cuban cutoff. Front-rank Dominican players of the sixties included Juan Marichal, San Francisco's brilliant right-hander; the brothers Felipe, Matty, and Jesus Alou, all members of the Giants in 1963; Cardinals second baseman Julian Javier; and Rico Carty, who in 1970, playing for the Atlanta Braves, became the first Dominican player to win a major-league batting title.

Like native-U.S. black players, Hispanic Americans often performed with more flash and dash than their white peers, and by the mid-sixties it was manifest that one of the major consequences of racial integration had been to boost base-stealing. In 1950, for example, stolen bases in the AL and NL totaled 650, with Sam Jethroe's thirty-five leading the NL and Dom DiMaggio's fifteen topping all American Leaguers. By 1960, the last year of the sixteen-team majors, base runners in the two leagues stole 923 times—a forty-two percent jump in ten years. After that, aggregate league statistics became skewed by the addition of new teams, but by 1965 (a season in which Maury Wills stole ninety-four bases), major-league clubs averaged seventy-two steals; within another three years, that number had jumped to eighty-five.

Besides the influx of speed-oriented Hispanic-American and native-U.S. black players, base-stealing benefited from several additional factors. The artificial surfaces installed in a number of ballparks by the late 1960s and early 1970s, together with lighter-weight uniforms and shoes, added perhaps two steps to a fast runner's getaway. By the 1960s, moreover, pitchers worked under such restrictive rules that umpires were inclined to call balks for little more than a raised eyebrow. Tightened balk rules gave runners an obvious advantage, at the same time that they made for more throws to first and second bases, as pitchers worked to cut down runners' leads. (One could only fantasize about how many bases Ty Cobb might have stolen under the balk rules put into force decades after he retired.)

As a group, NL managers proved more disposed to send base runners than their AL counterparts. In 1968, for example, the two least-active teams on the bases were both in the AL: the last-place

Washington Senators, with twenty-nine steals, and the pennant-winning Detroit Tigers, with a grand total of twenty-five for the entire season.

In earlier periods in baseball's history, base-stealing had correlated inversely with home-run hitting. That still held true in the sixties, albeit to a lesser extent than in the years before and after 1920. In 1950 a total of 2,073 home runs were hit in the major leagues; ten years later homer-hitting had increased modestly—to 2,128. Then, in the expansion era, even with the presence of twenty or so pitchers who would have been pre-1961 minor-leaguers, total home runs in the majors actually *decreased*. In 1950 the sixteen big-league teams had averaged about 130 homers each, against slightly less than a hundred for each of the twenty teams in 1968.

Aggregate run-scoring declined in similar fashion—from 12,013 runs in 1950 (sixteen teams) to 11,109 in 1968 (twenty teams). That came out to an average drop per major-league club of nearly two hundred runs. Despite the thinning out of mound talent, pitchers were obviously getting batters out more consistently than at any time in some fifty years. Combined major-league earned run averages fell from 4.36 in 1950 to 2.98 in 1968.

For the same eighteen-year period, combined batting averages in the two leagues shrank thirty points—from .266 to .236. It would have been even worse if, in 1954, the AL-NL rules and scoring committee hadn't reinstituted the sacrifice-fly rule, done away with after the 1931 season. Ty Cobb had predicted that someday nobody in the majors would bat .300, and in 1968, in the AL, that almost happened. Boston outfielder Carl Yastrzemski won his third batting title, and second in a row, by hitting only .301, the lowest mark ever for a league leader. The AL's next-highest man batted eleven points below Yastrzemski.

Better defensive play—a consequence of bigger and better gloves (elaborate hinged devices averaging about fifteen inches across that, among other effects, popularized the one-handed catch) and closer attention to hitting patterns and the positioning of fielders—contributed to the batting falloff. (Fielding averages improved by three points in the AL and two in the NL from 1950 to 1968.) Yet as they pondered why pitchers were so much in charge, knowledgeable baseball people were inclined to zero in on the slider as, in the phrase of one pundit, "the pitch that changed baseball."

As far back as 1953 New York sports columnist Tom Meany, pointing to the fact that only seventeen major-leaguers had reached the .300 plateau the previous season, had sounded an alarm over the decline of batting. One of the factors Meany cited was the advent of a new pitch called the slider, which, at various times before their playing days were over, Joe DiMaggio, Stan Musial, and Ted Williams had all complained about. Thrown like a fastball with a stiff wrist, but then with a snap at the moment of release that caused the ball—traveling at greater velocity than the usual curve pitch—to break a few inches at the last instant, the slider gave a hurler who had trouble mastering the curve an effective pitch to go with his fast one. Old-timers such as Rogers Hornsby dismissed the slider as a "nickel curve" and noted that nonbreaking sliders frequently ended up in the outfield seats, but others were convinced that it made a lot of pitchers more effective— and in a shorter time. Said Sal Maglie, one of the new full-time pitching coaches teams were hiring in the sixties, "All the young pitchers today are lazy. They all look for the easiest way out, and the slider gives them that pitch."

The slider might be relatively new; the spitball had a long if less-than-honorable history. In the 1960s batters voiced a common complaint: Just about everybody who took the mound was "loading up." Nowadays that meant less the application of saliva (inasmuch as tobacco-chewing had declined noticeably) than the use of petroleum jelly and various other lubricants, together with scuffing by such covert but old-fashioned means as belt buckles, razor blades, and emery boards. Although doctoring of the ball was probably less prevalent than batters thought (one 1967 estimate put the number of pitchers using the generic "spitter" at twenty-five percent), it was generally agreed that more illegal pitches were being thrown than at any time since 1919. By early 1972, when he was traded from San Francisco to Cleveland, a big right-hander from North Carolina named Gaylord Perry had won 134 big-league decisions in eleven seasons and gained a well-deserved reputation as the cleverest spit-baller in the majors.

Among the various signs of pitching ascendancy were per-season strikeout and shutout totals. In 1950 pitching staffs averaged 597 strikeouts; by 1960 that had grown to 801, and eight years later the twenty staffs struck out an *average* of 957 batters. For shutouts, the staff averages were nine, ten, and then seventeen for 1950, 1960, and 1968, respectively.

So the prevalent playing style in major-league baseball in the 1960s came down to considerably more base-stealing, a lot less base-hitting and somewhat less long-ball hitting, substantially fewer runs, and decidedly stronger pitching.

In 1965 the Los Angeles Dodgers managed to put runners across the plate only 608 times but held opponents to 2.81 earned runs per game in compiling a 97–65 record, two games better than second-place San Francisco. Don Drysdale won twenty-three games, while Sandy Koufax reestablished himself as baseball's premier pitcher by running up a 26–8 record, in the course of which he threw his third no-hitter and struck out 382 batters to surpass Bob Feller and Rube Waddell for the highest total in one season.

Meanwhile the Minnesota Twins became the first AL team in the sixties besides the Yankees to win a pennant. Tony Oliva's .321 average gave the second-year Cuban his second batting title; the Twins led the AL in homers and scoring while batting only .256 as a club.

In the World Series, Jim "Mudcat" Grant, Minnesota's twenty-three-game winner, went the distance in beating the Dodgers twice, the latter victory sending the teams into the seventh game. At Metropolitan Stadium in Bloomington, Koufax threw his second Series shutout; Lou Johnson's homer off Jim Kaat provided the margin of victory for the Dodgers.

The next March, Koufax and Drysdale staged an unprecedented tandem holdout, demanding a combined $250,000 from Walter O'Malley. What was equally unprecedented was that the two pitching stars forced O'Malley to deal not with them but with their agent, a lawyer named J. William Hayes. Declaring that he objected more to the players' agent than to their money demands, O'Malley delayed more than a month before signing Koufax for $130,000 and Drysdale for $90,000, which amounted to a $60,000 raise in each case. The pitchers' example in working through an agent to get what they wanted wasn't at all lost on their peers.

Although Drysdale struggled to a 13–16 record in 1966, Koufax proved himself worth his new salary and plenty more. Without him the Dodgers couldn't possibly have won their fourth pennant since moving west, and as it was, they came out ahead of the determined but unlucky Giants by only a game and a half. Allowing 1.79 earned runs per nine innings, Koufax compiled a 27–9 record, struck out 317 in 323 innings, and pitched a perfect game on September 5 versus the Chicago Cubs—his fourth no-hitter.

Koufax had achieved his glittering 129–47 record since 1961 at the cost of a worsening arthritic condition in his pitching arm and hand. Weary of pain and frequent cortisone injections and warned that, if he continued to pitch, he might end up losing the use of his left arm, Koufax, at the age of thirty, decided to retire once the 1966 World Series was over.

It was anything but a grand exit for the great lefty. The opponents were the Baltimore Orioles, managed by ex-Yankee Hank Bauer, and in losing four straight times, Los Angeles could marshal exactly two runs. Drysdale opened for the Dodgers rather than Koufax, who sat out the game in observance of Yom Kippur. The hero of the opening contest was veteran right-hander Myron "Moe" Drabowsky, who ignored Yom Kippur, relieved Dave McNally in the third inning, and struck out eleven Dodgers to preserve the Orioles' 5–2 victory. In game two, a Series record three errors in one inning by center fielder Willie Davis and mistakes by Koufax led to six runs, five more than were necessary for Jim Palmer, a tall, handsome twenty-year-old. In the third and fourth games, McNally and Wally Bunker, both only a little older than Palmer, also pitched shutouts.

As they had all year, outfielder Frank Robinson, first baseman John "Boog" Powell, and Brooks Robinson, a third-base wizard in his twelfth big-league season at twenty-nine, provided the bulk of Baltimore's offense. Frank Robinson, acquired from Cincinnati late in 1965 after the Reds' front office judged him "an old thirty," led American Leaguers in batting, homers, and runs batted in. That accomplishment made him the AL's Most Valuable Player—to this day the only man ever so honored in *both* leagues.

In 1967, without Koufax, the Dodgers fell all the way to eighth place, and they could do no better than seventh the next year. Under the direction of Red Schoendienst, the St. Louis Cardinals returned to the top in the NL, finishing well ahead of the San Francisco Giants in both 1967 and 1968. Roger Maris, traded by the Yankees after the '66 season, contributed significantly to both of the Cardinals' titles, then retired at thirty-four. The heart of the St. Louis pennant winners, though, consisted of hard-hitting Orlando Cepeda (obtained from the Giants the previous year) at first base, fleet Curt Flood and Lou Brock in the outfield, quick and smart Tim McCarver behind the plate, and truculent Bob Gibson on the mound.

In 1967, despite a broken leg, Gibson ended up with fourteen victories, and in 1968 he was simply overpowering—nailing down twenty-two games, striking out 268, pitching a dazzling thirteen shut-outs, and registering a 1.12 earned run average, the lowest in the majors since 1914. Meanwhile Brock, all but given away by the Cubs in 1964, emerged as the game's best leadoff man and Maury Wills's successor as its foremost base stealer.

With their young pitchers all nursing sore arms, Baltimore sank to sixth in 1967. The Boston Red Sox, a disorganized ninth-place outfit the previous year, took the '67 AL pennant after an exhausting four-team struggle and despite the loss of slugging young Tony Conigliaro, disabled on August 18 when an errant pitch shattered his face. At season's end Boston was one game ahead of Detroit and Minnesota and only three ahead of the Chicago White Sox. Rookie manager Dick Williams could mostly thank Carl Yastrzemski, who led the AL in nearly every batting category and was named its Most Valuable Player, and Jim Lonborg, a young right-hander who won twenty-two games and carried an otherwise mediocre pitching staff.

Lou Brock's record seven stolen bases and .414 batting average made the 1967 World Series especially memorable, as did Gibson's three complete-game victories and twenty-six strikeouts. Lonborg pitched superbly to win games two and five; then two homers by third baseman Rico Petrocelli and single shots by Yastrzemski and rookie outfielder Reggie Smith gave Boston an 8–4 win to tie the Series. It ended at Fenway Park, where the Cardinals pounded a tired Lonborg for six runs en route to a 7–2 triumph. Besides throwing a three-hitter and striking out ten, Gibson, an all-around athlete, also helped himself with a home run.

In 1968, batting averages sank to all-time lows, while pitchers dominated as they hadn't since pre–World War I days. National Leaguers averaged .243 and hit only 891 home runs, the fewest in the senior circuit since 1948 (when, of course, there had been two fewer teams). Cincinnati's fiery, switch-hitting Pete Rose won the first of his three NL batting crowns with a .335 average, but only four other National Leaguers topped .300. Although they hit substantially more home runs, American Leaguers produced a solitary .300 batter and averaged .230, the poorest league mark in major-league history. Fittingly, the 1968 All-Star Game ended 1–0, the NL scoring on a double play.

Bob Gibson's relentless brilliance overshadowed Juan Marichal's twenty-six victories, almost equally superlative work by the Cubs' Ferguson Jenkins, and even Don Drysdale's six consecutive shutouts and fifty-eight scoreless innings, which broke Walter Johnson's record of fifty-six, set in 1913. Yet even Gibson was partially eclipsed by Denny McLain, Detroit's stocky, free-spirited young right-hander.

With a total of forty-three victories between 1965 and 1967, McLain had established himself as a solid but not extraordinary major-league pitcher. Then, in 1968, he became the first pitcher since Dizzy Dean thirty-four years earlier to reach the thirty-win plateau. McLain finished with a 31–6 record, a 1.96 earned run average, and 280 strikeouts. McLain and his teammates batted only .235, but they also clouted 185 homers and made only 105 errors. Power, defense, and McLain's pitching produced 103 Detroit wins, nine more than Baltimore.

The Cardinals looked stronger than ever in taking a three-game-to-one lead in the World Series; in two of those wins they drove McLain from the mound. In the opener Gibson pitched a shutout and fanned seventeen to break Koufax's Series strikeout record; then he eased through a 10–1 victory in game four. But Mickey Lolich, a paunchy left-hander who'd defeated St. Louis in game two, came back in the fifth encounter to overcome nineteen-game-winner Nelson Briles. The next day Jim Northrup's bases-loaded homer keyed a 13–1 slaughter to tie the Series.

In the deciding game, at St. Louis, Detroit manager Mayo Smith called on Lolich again. The Cardinals lost sixth-inning scoring chances when Lolich picked both Brock and Flood off first base, and Northrup's two-run triple off Gibson in the seventh put the Tigers ahead to stay. It ended 4–1, Lolich's five-hitter giving him three complete-game wins.

Coming off several close pennant races and two tightly fought World Series, baseball looked healthy. Major-league attendance for 1968 exceeded twenty-three million, the largest total so far, and the Los Angeles Dodgers had supplanted the Yankees as baseball's richest franchise. Playing in new, ultramodern Busch Stadium, the Cardinals had broken attendance records three years in a row, while the New York Mets were drawing close to two million per season despite remaining at or near the bottom of the NL under various managers who followed Casey Stengel.

Beginning in 1965, moreover, curious people from all over North America traveled to Houston, less to watch baseball than to marvel at the new Harris County Domed Stadium. Described locally (with characteristic Texan understatement) as "the eighth wonder of the world," the stadium was the first to have an artificial playing surface— an innovation necessitated when the original grass turf withered under the dome's opaque panels. The lackluster Astros, as they were now called, had already hit the two-million mark in what owner Roy Hofheinz grandiloquently dubbed the "Astrodome."

Yet on a per-team basis, baseball was drawing fewer people than in 1948, despite a twenty-five to thirty percent increase in the general population. Several franchises were on shaky ground; two had relocated in recent years. After the 1965 season, a Chicago group that had purchased the Milwaukee Braves moved the franchise to Atlanta, where new Fulton County Stadium as well as a more lucrative television deal were waiting. Less than a decade earlier, Milwaukee had been the best baseball town in the world; even as late as 1964, with rumors in the air that the new owners intended to move, nearly a million had paid to watch a fifth-place team. As of 1966, though, the Braves' Eddie Mathews became the first player to perform for the same franchise in three different cities.

In the 1967–1968 off-season Charles O. Finley, owner of the Kansas City A's (as they were now modishly known), finally mustered the necessary three-fourths approval from his AL colleagues to move his operation. After buying the Kansas City team late in 1960, Finley stopped trading with the Yankees, tried to lure customers with a variety of promotional gimmicks (including keeping a mule named "Charlie O" as well as sheep, monkeys, and other animals behind a fence in right field), and even abandoned baseball's conservative dress code by outfitting his players in garish green-and-gold-trimmed uniforms and white shoes. Yet the A's plodded along in the bottom reaches of the league, drawing six to seven hundred thousand and realizing only about $350,000 in radio-television revenues per season.

For 1968 Finley opened for business across San Francisco Bay from the Giants, in newly constructed Oakland–Alameda County Coliseum. By that time he owned several gifted young players—Reggie Jackson, Jim "Catfish" Hunter, Joe Rudi, and Bert Campaneris—who would soon effect a transformation in the A's fortunes on the ballfield, if not at the ticket windows.

Sooner in some cases, later in others, all the major-league franchises sought to attract customers with methods that were reminiscent (in more sophisticated form) not only of Bill Veeck's schemes but of practices common to minor-league operations for several decades. It amounted to a new way of merchandising a baseball game, not merely as an athletic contest on the field but as a spectacle in which customers were catered to as never before.

Ballpark food became increasingly varied and appetizing (and expensive); clubs marketed a profusion of "novelty items" bearing distinctive team logos; fans received such favors as caps, pennants, posters, and miniature bats on designated promotional dates; more and more people came to games as the guests of business firms that bought blocks of tickets and distributed them to clients and employees. In the newer stadia, spectators sat in comfortable seats with unobstructed views, and wealthy patrons could lease plush "sky boxes"—first installed by Roy Hofheinz in the Astrodome—where they could either peer at the small figures far below or watch the action on closed-circuit television monitors.

Once inside the ballpark, fans confronted huge electronic scoreboards providing an incessant flow of statistics, greetings, and advertisements. The new scoreboards also exhorted spectators in various ways, such as the trumpeted "Charge!"—originated at Dodger Stadium and eventually copied almost everywhere. The Astrodome score-board commanded them to "Make Noise!" and then, if a Houston player happened to hit a home run, emitted sirens, bull snorts, and a variety of other clamors. "Once the great iconoclast among spectators," wrote Charles Einstein in 1967, "the baseball fan today travels in groups, performs on cue, and, as often as not, shamelessly apes the tribal customs of other fans in other cities."

Yet with all the attractive new physical plants and sophisticated techniques for capturing fans' interest, baseball, according to a view that gained wide currency in the late 1960s, was no longer the Na-tional Pastime. Other sports had supposedly displaced baseball in the affections of a majority of Americans. Although college football and college and professional basketball had huge followings, most com-mentators agreed that professional football was the new favorite for most sports-minded citizens. A 1965 *Newsweek* poll, indicating a wide preference for pro football in the twenty-one to thirty-four age group, stirred a great deal of media attention and confirmed what many had suspected for some time.

The rising popularity of pro football was a direct consequence of television's discovery of that sport—and the sport's discovery of television—beginning in the mid-1950s. Americans who'd previously seen only high-school and college football were captivated by the power and finesse of the pro game they watched on their home TV sets. The epic 1958 National Football League championship game, in which the Baltimore Colts defeated the New York Giants in sudden-death over-time at Yankee Stadium, won over tens of millions of people who up to then had followed pro football only casually, if at all.

In 1960 Alvin "Pete" Rozelle, recently elected NFL commis-sioner, negotiated a $4.5 million television contract with CBS. What made that agreement—plus a much smaller one signed by the fledg-ling American Football League with ABC—of lasting significance was that henceforth all the franchises would share equally in all TV revenues. By contrast, baseball franchises divided only All-Star Game and World Series broadcasting revenues; each franchise negotiated its own separate deal for regular-season rights, which of course made for big disparities in how much money each realized.

By 1964 CBS, under a new contract, was willing to pay the

National Football League $14 million per year, which meant that annually each franchise would receive $1 million, regardless of how well or poorly its team did on the field or how many people paid to see its home games. Meanwhile NBC solidified the future of the American Football League by agreeing to pay $42 million over five years for rights to regular-season and championship games. More than ever, the networks hyped professional football, pushing it as a brand of fast, exciting, compact action that came across even better on television than as a "live" spectator event.

While pro football teams both filled their stadia and won higher and higher ratings from the services gauging TV audiences, nearly all minor-league and a number of major-league baseball teams continued to draw poorly, and nationally broadcast weekend baseball games (carried exclusively on NBC in the late sixties) were among the lowest-rated programs on television. A host of commentators sought to explain why baseball had become, in the phrase of the New York sports journalist Leonard Koppett, "the ex-national sport." Although Koppett tended to blame baseball itself—its weak leadership and greedy owners and players—others looked for broader explanations.

Baseball, declared George Preston Marshall, owner of the NFL's Washington Redskins, "is a bloodless, unemotional spectacle compared to football." Baseball was "too tame for the times," added Robert Daley in *Esquire* magazine, and was "an exceedingly dull game." Everywhere he went, Daley reported, "in the schools, offices, living rooms and cocktail parties from coast to coast," people talked of pro football, not baseball, "and the [baseball] heroes of the past are dead."

Still others explained football's ascendancy in terms of its greater suitability for television. Because its action was confined within distances easily comprehended by the cameras, football was at its best on television, whereas baseball's greater distances and dispersed action made it basically incompatible to the small screen. The veteran sportswriter Tim Cohane added that whether on TV or in the flesh, baseball games lasted too long and involved too much inactivity—a situation he blamed on dilatory pitchers and indulgent umpires.

By the late 1960s and early 1970s, some writers were even prepared to equate pro football's popularity with the ongoing Vietnam War and militaristic, aggressive tendencies supposedly ingrained in Ameri-

can society. Replete with martial analogies, offering violence detached
from ordinary experience, humorless, relentless, dedicated to victory
at any cost, professional football supposedly fulfilled machismo fanta-
sies for people who led humdrum, basically passive lives. Novelist and
social critic Anton Myrer saw President Richard M. Nixon as a highly
symbolic figure, in being both a football enthusiast and "the most
sedentary of all our chief executives." Vice President Spiro Agnew
reminded Myrer of nothing so much as a pro middle linebacker.

In its obsessive time-consciousness, moreover, football supposedly mirrored the anxious, driven character of contemporary
American society. Baseball, with its leisurely pace and pastoral setting, its essentially nonviolent character, seemed less and less relevant
to modern existence. Baseball was in trouble, wrote David Halberstam
in 1970, "because it has not kept up with the velocity of American life,
the jet age, instant gratification, instant action." "Maybe," Myrer
addressed baseball, "you're too artful, too individualistic—maybe
you're just too *gentle* to survive."

Whether or not one believed that baseball was losing its hold on
the sporting public, everybody seemed to agree that the sport needed
more effective leadership than it had gotten since the passing of Judge
Landis. Not quite seventy-one, the pleasant but ineffectual Ford Frick
retired when his term as commissioner expired in December 1965,
and the owners' choice for his successor was William D. Eckert, a
retired U.S. Air Force general. Eckert was such an obscure figure that
Dick Young of the New York *Daily News* waggishly referred to him as
"the unknown soldier."

Eckert, who'd been comptroller of the air force when he retired,
was a capable administrator but a colorless, indecisive man who soon
showed that he was out of his element. His refusal to cancel games in
April and June 1968, following the assassinations of Martin Luther
King, Jr., the nation's foremost black leader, and U.S. Senator Robert
F. Kennedy, the main hope of the country's political liberals, prompted
acute criticism. By 1968, moreover, Eckert found himself caught
between mounting player grievances and demands and the stubborn-
ness of the owners.

If baseball needed fixing, then the quickest and therefore most
appealing fix was to put more offense back into the game. The men

who ran the sport had turned to that expedient in the early 1890s and again in 1920, with contrasting results. Despite lots of base hits and runs beginning in 1893, most franchises had lost money in the twelve-team National League, whereas soaring attendance had accompanied the batting boom after 1920. Working on the premise that most people preferred hitting and scoring to tightly pitched contests, for 1969 the NL-AL rules committee sought to make things more congenial for hitters—and presumably more attractive for fans.

In 1969 pitchers would have to throw off mounds that could be no higher than ten inches above the surface of the infield, versus the fifteen-inch mound allowed up to then. The strike zone, defined in 1963 as extending from the top of the shoulder to the bottom of the knee, was narrowed to the area between the armpit and the top of the knee—a difference of about eight inches. To inhibit actual or would-be spitballers, the rule-makers made it illegal for pitchers to put their hands to their mouths unless they first stepped completely off the mound.

The new rules for 1969 helped boost NL batting averages by seven points and AL averages by sixteen points, average home runs per team by thirty-three in the NL and twenty-seven in the AL, and average runs per team by 102 (NL) and 110 (AL). Earned run averages increased by about .6 of a run in each league. Apparently the fans really did prefer slugfests to pitching duels, because an average of about twenty-seven hundred more attended games in 1969 than in the previous year.

But rule-tinkering was only part of the story. The simple fact is that NL and AL pitching wasn't as good in 1969 as it had been in recent years. As in 1961–1962, it was a matter of more teams using the same number of big-league-quality pitchers, and more minor-league-quality pitchers pitching to major-league hitters.

In 1969 both major leagues underwent a second expansion—to twelve franchises each. The admission fee for the new members was $10 million in the AL, $5.25 million in the NL. A group headed by Ewing Kauffman reestablished the American League in Kansas City, which the A's had deserted for Oakland before the 1968 season. Municipal Stadium would still be the home of the Kansas City team, called the Royals, but plans were going forward for a new, exclusively baseball facility, intended to rival Dodger Stadium. Seattle, long a member of the Pacific Coast League, joined the AL with only inadequate Sick's Stadium to accommodate the Pilots—and with nothing better in the works.

The National League also took in a former PCL city. Still known as the Padres, the San Diego team would perform in the year-old stadium that had originally been planned mainly with the American Football League Chargers in mind, and for the first time, major-league baseball wouldn't be played entirely within the United States. Long a bastion of the International League, the French-Canadian city of Montreal acquired a big-league franchise with only a minor-league facility for its team. The Expos—so named after the 1967 Montreal world's fair (or *Exposition*)—would play their home games in Jarry Park, which could seat only twenty-eight thousand.

Once again expansion entries filled their rosters with players from the existing clubs, who again contributed their expendables to a draft pool—this time at $175,000 per man. Once again the existing amount of baseball talent was thinned to accommodate the need for one hundred additional "big-leaguers." And once again, with pitching staffs weakened, good hitters gained an edge.

Accompanying the majors' second expansion was a restructuring of the two leagues into two divisions each—the first time any major league had departed from a full top-to-bottom competitive structure. While keeping the 162-game schedule, both leagues re-formed into six-team eastern and western divisions, with the league championships to be decided in three-of-five-game playoffs between the division winners.

The NL disregarded geographical logic. Besides Los Angeles, San Francisco, Houston, and San Diego, Cincinnati and Atlanta also ended up in the NL West—despite the fact that those two cities were, respectively, three hundred and three hundred fifty miles east of St. Louis, which was grouped in the NL East. Other Eastern Division clubs were Chicago (also west of Atlanta and Cincinnati), Pittsburgh, Philadelphia, Montreal, and New York. Both of the AL's expansion teams were placed in its Western Division, which would also consist of

California, Oakland, Chicago, and Minnesota. Making up the comparatively compact AL East would be New York, Boston, Cleveland, Washington, Baltimore, and Detroit.

Late in 1968 William D. Eckert, having pleased nobody, was forced to resign. Presiding over the majors in their new, expanded division setup was a new commissioner—a tall, forty-two-year-old Washington attorney named Bowie Kuhn, who'd earlier represented the owners in their dealings with the ballplayers. Kuhn was initially elected commissioner pro tem, then in August 1969 was given a seven-year contract.

Kuhn stepped into a situation that, though different from what Judge Landis had faced in 1921, was just as troublesome. Unlike Landis (at least in the first decade or so of his reign), Kuhn couldn't dictate to the owners; nor were the players disorganized and passive, as they'd been in Landis's time. Besides the arrogance and shortsightedness that still typified the thinking of most club owners, Kuhn would also have to deal with the most powerfully organized players' movement since the Brotherhood war.

In 1954, fearing that the owners might do away with the pension system they'd gained shortly after World War II, sixteen elected player representatives, led by Ralph Kiner and Allie Reynolds, met in Cleveland on the eve of the All-Star Game and formed the Major League Baseball Players Association (MLBPA). Kiner and Reynolds expressly denied that the new body was a union, whereupon the owners assured the players that the pension fund wouldn't be tampered with. From then until the mid-1960s, the MLBPA, numbering only about half the players in the majors, remained watchful but generally compliant.

But starting in 1966, the MLBPA became a more representative and militant organization—a players' union in nearly every respect. In that year the MLBPA created the full-time post of executive director and hired Marvin Miller, who resigned his job as assistant to the president of the United Steel Workers of America to take on the players' cause. Trained in economics at New York University and in practical labor relations with the National Labor Relations Board during World War II, the patient, soft-spoken Miller understood the mechanics of mediation and negotiation better than anybody the owners could pit against him. Over the next fifteen years, Miller's influence would permanently change the business of baseball.

Dealing with men who'd been conditioned to think of their worth in terms of individual achievement, Miller worked tirelessly to create a sense of shared interest. Within a year of his appointment, the MLBPA had become a sufficiently united front that Miller was able to negotiate what was termed a Basic Agreement, by which the players received an increase in the minimum salary from $7,000 (where it had remained for the past ten years) to $10,000, as well as bigger owners' contributions to the pension fund. The owners also promised to consider modifying the reserve clause.

That first Basic Agreement expired early in 1969, shortly after Bowie Kuhn became commissioner. When the MLBPA threatened to strike, the owners, at Kuhn's urging, reluctantly got down to serious talks with Miller and the player representatives. Thirteen months later, under the second Basic Agreement, the owners finally recognized the MLBPA as the players' official bargaining agent in everything except salaries. As for salary negotiations, for the first time the owners agreed to deal individually with agents designated by their player-clients. Although the reserve clause remained intact, the arrival of professional agents—tough-minded men working for at least ten percent of whatever they got for their clients—wrought a profound change in the sport's historic employer-employee relationship.

Confused and irritated by the off-the-field labor-management machinations, baseball fans in 1969 watched lower-quality play and tried to adjust to the division alignments and to the fact that, at the completion of the 162-game schedule, the pennant winners still wouldn't be determined. As everybody expected, the expansion teams did poorly, although the Kansas City Royals did finish fourth in the AL West, ahead of the Chicago White Sox and Seattle. Both Montreal in the NL East and San Diego in the West finished last, with identical 52–110 records.

The Seattle Pilots fared twelve games better than that, but only 678,000 people paid to see them, and even before the season ended, the Seattle operators turned their bankrupt franchise back to the AL. Only four days before the 1970 season was to open, the league would finally conclude a deal with a group of Milwaukee investors; the

Western Division Brewers would play in County Stadium, once the home of the NL Milwaukee Braves.

In winning 109 games (nineteen more than Detroit) and then sweeping the playoff series from the Minnesota Twins, winners in the AL West, the 1969 Baltimore Orioles looked like the finest team since the '61 Yankees. Managed by Earl Weaver, a chain-smoking, pugnacious career minor-leaguer who, as an umpire-baiter, was in a class with John McGraw and Leo Durocher, the Orioles still drew on the talents of Frank Robinson, Boog Powell, and Brooks Robinson, plus two of their aces from the 1966 champions: Dave McNally, a twenty-game winner, and Jim Palmer, who'd overcome his arm troubles and posted sixteen wins. Mike Cuellar, a screwball-throwing Cuban left-hander obtained from Houston in the off-season, topped the staff with a 23–11 record.

In a scenario reminiscent of the Miracle Boston Braves of 1914, the long-hapless New York Mets rose from a ninth-place finish in 1968 to win thirty-eight of their last forty-nine games, overcome a big lead built by Durocher's Chicago Cubs, and capture the NL Eastern Division by eight games. Managed by Gil Hodges, the Mets' third field leader since Casey Stengel's departure in 1965, the Mets were a collection of perpetually platooned everyday mediocrities, combined with a young pitching staff led by Tom Seaver (twenty-five wins) and Jerry Koosman (seventeen). In the NL playoff the Mets swept the Atlanta Braves—a team that included still-powerful Orlando Cepeda, Phil Niekro, who won twenty-three, and Henry Aaron, who hit forty-four home runs to continue what few people yet recognized as an all-out assault on Babe Ruth's career homer record.

The amazing season of the "amazin' Mets" climaxed with a World Series triumph over the Baltimore powerhouse. After Cuellar defeated Seaver in the opener at Baltimore, the Mets won four straight, allowing the Orioles only five runs. Koosman bested McNally 2–1 in game two; Gary Gentry and a wild, blazingly fast youngster named Nolan Ryan combined on a shutout in game three; and Seaver stalled the Baltimore bats 2–1 in game four. Before a delirious assemblage at Shea Stadium, the Mets scored five times in their last three turns at bat to win the Series 5–3 behind Koosman. Except for skillful managing, superb pitching, spectacular fielding, and timely hitting (often from the unlikeliest sources), nobody could explain how the Mets had pulled it off.

The Mets played more nearly normal baseball in 1970, finishing third in the NL East behind the Cubs and the Pittsburgh Pirates, whose owners had persuaded an unwell Danny Murtaugh to leave the front office and resume dugout duties. Although their pitching was spotty, the Pirates had a strong-hitting team led by Roberto Clemente (.352), an ebullient Panamanian catcher named Manny Sanguillen (.325), and big Willie Stargell, who hammered thirty-one homers. In the playoffs the Pirates went quietly, dropping three straight to the Cincinnati Reds.

The Reds' first-year manager was thirty-six-year-old George "Sparky" Anderson, who, like Earl Weaver, had followed an undistinguished playing career with years of patient service in minor-league dugouts. Tagged the "Big Red Machine," Anderson's team won 102 games, fifteen better than the Dodgers, and hit 191 home runs. Reds catcher Johnny Bench, so skilled that, at twenty-two, he was already compared to the best who'd ever squatted behind the plate, led the majors with forty-five homers and 145 runs batted in. Third baseman Tony Perez, another Cuban playing in Organized Baseball before Castro's revolution, batted .317, with forty homers and 129 rbi's. Switch-hitting Pete Rose, then still stationed at second base, batted .316, as did outfielder Bobby Tolan, whose fifty-seven stolen bases led the majors. Lefty Jim Merritt, with twenty wins; righty Gary Nolan, with eighteen; and Wayne Granger, a skinny right-hander who relieved seventy-eight times and saved thirty-five games, were the backbone of the pitching staff.

In midseason 1970 both the Pirates and the Reds moved out of their old ballparks and into new multipurpose, barely distinguishable, even similarly named stadia: Riverfront in Cincinnati, Three Rivers in Pittsburgh. Like most of the other recently built sports plants, they offered seating for fifty to fifty-five thousand. Although Three Rivers and Riverfront were open-air facilities, they both featured the ruglike, plastic playing surface first installed out of necessity under Houston's dome, and subsequently also put down at Busch Stadium in St. Louis. In the 1970s "artificial grass" would become the faddish thing in new-stadium furnishings. Once in place, the new surfaces cost less to maintain; because water could be easily suctioned off, they minimized rainouts; and by affecting the speed and bounce of batted balls, they also significantly influenced the art of fielding.

The Detroit Tigers, world's champions only two seasons earlier, finished a poor fourth in the AL East in 1970, mainly because of what befell Denny McLain. Early in the year the weekly *Sports Illustrated* reported that in 1967 McLain had been a partner with a group of Detroit-area gamblers in a bookmaking scheme. The venture had gone sour when a friend of local big-time mobster Tony Giacalone won such a heavy bet that McLain and associates couldn't pay off. While McLain apparently got out of that predicament unscathed, at present, said *Sports Illustrated*, he owed large amounts of back taxes to the Internal Revenue Service and was again in debt to organized-crime figures. All that despite earning $200,000 during a 1969 season in which he won twenty-four games.

Having satisfied himself that the magazine had its facts straight, commissioner Kuhn declared McLain indefinitely suspended. Subsequently, in announcing that the suspension would end on July 1, 1970, Kuhn said, "Our society shows compassion for people who have gone wrong, and baseball is part of that society." Much of the news media and plenty of ordinary fans found Kuhn's behavior indecisive and weak-kneed, especially when contrasted to the season-long suspensions Pete Rozelle had laid on NFL stars Paul Hornung and Alex Karras a few years earlier for betting small amounts on league games.

McLain turned in a 3–5 record during the last half of the 1970 season, after which he was traded to lowly Washington, where he *lost* twenty-two games. Within a couple of years he would be out of baseball altogether and headed for disaster.

The first week of October 1970 brought a second cycle of division playoffs. Winning one less time than in '69, Baltimore again took the AL East—by fifteen games over the Yankees, who played their best baseball since 1964. The Orioles' McNally won twenty-four, Cuellar a like number, and Palmer twenty. Again the Orioles dispatched the Minnesota Twins, still the best in the West, in three games. The Twins were a good ball club in those years, with such stars as master batsmen Tony Oliva and Rod Carew, slugging Harmon Killebrew, and pitchers Jim Perry (Gaylord's older brother) and Jim Kaat. The 1970 Orioles, though, were close to being a *great* club, as they demonstrated by throttling Cincinnati's Big Red Machine in five games.

Lee May's eighth-inning, three-run homer in game four saved Cincinnati from a sweep, but the next day, at Baltimore, Frank Robinson and Merv Rettenmund homered and drove in two runs apiece, while Cuellar shut down the heavy-hitting Reds after a shaky start. When the game ended 9–3, the city of Baltimore celebrated its second world's title since inheriting the St. Louis Browns. The Series' outstanding player was Brooks Robinson, who batted .429, drove in six runs, and repeatedly made stops and throws at third base that left even the crustiest old-timers gasping in amazement.

Despite having never drawn more than 1,203,000 at home, the Baltimore Orioles were a lean, highly motivated organization, featuring excellent front-office and field management and a productive farm system. The 1971 season brought 101 victories, a third straight Eastern Division title, and a third straight playoff sweep of the AL West representative. That year's Orioles' pitching staff featured *four* twenty-game winners: McNally won twenty-one, and Cuellar, Palmer, and Pat Dobson (acquired from San Diego) all recorded twenty each.

The Orioles' playoff victim in '71 was Charlie Finley's Oakland club, managed by former Red Sox leader Dick Williams. While Minnesota faded to fifth, the A's, a young, frugally paid outfit, matched Baltimore's 101 wins to finish way ahead of a surprisingly good Kansas City team. Over the first half of the season, A's rookie left-hander Vida Blue seemed a good bet to win thirty games; he didn't reach that lofty figure, but still ended up 24–8 with a 1.82 earned run average and 301 strikeouts. Catfish Hunter added twenty-one victories for a team that seemed on the verge of becoming a powerhouse to rival the Orioles.

Hardly anybody pitched well for Cincinnati in 1971; that and deep batting slumps on the part of Bench and Perez sent the Reds skidding to fourth in the NL West. The San Francisco Giants came out on top after a season-long struggle with the Dodgers, who finished only a game short. Juan Marichal and Gaylord Perry were San Francisco's pitching mainstays; with Willie Mays in decline, the Giants' main offensive weapons were Willie McCovey, their big first baseman, and center fielder Bobby Bonds, who typified a growing number of contemporary players in combining speed, power, and a proclivity for striking out.

Following a quick exit in the 1970 NL playoff, Pittsburgh won everything in 1971. Led by Clemente's .341 batting average and Stargell's forty-eight homers and 125 rbi's, the Pirates outdistanced St. Louis by seven games to win the NL East, then knocked off San Francisco, three games to one. The Giants' victory was the first one for a losing team since the start of division-playoff competition.

Underdogs going into the World Series, the Pirates lost the first two games at Baltimore. Back home, though, they captured three straight behind the stout mound work of Steve Blass, Nelson Briles, and rookie Bruce Kison, who pitched six and one third scoreless innings in relief to win game four—the first in Series history played at night. The Orioles evened the Series in Baltimore on Brooks Robinson's tenth-inning sacrifice fly, but in the deciding game, at Memorial Stadium, Clemente homered for the second day in a row to win Blass's four-hitter, 2–1.

At the end of the third season of its existence, the divisional structure within the two major leagues still left traditionalists muttering that it diminished the importance of regular-season competition, besides permitting weaker teams to come into the playoffs and oust stronger, more deserving outfits. Yet most fans seemed to like the new competitive setup, which did, after all, double the number of races and suspend the outcome until the final games of the playoffs.

Both average attendance per club and baseball's television ratings had risen moderately since 1969, but plenty of major-league franchises still reported big deficits. As a whole, American League owners claimed greater financial ills, and at the end of the 1971 season one of them, Robert Short of the Washington Senators, announced that he could carry on no longer in the nation's capital.

Despite Frank Howard's long-distance home runs and the presence of Gil Hodges (1963–1967) and Ted Williams (since 1969) as managers, the Senators finished above .500 only once in the franchise's eleven-year history and never drew more than 918,000. Publicly, Short cited the Senators' inability to compete for customers with the Orioles, only twenty-nine miles to the north, and the high crime rate in the District of Columbia. Off the record he complained that the District's preponderantly black population just wouldn't support baseball. That winter Short convinced his AL colleagues to approve the Senators' removal to the Dallas–Fort Worth area. For 1972 Ted Williams's charges—as the Texas Rangers—would transfer to the AL West (with Milwaukee transferring to the East) and take the field in a recently enlarged minor-league ballpark at Arlington, Texas, just off the Dallas–Fort Worth Turnpike.

The most memorable thing about the 1972 season, though, wouldn't be baseball's most recent franchise shift, but the fact that the season would open only after the first comprehensive players' strike in the sport's long history—the first, but by no means the last. In the offing was a succession of wrenching changes that would profoundly affect baseball's financial structure, and put a permanent end to baseball feudalism.

12.
The End
of
Feudalism

In the spring of 1972 a players' strike, narrowly averted in 1969, finally happened. Upon the expiration of the second Basic Agreement, the Major League Baseball Players Association sought a twenty-five percent increase in the club owners' contributions to the pension fund, as well as improvements in medical benefits. When the owners stood together and refused to budge on the pension issue, the players voted 663–10 to follow executive director Marvin Miller's counsel and walk out of the spring-training camps.

In 1889 the Louisville players of the old American Association had struck for a couple of days; in 1912 the Detroit Tigers had sat out one game to protest Ty Cobb's suspension for going into the stands after a heckler. But nothing even close to the 1972 walkout had ever taken place. Big-league baseball players—most particularly the twenty-five now making $100,000 or more—just weren't supposed to act like people who made their livings on assembly lines or construction sites. The typical fan's attitude, thought Roger Angell, was that while unionism and strikes might be all right for ordinary Americans, professional athletes were obliged to remain lonely, individualistic heroes.

In mid-April, in exchange for an immediate $500,000 pension-fund contribution, the players rejoined their clubs and started the 1972 season, despite not having a new Basic Agreement. The strike, lasting about a week past the scheduled opening dates, cost the club owners some $5 million in gate receipts and the players close to $1 million in salaries. The missed games (five for some teams, six for others) were never made up, so that for once what sportswriters had long termed "the all-important loss column" wasn't all-important. In the American League Eastern Division that year, Detroit and Boston both lost seventy games; but the Tigers, having played and won one more time, took the division championship.

Early the next year the players ratified a new (third) Basic Agreement. Although the owners still refused to concede anything on the reserve clause, Marvin Miller did negotiate an increase in the minimum salary (to $16,500) and more in the way of pension money and medical benefits, as well as a provision that players with ten years' major-league service and five years with the same club could veto trades—the so-called 10–5 rule. In a further concession whose significance wasn't fully apparent at the time, the owners agreed to accept binding arbitration in contract disputes with players having at least two years in the majors, starting in 1974.

Although near-solidarity in the MLBPA gave ballplayers more leverage than they'd known at any time since the Federal League years, the reserve clause remained intact. The U.S. Supreme Court made sure of that when, in June 1973, it ruled against Curt Flood, thereby again upholding Organized Baseball's privileged position under the antitrust laws.

Although he was still the National League's top center fielder, in 1969 Flood had batted only .285 (following .335 and .301 years). At the end of that season the St. Louis Cardinals traded Flood, Tim Mc-Carver, and two others to the Philadelphia Phillies in a four-for-four deal, the Cardinals' key acquisition being the gifted but cantankerous Richie (or "Dick," as he later insisted on being called) Allen. The Phillies offered Flood a contract for $110,000—$20,000 more than he had made in 1969 with the Cardinals.

Flood, though, resented being uprooted from his life and business interests in St. Louis, and resented even more being shipped off again (the Cardinals had acquired him from the Cincinnati organization in 1957). He hired an attorney and brought suit in the federal courts, arguing that baseball's reserve clause violated his right to make a free choice of his employer. During the two years it took for his case to work its way to the U.S. Supreme Court, Flood sat out one season, tried a comeback in 1971 with Ted Williams's Washington Senators, and then officially retired.

The Court's decision in the case of *Flood vs. Kuhn* was the third involving baseball and the antitrust laws, following the landmark Federal League case in 1922 and *Toolson vs. New York* in 1953. By a 5–3 vote, with Justice Harry Blackmun writing the majority opinion, the Court termed baseball's antitrust exemption an "anomaly" and an "aberration" and suggested that the "inconsistency and illogic" of baseball's unique position—in contrast to pro football, basketball, and hockey, for which the federal courts had already established the applicability of antitrust actions—ought to be remedied by congressional legislation. Absent such legislation, though, the Court had no choice but to affirm the precedents in the Federal League and Toolson decisions.

So in its 103rd year, organized professional baseball still held its unique position among professional sports. By 1973, moreover, the Columbia Broadcasting System's ownership of the New York Yankees—the subject of a 1965 inquiry by a U.S. Senate subcommittee—had become a moot issue. Cutting its losses, CBS disposed of the franchise for $10 million to a syndicate headed by George Steinbrenner III, a multimillionaire Clevelander involved in shipbuilding and numerous other enterprises, who became the Yankees' new president (officially, "chief partner").

Part of the attraction of the deal for Steinbrenner and his associates—apart from the bargain-basement price for what was still one of the best franchises in professional sports—was that the city of New York had already pledged to pay for a new Yankee Stadium. For 1974–1975 the Yankees would lease Shea Stadium for their home games; then they would move back into a completely reconstructed facility on the same site as the original in the South Bronx. Completed in 1976, at least a year behind schedule and at enormous cost overrun, the second-edition Yankee Stadium was admittedly more usable and comfortable; and yet, for those who cherished memories of "The House That Ruth Built," it was sadly deficient in charm and dignity—not to mention nostalgia.

In an age of player unionism, legal battles, complicated shifts in corporate-franchise ownership, and the political controversies that commonly accompanied new stadium projects, it wasn't always easy to concentrate on the actual competition on the playing field. Yet the baseball of the seventies, if watered down by decades of big-league inflation and minor-league deflation, still held plenty of interest, excitement, and even originality.

From 1972 to 1974 Charlie Finley's Oakland A's captured three consecutive World Series—something only the Yankees had achieved. The A's, according to a popularly held notion that neither Finley nor his players did anything to discourage, aptly suited the times. After years of mounting protest against the United States' massive military involvement in the Indochina war, many young Americans found it fashionable, even *de rigueur*, to flout traditional standards of speech, dress, and decorum. While the Oakland players were hardly political dissidents, their flashy uniforms and white shoes, hitherto-taboo mustaches, beards, and shaggy hair, and frequent (often public) spats with Finley and each other made them something of a cultural symbol.

They were also a very good baseball team, one that combined long-ball hitting, speed, tight defense, and excellent pitching. In 1972, while Billy Martin's Detroit team slipped in under the vagaries of the strike-altered schedule, Oakland won the AL West by five games over the Chicago White Sox and a Minnesota team that found itself mostly—and suddenly—over the hill. The A's then edged the Tigers in a taut five-game playoff and entered the World Series against the Cincinnati Reds, who'd also needed the full five games to overcome the Pittsburgh Pirates. For the first time in either league, both playoffs had gone the limit.

None of Oakland's three Series triumphs was a cakewalk. Still featuring Pete Rose, Johnny Bench, and Tony Perez, the Reds were considerably stronger than in 1970, mainly because of the addition of Joe Morgan, a speedy, hard-hitting second baseman obtained from Houston for Lee May.

With the 1972 Series tied at three games apiece, Catfish Hunter, Oakland's superlative right-hander, relieved John "Blue Moon" Odom in time to benefit from two Oakland runs in the top of the sixth inning. Relief ace Rollie Fingers (his handlebar mustache waxed to perfection) came on to save Hunter's second Series win and the first world's title since 1930 for the Philadelphia–Kansas City–Oakland franchise.

Oakland played the 1972 Series without outfielder Reggie Jackson, disabled by a leg injury in the playoff. At the age of twenty-six, the bespectacled, left-handed Arizona State University product had already accumulated 152 major-league home runs—as well as 780 major-league strikeouts. Flamboyant and outspoken, the powerfully built Jackson belonged to a new breed of athletes who understood the value of self-promotion and generally enjoyed media attention. Jackson's favorite gesture (subsequently copied by other sluggers) was to linger at home plate and follow the flight of his home-run drives. Not really a good hitter, Jackson, like most other contemporary sluggers, worried little about batting averages or strikeouts, so long as he continued to hammer the ball for distance and drive in runs.

While Jackson's star was ascendant, most of the men who'd reached the top in the 1950s and early 1960s were either already gone or playing out the string. The saddest loss was Roberto Clemente, who made his three thousandth major-league base hit on the last day of the 1972 season and then, the following February, died in the crash of an aircraft that was ferrying supplies from his native Puerto Rico to earthquake-devastated Nicaragua. Shortly thereafter the Baseball Writers Association of America, as it had done in 1939 for Lou Gehrig, waived the five-year retirement rule and elected Clemente to the National Baseball Hall of Fame.

Mickey Mantle hit eighteen homers in 1968 and then quit with a career total of 536 (still, some would always insist, not having lived up to his full potential); and Don Drysdale, with 209 wins and the all-time record for consecutive scoreless innings, retired the next year. Two years later sunny-dispositioned Ernie Banks, the most popular player in Chicago Cubs history and the most prolific home-run hitter ever to play shortstop, hung it up at the end of a season in which he struck his 510th, 511th, and 512th homers. Willie Mays, traded from San Francisco to the New York Mets, struggled to bat .211 in 1973, then finally retired at age forty-three with his fourth World Series check, plus 660 home runs, 1,903 rbi's, more than two thousand runs scored, and a .302 lifetime batting average.

Bob Gibson and Juan Marichal would last a couple more years before quitting with 251 and 243 victories, respectively. Meanwhile Harmon Killebrew was winding down a career that produced 573 homers but also 1,699 strikeouts and only a .256 cumulative batting average. Al Kaline, the youngest player ever to win a big-league batting title (in 1955), retired in 1974 after twenty-two seasons as a Detroit Tiger—the first major-leaguer to accumulate three thousand base hits and yet still finish with a sub-.300 career average.

As a group, ballplayers had become far more record-conscious than their forebears. When Ty Cobb collected his four thousandth hit in Detroit on July 19, 1927, he learned about what he'd done by reading that evening's edition of a local newspaper. By contrast, nobody had the slightest doubt that the Atlanta Braves' Henry Aaron, starting the 1973 season with 673 homers, would play however long it took to surpass Babe Ruth's majestic total of 714.

Of modest size (slightly under six feet tall and about 175 pounds), Aaron performed with unostentatious brilliance and remarkable consistency; from 1955 to 1972 he never hit fewer than twenty-four (or more than forty-seven) home runs. In 1973 he added forty more to pull within one of Ruth's mark, then tied the record in the season opener at Cincinnati the following spring. On Monday night, April 8, 1974, in his second time up—and before a national television audience watching the Braves' home opener—Aaron lined a pitch from Los Angeles left-hander Al Downing over the wire fence enclosing the bullpen in left field.

Among a number of ironies associated with the moment was that not only had Ruth's record fallen to a black man who couldn't have played in the majors in Ruth's day, but the homer had also come off a black pitcher, in a city that until fairly recently had remained wedded to segregation in athletics and nearly everything else. On hand to congratulate Aaron as the commissioner's representative was Monte Irvin, who'd been one of the first generation to cross the color line.

As he neared Ruth's record, Aaron had become the object of a media onslaught surpassing even what Roger Maris had endured. The Braves outfielder also received lots of hate mail from people who, for racial or whatever reasons, despised him because he was about to eclipse what many viewed as baseball's most monumental achievement. Through it all Aaron continued to carry himself with the same quiet dignity he'd shown ever since leaving Mobile, Alabama, at age seventeen to join the Indianapolis Clowns.

In part-time duty over the remainder of the 1974 season, Aaron was able to add eighteen more homers to his career total. Traded to the Milwaukee Brewers that fall, he would play his final two seasons in the city where he broke in as a Milwaukee Brave; and by the time he finally stopped swinging the bat in the fall of 1976, Aaron would have accumulated 755 home runs, 3,771 hits, and a .305 career batting average. His 2,297 runs batted in also put him ahead of the Babe and everybody else in that category, and only Cobb had scored more runs.

Oakland's Reggie Jackson, twelve years Aaron's junior, was as numbers-conscious as any young player who'd ever come along. In 1973 Jackson led the AL in homers and runs batted in, while Oakland third baseman Sal Bando batted in ninety-eight tallies. With Rollie Fingers's help, Catfish Hunter, Vida Blue, and Ken Holtzman all won at least twenty games for the A's, who cruised to another division title in front of Kansas City, then beat Earl Weaver's Baltimore team in five games in the playoff.

In the National League West, Cincinnati won again, with Pete Rose gaining his third batting championship and Johnny Bench, Tony Perez, and Joe Morgan again enjoying productive seasons. The Reds went into the playoffs as heavy favorites over the New York Mets, first-place finishers in the NL East with a lackluster 82–79 record—a game and a half and two and a half better than St. Louis and Pittsburgh, respectively. Managed by Yogi Berra, who'd taken the job following Gil Hodges's fatal heart attack in the spring of 1972, the Mets owed their inelegant success principally to starting pitchers Tom Seaver and Jerry Koosman and reliever Frank "Tug" McGraw.

Berra's charges came close to duplicating what Hodges's "amazin' Mets" had done in 1969. In the NL playoff, the proud and powerful Reds fell in five games. In the clincher, a 7–2 victory behind Seaver at New York, things took an ugly turn when Rose and Mets shortstop Derrel "Bud" Harrelson scuffled at second base and police had to block menacing fans from coming onto the field after the Cincinnati star. When McGraw got the last two outs for Seaver, thousands of overwrought New Yorkers did surge across the Shea Stadium turf to rip up bases and chunks of grass, in a replay of 1969.

The pesky Mets then pushed Oakland to the limit. In a Series in which nobody on either staff pitched a complete game and Dick Williams went to his bullpen seventeen times, the A's finally prevailed in seven, with two-run homers by Jackson and shortstop Bert Campaneris deciding it. No longer able to endure owner Finley's meddling in on-field affairs, Williams then announced his resignation between postgame champagne dousings.

In 1974 the Los Angeles Dodgers won their first pennant since 1966 (and Walter Alston's sixth in Brooklyn-Los Angeles), and then became the third different NL champion to succumb to the A's. The Dodgers had to win 102 games to overcome the Reds, who won ninety-eight. Right-handers Andy Messersmith (20–6) and Don Sutton (19–9) were the Dodgers' most dependable starters, while Mike Marshall, who held a graduate degree in physical education from Michigan State University and practiced gruelling conditioning regimens, relieved 106 times to break the record of ninety-two he himself had set the previous season at Montreal. In 1974 Marshall saved twenty-two games and was the winner in fifteen, and in the playoff he finished up twice for Sutton and once for Messersmith, as Los Angeles beat Pittsburgh three games to one.

Again Baltimore was Oakland's AL playoff victim, this time in only four games. Consistent pitching had carried the Orioles to a two-game winning margin over the resurgent Yankees, now managed by Bill Virdon, successor to Ralph Houk in the first of George Steinbrenner's numerous changes in field leadership. The A's continued their swashbuckling ways despite the example of manager Alvin Dark, a pious Baptist who followed the notably impious Dick Williams. Getting high-powered output from Jackson, Bando, Joe Rudi, and Gene Tenace and twenty-five, nineteen, and seventeen wins from Hunter, Holtzman, and Blue, respectively, Oakland finished six games in front of the Texas Rangers—a one-season contender under new manager Billy Martin.

The World Series lasted only five games, but four of those games were decided by 3–2 scores. At Oakland in game five, Rudi broke a 2–2 tie in the seventh by hitting one of Marshall's pitches into the left-field seats, after which Fingers pitched two shutout innings to save his third game of the Series. If three straight world's titles made a baseball dynasty, the Oakland A's had built theirs.

The 1974 Series—the third straight in which no complete games were recorded—highlighted the central importance of relief pitching in contemporary baseball thinking. Not since Steve Blass defeated Baltimore to clinch Pittsburgh's victory in 1971 had anybody gone the route in Series competition. For relief pitchers, "saves"—an officially recognized statistical category beginning in 1969, when a complicated new scoring rule was adopted—had become the standard of achievement, rather than won-lost records. In the seventies such late-inning specialists as Oakland's Fingers, the Dodgers' Marshall, the Mets' McGraw, Detroit's John Hiller, the Yankees' Al "Sparky" Lyle, and the Cardinals' Al "Mad Hungarian" Hrabosky reached a level of eminence and affluence undreamed of by Johnny Murphy, Hugh Casey, Joe Page, Jim Konstanty, and other pioneer "firemen." As Sparky Lyle quipped, "Why pitch nine innings when you can get just as famous pitching two?"

Baseball traditionalists, who'd always assumed that pitchers ought to finish what they started, cherished such gems as Vida Blue's two-hitter to beat Jim Palmer 1–0 in game four of the 1974 AL playoff, but old-fashioned pitchers' battles were increasingly hard to come by, especially in the National League. In '74, hurlers in the older circuit completed only 439 games, somewhat less than one in every four played.

In American League regular-season play, on the other hand, the relief-pitching trend had slowed temporarily as a consequence of the AL's adoption of the designated hitter—the most far-reaching rule change since the pitching distance was extended to sixty feet six inches for the 1893 season. Like most of the important rule changes since that time, it was designed to put more offense into the game and thereby make it more appealing to actual and prospective customers.

Since the early 1950s the American League had consistently trailed the National in overall attendance; from 1963 through 1972, some thirty million more people saw NL games. Among NL franchises in '72, only Atlanta, San Diego, and San Francisco fell short of one million paid admissions, while in the AL only Detroit, Boston, and

Chicago reached that figure. In their first year in their new surroundings, the Texas Rangers could muster only about 663,000 fans, while Baltimore, coming off three straight pennants, totaled 921,323. In drawing 966,328 during the 1972 regular season, Oakland became the first World Series champion since the 1944 Cardinals to miss the million mark.

Part of the explanation for the attendance gap between the two leagues obviously had to do with the decline of the Yankees—the AL's biggest attraction both at home and away from 1920 until the mid-1960s. Hard times for the Yankees coincided with the Mets' rising popularity and the Dodgers' record-setting turnouts since their move to Los Angeles. Then, too, most fans seemed to prefer new stadia to the old ballparks, and NL playing facilities were generally more modern. As of 1974, only the Chicago Cubs and Montreal Expos still used pre-1960 plants, and within three years the Expos would occupy the stadium built for the 1976 Olympic Games. In the AL only Kansas City, Oakland, California, and Texas played in facilities built (or rebuilt) since 1960, although the new-edition Yankee Stadium would finally be ready for 1976.

Undoubtedly another reason more people paid to see NL games was the opinion—widely held since the 1950s—that on the whole the NL played better baseball. The NL's continuing domination of All-Star Game competition fortified such thinking; from 1950 through 1982, National Leaguers won twenty-eight All-Star meetings to only nine for the AL (with one ending in a rain-shortened tie). World Series play was much more competitive—the NL had a 17–16 edge over the same period—but after 1962, when the Yankees took their last world's title in the Stengel-Houk period, National League clubs won twelve of the next twenty Series.

Attracting substantially fewer paying customers and struggling with a reputation for being the lesser league, AL owners and officials again sought a quick fix. They pointed to the fact that in 1972 NL teams scored 824 more runs, hit 186 more homers, and compiled batting averages nine points higher than their AL counterparts. Thus they seized upon an expedient that had first been proposed by NL president John Heydler as far back as 1929, and that had actually been adopted starting in 1969 in the Class AAA International League:

designating an extra player to bat for the pitcher each time it was the pitcher's turn to hit.

With commissioner Kuhn speaking in its favor, AL owners and general managers unanimously approved the new rule at that winter's annual major-league meeting at Rosemont, Illinois. Voting separately, the National Leaguers turned it down. Henceforth, in the AL, pitchers wouldn't have to bat and run the bases; the new class of designated hitters wouldn't have to catch and throw the ball. Although it might be argued (and was) that the designated-hitter rule only represented the next logical progression beyond platooning and relief pitching, others protested that the AL had fundamentally changed the world's most nearly perfect team sport.

Initially approved on a three-year trial, the DH rule proved so popular with AL people that it was made permanent after the 1975 season, and the rule spread throughout baseball. The National Collegiate Athletic Association and every professional minor league adopted it, as did the Little League, the Babe Ruth League, the American Legion, and interscholastic baseball, plus professional leagues in Mexico, Nicaragua, Venezuela, and throughout the Caribbean (including Cuba), and one of the two Japanese major leagues. Within a few years, the only place in the Western Hemisphere where non-DH baseball could still be watched was the National League.

The DH did give the American League its hoped-for offensive boost: AL batters in 1973 averaged .254, a fifteen-point jump, and scoring and home-run hitting increased by nearly a third. The rule also had some unanticipated consequences. Inasmuch as AL managers no longer pinch-hit for their pitchers in late-inning situations, pitchers finished more games and accumulated more innings—at least in the early years of the DH. In 1974, for example, AL moundsmen threw about thirty percent more complete games than they had two years earlier, and about twenty-five percent more than were pitched in the NL. That proved a temporary phenomenon. A decade after the advent of the DH, the AL actually had *fewer* 250-innings-plus pitchers than the NL.

Facing nine legitimate big-league batters, including a designated hitter who was typically a slugger, AL pitchers tended to throw more curveballs than their NL peers. Yet because they never had to worry about retaliation by the opposing pitcher if they hit somebody, they also tended to throw inside more often. But because they had to be careful with every batter, they also issued more walks, and that and the fact that managers nearly always removed pitchers *during* innings (as opposed to pinch-hitting for them) made for longer games in the AL.

Finally, the designated-hitter rule extended by a few seasons the careers of players (commonly ex-National Leaguers) whose legs were about gone but who could still swing the bat. In the early years of the DH, Frank Robinson (California), Orlando Cepeda (Boston), Tony Oliva (Minnesota), Billy Williams (Oakland), Tommy Davis (Baltimore and Oakland), Henry Aaron (Milwaukee), and Rico Carty (various teams) were among the slow-footed veterans who gained new life from the rule. Hal McRae, an erratic outfielder for Cincinnati, was a different case. Traded to Kansas City in 1973 when he was only twenty-nine, McRae became the AL's DH par excellence for many years.

The problem with equating the DH rule with AL attendance growth is that crowds generally improved in both leagues from 1973 on, as did batting. In '73 total major-league attendance topped thirty million for the first time; another thirty-million-plus watched games the next season. Yet while AL franchises improved at the gate, collectively they still ran three or four million behind the NL season after season.

One of the reasons for the NL's bigger attendance in the mid-seventies was that the Cincinnati Reds—the Big Red Machine, third edition—became one of baseball's most appealing teams, both at home and away. In both 1975 and 1976—years in which they won back-to-back world's championships—the Reds attracted well over two million people into Riverfront Stadium, drawing from a wide radius in Ohio, West Virginia, Indiana, and Kentucky.

In 1975 Cincinnati won 108 games, ran away from the rest of the NL West, and then dispatched Danny Murtaugh's Pittsburgh club (NL East winners five of the last six years) in three straight. Earning the nickname "Captain Hook," Sparky Anderson allowed his starters to complete only twenty-two games, lowest in the majors. Left-hander

Will McEnaney and right-handers Rawly Eastwick, Clay Carroll, and Pedro Borbon, who together saved forty-nine games, were Anderson's indispensable moundsmen.

Besides their unmatched bullpen strength, the 1975–1976 Reds featured superb defensive play and the NL's most powerful attack since the Brooklyn, Milwaukee, and Cincinnati teams of the 1950s. While committing only 102 errors, the '75 Reds scored 840 runs, most in the majors since 1962. The only relatively soft spots in the batting order were Venezuelan shortstop Dave Concepcion and Dominican center fielder Cesar Geronimo, both outstanding glovemen. Besides the stellar foursome of Pete Rose (.317), Joe Morgan (.327, ninety-four rbi's, sixty-seven steals), Tony Perez (twenty homers, 109 rbi's), and Johnny Bench (twenty-eight homers, 110 rbi's), NL pitchers also had to face George Foster (.300, twenty-three homers) and second-year man Ken Griffey (.305).

Although they lost Catfish Hunter when a federal arbitrator ruled him a free agent, the Oakland A's were still far better than anybody else in the AL West. Ninety-eight victories, their most so far, gave them a fifth straight division title. Blue, Holtzman, and Fingers continued to be among baseball's top pitchers; Jackson, Rudi, Bando, and Tenace were still good for plenty of offense; and Billy Williams, for many years a NL star with the Cubs, contributed twenty-three homers and eighty-three rbi's as the team's designated hitter.

Hunter, after signing a huge contract with the Yankees, pitched twenty-three wins for his new team, but the New Yorkers still finished the season a poor third under the peripatetic Billy Martin, fired at Texas in August and quickly brought in to replace Bill Virdon. Despite strong pitching by Jim Palmer and Mike Torrez (acquired from Montreal in a deal involving Dave McNally), Baltimore fell four and one-half games short of the Boston Red Sox.

Managed by Darrell Johnson, the Red Sox won even though Carl Yastrzemski suffered through a season-long slump and Carlton Fisk, their hard-hitting catcher, was injured more than half the season. Five Boston pitchers recorded at least fourteen wins, but two outstanding rookies—left fielder Jim Rice (.309, twenty-two homers, 102 rbi's) and center fielder Fred Lynn (.331, twenty-one homers, 105 rbi's)— made the biggest difference in the team's fortunes. A former University of Southern California All-American, Lynn became the only man ever named both Rookie of the Year and Most Valuable Player in the same season.

The A's looked to be stronger than anybody in the AL East, especially after Rice suffered a late-season injury that kept him out of postseason play; but with Yastrzemski's bat finally alive, the Boston lineup pounded Oakland pitching for thirty-one hits and eighteen runs in a three-game sweep.

Chiefly because it was one of the most witnessed events in sports history—with five of the seven games played at night and some seventy-six million people viewing the finale—the 1975 World Series would often be described as the greatest ever played. If it wasn't, it still offered as much as anybody could ever have wanted.

It opened at fifty-three-year-old Fenway Park, where Boston's Luis Tiant, Jr., a crafty Cuban who'd won eighteen games in 1975 and 158 in his big-league career, pitched a five-hit shutout. The Reds took game two by scoring twice in the top of the ninth on doubles by Bench and Griffey. In the tenth inning of game three, at Riverfront Stadium, catcher Fisk protested vainly that he was interfered with by Reds pinch hitter Ed Armbrister as he tried to throw to second base; a few minutes later Cincinnati scored the winning run. Less masterful in game four, Tiant still outlasted four Reds hurlers for a 5–4 victory. Two homers and four rbi's by Tony Perez and strong pitching by young Don Gullett gave the Reds the fifth game, 6–2, and put them within one of the title.

They seemed to have matters well in hand at Fenway Park the next night, when they went into the bottom of the eighth inning leading 6–3, but a three-run pinch-hit homer by Bernie Carbo (a former Red) tied it up. The epic struggle ended in the bottom of the twelfth (long past midnight in the East), when Pat Darcy, Sparky Anderson's eighth pitcher, threw one too close to Fisk, who lined the ball off the left-field foul pole to win it for Boston, 7–6.

The night after that, most of New England rejoiced when the Red Sox pulled out to a 3–0 lead in the third inning. Bill "Spaceman" Lee, a whimsical lefty who espoused leftish social causes (and riled Bowie Kuhn with references to marijuana-smoking), nursed the lead into the sixth inning, when Perez lifted a two-run homer over Fenway's short, high, left-field fence. Another run in the seventh tied the score and drove Lee to the showers, and two innings later, with left-hander Jim Burton on the mound, Joe Morgan blooped a single behind second base to drive in the go-ahead run. Will McEnaney then retired Boston without incident to wrap up Cincinnati's first Series victory in thirty-five years.

In 1976 it was a lot easier for the Reds. Bench struggled through a terrible year at bat and Perez slumped mildly; but Rose (.323), Morgan (.320), Griffey (.336), Foster (.307), and Geronimo (.307) showered opponents with base hits. Foster's 121 rbi's led the majors; Morgan's twenty-seven homers, 111 rbi's, and sixty steals clinched his second consecutive Most Valuable Player Award. Anderson, usually content to get five or six decent innings from his starters, again looked to his bullpen. Eastwick, Borbon, and McEnaney combined for forty-one saves in the Reds' 102 wins—ten more victories than Los Angeles managed.

Under the direction of laconic Danny Ozark, the Philadelphia Phillies piled up 101 victories to win the NL East, as Steve Carlton, a big, temperamental left-hander, led the staff with twenty wins. (Four years earlier Carlton had turned in possibly the finest one-season pitching performance in the game's history, accounting for twenty-seven of the tail-end Phillies' fifty-nine wins.) Jim Lonborg, hero of Boston's 1967 near-miracle, added eighteen. Burly Greg Luzinski (.304, twenty-one homers, ninety-five rbi's) and third baseman Mike Schmidt (thirty-eight homers, 107 rbi's) were the nucleus of the Phillies' offense. But it wasn't enough to match the Reds', and Foster's and Bench's successive homers keyed a ninth-inning rally at Riverfront that completed a Cincinnati sweep.

In the AL, meanwhile, George Steinbrenner set out to prove that it was still possible to buy a winner. In fact, Steinbrenner had given Billy Martin a pretty good ball club, although as Yankees teams went, the 1976 version would have to rank behind a score of others. Besides signing free agent Catfish Hunter, Steinbrenner spent money and players to obtain Dock Ellis (17–8), an erratic right-hander who came from Pittsburgh, and righty Ed Figueroa (19–10) and fleet center fielder Mickey Rivers (.313) from California. The team was largely built around catcher Thurman Munson, a moody, combative Ohioan who in 1976 batted .302, drove in 105 runs, and generally performed as the AL's answer to Johnny Bench.

A smooth-running, well-put-together operation, the Kansas City franchise had fielded the most successful expansion ball clubs thus far. In 1976 manager Dorrel "Whitey" Herzog's Royals finally dethroned Oakland in the AL West, then pushed New York to the limit in the playoff. In the deciding game, at rebuilt Yankee Stadium, the Royals gained a 6–6 tie on an eighth-inning three-run homer by AL batting titlist George Brett, only to lose it in the bottom of the ninth on Chris Chambliss's homer off ace reliever Mark Littell.

Having made it to the World Series for the first time in twelve years, the Yankees then suffered the second Series sweep in their history. The bitterly cold nighttime weather in which all four games were played evidently didn't bother the Cincinnati batters, who averaged .313 and cuffed Hunter and his mates for twenty-two runs. In the first Series featuring designated hitters (under Kuhn's ruling authorizing the DH in alternate years), Reds utilityman Dan Driessen totaled five hits to three for the Yankees' platooned tenth men. Johnny Bench largely redeemed his poor season by making eight hits, including two homers, and driving home six runs.

The Cincinnati Reds—winners of six division, four league, and two world's championships in the 1970s—consciously sought to project an image of disciplined, mature professionalism. The Cincinnati organization offered fans only baseball, shunning the promotions and giveaways (and the various outlandishly costumed "mascots" inspired by San Diego's "Chicken") with which nearly everybody else sought to hype attendance. For some people, the Reds were old-fashioned and "uptight"; for others, they were an organization with class.

Like baseball teams everywhere, the Reds had discarded their old flannel uniforms for the stretchable, form-fitting, nylon-knit garments introduced by Pittsburgh in midseason 1970. Yet the Reds still played in plain black shoes while other teams went to white or colored footwear, still wore their outer stockings with low-cut "stirrups" while most players favored only a thin strip between pant and shoe, still had clean-shaven faces and neatly trimmed hair while beards, long sideburns, and flowing locks (for whites) or bushy Afros (for blacks) became the rule in baseball and throughout American society. If the Oakland A's seemed right for the laid-back, permissive Bay area, the Reds seemed right for a basically conservative midwestern city known as the birthplace of professional baseball.

Amid the obligatory champagne showers in the victorious Reds' dressing room at Yankee Stadium, Cincinnati president Robert Howsam wistfully advised everyone to savor the moment, because in the future teams wouldn't hold together for seven or eight years around the same outstanding players as the Reds had done—up to that point. What prompted Howsam's remark was a circumstance—still but dimly understood by most baseball fans—that was about to transform nearly everything for both owners and players.

Beginning in 1974, established big-leaguers were often able to use compulsory salary arbitration—a provision of the 1973 Basic Agreement—to get substantially bigger pay boosts, and in other instances general managers granted much or all of what players wanted to avoid going into arbitration. Meanwhile Catfish Hunter won release from Oakland's hold on him when an arbitrator ruled that Charlie Finley, by paying Hunter his entire $100,000 salary for 1974 instead of deferring half of it, had violated the pitcher's contract. Baseball's first top-performer free agent since the 1870s, Hunter eventually accepted George Steinbrenner's bid—$3.75 million over five years—but contrary to popular misunderstanding, the Hunter case didn't threaten the basic viability of the reserve clause.

After 1975, though, the reserve clause would never be the same. In the spring of that year Andy Messersmith, a 112-game winner in seven seasons with the California Angels and Los Angeles Dodgers, and Dave McNally, longtime Baltimore ace who'd just been traded to Montreal, acted on the advice of their attorneys and refused to sign the contracts they were offered for 1975. Instead of holding out in the traditional manner, both pitchers went ahead and played the season for their respective clubs—without contracts. Messersmith had another good year, leading the NL in innings pitched and recording nineteen wins and a 2.29 earned run average, while McNally, hampered by arm trouble, won only three games for the Expos.

At the end of the 1975 season, pursuing the strategy laid out by their legal advisers, the two pitchers persuaded the Players Association to file for an arbitration hearing in their behalf. A three-man panel—Marvin Miller of the MLBPA, John Gaherin for the club owners, and a professional arbiter named Peter Seitz—judged the case. Seitz sided with Miller in ruling that, by playing a full season without being under contract, Messersmith and McNally had freed themselves from their clubs' reserve rights. Although the club owners promptly fired Seitz, the hitherto-obscure lawyer and labor-management specialist had gained a permanent place in baseball history.

The owners' efforts to overturn the "Seitz decision" in the courts failed first at the U.S. district level, then in federal appeals court. In April 1976, while the sore-armed McNally decided to retire from baseball, Messersmith signed a three-year contract for about $600,000 per year with Ted Turner, the brash young satellite-television tycoon who now owned the Atlanta Braves.

As everyone within baseball quickly grasped, the Messersmith-McNally strategy offered a ready means by which players could break the hold of the reserve clause and sell their services to the highest bidders. That would be a formula for financial disaster—or so the club owners argued and many other observers readily believed. Inasmuch as the third Basic Agreement expired at the end of 1975 and the owners weren't willing to go into another season without some kind of restriction on free agency, they refused to open the training camps late in February 1976. On March 17 commissioner Kuhn personally intervened to end the lockout, and the 1976 baseball season—intended to celebrate both the nation's bicentennial and the National League's centennial—got under way on schedule.

In the fourth Basic Agreement, which Miller negotiated and the players ratified that summer, the MLBPA made important concessions on free agency. Only at the end of six years of major-league service would a player become eligible for what was called the "reentry draft," where he could put his skills on the open market; and in compensation for losing a player to free agency, his former club would receive an additional selection from the annual amateur draft. At first seemingly mollified by those concessions, the owners soon were complaining that they were losing their best men, and getting in return only youngsters with uncertain futures.

The 1976 Basic Agreement, by ending the owners' perpetual hold on players' services, codified the most significant change in baseball's employer-employee relations since the advent of the reserve clause itself. As historian David Voight has remarked, "Truly, it turned the baseball world upside down." While ordinary fans struggled to understand the complex issues and stipulations, the owners, with Kuhn generally echoing their views, proclaimed the imminent bankruptcy of individual franchises and ultimately all professional baseball, not to mention domination of play by the richest clubs and skyrocketing ticket prices for everybody. To all of which Miller calmly replied that bigger radio-television revenues more than covered both increases in players' salaries and hikes in owners' contributions to the pension fund.

Yet Bob Howsam had been right in suggesting that henceforth it would be a lot harder to hold teams together—unless franchises were willing and able to spend what it took to keep their stars. Within four years, the mighty Big Red Machine had pretty much disintegrated; the Cincinnati front office simply wouldn't go after free agents, either their own or other clubs'.

Don Gullett was the first free agent to leave the Reds, taking several hundred thousand dollars from George Steinbrenner not long after the 1976 World Series. As other clubs quickly learned to do, the Reds unloaded some players—Tony Perez, Will McEnaney, and Rawly Eastwick—in trades shortly before they gained free agency. Pete Rose, a Cincinnati native and by far the most popular player in the franchise's history, became a free agent at the end of the 1978 season, following another .300 season that included a forty-four-game hitting streak (tying Willie Keeler's NL record). Rose signed a long-term contract with the Phillies for about $800,000 per year; the next year Joe Morgan signed with Houston. Meanwhile Sparky Anderson also left, fired in 1978 following a second straight runner-up showing in the NL East. Anderson quickly moved into the manager's job at Detroit under a multiyear contract.

The same thing that happened to the Reds also happened to the Oakland A's, only faster. Charlie Finley had always run the smallest and cheapest organization in the majors, handling the duties of general manager, business manager, and chief scout on his own, as well as taking a generally unwanted hand in the on-field direction of his players. Despite being one of the most interesting and successful teams in baseball history, the A's had always had trouble drawing crowds at home. Yet Finley made money in Oakland, mainly because he paid about the same stadium rent he had in Kansas City, controlled all parking and concessions revenues, and by 1975 was receiving $1.1 million for radio-television rights.

Finley nonetheless pleaded poverty and would have nothing to do with free agents, actual or imminent. After letting Catfish Hunter get away, he ran afoul of Bowie Kuhn when he tried to sell Joe Rudi, Rollie Fingers, and Vida Blue for prices totaling about $3.5 million. Kuhn intervened to stop the sales on the grounds that such profiteering was "devastating to baseball's reputation" and bound, he thought, to cluster the best talent on the richest teams. How the present situation differed from what had often happened in baseball history, the commissioner failed to say. After a U.S. district court judge in Chicago threw out Finley's suit against "the nation's idiot" (as Finley referred to Kuhn), the Oakland owner watched his stalwarts depart, sometimes with his active assistance, sometimes with his passive acquiescence.

In the spring of 1976 Finley traded Reggie Jackson and Ken Holtzman, scheduled to become free agents after another season, to Baltimore for pitcher Mike Torrez and Don Baylor, a hard-hitting young outfielder. That fall Sal Bando signed as a free agent with Milwaukee, Joe Rudi signed with California, Bert Campaneris with Texas, and Rollie Fingers with San Diego. Before the 1978 season, Finley sent Vida Blue to San Francisco for $390,000 and no fewer than seven run-of-the-mill players.

In 1977 the A's fell all the way to last in the AL West; the next year they finished a rung higher, only to settle on the bottom again in 1979. That season they attracted 306,763 customers, played under their sixth manager since 1973, and operated with the smallest payroll in the majors. For 1980 Finley was able to sell a grand total of seventy-five season tickets, versus the five to ten thousand most other clubs sold.

At the end of the 1976 season, fifty-eight major-leaguers became free agents. The signing or re-signing of those players, plus continuing upward pressure on salaries in the arbitration process, pushed big-leaguers' average pay from $45,000 in 1976 to above $100,000 by 1979. Yet attendance also continued its upward trend, and radio-television contracts were more lucrative than ever.

Late in 1976, moreover, the twelve AL franchises realized still another financial windfall when, ignoring their NL colleagues, they voted to put new franchises in Seattle (as they were obligated to do under a court order issued in 1970 when the first Seattle franchise moved to Milwaukee) and Toronto, Canada's second largest city. Again the newcomers paid fat entry fees and stiff prices for dispensable players. The 1977 Seattle Mariners, grouped in the AL West, opened for business in the brand-new Kingdome, baseball's second completely closed environment. The Eastern Division Toronto Blue Jays also played at home on artificial turf, but outdoors in Exhibition Stadium, a facility far more suited to accommodate Canadian-style football and the annual national fair.

In each of its divisions, the American League now numbered only one less team than the entire league had included in 1960. As expected, Toronto finished its first major-league season buried deep in seventh place, and although Seattle won one more game than Oakland and stayed out of the Western Division cellar, AL hitters benefited from facing two additional weak pitching staffs. The league as a whole batted .266, ten points better than in 1976, and hammered 2,013 home runs—about 144 per team.

Yet overall batting averages in the NL also increased by seven points, while homers per team jumped only slightly less than in the AL. Clearly something was at work besides watered-down pitching.

The baseball itself had always critically affected the ever-tenuous balance between pitcher and batter. In 1973 Spalding—in line with what numerous U.S. firms were doing—moved part of its manufacturing process to the poverty-stricken Republic of Haiti (ironically, the only country in the Caribbean that had never embraced baseball). There the ball covers were hand-stitched, although laminating, yarn-winding, and cover-cutting by machines continued at the Spalding factory in Chicopee, Massachusetts. Four years later Spalding yielded its 101-year-old contract as Organized Baseball's exclusive supplier to Rawlings, which located the whole manufacturing process in Haiti.

Moreover, as Spalding had been doing since 1974, Rawlings continued to use cowhide covers, now cheaper and more readily available than horsehide.

While tests of balls from 1977 and previous years (commissioned by *Sports Illustrated*) were inconclusive, experienced baseball people were certain that Rawlings's "Haitian voodoo ball" was a lot livelier. Jimmy Reese, onetime roommate of Babe Ruth and now a coach and renowned fungo-hitter for the California Angels, declared that the current ball was the liveliest he'd seen in his fifty-plus years in the game. Now, said Reese, he had to ease up to keep from fungoing everything over the fence in pregame practice.

The 1977 New York Yankees totaled 184 home runs (only third best in the AL) and batted .281 as a team, in part because Reggie Jackson, after spending 1976 at Baltimore under a one-year contract, signed a big five-year pact with George Steinbrenner. Jackson boasted that he and the "Big Apple" were made for each other—that he was "the stick that stirs the drink." In truth, Jackson's presence transformed a good Yankees team into a powerhouse.

Besides Jackson's thirty-two homers and 110 rbi's, Billy Martin got strong seasons from Thurman Munson, Chris Chambliss, designated hitter Lou Piniella, and third baseman Graig Nettles. Although Catfish Hunter had run into arm trouble, holdovers Ed Figueroa and Sparky Lyle, rookie left-hander Ron Guidry, free-agent acquisition Don Gullett, and Mike Torrez, obtained in a multiplayer trade with Oakland, were a solid pitching combination.

The Yankees won one hundred games, three more than Baltimore and Boston, and again met Kansas City, which finished on top without much trouble in the West. It was another bitterly contested five-game playoff, finally won by the Yankees on a three-run rally in the top of the ninth at Royals Stadium. For the second night in a row, Lyle was the victor in relief.

Walter Alston had resigned as the Los Angeles Dodgers' manager with four games left in the 1976 season, having not quite completed his twenty-third one-year contract. His successor was as different from Alston as Alston had been from Charlie Dressen, whom he'd succeeded at Brooklyn. Tom Lasorda, long a coach under Alston, had been a good minor-league lefty, a career farmhand in the Brooklyn system. So devoted was he to his organization, proclaimed the pudgy Lasorda, that if he cut himself, he'd "bleed Dodger blue."

A considerable windbag, Lasorda showed that he was also a solid baseball man in directing the Dodgers to division and league titles in his first season. Lasorda inherited a veteran team, one that featured baseball's best infield in Steve Garvey, Davey Lopes, Bill Russell, and Ron Cey; outfield punch from Reggie Smith and Johnnie "Dusty" Baker; and well-distributed pitching strength, with Tommy John, a left-hander whose dead arm had been rejuvenated by innovative muscle-tendon transplant surgery, leading the staff at 20–7.

Already hurt by free agency and destined for even worse damage, Cincinnati finished twelve games behind Los Angeles, despite George Foster's fifty-two homers (the most since Maris and Mantle in 1961) and the arrival of Tom Seaver, dealt away by the Mets before he gained free agency.

In the NL East, the St. Louis Cardinals finished a distant third, but local fan interest remained high because Lou Brock was chasing Ty Cobb's career stolen-base record of 892. Three seasons earlier Brock had shattered Maury Wills's eleven-year-old mark for single-season steals, ending up with 118, and in 1977, at age thirty-eight, Brock dashed to thirty-five thefts, pushing his own career total to an even nine hundred. By the time he retired two years later, at age forty, that total would have reached a seemingly unassailable 938.

The Philadelphia Phillies enjoyed a second straight 101–61 season and another division title, mostly because of Steve Carlton's twenty-three victories and big years at bat for Mike Schmidt and Greg Luzinski. Pittsburgh finished second under the affable Chuck Tanner, fired at Oakland and hired to manage the Pirates when Danny Murtaugh succumbed to heart disease late in 1976. The Phillies again stumbled badly in the playoff, winning only one game from Los Angeles.

In the first Yankees-Dodgers World Series since 1963, the New Yorkers, acidly described as "the best team money could buy," proved how good they really were. In the twelve-inning opener, Sparky Lyle's sterling relief work was decisive, and subsequently Torrez pitched two complete-game wins and Guidry one. Jackson was overpowering at bat, with nine hits in twenty times up, ten runs scored, eight rbi's, and five homers. Three of those round-trippers came in game six, at Yankee Stadium, when Jackson connected on the first pitch from three different Dodgers in an 8–4 clincher. Not even the Babe had ever done that.

In 1978 the Phillies won their third division title in a row, although this time Pittsburgh fell short by only a game and a half. It was closer in the West as well, Lasorda's men beating out the Reds by two and a half, with Foster (forty homers, 120 rbi's) again wielding the biggest bat for Cincinnati. Whitey Herzog's Kansas City club made it three in a row in the AL West, with four pitchers—Dennis Leonard, Paul Splittorff, Larry Gura, and Rich Gale—accounting for seventy of the Royals' ninety-two victories.

The AL East provided the hottest competition since the NL's dead heat in 1962. The Yankees grabbed an early lead, then watched it disappear as the Boston Red Sox, managed by rotund, tobacco-chewing Don Zimmer, went into high gear and, by July 9, built a seemingly insurmountable fourteen-and-one-half-game advantage. Later that month, after Billy Martin wrangled with several players and almost came to blows with Jackson in front of a national television audience, Steinbrenner fired his high-strung manager and brought in low-keyed Bob Lemon, just fired by the Chicago White Sox.

Under the Hall of Fame right-hander, the Yankees put on a terrific surge—highlighted by a four-game slaughter of the Red Sox at Fenway Park late in September—and finished the regular season tied with Boston at 99–63. Jackson and Munson tailed off from their 1977 numbers, but Chambliss, Nettles, and Piniella all pounded the ball with authority. Guidry, a left-hander from Louisiana's Cajun Country, pitched with rare brilliance, winning twenty-five, losing only three, fanning 248, throwing nine shutouts, and holding opponents to 1.74 earned runs per nine innings. Guidry's performance overshadowed Ed Figueroa's 20–9 season and outstanding relief work by Rich "Goose" Gossage, a big right-handed fastballer who'd left Pittsburgh as a free agent.

For Boston, Dennis Eckersley posted twenty victories, the much-traveled Mike Torrez (signed as a free agent the previous fall) added sixteen, and Jim Rice put in an outstanding year (.315, forty-six homers, 139 rbi's). Dazed and frustrated at season's end, the Red Sox faced a one-game playoff for the division title.

That playoff—like the one-game pennant showdown with Cleveland thirty years earlier—proved a bitter experience for the Fenway Park faithful. With Boston ahead 2–1 in the top of the seventh inning, light-hitting Yankees shortstop Russell "Bucky" Dent lofted the ball into the screen atop the left-field fence to put New York ahead by two runs. After Jackson's homer made it 5–2 in the top of the eighth, Boston rallied for two runs in its half of the inning. Then, in the bottom of the ninth, designated hitter Yastrzemski popped out to end the game, leaving the tying run on third.

After fighting off the Red Sox, the Yankees found Kansas City fairly easy; the Royals were eliminated in four games. Even George Brett's three home runs couldn't stop the Yankees in game three, which Gossage won in relief, and Gossage also saved the clincher for Guidry at Yankee Stadium. Jackson, rapidly building his reputation as "Mr. October," homered twice, drove in six runs, and batted .462 for the playoff.

The outcome of the eleventh Yankees-Dodgers World Series was the same as all but two of the others. As they had in 1977, the Dodgers submitted in six games. With the Series tied 2–2, the Yankees pounded three Los Angeles pitchers for eighteen hits and a 12–2 victory behind little-known right-hander Jim Beattie, and two nights later, at Dodger Stadium, Jackson homered for the second time in the Series and the Yankees collected ten more hits, good for seven runs off Don Sutton and two successors. In the last good outing of his splendid career, Catfish Hunter threw seven strong innings, then gave way to Gossage, who blanked Los Angeles the rest of the way. It was the twenty-second world's championship for the Yankees franchise.

The 1979 baseball season began with another strike—this time by the umpires. A decade earlier, after years of bitter dispute with the league presidents and commissioner's office, the umpires had won a ruling from the National Labor Relations Board that enabled them to organize the Major League Umpires Association (MLUA). By 1978, with all regular-season games being worked by four umpires (the standard practice since the mid-fifties), the MLUA numbered fifty-two men, paid an average annual salary of $31,000.

In the middle of that season, when they got no action on demands for more money and an end to the rule whereby they could be fired with only ten days' severance pay, the umpires staged a one-day walk-out, only to be forced back to work by a U.S. district court injunction secured by the AL and NL presidents. The next spring the arbiters collectively refused to sign their contracts and wouldn't take the field. The 1979 season started with regular umpires picketing outside the stadia; inside, hurriedly recruited umpires from amateur, semipro, and minor-league baseball—denounced as "scabs" by the MLUA—did the best they could.

By May 18, when the league presidents finally gave in, nearly everybody was complaining that, however earnest and hardworking the substitute umpires might be, they just couldn't do the job at big-league standards. The MLUA won substantial boosts in salary and expense money, plus in-season paid vacations (which necessitated an increase in the umpiring staff) and a stipulation that no umpire could be fired during the season. Beyond all that, the umps had made their point: Their skills and experience were just about as important to sustaining quality baseball as those of the players.

The 1979 umpires' strike signaled not only the determination of the game officials to share in baseball's swelling revenues but also their growing professional militance. Umpires were no longer willing to take the kind of abuse their predecessors had often endured; managers and players in both leagues now complained of umpires' "short fuses" and "hair triggers." Anybody who'd watched baseball for decades would have to agree that umpires had become less patient and acquiescent, more argumentative and confrontational in on-field disputes. Unionized and determined, the new breed of umpire often seemed to echo the psychotic newscaster in the 1976 motion picture *Network*: "I'm mad as hell and I'm not going to take it anymore!"

For the rest of the 1979 season, managers lamented that such-and-such calls by the sub umps had cost their team such-and-such games, but only in the NL West would a game or two decided by bad calls have affected the outcome. While the Dodgers, hurt by the loss of Tommy John to the Yankees through free agency, faded to third, the first Cincinnati team since 1963 that didn't have Pete Rose in the lineup barely slipped in ahead of the increasingly menacing Houston Astros. Directed by John McNamara, earlier fired at both San Diego and Oakland, the Reds won with a rebuilt pitching staff headed by

Tom Seaver (16–6), plus solid efforts by Johnny Bench, George Foster, and Ray Knight, Rose's successor at third base.

Pittsburgh took the NL East by three games over Montreal, which under Dick Williams set a franchise record with ninety-five wins. For Chuck Tanner's Pirates, a tall, bony, right-handed submariner out of Marietta College named Kent Tekulve relieved ninety-four times, saved thirty-one games, and got credit for ten victories. The Pirates' most potent bats belonged to first baseman Willie Stargell and outfielder Dave Parker. Under a five-year contract he'd signed over the winter, the lefty-hitting Parker, at twenty-eight, had become baseball's first million-dollar-per-year player. NL batting champion in 1977 and 1978, the massive (6-5, 230 pounds) Parker batted .310 in 1979, besides clubbing twenty-five homers, driving in ninety-four runs, and intimidating base runners with his outstanding throwing arm.

Despite free agent Tommy John's twenty-one victories, Ron Guidry's eighteen, and thirteen from aging Luis Tiant (another free agent signed), the Yankees tumbled to fourth in the AL East, playing the last two months of the season without Thurman Munson, killed when his private aircraft crashed near his home at Canton, Ohio. After firing Bob Lemon in June, Steinbrenner brought back an embarrassingly appreciative Billy Martin. It was still another episode in a seemingly endless soap opera starring Steinbrenner, Martin, and a large cast of other equally bad actors.

While the Yankees gave their fans *angst*, Baltimore, still guided by Earl Weaver, ran off a 102–57 record to outdistance the upstart Milwaukee Brewers by seven games in the AL East. In the West, the California Angels beat out Kansas City by three to win the franchise's first title of any kind in its eighteen-year history.

The AL's two division titlists represented contrasting responses to the changing circumstances of the seventies. Although Jim Palmer was the sole survivor from the 1966–1974 teams, the Orioles remained almost entirely homegrown; right-hander Steve Stone, formerly of the White Sox, was the only Oriole gained through free agency. Lefties Mike Flanagan (23–9) and Scott McGregor (13–6) and righty Dennis Martinez (15–6) led the pitchers, while the switch-hitting tandem of first baseman Eddie Murray (.295, twenty-five homers, ninety-nine rbi's) and right fielder Ken Singleton (.295, thirty-five homers, 111 rbi's) carried the Baltimore offense.

By contrast, California's Jim Fregosi, at thirty-five the majors' youngest manager, oversaw a team built around free agents. Gene Autry had spent big chunks of his fortune to secure second baseman Bobby Grich (Baltimore) and outfielders Joe Rudi and Don Baylor (Oakland), among others who'd put themselves on the market and signed with the Angels. Meanwhile outfielder Dan Ford and seven-time AL batting champ Rod Carew had arrived in separate deals with Minnesota, in exchange for a total of seven players.

All of the ex-singing cowboy's money could buy no more than a division title. After failing twice in Baltimore and winning once at Anaheim Stadium, the Angels suffered an 8–0 drubbing at the hands of McGregor and mates, with designated hitter Pat Kelly's three-run homer doing the most damage.

Meanwhile Pittsburgh fans vengefully cheered their favorites to three straight victories over the Reds, before whom the Pirates had fallen three times in previous playoffs. Dutch-born righty Bert Blyleven scattered eight hits to clinch the pennant by a 7–1 score at Three Rivers Stadium.

The favored Orioles took three of the first four games in the World Series on fine pitching by Flanagan and McGregor, who went the distance in games one and three, and Tim Stoddard, a 6-7 reliever who rendered three shutout innings after Baltimore staged a six-run rally in game four. But the next night—with the Three Rivers public-address system blasting out Sister Sledge's "We Are Family" (the home team's unofficial anthem) and the players' wives beaming for the TV cameras—the Pirates slapped Flanagan and four other hurlers for thirteen hits and seven runs. Back in Baltimore, tall John Candelaria and Kent Tekulve combined on a 4–0 shutout, with Palmer taking the loss. Then, in game seven, Willie Stargell hit one of McGregor's pitches over the fence with a man aboard; Tanner received effective work from four pitchers; and the Pirates triumphed 4–1, thereby becoming only the fourth team in seventy-five World Series to recover from a three-games-to-one deficit.

Within a short time after signing free agent Pete Rose late in

1978, the Philadelphia Phillies sold four thousand more season tickets and exacted an additional $600,000 for local broadcast rights, thereby covering Rose's annual salary with about $200,000 to spare. Although the Phillies' pitching fell apart in 1979 and the team slumped to fourth, Rose registered another fine season, batting .331 (second in the NL to the Cardinals' Keith Hernandez), rapping out 200-plus hits for the tenth time, making only eight errors at first base (a position he'd never before played), and generally proving that, at thirty-eight, he still had plenty of good baseball left.

Nicknamed "Charlie Hustle" in his early years in the NL, Rose was an updated version of what people assumed ballplayers must have been like in Ty Cobb's time. Never a fast man on the bases, Rose was nonetheless a smart and aggressive runner who repopularized the headfirst slide—a technique in general disfavor at least since the turn of the century. (John McGraw, for one, had always disliked that way of sliding, arguing that it simply ran the runner directly into the tag, whereas a well-executed, feet-first hook slide gave the baseman nothing but a toe to touch.) One suspected that Rose's trademark dives into bases were as much a matter of self-expression as studied technique, but his style influenced a whole generation of belly-flopping youngsters.

Often compared to Cobb, Rose was peppery, intense, hardworking, a nondrinker and nonsmoker who stayed in shape year-round. Like Cobb, the native Cincinnatian was an overachiever—a man who did as much as possible with less physical skills than many other players possessed. Unlike Cobb, Rose usually kept his temper in check and enjoyed the goodwill as well as respect of most of his peers. (But like Cobb, Rose had trouble being a husband and father: Cobb was married and divorced twice and became estranged from his five children; Rose settled out of court on a paternity suit and later divorced his first wife. And unlike Cobb, Rose proved to be a compulsive gambler.)

Although he batted only .282 in 1980, Rose again emerged as the acknowledged leader of a strong team—strong enough to win the Phillies' fourth division title in five years, by a bare one game over Dick Williams's tough Montreal Expos. Now managed by Dallas Green, Philadelphia still featured the superlative Steve Carlton, who posted a 24–9 record while leading the NL in innings pitched and strikeouts, and slugging Mike Schmidt. Schmidt, an Ohio University alumnus who set a rookie record by striking out 136 times in 1973 and then recorded a staggering 180 whiffs two years later, had worked hard to make himself a better contact hitter, and by the late seventies he was one of the majors' top home-run and rbi men and a superior third baseman. In 1980 Schmidt powered a career-high forty-eight homers, drove in 121 runs, batted a solid .286, and took NL Most Valuable Player honors.

That year the Dodgers, with a history of playing to ties in the old top-to-bottom NL, were also participants in the second division tie. After beating Bill Virdon's Houston Astros in the season's last three games to pull even, Los Angeles then lost a one-game playoff at Dodger Stadium. The Astros' Joe Niekro throttled Dodgers batters while his usually light-hitting teammates piled up seven runs.

Finally winning something after nineteen NL seasons, the Astros survived despite scoring only 637 runs and losing J. R. Richard, their giant right-hander, who'd won eighteen games and fanned 313 in 1979. In mid-1980 Richard suffered a stroke that almost took his life and did finish his career. Meanwhile Nolan Ryan—frequently awe-inspiring in winning 138 games, throwing four no-hitters, and breaking Sandy Koufax's season strikeout record during eight seasons with the California Angels—pitched disappointingly at the start of a long-term contract paying him well over $1 million per year at Houston.

The most expensive free agent thus far, Ryan again disappointed in the NL pennant playoff. It was the best such series since the inception of the playoff format, full of controversial plays and dramatic finishes, with four of the five games extending into extra innings. In game five, at Houston, Ryan took a 5–0 lead into the seventh, only to collapse under a six-run assault that was helped by his own inept fielding. The Astros rallied for two runs in the bottom of the inning to move ahead 7–6, but the Phillies pushed across a single run in the ninth, then won it in the tenth on Gary Maddox's double off reliever Frank LaCorte.

The Yankees rebounded from a bad 1979 season to win a fourth AL East title in five years. Billy Martin, who'd returned with such *éclat* the previous August, was fired even before the 1980 season began, the victim of Steinbrenner's wrath after the hot-tempered manager got involved in a well-publicized off-season fistfight. Coach Dick Howser took the helm and guided the Yankees to 103 wins, based largely on Reggie Jackson's best all-around season: a .300 batting average, forty-one homers, 111 rbi's. Tommy John won twenty-three times, Ron Guidry seventeen, and Goose Gossage was again the big man out of the bullpen, saving thirty-three of the Yankees' victories. At the end, New York was three games better than Weaver's stubborn Baltimore team, for whom Steve Stone pitched twenty-five wins and Scott McGregor twenty.

In the West, Jim Frey succeeded Whitey Herzog as manager of the Kansas City Royals, who exactly matched the Yankees' run of division successes since 1976. Pulling ahead early, Kansas City finished fourteen games in front of Oakland, where Billy Martin had again landed on his feet and sparked something of a revival. For the Royals, the gifted George Brett threatened the .400 mark almost to the end of the season before finishing at .390. Besides achieving the highest average since Ted Williams's .406 thirty-nine years earlier, Brett connected for twenty-four home runs and drove in 124 runs—an indubitably Most Valuable Player performance. Designated hitter Hal McRae had his usual solid season; free agent Willie Mays Aikens contributed twenty homers and ninety-eight rbi's; Dennis Leonard and Larry Gura racked up twenty and eighteen wins, respectively; and free agent Dan Quisenberry, a submarine reliever who reminded NL fans of Kent Tekulve, finished with a 12–7 record and thirty-three saves.

At last, Kansas City disposed of the New York nemesis—and in short order. It took only three games for the Royals to wrap up the AL playoff, with Brett's homer with two aboard off Gossage deciding game three at Yankee Stadium.

The 1980 World Series—a matchup of one team that had never been there and another that hadn't since 1950—excited extraordinary interest. Philadelphia prevailed in a hard-hitting six-game set that featured eleven home runs and the highest combined batting average (.292) of any Series thus far. With Brett troubled in the early going by a hemorrhoid flare-up ("It's all behind me," he noted before resuming play), the Royals lost the first two games at Veterans Stadium in Philadelphia, rallied for two wins in Kansas City, then dropped game five in Royals Stadium.

Back at Veterans Stadium, before sixty thousand rowdy fans and an on-field cordon of policemen with German shepherds, Schmidt knocked in two runs to give Carlton a 4–1 lead, which reliever Tug McGraw, one of the New York Mets' 1973 heroes, preserved over the last two innings. The Phillies, representatives of a NL franchise dating back to 1876, had finally won a World Series.

In many respects, the 1980 season was the high-water mark thus far in major-league baseball history. Some forty-three million people paid their way in to see American and National League games; television audiences for the World Series were the biggest ever; and minor-league baseball, after many years of struggle, was finally showing strong signs of revival. Even more, there were indications that the popularity of professional football—ballyhooed as the new National Pastime for the past fifteen years—had finally crested. And at least so far, free-agent spending hadn't driven a single owner into bankruptcy.

For all the good news, the Major League Baseball Players Association and the club owners remained unreconciled on issues that had divided them for a decade and more. The reserve clause, as it had functioned for a century, was no longer viable, and baseball feudalism was at an end. In the coming decade, profits, salaries, attendance, and general excitement over things baseball would be greater than ever, but it would be an unprecedentedly strife-filled period. If baseball's best of times, the 1980s, in some ways, would also be its worst.

13.
The
Embattled
Eighties

"The game is heading toward banditry," lamented R. R. M. "Ruly" Carpenter, president and principal owner of the Philadelphia Phillies, early in 1981. Although Carpenter himself carried one of the highest payrolls in baseball—about $7 million in 1980, counting bonuses and deferred payments—what he particularly had in mind was George Steinbrenner's recent acquisition of free agent Dave Winfield under a ten-year contract whose total worth was estimated at $25 million. By a considerable margin, Winfield's was the fattest deal any free agent had made so far. In eight years of toiling for bad teams in San Diego, the former University of Minnesota basketball and baseball star had become one of the National League's headline performers. If anybody could possibly be worth that kind of money, then the big outfielder might be.

But as Carpenter and other owners complained, between the huge contracts necessary to keep or acquire top players, the effects of arbitration and aggressive players' agents, and the sheer foolishness of some club owners (such as San Francisco's Bob Lurie, who'd agreed to pay Rennie Stennett, an all-but-washed-up infielder, $3 million over six years), baseball's financial structure was in peril. In the past two years, eight big-league franchises had changed ownership—proof, claimed the owners, that baseball had become a losing proposition.

Nonsense, replied executive director Marvin Miller, Phillies catcher Bob Boone, and Orioles shortstop Mark Belanger, the foremost figures in the Major League Baseball Players Association. Major-league attendance in 1980 had soared to forty-three million, and for 1981, baseball could expect to receive about $90 million in radio-television revenues alone. Moreover, since the advent of free agency in 1976, ten of the twelve biggest-spending ball clubs had set new franchise attendance records. The Yankees, loaded with free agents, had drawn record numbers of people both at home and away, whereas the Mets, shunning the free-agent market, had finished on the bottom the past three years and lost about half their fans.

Players' salaries, noted the MLBPA, still were only twenty-eight percent of the gross revenue received in 1980 by the twenty-six big-league franchises. For tax purposes, moreover, club owners could treat players as capital assets and depreciate up to fifty percent of total salary costs over five years. When owners complained about how much money they'd lost because of salary escalation, frequently they were talking about paper losses. As for the rapid turnover in ownership, that resulted both from the sport's generally good financial health and from investors seeking new tax advantages. When Ruly Carpenter put the Phillies on the market in 1981, he eventually received $30 million for the franchise—hardly a sign of diminishing investor confidence.

With the fourth Basic Agreement between club owners and the MLBPA due to expire in the spring of 1980, negotiations between the players, led by Marvin Miller, and the owners, with Boston attorney Ray Grebey bargaining for them, had commenced late in 1979. Insisting that an extra choice in the annual amateur draft just wasn't enough compensation for the loss of a player through free agency, the owners demanded compensation in the form of a "ranking" player, to be drawn from what would be left after a team listed eighteen men (fifteen when a "ranking" player went free agent) on a "protected list."

Miller and the MLBPA rejected that demand outright, on the grounds that such upgraded compensation would curtail the free-agent market, as had already happened in the National Football League under the notorious "Rozelle rule." As Miller put it, "The owners are trying to force the players to force the owners to regulate themselves. That is not the players' responsibility."

When the negotiations broke off at the beginning of April 1980, the players walked out of the training camps in what was effectively baseball's second general strike. The season started on time after the MLBPA agreed to begin play while negotiations went forward, but when the deadlock continued, the two sides agreed simply to adjourn, with the owners promising to implement the "protected list" compensation plan in 1981 and the players promising to strike on June 1 of that year if they still found the plan unacceptable.

The timetable worked inexorably. On February 20, 1981, club owners proclaimed the new plan in force; the MLBPA refused to recognize it. Spring training proceeded as usual, as did the start of the season, but all under a darkening cloud and amid a drumfire of accusations, claims, and counterclaims. Negotiations went on fitfully and fruitlessly, although they did extend past the original June 1 deadline. Finally, on June 11, all efforts to achieve a *modus vivendi* broke down and the MLBPA called a strike.

It turned out to be baseball's most damaging labor-management conflict since the 1890 Brotherhood war. The strike lasted fifty days and cost the players some $30 million in salaries; the owners' estimated losses were $116 million, although their suffering was alleviated by $50 million in strike insurance they'd collectively secured. City officials and chambers of commerce in the big-league cities bemoaned lost tax revenue and hotel, restaurant, and other baseball-related income. As the weeks passed, everybody looked to Bowie Kuhn to do something—anything—but the commissioner, while basically in sympathy with the owners' predicament, remained officially aloof.

An opinion poll taken by the National Broadcasting Company indicated that by about fifty-three to forty-seven percent, fans supported the owners over the MLBPA; a New York *Daily News* poll gave owners a two-to-one advantage. Impressionistic evidence also suggested widespread public hostility toward the players, whose average salaries had at least tripled in the five years of free agency and now stood either at $180,000 (the owners' figure) or $130,000 (the MLBPA's figure). Recent published comments by a number of present and former players contributed to suspicions that highly paid performers—especially those under long-term contracts—often became arrogant, lazy, and unwilling to play with minor injuries.

Said Frank Robinson, now a Baltimore coach, "You used to be able to fine a guy $100 and he'd step back into line. Now $1,000 doesn't mean a thing to him." "Up until 1975," remarked Jim Palmer, "my next year's salary always depended on every pitch I threw. I never relaxed." Under the present multiyear contracts, thought Palmer, "it would seem hard for some players to have that kind of intensity." Onetime Yankees ace Jim Bouton—who'd gained literary fame and offended Bowie Kuhn (among many others) with *Ball Four* (1970), his racy, raucous look at ballplayers and their world—thought young players demanded more and became discouraged more easily than when he came up in the early 1960s. For Curt Flood, unsuccessful in a variety of undertakings since leaving baseball, the situation was bitterly ironic. "When I started my case," Flood said, "we tried to get owners to agree to a middle ground, where players would have some rights. But now it's swung too far in the other direction."

As the weeks passed with no settlement, Miller's and Grebey's faces, seen almost nightly on television news reports, became two of the most familiar in the country. Deprived of big-league ball, some fans rediscovered (or first discovered) accessible minor-league competition, while others disgustedly announced they'd sworn off baseball for good. No one felt the strike more keenly than Pete Rose, who at thirty-nine had set his sights on Ty Cobb's career base-hit record of 4,191 and needed about six hundred more safeties to get there.

After tearing a fifty-day hole in the schedule, the strike finally ended on the last day of July. Under the new Basic Agreement ratified a few days later by the MLBPA membership, the players compromised on the critical compensation issue. Instead of direct compensation from the organization that signed its former player, a team could choose from a pool consisting of surplus men contributed by all twenty-six major-league franchises, with the team losing a player from the pool receiving a flat $150,000. The Agreement also clarified the method for figuring a player's performance in arbitration hearings, by stipulating reliance on his previous year's output rather than his cumulative record.

With the strike over, it was easy enough to arrange for the All-Star Game to be played on August 9, just before the resumption of regular-season play. That night in Cleveland's huge stadium, seventy-two thousand people, the biggest crowd in All-Star history, cheered baseball's return and also saw a fine exhibition. Two homers by Montreal catcher Gary Carter and one each by Mike Schmidt and Dave Parker powered the Nationals to still another victory, 5–4.

But the regular-season schedule was a shambles. Inasmuch as making up some fifty games per team was out of the question, Bowie Kuhn decreed a split-season format, akin to ancient practices in the Negro and minor leagues, as well as what the National League had tried back in 1892. Under Kuhn's plan, the division leaders as of June 11 were declared first-half winners. The first- and second-half winners in each division would meet in a three-of-five-game "mini-playoff," followed by the regular playoff between division champs.

Assured of a place in the mini-playoffs, the first-half winners generally played at half-throttle and drew poorly at home in what remained of the season. Kuhn's plan also produced various freakish effects. The Yankees, for example, finished first in the AL East second half, then defeated the Milwaukee Brewers, first-half winners, in five games for the division title. But whereas the Brewers accumulated the best overall record in the division (62–47), the Yankees made only the third-best showing (59–48). Kansas City won the second half in the AL West, then went into the mini-playoffs against Oakland as the only team with a sub-.500 overall record (50–53).

In the NL East, the St. Louis Cardinals ended up with the best winning percentage but had to watch while Montreal, the division's best in the final fifty-three games of the season, took three of five mini-playoff games from Philadelphia, first-half winners. The most grotesque outcome of all occurred in the NL West, where Cincinnati's 66–42 record was the best in the majors in 1981, but still not enough to get the Reds into the mini-playoff. Los Angeles, prestrike leaders, played barely above .500 in poststrike competition but took the division title by beating Houston, second-half winners, in five games.

The Dodgers' pennant was their first since Walter O'Malley's death in 1979. Tom Lasorda's championship club—his third—took five games to beat a young, very talented Montreal team. In the finale, played in snow flurries at Montreal's Olympic Stadium, pinch hitter Rick Monday broke a 1–1 tie in the top of the ninth with a pinch-hit homer off Expos starter Ray Burris, and a few minutes later Bob Welch came on to get the last out for Fernando Valenzuela, the Dodgers' brilliant young Mexican left-hander.

The Oakland A's had come up with a fine group of young players, harvested at relatively little cost in Charlie Finley's bare-bones farm system. "Charlie O" himself, though, was no longer in charge of the Oakland situation, having sold the franchise in May 1980 to Walter A. Haas, Jr., chairman of the board of Levi Strauss & Co., for $12.7 million. A's manager Billy Martin, given to dirt-kicking forays against the umpires, again showed an extraordinary ability to work quick changes in his team's fortunes. After managing the 1981 A's to a first-place position at strike time and a 65–45 overall mark, he inspired his youthful charges to three wins in a row over Kansas City in the AL West mini-playoff.

Martin relied on abundant speed in his everyday lineup and a corps of sturdy young pitchers. Having stolen an even one hundred bases in 1980 to establish a new AL record, third-year man Rickey Henderson was good for fifty-six more in '81, along with a .319 batting average. Martin's starting pitchers followed up their ninety-four complete games in 1980 (the most for any team in thirty-four years) with sixty route-going outings in 1981. Right-handers Rick Langford and Mike Norris and left-handers Steve McCatty and Marty Keough accounted for fifty-six complete games—and forty-eight of the team's wins.

Oakland's bubble popped in the playoff, which the Yankees swept mainly on strong batting by Graig Nettles, Lou Piniella, and Larry Milbourne—the last an unlikely hero filling in for the injured Bucky Dent at shortstop. Yet even with Dave Winfield in the lineup, it was a comparatively weak Yankees team. In fact Winfield, following a solid regular season, managed only a .181 batting average in fourteen games of postseason play, including just one single in the World Series. (That feeble showing appears to have been the origin of George Steinbrenner's bitter, long-running feud with his multimillionaire outfielder.) Meanwhile Reggie Jackson, who batted only .237 during the abbreviated season and was about to become a free agent, often seemed to be just going through the motions.

After winning the first two Series meetings at home, the New Yorkers dropped three in Los Angeles. Back at chilled Yankee Stadium on October 28 (the latest game date in Series history), Pedro Guerrero, a powerful Dominican, homered for one of the Dodgers' thirteen hits and one of nine tallies off Tommy John and five other pitchers. New York's George Frazier ended up as the first man since Lefty Williams of the White Sox in 1919 to take three Series losses.

Following the previous year's playoff loss to Kansas City, Steinbrenner had fired Dick Howser and promoted Gene Michael from the Yankees' Columbus (International League) farm club. Then, with about a month left in the 1981 season, Michael got the axe and Bob Lemon returned. Although Lemon steered the Yankees to victories in the mini-playoff and the regular playoff, his failure to win the '81 Series left the mercurial Steinbrenner in an off-season funk. Lemon would last only fourteen games into the 1982 season, and Michael would return, only to be fired again with a third of the season left in favor of pitching coach Clyde King, under whom the Yankees would end up a dreary fifth.

In an age in which the baseball business, like other areas of the American economy, had become increasingly dominated by faceless corporate ownership, Steinbrenner and the now-departed Charlie Finley, as well as Atlanta's Ted Turner and San Diego's Ray Kroc, often behaved as throwbacks to the strong-minded, high-profile baseball capitalists of past times. Their ball clubs, like Chris Von der Ahe's and Andrew Freedman's in the late nineteenth century, served as extensions of their own tumescent egos. Keeping a close eye and firm hand on virtually every aspect of franchise operations, they felt free to meddle in game-by-game field management.

In his early years as Braves owner, for example, Turner sat in his field box chewing tobacco, leading cheers, and barking advice to his managers. In 1977 he even undertook to manage the team himself; after one night in the dugout, he handed the job back to Dave Bristol. Kroc, owner of the far-flung and fabulously successful McDonald's hamburger empire, was less inclined to dictate to his managers, but he did relish the public attention that came with being Padres owner— and the prerogative to do pretty much as he wished with his ball club. Toward the end of a one-sided loss in San Diego's 1974 home opener, Kroc grabbed the public-address-system microphone to apologize for his team's inept performance.

While Steinbrenner, Finley, Turner, and Kroc had all gained their wealth from nonbaseball endeavors, Minnesota's Calvin Griffith was the sole surviving owner who depended chiefly on franchise earnings. Like many such baseball entrepreneurs before him—perhaps most notably Connie Mack—Griffith operated as economically as possible and, in lean years, sought to trim his payroll. In the late seventies he traded Rod Carew, the finest hitter of his time, and gave up several other key men through trades or free agency. Although the 1980 Twins finished third in the AL West, they trailed everybody in the majors in home attendance—769,206—and that year Griffith received $1.25 million for radio-television rights, as compared to Steinbrenner's $4 million.

In 1982 Griffith moved his operations into the newly constructed Metrodome in downtown Minneapolis, and although attendance increased in the enclosed environment, the team brought up the rear in the AL West. But by 1984, with a number of fine young players beginning to reach their potential, the Twins' prospects had improved considerably—as had their market value. Late that year Griffith sold his holdings to a group headed by Carl Pohlad, thus ending the Griffith family's seventy-two-year association with the Washington-Minnesota franchise.

Despite judgments by many pundits that the great strike of 1981 had permanently alienated huge numbers of fans, total major-league attendance for 1982 surpassed the record 1980 turnouts. Much of the reason was the hot race in the AL East, where, with the collapse of the Yankees, a struggle ensued between Baltimore and Milwaukee. The Orioles fell short by one game, at which point Earl Weaver—with a world's championship, four pennants, and six division titles to his credit—announced his retirement. (Prematurely: Weaver would make an ill-advised comeback in mid-1985; after a fourth-place finish that season and a last-place showing the next, he quit for good.)

To win their first title, manager Harvey Kuenn's Milwaukee Brewers had to score 891 runs, bat .279 as a team, and clout 216 homers. Shortstop Robin Yount (.331, twenty-nine homers, 114 rbi's) was the AL's Most Valuable Player; first baseman Cecil Cooper batted .313, with thirty-two homers and 121 rbi's; and center fielder Gorman Thomas was good for thirty-nine homers and 112 rbi's (while batting only .245). Longtime relief star Rollie Fingers saved twenty-nine games.

The most sensational event that year in the AL West—in the majors as a whole, for that matter—was Rickey Henderson's feat of stealing 130 bases to top Lou Brock's single-season record by twelve. Billy Martin's intrepid A's stole 232 bases overall and set a franchise attendance record—1,735,489—but with their young pitchers hit by an epidemic of sore arms and personal troubles, they still skidded to fifth place.

Manager Gene Mauch's California Angels recorded only fifty-five steals, but they won the AL West with a star-studded lineup that now included Fred Lynn and Reggie Jackson in addition to Rod Carew, Bobby Grich, and Don Baylor, although the late-season acquisition of Tommy John from the Yankees did little to strengthen a ragged pitching staff. After winning the first two playoff games, at Anaheim, Mauch's men dropped three in a row at Milwaukee County Stadium.

The Atlanta Braves, a lackluster outfit for more than a decade, shot ahead of everybody by winning their first thirteen outings of the season, then barely held off Los Angeles and San Francisco. Manager Joe Torre's only reliable starter was Phil Niekro (17–4), a forty-three-year-old knuckleballer, but Gene Garber came out of the bullpen to save thirty of the Braves' eighty-nine wins. Atlanta's biggest bats were swung by center fielder Dale Murphy (thirty-six homers, 109 rbi's) and by third baseman Bob Horner (thirty-two homers, ninety-seven rbi's), one of the few players to enter a big-league lineup directly from college baseball (Arizona State, in Horner's case).

Atlanta folded in three games against the St. Louis Cardinals, now managed by Whitey Herzog. While defending division champ Montreal fell to third in the NL East, the Cardinals finished three ahead of Philadelphia. Herzog depended on valiant bullpen work from right-hander Bruce Sutter (thirty-six saves) and a slashing, speed-oriented attack. Although they were last in the majors in homers and scored only 685 runs, the Cardinals stole an even two hundred bases, used bunts, squeezes, and hit-and-run-plays with greater effectiveness than any team in decades, and generally scrounged to win games in a fashion reminiscent of the dead-ball era. The St. Louis team was tailored to spacious, artificially surfaced Busch Stadium, where

Cardinals batters slapped high hoppers for singles and raced for doubles and triples on shots between opposing outfielders. Meanwhile Ozzie Smith, an extraordinarily acrobatic shortstop, could expect true bounces as he ranged far and wide to squelch base hits.

Down three games to two in the World Series, the Cardinals returned to Busch Stadium and pounded out a 13–1 victory behind right-hander John Stuper, who had to wait through more than two hours of rain delays. The next night St. Louis overcame a three-run lead with three runs in the sixth inning and two in the eighth, and Sutter came on to preserve a 6–3 victory for Joaquin Andujar, a quick-tempered Dominican right-hander.

That off-season Milwaukee's Robin Yount, who became a free agent coming off his MVP year, enjoyed an extraordinary advantage in dealing with the Brewers' front office. At age twenty-seven, Yount signed a complicated six-year contract that was fairly typical of the deals top-level free agents were making in the 1980s. Yount's contract included a clause whereby the *player*, not the franchise, could exercise an option not to fulfill the final three years of the contractual term. Besides a yearly salary of $850,000, Yount would also earn a $50,000 bonus per season for appearing in at least one hundred games, another $50,000 for 350 times at bat, and still another $50,000 if the Brewers' home attendance reached 1.9 million. The free use of an automobile, a $600,000 interest-free loan from the Milwaukee franchise, and a $3 million bank loan, with the Brewers paying the difference between a nominal six percent interest rate and whatever the actual rate might be, were other features of the deal. Finally, if in 1986 Yount opted to fulfill the remaining three years of his contract (as in fact he would), the Brewers would arrange another loan for $2 million and continue to subsidize his interest payments.

While Milwaukee thus induced Yount to stay put, plenty of other free agents were on the move. Free agency was obviously a big reason why the major leagues were experiencing unprecedented competitive parity; the 1982 World Series marked the fourth straight year in which neither participant from the previous year had repeated. Besides free agency, liberalized trading rules, the amateur draft, and the contraction of farm systems helped even out year-by-year competition, as did expansion. With players spread over twenty-six teams, it was harder to load up with talent and sustain winning ball clubs than in the decades before free agency and expansion.

The pattern continued in 1983, when the Philadelphia Phillies and Baltimore Orioles met in the Series. Easygoing Joe Altobelli, who'd managed San Francisco in the late seventies, succeeded the volatile Earl Weaver and won with basically the same club Weaver hadn't won with in 1982. Still consisting almost entirely of players developed in the Orioles' farm system, Altobelli's club finished six games ahead of Sparky Anderson's rapidly improving Detroit Tigers.

Switch-hitting Eddie Murray (.306, thirty-three homers, 111 rbi's) continued to be the most dangerous man in the Orioles' batting order, but second-year man Cal Ripken, Jr., son of one of the Orioles' coaches, arrived as the heaviest-hitting shortstop since Ernie Banks. At 6-4 and two hundred pounds, Ripken was also one of the biggest men to play the position. Besides doing a capable job on defense, he batted .318, clouted twenty-seven homers, and drove across 102 runs. Pitchers Scott McGregor, Mike Flanagan, and Dennis Martinez were still on hand from the 1979 pennant winners, while rookie Mike Boddicker (16–8) solidified the staff.

The sentimental favorites in the AL playoff were the Chicago White Sox, whose Western Division title was the second-best thing that had happened for South Side fans in sixty-three years. Unfortunately, Bill Veeck could only watch from the outside. White Sox president in 1959 when they'd last won a pennant, Veeck had sold his holdings a few years later, then repurchased the club in 1976. Since 1980, when Veeck's failing health forced him to sell again, the franchise had been owned by television entrepreneurs Jerry Reinsdorf and Eddie Einhorn. Managed by poker-faced Tony LaRussa, the White Sox were the class of a weak division. Their twenty-two-game bulge over Kansas City was the widest margin of victory since the inception of division play.

In the NL West, Tom Lasorda's Los Angeles Dodgers beat out Atlanta by three games, mainly by having the lowest staff earned run average in the majors, plus Pedro Guerrero's potent bat. The Phillies finished strong under Paul Owens, who descended from the general manager's office in midseason to take over a floundering team. Pete Rose, in the last year of his five-year contract, continued his relentless quest for Ty Cobb's record but could do no better than a .245 average. Although aging Joe Morgan and Tony Perez rejoined Rose on the '83 Phillies, Mike Schmidt was still the big threat, hitting forty homers and driving in 109 runs. Thirty-eight-year-old Steve Carlton slipped to a 15–16 record, but right-hander John Denny came through with nineteen wins and lefty Al Holland led the NL with twenty-five saves.

Both playoffs ended in four games. After splitting at Dodger Stadium, the Phillies slammed Lasorda's pitchers for twenty-two hits and fourteen runs to take back-to-back victories at Veterans Stadium. And on a drizzly Saturday afternoon at aged Comiskey Park, in the top of the tenth inning of a scoreless tie, pinch hitter Terry "Tito" Landrum homered into the left-field upper deck to trigger a rally that won it for the Orioles, 3–0.

The 1983 World Series was the most one-sided since 1976. The Phillies won game one, at Baltimore, behind Denny and Holland; then Baltimore took four straight, highlighted by Boddicker's superlative mound work in game two and Flanagan's in game five. At Veterans Stadium on October 16, two homers by Murray and one by catcher Rick Dempsey gave Flanagan five runs—four more than he needed in twirling a five-hit shutout.

Bowie Kuhn attended the games in Baltimore and Philadelphia as a lame-duck commissioner of baseball. The previous August 12 Kuhn had failed by one vote to muster the three-fourths majority of the franchise presidents needed to renew his contract, but inasmuch as they hadn't come up with a successor, Kuhn obligingly agreed to stay on until one could be chosen.

Kuhn's tenure had been an extraordinarily trying time, what with the inauguration of division play, another expansion by the American League, the rise of the players' union, the advent of arbitration and free agency, the wrenching 1981 strike, and numerous other difficult and divisive matters. Besides his run-ins with Charlie Finley, Kuhn had barred George Steinbrenner from serving as Yankees president during 1974 after Steinbrenner admitted to having made illegal contributions to President Richard Nixon's reelection campaign two years earlier.

Yet for all the storm and stress that had marked his tenure, Kuhn could point to one final accomplishment: the signing of a five-year contract with NBC and ABC, effective in 1985, whereby the two networks would continue to alternate All-Star Game, playoff, and World Series radio and television coverage, in exchange for a cumulative $1.1 *billion*. In the period 1985–1989, in other words, the twenty-six major-league franchises would annually receive from $5.7 to $7.9 million apiece from the new contract, in addition to what they gained for local radio-TV rights.

In some ways, Kuhn got out just in time. His successor, elected in March 1984, was Peter Ueberroth, who delayed assuming the commissionership until he completed his work as chief organizer of the Olympic Games in Los Angeles. On October 1, 1984, fresh from his spectacular success—financial, artistic, and otherwise—with the Olympic extravaganza, the urbane Ueberroth began a five-year term as the sixth commissioner of baseball. He inherited the biggest mess since the Black Sox scandal.

In 1965, in bemoaning the disappearance of the rollicking old-time players—"the drunks of yesteryear"—Bill Veeck had proclaimed: "What baseball needs more than anything else is the simple courage to become disreputable." Veeck couldn't possibly have imagined how utterly ironic that sentiment would become by the time he died twenty years later. By then, plenty of major-league players had acquired public reputations for thorough disreputability—as sustained and systematic transgressors of the drug laws of the United States.

Legalized indulgence in beveraged alcohol—termed a "controlled substance" in the legal-medical jargon that came to pepper the sports pages—still caused trouble for ballplayers, as had always been the case. Mickey Mantle, Whitey Ford, Hank Bauer, and Billy Martin had recorded some legendary nightclub scrapes during their Yankees days; Martin's boorish barroom behavior continued into his fifties. Some former players—among others, Don Newcombe, Ryne Duren, Lou Johnson, Sam McDowell (a gifted left-hander who won 116 games and struck out 1,844 for Cleveland between 1964 and 1971)—were eventually willing to talk openly about their personal battles with alcoholism. In 1982 young Bob Welch of the Dodgers rendered his own poignant version of that battle under the book title *Five O'Clock Comes Early*.

But the late 1970s and early 1980s brought something new:

repeated revelations about professional athletes who'd become "addicted to" or "dependent upon" what were euphemistically designated "illegal substances." That nearly always meant snorting cocaine. (Over the past decade, smoking marijuana, though still illegal, had gained a considerable degree of social toleration.) Whatever changes in cocaine's legal status Americans might be willing to accept someday, in the 1980s the great majority viewed it as a public menace—far more menacing than alcohol had ever been.

For white Americans, cocaine was relatively new. It also was much more addictive than alcohol, or so a rapidly accumulating body of research indicated. And, of course, it was illegal everywhere in the U.S.—whether to possess, to use, or to traffic in. Actually, cocaine had been a significant factor in the life of urban black Americans at least since the 1920s, when Carl Van Vechten built his novel *Nigger Heaven* largely around the trade in "happy dust" in Harlem. Yet in the post–World War II period, heroin had loomed as the deadly drug of the streets, whereas cocaine had appeared to be a relatively harmless "recreational" indulgence, thought to be fashionable among the chicly rich in New York and Hollywood.

By the late 1970s cocaine-smuggling had expanded enormously, with inevitable reductions in price. Reports began surfacing about cocaine addiction among players in the National Basketball Association and National Football League, but it wasn't until 1980 that the first well-known and still-active baseball player was arrested for cocaine possession.

On August 25, 1980, Ferguson Jenkins, an outstanding pitcher for the past fourteen seasons with the Cubs, Red Sox, and Rangers, arrived at the Toronto airport with his Texas teammates. After waiting vainly for his personal luggage, Jenkins accompanied the team to its hotel. When Jenkins's bag finally arrived on a later flight, it was taken to an anteroom and opened, presumably to establish its ownership. Small amounts of cocaine as well as marijuana and hashish were found, whereupon police went to the Rangers' hotel and arrested the pitcher for possessing and transporting illegal drugs.

Released pending trial, Jenkins (ironically, one of the few native Canadians in Organized Baseball and the *only* black Canadian) traveled to New York to meet with commissioner Kuhn. When Jenkins refused to answer questions about whether and to what extent he used drugs, Kuhn suspended him indefinitely, whereupon the pitcher filed a grievance through the Players Association. A federal arbitrator overruled Kuhn's suspension order, although by that time the 1980 season had already ended. Meanwhile, in a court in Brampton, Ontario, Jenkins pleaded guilty and received an "absolute discharge"—equivalent to a suspended sentence.

Blocked by the MLBPA's intervention, Kuhn eventually settled for having Jenkins contribute $10,000 to a Dallas drug-education program. The big right-hander would pitch another season for the Rangers, then return to the Cubs for 1982 and 1983, finishing his nineteen-year career with 284 victories.

The Jenkins affair foreshadowed the coming cocaine scourge in big-league baseball, and the difficulty baseball officials would experience in trying to quell its use and discipline users. The warning signs were clearly up. About a year after Jenkins's arrest, Dick Young of the New York *Daily News* became one of the first sportswriters to acknowledge widespread cocaine use within baseball and to call for a crackdown. If Marvin Miller really cared about the MLBPA's members, said Young, he would jump into the fight against drugs instead of arraying the MLBPA against baseball officialdom on that issue, as in everything else. Yet as Bill Conlin noted in the *Sporting News*, unlike the situation with alcohol, players didn't talk openly about cocaine, didn't use it publicly, and didn't show its obvious effects. If officials, owners, and managers had never been able to control drunkenness, commonly a public activity, how could they possibly control the secret use of cocaine?

Season by season the number of players identified at the time or later as cocaine users continued to grow. Several years after the fact, Whitey Herzog put the number of Cardinals who were "heavy users" during the 1980 season at "about 11"—close to half the roster. At Kansas City in the late seventies, added Herzog, cocaine had probably "cost me a world title."

John McHale, president of the Montreal franchise, said that he was convinced cocaine kept the Expos from winning the 1982 NL Eastern Division title. At least eight Expos, McHale estimated, were regular users that season. The only one to admit as much was Tim

Raines, a fleet outfielder who stole seventy-eight bases while, he later admitted, ingesting cocaine every day and far into the night. Keeping gram bottles of the powdery substance in the back pockets of his uniform, Raines frequently left the dugout to take snorts in the tunnelway outside the dressing room. He always slid headfirst, Raines added, for fear of breaking the containers in his pockets.

Much of what became known about the cocaine problem resulted from two trials involving drug-using players. In November 1983, confronted with wiretapped evidence gathered by F.B.I. agents, Kansas City Royals outfielders Willie Wilson and Jerry Martin, first baseman Willie Mays Aikens, and pitcher Vida Blue pled guilty in U.S. district court to possessing or trying to purchase cocaine. The players spent three months apiece in prison and paid $2,500 to $5,000 fines. The Royals released Blue and Martin and traded Aikens to Toronto. Kuhn, in his capacity as lame-duck commissioner, reinstated the players in May 1984 when they'd finished their sentences, but with the exception of Wilson their careers were virtually over.

By the spring of 1984 the dimensions of the situation were starting to be apparent, as were its ambiguities. Over the past five years, by one estimate, sixteen active major-leaguers either had been convicted on drug charges or had voluntarily submitted to treatment for drug addiction. Then there were such former ballplayers as Orlando Cepeda (sent to prison in Puerto Rico for transporting a large quantity of marijuana), and Maury Wills (arrested in Los Angeles for cocaine possession late in 1983, after having undergone treatment twice in the previous six months), and John "Blue Moon" Odom (convicted in 1986 in Santa Ana, California, of dealing drugs), and Denny McLain (sentenced in Florida in 1985 to concurrent eight-year prison terms for racketeering and conspiracy, plus fifteen years for cocaine-trafficking).

According to most reformed users, protracted cocaine indulgence eventually hurt both physical skills and emotional stability. In 1985 Bill Conlin judged that of the many players traded by Philadelphia since 1981—beginning with outfielder Lonnie Smith and extending through pitcher Al Holland—the majority had been suspected drug users. Now one of the first questions that came up in trade talks, according to Phillies president Bill Giles, was, "Is he clean?"

Yet athletes seemed to perform quite well in the early phases of their involvement with cocaine. Lonnie Smith, for example, put in four straight productive seasons (1980–1983) with the Phillies and Cardinals—seasons in which, he later testified, he was a steady snorter. Catcher Darrell Porter enjoyed his best season with Kansas City (1979) at a time when he was heavily involved not only with cocaine but with amphetamines and alcohol, and Pascual Perez, a Dominican right-hander, accumulated twenty-nine wins for Atlanta in 1982 and 1983 while becoming steadily more dependent on cocaine.

Apparently the situation on the Pittsburgh Pirates was the worst in baseball. It turned out that the Pirates' celebrated "family" of 1979 had included several men who regularly ingested cocaine. (Dock Ellis, a reformed drug user who finished up his career at Pittsburgh in 1979, later ruefully observed that the carpet in the Pirates' Three Rivers Stadium clubhouse was "the whitest I ever saw.") The word around the league was that Pittsburgh, not Los Angeles or New York, offered the readiest cocaine action in the majors.

In the spring of 1985 more than twenty ballplayers, all previously granted immunity from prosecution, testified before a federal grand jury in Pittsburgh, and mainly on the strength of their testimony, seven Pittsburgh-area men were indicted on cocaine-trafficking charges. At the trials beginning the following October, six active and one retired player—all, of course, still under immunity—named themselves and seventeen others as users.

Lonnie Smith (with Kansas City by 1985) related his personal drug history and identified those under indictment as dealers. Keith Hernandez—1979 NL batting champion with the Cardinals, and four years later traded to the Mets—did the same, then went on to suggest that in 1980 as many as forty percent of the players in the majors at least experimented with cocaine. Dale Berra, Yogi's son and a former Pirate, testified that manager Chuck Tanner had tolerated the presence in the clubhouse of people he knew to be cocaine dealers. (Tanner was cashiered following a last-place finish in 1985.)

Ultimately all seven accused dealers were either convicted or pled guilty. To Alan Dershowitz, professor of law at Harvard University, the whole business seemed awry. "These players were not innocents lured into a trap," protested Dershowitz. Immunity from prosecution in drug cases, he noted, usually went to "obscure mules" in return for testimony against the big boys. "Here, the powerful have immunity to help prosecute the unknown."

Meanwhile Peter Ueberroth, who confessed to having had no idea how big baseball's drug problem really was when he'd accepted the commissioner's job, sought ways to curb drug use throughout Organized Baseball. Speaking at Loyola Marymount University's spring 1985 commencement, Ueberroth raised the ominous prospect that ultimately professional gamblers might be able to exploit players with drug addictions. Shortly thereafter he decreed random, mandatory drug-testing for everybody in baseball—owners, front-office and clubhouse people, batboys, umpires, some three thousand minor-league players.

Everybody, that is, except players on major-league rosters, for whom the MLBPA absolutely refused to agree to any kind of drug-testing—random or otherwise. That intransigence did little to endear the MLBPA to baseball fans, many of whom had become convinced that ballplayers were a bunch of pampered, overpaid, cocaine-snorting millionaires. Art Spander of the *Sporting News* voiced a common plaint: "When did Jack Armstrong, the All-American Boy, go from Wheaties to Johnnie Walker Red—or to cocaine?"

Similarly unendearing were comments by Dave Parker, former Pittsburgh star, who testified under immunity and was linked to four counts in the conviction of Curtis Strong, the principal Three Rivers Stadium drug peddler. After playing in 1984 and 1985 with Cincinnati and then signing another two-year contract for 1985 and 1986 with the Reds (for close to $1 million a season), Parker seemed unrepentant: "Why should I be sorry? I'm not sorry about anything I do. It was a fad. . . . I never missed a game." Early in May 1986, the Pittsburgh franchise sued Parker for $5.3 million—the amount the Pirates still owed him in deferred payments on his 1979 contract—on the grounds that his cocaine involvement had hurt his productivity at Pittsburgh.

A muted aspect of the cocaine phenomenon was that whereas roughly eighty percent of the six hundred fifty to seven hundred major-league players were white, about three-fourths of those implicated as illegal drug users were black. Reggie Jackson, for one, expressed hurt and dismay over a situation he feared would disparage black people in general. Equally dismayed was Henry Aaron, now vice president for player development in the Atlanta organization, who vigorously endorsed Ueberroth's drug-testing campaign.

Ueberroth did persuade the MLBPA to accept punishments for thirty-one players who admitted to using cocaine. Besides fining the players five to ten percent of their 1986 salaries, he put them under random drug-testing and required up to two hundred hours of "community service" from each man. In the meantime, the owners collectively withdrew from an agreement with the MLBPA (dating from mid-1984) premised on players' voluntary submission to diagnosis, treatment, and rehabilitation. Instead they sought, with mixed success, to get individual players to accept drug-testing clauses in their contracts.

Anybody with any awareness of the continuing spread of cocaine and other illegal drugs throughout American society could see the hollowness of Ueberroth's claim—in the aftermath of his disciplinary actions in the spring of 1986—that baseball had overcome its drug problem. Yet while particular players would continue to run afoul of the drug laws, it did seem that by the end of 1986 the worst had come and passed.

As with predictions that the 1981 strike would cost baseball millions of fans, fears that drug disclosures would badly damage attendance also proved unfounded. Nothing, it seemed, could really slow the baseball boom of the eighties. For 1984 total major-league attendance did fall about eight hundred thousand below the 46.5 million who watched games the previous year, even with the Dodgers becoming the first franchise to top three million (3,134,797, to be exact); yet the upward trend resumed in 1985, when nearly forty-seven million turned out. Meanwhile the comeback in the minor leagues that had started in the late seventies reached remarkable proportions.

In 1987 the seventeen operating minor-league circuits drew some twenty million people, which represented an increase of about seventy percent since the mid-1970s. Forty years earlier, more than half of all minor-league franchises had been owned by major-league clubs. Now only twelve were still owned outright; the remainder operated under "working agreements" whereby the big-league parent club picked up nearly all salary, equipment, meal, and lodging costs, at the same time that all revenues stayed with the local franchise. Low ticket prices, cozy but comfortable ballparks, and many, many promotions and special events also helped explain why, by 1988, an estimated three-quarters of all minor-league franchises were operating in the black. Remarked Joe Buzas, owner of the prosperous Portland Beavers of the Pacific Coast League, "Television killed us, and now television is bringing us back. Americans are bored with the tube. They want to get out for some cheap, local, live entertainment."

What occurred in some cities was astonishing. In 1983 the Louisville Redbirds of the American Association, despite being only about a hundred miles from Cincinnati, became the first minor-league franchise in history to reach the one-million attendance mark. Four years later Redbirds owner A. Ray Smith sold his holdings for an eye-popping $5 million. In 1988 the International League's Buffalo Bisons also pushed past the one-million mark, playing in a new downtown facility designed solely for baseball and seating some twenty thousand.

The boom in college baseball was equally remarkable. By the mid-eighties, approximately ten million people were attending college games from February into mid-June, when the college season climaxed with the NCAA's championship tournament at Omaha, Nebraska. College baseball facilities now frequently equaled the best in the minors, with stadia that were lighted, seated ten thousand or more, and frequently had artificial surfaces. Employing the designated-hitter rule as well as aluminum bats that put an extra five to ten feet on fly balls, college baseball offered a heavy-hitting game that appealed to the record numbers of young people seeking degrees in the eighties. Teams in the so-called sunbelt, stretching from Florida to the central California coast, dominated postseason competition, mainly because, playing some seventy-five games per year, they generated far more revenue than northern schools. College baseball—especially programs such as those at Arizona State, Louisiana State, Miami, Mississippi State, Texas, Southern California, Stanford, Florida State, and Oklahoma State—now supplied about seventy-five percent of all eventual major-leaguers.

Undoubtedly much of the reason why major-league attendance records were broken nearly every season was the inability of one team to dominate the competition more than a year at a time. In 1984, while

Baltimore went into decline, the Detroit Tigers blasted off to a 32–5 record and won the AL East by a fifteen-game margin. Sparky Anderson, in his sixth year as Tigers manager, could call on three reliable starters in Jack Morris, Dan Petry, and Milt Wilcox; that year's top reliever in lefty Willie Hernandez; and a lineup that excelled at clutch hitting. In the playoff Detroit swept a Kansas City club that was still recovering from drug troubles. The 1984 Royals were the only major-league team ever to get into postseason play with a deficit in runs scored.

The NL playoff matched a team that won for the first time against one that hadn't been in postseason play since 1945. The San Diego Padres, managed by a somewhat mellowed Dick Williams, were the NL's last expansion team to win a division title—and the only Western Division club to play .500 ball in 1984. Goose Gossage, who left the Yankees as a free agent, propped up a middling pitching staff with ten victories and twenty-five saves; Steve Garvey, another free-agent acquisition, and Graig Nettles, obtained in a trade with the Yankees, stabilized the San Diego infield. Garvey also drove in eighty-six runs, even while complaining that the Padres' brown-orange-and-gold-decorated uniforms (with white shoes) "make us look like a lot of tacos." Second-year man Kevin McReynolds and third-year man Tony Gwynn provided most of the remaining offensive punch, Gwynn leading the majors with a .351 average.

The Chicago Cubs, 96–65 under Jim Frey, at least partly made up for thirty-nine years of frustration endured by baseball's most faithful fans. Now the property of the *Chicago Tribune* and WGN satellite television, the Cubs still played without lights at home. Despite that stubborn traditionalism (or maybe because of it), the Cubs drew 2,104,000 paid admissions into lovely old Wrigley Field. Six Cubs drove in eighty or more runs, including second baseman Ryne Sandberg, the NL's Most Valuable Player, who also batted .314 and made only six errors in 156 games. The main reason the Cubs won, though, was Rick Sutcliffe, a 6-7, red-bearded righty gained in June in a multiplayer deal with Cleveland, in time to win sixteen of seventeen decisions.

Like the crosstown White Sox a year earlier, the Cubs were sentimental favorites in the NL playoff; also like the White Sox, they went down after a struggle. Trounced twice at Wrigley Field, San Diego won three in a row at home. A four-run rally in the seventh inning put the Padres ahead for good in game five, and Gossage pitched two shutout innings in relief to nail down San Diego's pennant.

Against the Tigers in the World Series, Williams's starters fell apart. San Diego won only once—at home in game two—as Detroit hammered seven home runs, including two in the clincher at Tiger Stadium by Kirk Gibson, a big, balding, remarkably unkempt twenty-seven-year old who'd played football at Michigan State. With Gibson personally accounting for six of Detroit's eight runs, Sparky Anderson became the first man to manage Series champions in both leagues.

The 1985 season was a memorable one for a number of reasons. For one, it brought still another players' strike—a mercifully short one this time around. Ill health had forced Marvin Miller's retirement as MLBPA executive director, and his successor was Donald Fehr, a younger, less articulate, far less charismatic figure. In May, with the fourth Basic Agreement about to expire, the executive board of the MLBPA voted to authorize a walkout if negotiations broke down. The issues boiled down to the MLBPA's determination to keep what it had gained versus the owners' efforts to redress the balance they were convinced had tilted in the players' favor. Specifically, the owners sought to lengthen the eligibility term for arbitration; to establish a "payroll plan" that would cap per-club salaries and thus curb free-agent signings (similar to what had happened in the National Basketball Association); and, in light of the huge current contract with NBC and ABC, to reduce the percentage of the owners' pension contributions from common radio-television revenues.

The players wouldn't buy any of it, and on August 6 they struck. Unlike Bowie Kuhn in 1981, commissioner Ueberroth assumed an active role, pressuring the owners to disclose their real financial circumstances, give up their dream of overturning free agency, and drop their salary-cap project. Largely through Ueberroth's efforts, a settlement was reached in New York early on the morning of August 8. The two-day strike wiped out only twenty-five games that, among many other things specified in a new Basic Agreement, would all be made up.

Under the 1985 Basic Agreement, the players surrendered quite a lot: a year on the two-year arbitration rule in force since 1976, plus a reduction in owners' radio-TV contributions from thirty-three to eighteen percent. (Somebody calculated that at age sixty-two, a ten-year big-league veteran would still be eligible for a $91,000 pension.) At the same time, the minimum salary was raised from $48,000 to $60,000. On free-agent compensation, a central issue in the 1981 struggle, most owners decided they lost more than they gained by having to contribute players to an annual compensation pool, and the MLBPA was delighted to have the compensation system restored to its original reliance on the amateur draft.

Incessantly talking bankruptcy, the owners moaned that collectively they owned half a billion dollars in deferred contract obligations to players who, in a number of cases, were already out of baseball. For forty-eight players given their releases at the end of the 1986 season, major-league franchises would still owe $33 million in guaranteed income; but if that be madness, it was madness of the purely free-market variety.

While the MLBPA pointed to owners' tax-depreciation advantages, swelling moneys from broadcast rights, and some $625 million in aggregate gross revenues for 1985, the fact remained that the average cost of running a big-league franchise had climbed to $20 million —nearly a threefold increase in ten years. Even the MLBPA agreed that such franchises as Cleveland, Pittsburgh, San Francisco, and Seattle were losing heavily. In the end, opinions on the financial future of baseball came down to how much emphasis one placed on the disparate factors of current salaries, guaranteed payments, revenues, and tax breaks. For ordinary fans, it had all become too much to comprehend.

The 1985 season also saw another hoary record fall when, on the night of September 11, before more than fifty thousand people at Cincinnati's Riverfront Stadium, Pete Rose lined a pitch from San Diego's Eric Show into left field for his 4,192nd base hit, one more than Ty Cobb had amassed. Gigantic media coverage—bigger than anything Henry Aaron, Roger Maris, or any record-seeker in any sport had experienced—focused on Rose's hit-by-hit progression. Mediawise and supremely confident, the aging Charlie Hustle handled it all with something approaching aplomb.

That one number—4,191—had long been the central concern in Rose's life. Rose had returned to Cincinnati on August 16, 1984, from the Montreal Expos (with whom he'd signed at the end of his contract at Philadelphia), to succeed Vernon Rapp as Reds manager and continue his pursuit of Cobb. In 1985, as the majors' only player-manager, Rose finished with a .264 average on 107 safeties—a respectable showing, but hardly much of a boost for a team that remained in contention most of the way.

The 1985 New York Mets, managed by former Baltimore and Atlanta infielder Dave Johnson, finished only three games out of first in the NL East. Purchased five years earlier at a bargain $26.1 million by a group headed by Nelson Doubleday and Fred Wilpon, the Mets had plunged into the free-agent market to secure George Foster, who proved something of a disappointment, and Gary Carter, who continued to be the NL's hardest-hitting catcher. As their Shea Stadium attendance swelled from 789,000 in 1979 to more than two and a half million in 1985, the Mets again proved what had become increasingly obvious: The arrival of high-powered free agents reawakened fan interest and usually generated enough added income to cover larger salary outlays.

But the new arrival who made the greatest difference in the Mets' fortunes was Dwight Gooden, a nineteen-year-old right-hander who in 1984 broke in with more strikeouts (276) than any rookie in history, as well as seventeen victories. In his second season the youngster from Tampa was masterful: a 24–6 record, a 1.53 earned run average, eight shutouts, and 268 strikeouts. For adoring Mets fans, it wasn't too early to start work on Gooden's Hall of Fame plaque.

Despite Gooden's heroics, the 1985 Mets still couldn't catch Whitey Herzog's St. Louis club. The Cardinals stole 314 bases, the most in the majors since the 1912 New York Giants, and raced for fifty-nine triples while hitting only eighty-seven homers. Vince Coleman's 110 steals established new records for both the National League and for rookies; outfielder Willie McGee stole fifty-six while batting a league-best .353. Backed by a defense that erred only 108 times, St. Louis's pitching staff—featuring lefty John Tudor (21–8) and righties Joaquin Andujar (21–12) and Danny Cox (18–9)—allowed the fewest runs in the majors.

Los Angeles had plenty of speed and pitching of its own and more batting power, and the Dodgers finished nine games ahead of Pete Rose's Reds. Outfielders Pedro Guerrero and Mike Marshall were the offensive leaders for Lasorda's team; Fernando Valenzuela, Orel Hershiser, Bob Welch, and Jerry Reuss headed an excellent staff.

In the Yankees' ongoing managerial melodrama, Billy Martin had returned in 1983 and then, after a third-place finish, endured his fifth firing, his second by George Steinbrenner. Yogi Berra handled the Yankees through another third-place season in 1984, but after a slow start in '85, Berra himself fell under Steinbrenner's blade. Back scurried Martin to lead the New Yorkers to ninety-one wins, largely because Ron Guidry (22–6) pitched effectively for the last time and Dave Winfield (twenty-five homers, 114 rbi's) was in top form. First baseman Don Mattingly was in even better form. AL batting titlist at .343 the previous season, the young Indianian won 1985 Most Valuable Player kudos by averaging .325, stroking thirty-five homers, and driving home 145 runs. Yet at 97–64 for the season, the Yankees still fell two short of the Toronto Blue Jays, Eastern Division winners after nine seasons in the American League.

Toronto manager Bobby Cox called on one or all of five relief pitchers to bail out his starters, who went the distance only eighteen times. Of Cox's regulars, three players—second baseman Damaso Garcia, shortstop Tony Fernandez, and left fielder Jorge (George) Bell—were citizens of the Dominican Republic, and Fernandez, Bell, and utility infielder Manny Lee all had grown up in San Pedro de Macoris, on the island's southern coast. Over the past two decades, that city of about eighty thousand had produced close to two dozen big-league players; for whatever reason, San Pedro de Macoris seemed to have the densest concentration of baseball talent on earth.

Dick Howser again brought the Kansas City Royals in first, but only by a game over California. The Royals' assemblage of young pitching talent—especially right-handers Bret Saberhagen (20–6) and Mark Gubicza (14–10) and left-hander Danny Jackson (14–12)—prompted comparisons with the 1966 Orioles staff. Veteran lefty Charlie Leibrandt contributed seventeen victories, and submarine reliever Dan Quisenberry recorded thirty-seven saves, giving him 161 over the past four seasons. In a lineup of mostly journeymen, George

Brett enjoyed one of his most productive years: .335, thirty home runs, 112 runs batted in.

Under the huge broadcasting contract signed in 1983, NBC and ABC insisted upon going to a four-of-seven-game playoff format, and early in 1985—against protests that the season was already too long and that extending the playoffs would push the World Series as many as eight weeks into the college football schedule—holdover commissioner Kuhn acceded to the networks' wishes.

As it happened, both playoffs ended on October 16. The Cardinals eliminated Los Angeles in six games, with first baseman Jack Clark's three-run homer in the top of the ninth at Dodger Stadium (following Lasorda's decision to pitch to him with first base empty) providing the *coup de grâce*. Kansas City dropped three of its first four games in the AL playoff, then won three straight, the last two at Exhibition Stadium in Toronto. Brett was the playoff batting star: five rbi's on eight hits, including three homers.

The 1985 World Series, the first during Peter Ueberroth's commissionership, bore his personal stamp in at least one respect: Ueberroth modified what had been the prevailing practice on the use of designated hitters. Having been used since 1976 by both clubs every other year, the DH, under Ueberroth's ruling, would now be used every year, but only on the American Leaguers' home field.

Bringing together teams from opposite sides of Missouri, the Series lasted a rousing, controversy-filled seven games. The Royals again put themselves at a 3–1 deficit, Tudor pitching his club to victory in games one and four; then, as he'd done in game five of the playoff, Danny Jackson kept Kansas City alive with a complete-game performance. In game six, down 1–0 in their last at bat, the Royals capitalized on a hotly argued call by umpire Don Denkinger at first base to load the bases for pinch hitter Dane Iorg, whose single brought in the tying and winning runs.

The deciding game, on Sunday night, October 27, was an utter fiasco for Cardinals fans and, for the forty-thousand-plus Royals partisans, the greatest event in Kansas City's long baseball history. The Cardinals managed five hits and no runs off twenty-one-year-old Saberhagen in his second complete-game victory of the Series. Little-known Darryl Motley's two-run homer helped drive Tudor to the dressing room, and three other St. Louis pitchers came and went before Joaquin Andujar took the mound in a volcanic mood. After he yielded more runs and almost assaulted Denkinger (now working behind the plate), Andujar was ejected, in the company of Herzog. Three innings later the game ended 11–0—the most one-sided Series closer since 1934, when, ironically, the Cardinals had wrapped things up by the same score.

For 1986 the owners sought to economize by unilaterally cutting the June–September roster size by one—to twenty-four. Although most managers decided to get along with one less pitcher, they made more pitching changes than ever once games got under way; the twenty-six major-league pitching staffs averaged only twenty-two complete games. As managers commonly remarked about their starters, "We were hoping for five good innings so we could get into the bullpen."

For the eighth year in a row, both World Series participants were newcomers. Managed by much-fired John McNamara, the Boston Red Sox won the 1986 AL East by five and one-half games over runner-up New York, where Steinbrenner's revolving door had disgorged Billy Martin and brought in Lou Piniella. For Boston, designated hitter Don Baylor, right fielder Dwight Evans, and first baseman Bill Buckner drove in a total of 293 runs, while Jim Rice had a banner year: .324, twenty homers, 110 rbi's. Red Sox third baseman Wade Boggs was arguably the finest "pure hitter" since Ted Williams, with whom, as a left-handed swinger, he often drew comparisons (despite having nothing like Williams's power). Boggs's .357 average for 1986 gave him three batting titles in his first five years in the majors.

The main man on the mound for Boston—in either league, for that matter—was right-hander Roger Clemens. At 6-4 and 205 pounds (not much above average size for 1980s pitchers), the former University of Texas All-American threw an overpowering fastball—never more so than on April 29, 1986, when he struck out twenty Seattle Mariners to surpass the nine-inning record of nineteen set by Steve Carlton in 1969. For the season, Clemens was 24–8 with 238 strikeouts and a 2.48 earned run average.

Its young pitchers suddenly ineffective, world's champion Kansas

City finished a dismal third in the AL West; Dick Howser, found to have a fatally malignant brain tumor, never returned after the All-Star break. Still directed by Gene Mauch, the California Angels won their third division title—but again nothing else. With Reggie Jackson showing flashes of the old power in the DH slot, rookie Wally Joyner sparkling at the plate and first base, third baseman Doug DeCinces and left fielder Brian Downing driving in runs, and Bob Boone steadying the pitchers and surpassing Al Lopez's career record for games caught, the Angels overcame mediocre mound work to beat out the Texas Rangers by five games.

The Red Sox prevailed in a stirring seven-game playoff series. In the fifth contest, with his club down three games to one and only a strike away from elimination, Boston's Dave Henderson hit a pitch from Donnie Moore, the Angels' ace reliever, over the Anaheim Stadium center-field fence for a two-run homer to tie the score. About an hour later, in the eleventh inning, Henderson lofted a sacrifice fly to put Boston ahead for good, 7–6. Three days later the dispirited Angels yielded seven unearned runs and lost game seven.

After years of coming close, the New York Mets did everything right. With a roster that feverish New Yorkers compared to great teams of the past, the Mets ran up a 108–54 record and pulled away from everybody, finishing a whopping twenty-two and one-half games in front of second-place Philadelphia. A remarkably well-balanced club both on the mound and in the everyday lineup, the Mets nonetheless offered lots of star quality in Gary Carter, Keith Hernandez, Dwight Gooden, and Darryl Strawberry. A lean 6-6 twenty-four-year-old who was already a four-year veteran, Strawberry possessed unlimited potential—or so everybody said, almost *ad nauseam*. For 1986 he accumulated twenty-seven homers and ninety-seven rbi's, yet batted only .259 and struck out 141 times. For all his obvious gifts, the moody young Californian with the picture-perfect swing consistently disappointed those who expected greatness.

The 1986 Houston Astros—built on well-distributed pitching strength, timely hitting, and the intelligent leadership of manager Hal Lanier (son of the 1940s Cardinals lefty)—were the best team that franchise had fielded. A gruelling six-game struggle with the Mets finally ended late one afternoon in the Astrodome, when the Mets pushed across a run in the top of the fourteenth inning and Mets reliever Jesse Orosco held on for a 7–6 victory.

In their fourth World Series opportunity since 1918, the Red Sox made it a hard fight but again proved unequal to the task. Bill Buckner's misplay of a routine, two-out ground ball lost game six and enabled the Mets to tie the Series. In game seven, at Shea Stadium, Boston got off well on Dwight Evans's three-run homer in the second inning, only to see New York pounce on Calvin Schiraldi when he relieved starter Bruce Hurst. Scoring eight times in their last three at bats, the Mets won 8–5 and again produced mortification throughout New England.

By the time another spring training came around, Pete Rose, about to turn forty-six, had finally decided to quit playing. After batting a puny .219 in part-time action in 1986, Rose still showed a lifetime .303 average on 4,256 base hits, and nobody had come to bat more times or played in more games—or more *winning* games, as Rose was quick to remind people.

Nearly all of Rose's generation of major-leaguers were gone or soon would be. Willie McCovey, for example, retired in 1980 with 521 home runs and 1,555 rbi's, and two years later Willie Stargell, a favorite in Pittsburgh for two decades, quit with 475 homers and 1,540 rbi's—and 1,936 strikeouts, at that time the most ever. Johnny Bench decided to give his battered frame a permanent rest after the 1983 season; Carl Yastrzemski retired at the same time, having accumulated 452 homers, 1,844 rbi's, and 3,419 hits in his twenty-three seasons at Boston.

In 1983 Gaylord Perry threw his last spitball and won his 314th game pitching for Kansas City, his eighth stop in nine years. Abruptly released by Baltimore the next season, 268-game-winner Jim Palmer turned to broadcasting and modeling underwear. Rod Carew retired at the end of the 1985 campaign with 3,053 base hits and the highest lifetime batting average (.328) since Stan Musial, and Tom Seaver spent 1986 with the White Sox and Red Sox, picking up seven more victories and a World Series check before stepping down with 311 career wins.

For Don Sutton, Steve Carlton, Phil Niekro, and Reggie Jackson, the 1987 season would be the last before they, too, experienced what the novelist John Updike called "the little death that awaits athletes." Sutton, the archetypal seven-inning starter, finished up at California with eleven wins and 321 for his career, having completed only about one in four starts over twenty-two seasons. Carlton, unloaded by five teams in a year and a half, finally gave up with 329 victories, second only to Warren Spahn's 368 among left-handers. Niekro threw his last knuckleball for the Braves (his home team for twenty years before he went free agent in 1984), retiring at forty-eight with 318 wins, 274 losses. Rejoining Oakland as a free agent, Jackson, the erstwhile Mr. October, produced fifteen homers for a career total of 563, and also extended his career strikeout total to 2,597—a record nobody would aspire to break. (Yet it could be argued that, more than any player, Jackson had glamorized, or at least destigmatized, the strikeout.)

Meanwhile the Minnesota Twins, whose talented young players had accomplished little as a team up to now, capped a wholly improbable 1987 season by winning a world's championship. Managed by bespectacled, taciturn Tom Kelly, the Twins won only twenty-nine times on the road but played .691 ball in the cozy Metrodome, where about two and a half million victory-starved midwesterners paid to see them. Jeff Reardon, who'd left Montreal as a free agent, saved thirty-one games for a wobbly group of Minnesota starters, of whom Frank Viola (17–10) and Bert Blyleven (15–12) were the most reliable.

The Twins excelled on defense (erring only ninety-eight times) and at the plate. For reasons no one could really explain, fly balls carried exceptionally well in the Metrodome, and the home team whacked 196 homers, including thirty-four by first baseman Kent Hrbek, thirty-two by right fielder Tom Brunansky, thirty-one by third baseman Gary Gaetti, and twenty-eight by Kirby Puckett, a fireplug center fielder who also batted .332.

Minnesota edged Kansas City by two games and went into the playoff against the favored Detroit Tigers, who'd swept three games from Toronto at the close of the season to finish two games in front. Shortstop Alan Trammell hit twenty-eight home runs to go with a .343 average and 105 rbi's; and, with forty-year-old Darrell Evans contributing thirty-four homers and twenty-three-year-old Matt Nokes thirty-two, the Tigers banged even more round-trippers than the

Twins. Jack Morris, Walt Terrell, and Frank Tanana were the best on a pitching staff that wasn't much stronger than Minnesota's.

The teams combined for fifty-seven runs in the playoff, which the Twins won with surprising ease in five games. Brunansky, Gaetti, and shortstop Greg Gagne each homered twice, and Blyleven received credit for two of the Twins' wins. The veteran Doyle Alexander, 9–0 after being secured in August from Atlanta, took two of Detroit's losses.

The Mets didn't repeat in 1987, largely because Dwight Gooden spent the first part of the season in a drug-treatment center, ridding himself of cocaine dependency. Although Gooden returned in time to lead the staff with fifteen wins, his early absence, together with an accumulation of injuries among his teammates, doomed the defending world's champions to a second-place finish, three games behind St. Louis.

In winning their third NL pennant in six seasons, the Cardinals again featured speed (248 stolen bases) and tight defensive play. St. Louis's pitching, though, was considerably weaker than in 1982 and 1985; nobody won more than twelve games and the entire staff completed only ten starts. Todd Worrell, a brawny fireballer, relieved in seventy-five games, saved thirty-three, and generally made the difference for Whitey Herzog's club.

The San Francisco Giants, who'd played and drawn poorly most of the past fifteen years, finished comfortably ahead of Cincinnati in the NL West under the direction of Roger Craig, onetime twenty-four-game loser for the early Mets. Still performing at chilly Candlestick Park, the Giants topped two million paid admissions for the first time, only a few years after owner Bob Lurie had tried to move them to Denver.

Although they lacked consistently effective pitching (like everybody else in 1987), the Giants totaled 208 home runs, topped by Mississippi State alumnus Will Clark, who connected for thirty-five, drove in ninety-one teammates, and batted .308. Not an outstanding team by any means, they were nonetheless good enough to take a three-game-to-two lead in the playoff, at which juncture their bats fell silent. Unable to score in their last twenty-two innings, the Giants lost games six and seven at St. Louis on shutouts.

The Twins' strong attack and Frank Viola's clutch pitching brought the Washington-Minnesota franchise only its second-ever World Series victory. Evidently another factor was the environment in the Metrodome, where more than fifty-five thousand screaming, handkerchief-waving Twins fanatics created a din such as neither the Cardinals nor visitors from anywhere else had ever experienced. (A Washington University hearing-research specialist concluded that Metrodome decibel levels were at least twice as high as at Busch Stadium.) True to their regular-season pattern, the Twins lost all three games at St. Louis and won all four at home; by the time Reardon got the last out to save Viola's stout performance in the 4–2 clincher, outsiders were ready to agree that the Twins had given new meaning to the term "home-team advantage."

In 1988, overall major-league attendance soared to 52,957,752. The Twins drew more than three million at the Metrodome, completing a wonderful turnaround for a franchise that had been one of the majors' sickliest just a few years earlier. Twins followers watched plenty of good baseball—in fact, better than they'd seen in 1987. Yet even though the local heroes improved their record by six games and committed only eighty-four errors (fewest in major-league history), Minnesota could do no better than a distant second place, thirteen games behind Oakland.

Now again known as the Athletics, the Oakland team wore the tightest-fitting uniforms in the majors and featured players who were big even by contemporary standards. The restoration of the old white-elephant club symbol (originally contrived early in the century in answer to a slur by John McGraw) seemed eminently appropriate for the Oakland musclemen. The Athletics' headliners were Cuban-born, Miami-reared Jose Canseco, who at twenty-four became the first player ever to pair forty home runs and forty stolen bases; towering Mark McGwire, who slammed thirty-two homers after leading the majors with forty-nine in his rookie year; and pitchers Dave Stewart and Dennis Eckersley (both, coincidentally, Oakland natives). Stewart posted twenty wins for the second year in a row, while Eckersley, erstwhile starter for Cleveland, Boston, and the Cubs, qualified for a staggering forty-five saves. Managing the Athletics was Tony LaRussa, dismissed by the White Sox in 1986 and immediately hired at Oakland. Like Hughie Jennings, Branch Rickey, and Miller Huggins before him, LaRussa was licensed to practice law but preferred to practice baseball.

Oakland's 156 homers were the second-highest total (behind Toronto's 158) in either league, in a season in which home-run production fell by twenty-nine percent, scoring by thirteen percent, and overall batting averages by seven points in the AL and thirteen in the NL. Wade Boggs's .366 and runner-up Kirby Puckett's .352 were impressive enough in the AL, but Tony Gwynn's .313 (fifty-seven points below his 1987 mark) was the lowest winning average in NL history. The most common explanation for the falloff in batting was an off-season redefinition of the strike zone, now officially said to extend from the knees to the uniform letters. Some commentators also speculated that Rawlings had taken a little of the rabbit out of its Haitian-made balls, but as always, nobody had any conclusive proof and the manufacturer wouldn't tell.

In the AL East, the Boston Red Sox finished only one game ahead of Detroit, two ahead of Toronto and Milwaukee, and three and one half ahead of the fifth-place Yankees. Along the way Billy Martin, hired again as field manager while Lou Piniella moved into the front office, endured his fourth (and last) firing at New York. George Steinbrenner then reinstalled Piniella in the dugout.

The Red Sox won under former third-base coach Joe Morgan ("the other Joe Morgan," as he was invariably referred to), appointed manager when John McNamara was fired in midseason. Roger Clemens and Bruce Hurst, both eighteen-game winners, headed Boston's pitchers. Besides the remarkable Boggs, Boston's perennially power-packed lineup now included Mike Greenwell and Ellis Burks, two hard-hitting youngsters, plus Dwight Evans and a fading Jim Rice.

Everything went bad for the 1988 St. Louis Cardinals, who fell to sixth. Enjoying general good health and playing before more than three million at Shea Stadium, the New York Mets reestablished their supremacy in the NL East, outdistancing a young Pittsburgh team by fifteen games. Dwight Gooden (18–6), former Yale All-American Ron Darling (17–9), and second-year-man David Cone (20–3) showed the top numbers on an outstanding pitching staff. Darryl Strawberry (thirty-nine homers, 101 rbi's) and trade acquisition Kevin McReynolds (twenty-seven homers, ninety-nine rbi's) spearheaded the Mets' offense.

In the NL West, for the fourth year in a row, Pete Rose's Cincinnati team finished an unthreatening second. (Rose himself, under suspension for shoving an umpire, was absent from the dugout for a month in May and June.) Meanwhile Tom Lasorda's Los Angeles pitchers recorded the lowest earned run average in the majors, which was why, in a manner reminiscent of the Koufax-Drysdale years, the Dodgers won ninety-four games while scoring only 628 runs. With Pedro Guerrero traded to St. Louis, nobody hit much for Los Angeles besides free agent Kirk Gibson (.290, twenty-five homers, seventy-five rbi's) and Mike Marshall (.277, twenty-homers, eighty-two rbi's). But the Dodgers usually produced enough runs for Tim Belcher (12–6), Tim Leary (17–11), and particularly baby-faced Orel Hershiser, who pitched fifteen complete games—heroic work by 1980s standards—in compiling a 23–8 record. Hershiser's season included eight shutouts and a string of fifty-nine scoreless innings that broke Don Drysdale's record.

Speculation that Oakland might be the strongest team of the decade appeared abundantly confirmed when the Athletics dumped the Red Sox in four straight. Meanwhile the Dodgers pulled a big upset by winning in seven games from a New York team that had beaten them eleven of twelve times during the regular season. Belcher gained two victories; Hershiser started games one and three, relieved in game four, and then threw a five-hit shutout at Dodger Stadium to end the season for the cocky Mets. Impaired by a torn hamstring muscle, Gibson made the most of his four hits: two homers, six rbi's.

It was the second all–West Coast World Series, a rematch of the 1974 Oakland–Los Angeles clash. To maximize the television audience, all games started at 5:30 P.M. local time, which meant that for about half of every contest, batters had to look at pitches in twilight shadow. That may have been one reason why the underdog Dodgers' superior pitching determined the outcome. Held to a .177 team batting average, the mighty Athletics could win only once.

In the ninth inning of game one, at Dodger Stadium, in his only Series appearance, Gibson limped to the plate to hit Eckersley's two-strike pitch into the right-field stands for two runs, giving Los Angeles a 5–4 victory. The next night Hershiser permitted only three hits in a 6–0 shutout. Oakland's only win came in game three, when McGwire homered in the bottom of the ninth to break a 1–1 tie. Two scoreless innings from Jay Howell, in relief of Belcher, saved game four, 4–3, and in the clincher, before fifty thousand morose Bay area partisans, the light-hitting Mickey Hatcher and Mike Davis clouted two-run homers to back up Hershiser's four-hit pitching. After getting the final out, the pious pitcher knelt near the mound to give thanks for his team's 4–3 victory.

The Dodgers' unexpected triumph in the century's eighty-fifth World Series capped a tremendously successful baseball season, one that saw attendance and television ratings reach all-time highs. Peter Ueberroth—the "money commissioner," some writers called him—had presided over the richest period in baseball history. Between 1985 and 1987, the twenty-six major-league franchises had cleared $206 million; collective gross revenue for 1988 was $977 million, an increase of 7.4 percent over 1987.

Nearing the end of his five-year term, Ueberroth decided to go on to other things, and the owners had already agreed upon a successor: A. Bartlett Giamatti, a lifelong Red Sox fan who held a Ph.D. in Renaissance literature, had put in a stint as president of Yale University, and in 1986 had succeeded Charles "Chub" Feeney as president of the National League. If Giamatti seemed an unlikely baseball administrator, so, by earlier notions, were AL president Bobby Brown, M.D., a cardiologist who'd played third base for the Yankees in the late forties, and Bill White, a black man who'd been a National League star in the sixties and subsequently a successful sports announcer, and who now succeeded Giamatti as NL president.

As numerous people, including Giamatti himself, had long observed, baseball always tended to reflect what was best and worst in American society as a whole. And as students of baseball's or any other history would have to acknowledge, it's never a good idea to become complacent in the midst of success. The coming 1989 season would be scarred by scandal, untimely death, even natural disaster; and beyond that loomed the prospect of still another bitter, disruptive face-off between owners and players.

14.
Non-
Sesquicentennial
Reflections

One of the curious aspects of the 1989 baseball season was that nothing happened to commemorate the sesquicentennial of Abner Doubleday's mythical invention of the game—and nobody seemed to care. In 1939 baseball had made a considerable to-do over the Doubleday centennial, opening the National Baseball Hall of Fame and Museum and having teams wear centennial sleeve patches. Fifty years later, despite the persistence of sports journalists and the advertising media in trading on the Doubleday-Cooperstown fable, hardly anybody still considered it to be anything but a fable—albeit a charming one. Officials at the Hall of Fame, like Organized Baseball's hierarchy, were quite willing for 1989 to come and go as a non-sesquicentennial.

If an entire generation of Americans had rediscovered baseball in the 1980s, a sizable number had also developed a fond interest in the sport's incomparably rich heritage, together with a willingness to approach its past seriously and systematically. That meant scrutinizing a thick encrustation of myths and unverified anecdotes—the Doubleday business included. Working closely with the National Baseball Library, the rapidly growing Society for American Baseball Research (SABR) encouraged a deluge of books and articles, many of which were careful studies that significantly revised conventional wisdom about baseball's origins and evolution. As part of a broader interest in the role of competitive sports in modern society, baseball history even took on academic respectability, becoming a legitimate teaching and research specialty at a number of colleges and universities. It remains to be seen whether SABR—with its roughly five-thousand-plus members worldwide—will promote 1995–1996 as the sesquicentennial of the Knickerbocker Club and the advent of baseball-playing for adults.

A stronger historical awareness may even have had something to do with changing baseball fashion. By the late 1980s most ballplayers wore shorter haircuts; mustaches and beards, if still in evidence, were usually trimmed neatly. Plastic batting helmets remained mandatory both at the plate and on the basepaths; uniforms were still form-fitting; players had come to consider wristbands and batting gloves essential; and the Oakland Athletics and Houston Astros persisted in wearing white shoes. Yet they and most other teams again favored belts and button-up shirts over the elastic waistbands and pullovers popular in the seventies and early eighties; except for practice garb, colored shirts disappeared altogether. In general, teams had toned down their appearances, so that at least for older fans, baseball players looked a little more the way they ought to, not like recreation-league softballers.

The baseball boom also carried over into the popular arts. Besides a substantial increase in baseball-related fiction, motion pictures with baseball settings and characters—a film genre that usually hadn't fared well in the past—suddenly became money-makers. Beginning with the hugely successful *The Natural* (1984), such movies as *Long Gone* (an original pay-television production, 1987), *Bull Durham* and *Eight Men Out* (1988), and *Major League* and *Field of Dreams* (1989) scored with both critics and customers. *Eight Men Out*, based on Eliot Asinof's keen 1963 study of the Black Sox scandal, came considerably closer to historical verisimilitude than most movies ever had.

Had baseball recaptured its place as the National Pastime? Although baseball could never hope to dominate the American sports scene as it had early in the century, the evidence at hand—mostly impressionistic, to be sure—indicated that professional football's claims to be the new National Pastime had been laid to rest. The springtime United States Football League (1983–1985) had failed dismally, and the imperious National Football League had experienced a rocky decade. The cocaine blight common in professional sports (as well as deepening concern over the use of anabolic steroids), sagging television ratings, bitter labor-management conflict, and nomadic franchises troubled the NFL. Given the sixteen-game duration of the NFL's regular season, the protracted players' walkouts that hit pro football in 1982 and 1987 were actually more damaging than the 1981 baseball strike. And whereas baseball had undergone its last franchise shift following the 1971 season, in the eighties three relocations (Oakland to Los Angeles, Baltimore to Indianapolis, and St. Louis to Phoenix) took place in the midst of the NFL's vaunted prosperity.

"Whoever would know the mind and heart of America had better learn baseball," the Columbia University historian Jacques Barzun wrote in 1954 in *God's Country and Mine*—an effort by a French-born scholar to understand his adopted country. In the 1980s Barzun's aphorism was rediscovered and quoted by sports journalists, sociologists, and lots of other people who seemed to think it profoundly insightful, although no one could really explain why knowing baseball taught anything in particular about the mind and heart of America. Barzun himself hadn't been very helpful, except to speculate briefly on baseball as an example of Americans' penchant for rules and regulations, on how kids learned to play together, but competitively, and on the World Series as something of a national catharsis, à la Greek tragedy.

In the eighties such notables as Donald Hall, Roger Angell, Roger Kahn, George Will, and, not least, A. Bartlett Giamatti took up where Barzun left off, all writing in a vein that might be termed "baseball and the meaning of life, American and otherwise." They all spoke lyrically of the game on the field, its textures, rhythms, and symmetries, its rootedness in the national experience. Amid such paeans, the novelist and sportswriter Dan Jenkins offered a reminder that baseball was still an activity whose participants "mostly like to stand around, chew things, spit and scratch their nuts."

But for all its resurgent popularity, baseball had apparently lost its appeal for most black Americans. A 1987 survey indicated that despite far lower per-game prices, only 6.8 percent of the crowds at major-league baseball games consisted of black people, as opposed to 17 percent in the National Basketball Association and 7.5 percent in the National Football League. About 85 percent of the players in the

NBA and 55 to 60 percent in the NFL were black, but baseball actually seemed to be getting whiter. In 1980 one in five big-league players had been black or racially mixed, versus one in six at the end of the decade. If baseball wasn't again fully the National Pastime, was it possibly becoming White America's Game?

Part of the explanation for the preponderant whiteness in baseball lay in the fact that top-level college football and basketball players, from which the professional leagues directly drew their talent, were mostly black. College baseball, on which the American and National leagues indirectly but increasingly relied, had always been predominantly white. That left unanswered the question of why college baseball programs recruited mainly white athletes and the other two big intercollegiate team sports looked mainly to blacks. The question was complex and endlessly debatable, but for whatever reasons, youths in the inner cities, where most black Americans lived in the late twentieth century, had come to focus their interests and energies mainly on basketball and football, whereas baseball's hold was strongest in the predominantly white suburbs and towns. The baseball-crazy black urban environment that once produced both the Homestead Grays and the Pittsburgh Crawfords had vanished, apparently forever.

Baseball's standing among black Americans took another blow in the spring of 1987. During an interview on the ABC program "Nightline," Al Campanis, seventy-one-year-old director of player development for the Los Angeles Dodgers and once Jackie Robinson's teammate at Montreal, inarticulately blurted out that former black players "may not have the necessities to be, let's say, a field manager, or perhaps a general manager." At that time only three black men had ever handled big-league baseball clubs: Frank Robinson, who managed Cleveland between 1975 and 1977 and San Francisco between 1981 and 1984; Larry Doby, caretaker manager of the Chicago White Sox during the last half of 1978; and Maury Wills, who served an unhappy tenure with the Seattle Mariners, lasting only from August 1980 until May 1981. No black person had ever occupied a top-level front-office position in the major leagues.

Campanis's gaffe provoked a barrage of criticism from both black and white sources, and also got him fired within twenty-four hours. The Ueberroth regime quickly brought in Harry Edwards, an outspoken black sociologist, as special assistant for minority affairs; in turn, the following September, Edwards hired Campanis to help him convince the club owners to put more blacks into upper-echelon posts. "We're going to have to deal with the Campanises in baseball," said Edwards, "and it's good that I have a person in-house who knows how they think."

By 1988 some ten percent of front-office personnel were black or Hispanic, a fivefold increase in a year's time, and *Jet* magazine estimated that a third of all coaches, scouts, instructors, and trainers hired since 1987 were members of minority groups. The choice of Bill White as National League president in the fall of 1988 undoubtedly wouldn't have happened in a less racially sensitive atmosphere.

In 1989 the two strongest contenders for the American League Eastern Division championship both had black managers. Three games into the '88 season, early in what became an all-time-record losing streak of twenty-two straight, the Baltimore Orioles fired Cal Ripken, Sr., and gave the job to Frank Robinson, one of Ripken's coaches. Although the Orioles finished deep in the cellar that year, in 1989 they led the division most of the way with players who were mostly farm-bred, in the tradition of successful Baltimore teams of the past. Toronto's division-winning black manager was Clarence "Cito" Gaston, onetime slugging outfielder for San Diego, who succeeded Jimy Williams in midseason. Presumably Robinson's and Gaston's successes would influence club owners to draw more frequently from the reservoir of black baseball experience, instead of recycling fired white managers who'd lost more than they'd won.

The close AL East race—which produced more than two million paid admissions for the first time in Baltimore history and drew three-million-plus for Toronto's home games—was one reason total 1989 major-league attendance reached another all-time high of nearly fifty-six million. In the past few seasons, moreover, the AL had finally caught up with the NL in overall attendance, as it had competitively as well. (Since 1983 American Leaguers had won five of six World Series and four of seven All-Star games.)

Early in 1989, with the five-year radio-TV contract with NBC and ABC due to expire after that season, the commissioner's office negotiated a new four-year deal under which, beginning in 1990, CBS would carry All-Star, playoff, World Series, and Saturday games, and the Entertainment and Sports Programming Network (ESPN), a pay-TV satellite system, would show six regular-season games per week. Total revenue generated under the new arrangement (with two-thirds coming from CBS) would amount to $1.75 billion. The CBS-ESPN contract meant that starting in 1990, for the first time, major-league franchises earned more from radio and television than from in-stadium revenues. Local broadcasting fees still varied enormously from team to team—beginning in 1991, Madison Square Garden Television would pay the New York Mets $42 million per season, whereas Cincinnati received about $4 to $5 million from its broadcasters—but in its own characteristically uncertain way, baseball appeared to be moving toward something approximating the revenue-sharing practices pioneered by the National Football League.

Obviously players wanted the biggest possible slice of a rapidly expanding pie. Eight men who became free agents in the fall of 1989 signed multiyear contracts for at least $3 million per season, and by signing Mark Davis, former San Diego relief ace, as well as Storm Davis, a nineteen-game winner at Oakland, the Kansas City Royals acquired the costliest player payroll in the majors: more than $30 million. Midway through 1990 Jose Canseco agreed to remain with Oakland from 1991 through 1995 for a package worth more than $25 million, and a few weeks later Kevin Mitchell signed a comparable multiyear pact with San Francisco. Meanwhile, both directly and indirectly, the arbitration system continued to produce dramatic salary inflation; for 1990, arbitrators awarded fourteen players raises ranging from $373,179 to $909,000—an average increase of 141 percent.

Yet even when players lost their arbitration hearings (as had happened in 164 of 303 cases between 1974 and 1989), they still commonly ended up with a lot more money, simply because owners had already offered them big raises in an effort to forestall arbitration. For example, Atlanta's Lonnie Smith, coming off his best all-around season, wanted $2 million for 1990, more than twice what he'd made in 1989. Although the arbitrator's ruling went against him, Smith still signed for $1.75 million. Ten arbitration *losers* in the 1989–1990 off-season ended up gaining pay hikes averaging 106 percent.

At the start of the 1990 season, the average major-leaguer's salary was $578,930—an increase of sixteen percent over 1989—yet the Major League Baseball Players Association was far from satisfied with what its membership had been able to extract from club owners. Detailed studies concluded that by 1988, players were still receiving no more than thirty-three percent of total revenues, only an eight percent increase since the advent of free agency. During the 1985–1986 and 1986–1987 off-seasons, moreover, the MLBPA had protested that the owners were secretly conspiring *not* to sign free agents, so that such stars as Kirk Gibson and Tim Raines had no choice but to re-sign with their old teams for much less than they would have commanded in an open market. (Bob Horner refused and played the 1987 season in Japan.)

In 1988 a federal arbitrator agreed with the MLBPA's charge of "collusion" and ruled that the owners would have to compensate such players, in amounts to be negotiated by the MLBPA. MLBPA executive director Donald Fehr held Peter Ueberroth personally responsible for persuading the owners collectively to hide their checkbooks. "I can tell you," Fehr said in 1988, "collusion is concurrent with his term."

Ueberroth was gone by the spring of 1989, and while his successor inspired high expectations, A. Bartlett Giamatti quickly found the going extremely rugged. Baseball's century-old campaign to sustain a wholesome, family-oriented appeal, already marred by drug troubles, suffered further from the domestic tribulations of Wade Boggs and Steve Garvey, which the news media covered in titillating detail during the first part of the year.

Boggs, supposedly a dedicated family man whose wife's chicken recipes aided his success, had carried on a protracted, peripatetic affair with a real-estate broker named Margo Adams, who now tirelessly told all and sued the Red Sox star on various grounds. Garvey, an aspiring politician who throughout his nineteen-year career (1969–1987) had carefully nurtured his image as a muscular Christian, engaged in a bitter legal fight in California with his ex-wife over access to their children, at the same time that he publicly acknowledged fathering other children by other women.

All that was pretty mild, though, alongside the Pete Rose affair, which vexed Bartlett Giamatti throughout his sadly short commissionership. When Ueberroth gave way to Giamatti, the commissioner's staff already was scrutinizing Rose's gambling activities. Although Rose steadfastly denied betting on baseball, he did acknowledge wagering heavily (and losing up to $500,000 in a year's time) on horse and dog races, football, and basketball. Subsequently three close acquaintances of Rose testified that he'd also often bet on baseball games, including a number involving his own Cincinnati Reds. (Those three men and three other Rose associates eventually pled guilty to federal charges ranging from tax evasion to drug-trafficking.) As the investigation dragged through the spring and into the summer, questions also surfaced concerning whether Rose had been honest with the Internal Revenue Service about his income from gambling and autograph and memorabilia sales.

At last, after an Ohio appeals court overturned an injunction secured by Rose's lawyer blocking the commissioner from taking action, Giamatti was free to move in the Rose case. On August 24, 1989, he held a nationally televised press conference to say, yes, he was convinced Rose had bet on baseball games, and to announce the Cincinnati manager's lifetime suspension from Organized Baseball. Although he had the right to seek reinstatement after twelve months, by late August 1990 Rose was preoccupied not with getting back into baseball but with serving a five-month prison sentence for tax evasion, handed down the previous July 18 in federal district court in Cincinnati.

It was the worst episode of its kind since the Black Sox scandal: the banishment, imprisonment, and public disgrace of one of the most popular figures in baseball's history—not only its all-time base-hit leader but a man universally admired for his unsurpassed dedication to his craft.

As for Giamatti, even though he blundered early in the Rose investigation (unwisely signing a letter attesting to the honesty and cooperativeness of one of Rose's sleazy cohorts), he generally won accolades for his handling of an extraordinarily thorny, complex situation. An eloquent spokesman for a sport he loved in a way that none of his predecessors—at least not since Kenesaw Mountain Landis—had really loved it, Giamatti was an intellectual who proved he could operate with great effectiveness in the "real world." On September 2, 1989, nine days after announcing Rose's suspension, he was enjoying a respite on Martha's Vineyard when, at the age of fifty-one, he suffered a fatal heart attack.

Giamatti's interim successor (until he was formally elected commissioner a few months later) was deputy commissioner Francis "Fay" Vincent, who presided over the remainder of a season that saw attendance records broken and several happenings that served as merciful distractions from the dispiriting Rose affair.

In May 1989 Mike Schmidt decided that after 2,404 games, 548 home runs, 1,597 runs batted in, and 1,487 runs scored, he wouldn't risk embarrassment by trying to do what he could no longer do, at least not consistently. Although he hadn't always been happy in his eighteen years in Philadelphia (whose fans were reputed to be baseball's toughest), Schmidt left without voicing the kind of recriminations other retiring players had sometimes expressed—and without overstaying his welcome.

While Schmidt departed gracefully, Nolan Ryan, at forty-two, three years Schmidt's senior, didn't seem to be slowing down at all. After spending nine years at Houston, where, among other feats, he recorded his fifth no-hit game, Ryan had signed as a free agent with the Texas Rangers. In 1989, besides making thirty-two starts and winning sixteen times, the durable native Texan led the majors with 301 strikeouts. On August 22, 1989, at Texas Stadium in Arlington, Ryan fanned Oakland's Rickey Henderson for his five thousandth major-league strikeout; by season's end his total was nearly a thousand more than that of Steve Carlton, the number two man. Then in 1990 Ryan pitched his *sixth* no-hitter and posted his three hundredth major-league victory. (Ryan was also far in front of everybody in lifetime bases on balls and among the leaders in career losses.)

The 1989 season also was the first in which a father and son played in the majors at the same time. Ken Griffey, winding down a fine career, appeared in 106 games for Cincinnati, while Ken Griffey, Jr., put in an impressive rookie season with the Seattle Mariners until he was disabled in August. A year later, following his release by the Reds, Griffey, Sr., signed with Seattle, where father and son made still more baseball history by becoming teammates.

Jim Abbott, 6-3 and two hundred pounds, compiled a 12–12 record with the California Angels in 1989, his first big-league season.

What was distinctive about the twenty-one-year-old University of Michigan alumnus was that since birth he'd lacked a right hand. Exhibiting a dexterity that called up memories of Pete Gray, Abbott made fewer errors than many of his mound peers and showed enough stuff to register 115 strikeouts in 181 innings.

Baseball's physical environment continued to change. In 1986, after a ten-year delay, the public authorities in Montreal finally mustered sufficient funds to put a roof on Olympic Stadium; and in midseason 1989 the Toronto ball club vacated Exhibition Stadium for the Skydome. Featuring a retractable roof and built-in hotel accommodations (some of which overlooked the playing field), the Skydome was the poshest multipurpose facility yet. Major-league baseball was now played completely indoors in four stadia, indoors-outdoors in one, and on artificial surfaces in ten. New plants for the Orioles and White Sox, though, were being designed exclusively for baseball, with promises of real grass and at least something of the intimacy of the old ballparks.

As of August 1988, moreover, baseball was played at night in venerable Wrigley Field, where the Chicago Cubs installed light banks on the grandstand roof while keeping the bleachers free of obtrusive towers. In 1989 the Cubs played eighteen night home games, a figure they promised not to exceed for the next several seasons.

The Cubs, the only franchise operating continuously since 1876, packed in the customers both day and night in 1989, and won the NL East by six and seven games, respectively, over the injury-plagued Mets and the Cardinals. Hard-bitten Don Zimmer, who'd made managerial stops at San Diego, Boston, and Texas and carried a metal plate in his head (the legacy of a minor-league beaning), was the Cubs' manager. Young Greg Maddux, with nineteen wins; bearded Rick Sutcliffe, with sixteen; journeyman Mike Bielecki, with eighteen; and a shaggy, free-spirited lefty named Mitch Williams, who saved thirty-six games, were Chicago's mound mainstays. Although star outfielder Andre Dawson, NL Most Valuable Player in 1987, struggled through a lackluster year, second-year-man Mark Grace and rookie Jerome Walton enjoyed fine seasons, while Ryne Sandberg and rifle-armed Shawon Dunston formed baseball's best second base–shortstop combination.

As in 1984, though, the Cubs couldn't get past the playoff, losing in five games to Roger Craig's San Francisco Giants. While the world's champion Los Angeles Dodgers had experienced more trouble than ever scoring runs and had fallen to fifth place, the Giants had won three more games than an improving San Diego team. Will Clark (.333, twenty-three homers, 111 rbi's) and Kevin Mitchell (.291, forty-seven homers, 125 rbi's) were the most potent offensive tandem NL fans had watched in a long time. Portly forty-year-old Rick Reuschel led Craig's staff with seventeen wins (for a career total of 211), despite finishing only two starts.

Again the white-shod Oakland Athletics triumphed easily in the AL West, winning ninety-nine times and finishing comfortably ahead of Kansas City and California. The most exciting thing about the season for Royals fans was watching Vincent "Bo" Jackson, an extraordinary athlete out of Auburn University who powered homers and stole bases (and struck out a lot) in the summertime, then galloped for yardage in the autumn months for the NFL's Raiders.

Oakland's Dave Stewart (21–9), Mike Moore (19–11), Storm Davis (19–7), and Bob Welch (17–8) were the best starting foursome of the decade; Dennis Eckersley recorded thirty-three saves and won four decisions without defeat. Injuries caused Jose Canseco to miss two-thirds of the season, but Carney Lansford batted .336 and Mark McGwire, Dave Henderson, and designated hitter Dave Parker (the first big-leaguer to wear an earring) provided plenty of power. Leadoff man Rickey Henderson, obtained in a trade early in the season from the Yankees, finished with seventy-seven stolen bases, pushing his career total to 863 and, at thirty-one, becoming a sure bet to overcome Lou Brock's all-time steals record.

The Athletics also had little trouble in the playoff and thus became the first repeat pennant winner since the 1978–1979 Yankees and Dodgers. Toronto's Blue Jays, having narrowly finished ahead of Frank Robinson's rejuvenated Baltimore club in a weak Eastern Division field, could capture only one game, at the new Skydome. George Bell (.297, eighteen homers, 104 rbi's) continued to be Toronto's top hitter, while young Fred McGriff (thirty-six homers, 92 rbi's) struggled through a horrid late-season slump. Cito Gaston had to get along with even wobblier pitching than Toronto's 1985 division winners; veteran right-hander Dave Stieb (17–8) led the staff but failed twice against the Athletics in the playoff.

The World Series matched West Coast teams for the third time and Bay area representatives for the first time. Although the Athletics were stronger than the Giants in nearly every respect, the Series might have offered better baseball if it hadn't been interrupted by North America's worst earthquake since the 1906 cataclysm that destroyed San Francisco. This one killed between one hundred fifty and two hundred people, left thousands homeless, did billions of dollars in damage—and prompted a ten-day suspension of the Series.

Following 5–0 and 5–1 Athletics victories at Oakland behind Stewart and Moore, the teams moved to Candlestick Park. The quake struck on Tuesday evening, October 17, about fifteen minutes before the players took the field for game three; and while no one at Candlestick Park was injured, the severe tremor did minor damage to the stadium. Despite urgings that he either cancel the Series altogether or move it to another part of the country, acting commissioner Vincent ordered a delay while structural engineers verified Candlestick Park's soundness. Determined to go through with the Series according to plan, Vincent announced that play would resume on the Giants' home field on the night of October 27.

Soon after San Francisco's Scott Garrelts served up the first pitch of game three to Rickey Henderson, it was clear that only the Athletics had been able to sustain their competitive edge. A fourteen-hit, five-homer bombardment of Garrelts and three others sent the Giants to defeat, 13–7. Given Oakland's clearly demonstrated superiority, game four was an anticlimax to both the earthquake and the Series as a whole: It ended 9–6, Oakland, with Tony LaRussa using four pitchers in relief of Moore to shut down the Giants after the sixth inning.

Following that strange, almost surreal conclusion to baseball's non-sesquicentennial season, dedicated fans were nagged by off-season fears that, with the current Basic Agreement coming to an end, 1990 would bring another strike. Sure enough, players and owners again deadlocked on a range of issues, the most critical being the MLBPA's insistence that the term of eligibility for salary arbitration be restored to two years, as it was from 1972 through 1984, versus the three-year term specified in the 1985 Basic Agreement.

In a replay of 1976, the owners refused to open the spring-training camps, but, unlike Bowie Kuhn in that lockout, Fay Vincent wouldn't pressure the owners to open the gates. The lockout (which again many people misunderstood as a players' strike) lasted thirty-four days. Late on Sunday night, March 18 (appropriately enough, in the Versailles Room at the Helmsley Palace in New York City), owners and players agreed to a new four-year Basic Agreement.

Under a complicated compromise, some two-year-plus men would become eligible for arbitration; most wouldn't. The owners also agreed to raise the official minimum salary to $100,000 (from $68,000) and their annual collective contribution to the players' pension fund to $55 million (from about $31 million). The 1990 season would start on April 9, a week late. The lost week's worth of games would be made up on off days and at the end of the official schedule.

"Baseball has to be a great thing," goes an old saying, "or it couldn't survive the people in it." By the end of July 1990, George Steinbrenner, without doubt the most unpopular man in the sport, had taken his leave. When Vincent learned that Steinbrenner had paid a professional gambler named Howard Spira to dig up damaging information on Dave Winfield, with whom the Yankees president had feuded for nine years, the commissioner decided that enough was enough. While Winfield agreed to be traded to the California Angels, Vincent determined that Steinbrenner's conduct—"a pattern of behavior that borders on the bizarre," in Vincent's words—had become a detriment to baseball. On July 30 the commissioner ordered Steinbrenner to relinquish his controlling interest in the Yankees franchise, and effectively barred him from the sport. That evening, when word of Steinbrenner's ouster reached Yankee Stadium, the crowd rose to chant, "No more George!"

But if Steinbrenner's departure removed one of baseball's irritants, fans remained resigned to others, especially periodic player-owner impasses and disruptions of the sport's seasonal cycle. Throughout professional baseball's long history, customers had proved amazingly tolerant and forgiving of rapacious, pigheaded owners; in recent decades they'd

learned to exercise the same forbearance where the apparently insatiable money demands of the players were concerned.

"Complaining about the lack of profit in baseball is a perennial
avocation of club owners," Gerald Scully has written in his study of
baseball economics; yet new enterprisers, eager to have their own ball
club and willing to pay for the chance, have never been scarce. And if
contemporary ballplayers seemed insufferably greedy by comparison
with the old-timers, it's worth remembering that men earning their
livings on the ballfield have always sought higher pay—and usually
considered themselves underpaid. As Waite Hoyt observed in 1935, in
the twilight of a distinguished pitching career, "A winning ballplayer is
motivated by two strong incentives—professional pride and the urge to
make money." Ballplayers, wrote the *Washington Post's* Thomas Boswell a half-century later, might be "stupefyingly overpaid," but "the
notion that such internally driven people can become slipshod over-
night . . . is bogus."

What it all came down to, finally, was whether one was willing to
put up with the trials and travails that went with being a baseball fan
near the end of the twentieth century. Apparently record numbers of
Americans were and are, although it might not make any sense to
people who've never been caught up in the quirky, stylized, deliberately paced, yet compellingly beautiful spectacle of a ballgame. "Some
adults think that to watch baseball is to waste one's time in a childish
way," the seventy-five-year-old novelist James T. Farrell, himself a
lifelong Chicago White Sox fan, wrote in 1979. "But I have always
loved the game. I don't care or not whether it is childish. Long before I
possessed any capacity to examine myself or the reason for the game's
appeal to me, I loved it."

Bibliographic Essay

To a great extent, the "serious" study of baseball history dates from Harold Seymour's *Baseball: The Early Years* (1960), followed by *Baseball: The Golden Age* (1971), which brings the story up to 1930. Seymour's *Baseball: The People's Game* (1990) deals copiously with the vast baseball universe outside Organized Baseball. The other standard general work is David Q. Voight's *American Baseball* (3 vols., 1970–1983), which extends up to the early 1980s. Briefer general accounts include Lee Allen's *100 Years of Baseball* (1950), *The National League Story* (1961), and *The American League Story* (1962); Glenn Dickey's *The History of American League Baseball Since 1901* (1980) and *The History of National League Baseball Since 1876* (1982); and Fred Lieb's *The Baseball Story* (1950). Robert Smith's *Baseball* (1970), Douglas Wallop's *Baseball: An Informal History* (1969), and Joseph Durso's *Baseball and the American Dream* (1986) are heavily anecdotal, while Branch Rickey's *The American Diamond: A Documentary History of the Game of Baseball* (1965) provides an overview by one of baseball's most important figures. Joel Zoss and John Bowman's *Diamonds in the Rough: The Untold History of Baseball* (1989) reexamines and revises conventional understanding about many aspects of baseball's development.

Of numerous pictorial histories—"coffee-table volumes"—five

are superior: David Q. Voight, *Baseball: An Illustrated History* (1987); Gerald Astor, ed., *The Baseball Hall of Fame 50th Anniversary* (1988); Donald Honig, *The National League* (1983); Lawrence S. Ritter and Donald Honig, *The Image of Their Greatness* (1979); and Daniel Okrent and Harris Lewine, eds., *The Ultimate Baseball Book* (1984).

On baseball's origins and early development in the United States, several recent studies are especially helpful: Melvin L. Adelman, *A Sporting Time: New York City and the Rise of Modern Athletics, 1820–1870* (1986); George B. Kirsch, *The Creation of American Team Sports: Baseball and Cricket, 1838–72* (1989); Warren Goldstein, *Playing for Keeps: A History of Early Baseball* (1990); Irving Leitner, *Baseball: Diamond in the Rough* (1972); Steven Riess, *City Games: The Evolution of American Society and the Rise of Sports* (1989); Steven M. Gelber, "Working at Playing: The Culture of the Workplace and the Rise of Baseball," *Journal of Social History*, 16 (Summer 1983), 3–22, and " 'Their Hands Are All Out Playing': Business and Amateur Baseball, 1845–1917," *Journal of Sport History*, 11 (Spring 1984), 5–27; Stephen Freedman, "The Baseball Fad in Chicago, 1965–1870: An Exploration of the Role of Sports in the Nineteenth-Century City," *Journal of Sport History*, 5 (Summer 1978), 42–64; and John M. Carroll, "The Doubleday Myth and Texas Baseball," *Southwestern Historical Quarterly*, 92 (April 1989), 597–612. A. G. Spalding, *Baseball: America's National Game* (1911) and Harry Ellard, *Base Ball in Cincinnati* (1908) are still worth looking into. Harvey Frommer's *Primitive Baseball: The First Quarter-Century of the National Pastime* (1988) is anecdotal and superficial.

Team histories (some quite dated) include Franklin Lewis, *The Cleveland Indians* (1949); Warren Brown, *The Chicago Cubs* (1946) and *The Chicago White Sox* (1952); Lonnie Wheeler, *The Cincinnati Game* (1988); Bob Buege, *The Milwaukee Braves* (1989); Neil Hynd, *The Giants of the Polo Grounds* (1988); Janet Bruce, *The Kansas City Monarchs: Champions of Black Baseball* (1985); Donald Honig, *Baseball's Ten Greatest Teams* (1982); Lee Allen, *The Cincinnati Reds* (1948); Frank Graham, *The New York Giants* (1952), *The New York Yankees* (1943), and *The Brooklyn Dodgers* (1945); Shirley Povich, *The Washington Senators* (1954); Robert Harris Walker, *Cincinnati and the Big Red Machine* (1988); Rick Talley, *The Cubs of '69* (1989); Jim Langford,

The Game Is Never Over: An Appreciative History of the Chicago Cubs (1980); Jack Lang and Peter Simon, *The New York Mets* (1987); John Mosedale, *Greatest of All: The 1927 New York Yankees* (1974); Richard A. Mayer, *The 1937 Newark Bears* (1980); Jack Mann, *The Decline and Fall of the New York Yankees* (1967); Ralph Houk and Robert W. Creamer, *Season of Glory: The Amazing Saga of the 1961 New York Yankees* (1988); Bill Madden and Moss Klein, *Damned Yankees* (1990); Harvey Frommer, *Baseball's Greatest Rivalry: The New York Yankees and Boston Red Sox* (1984); Peter Golenbock, *Bums: An Oral History of the Brooklyn Dodgers* (1984); Stanley Cohen, *Dodgers! The First 100 Years* (1990); and several by the prolific Fred Lieb: *The Baltimore Orioles* (1955), *The Boston Red Sox* (1947), *The Detroit Tigers* (1946), and *The Pittsburgh Pirates* (1948).

James E. Miller's *The Baseball Business: Pursuing Pennants and Profits in Baltimore* (1990), a meticulously researched study that places the Baltimore Orioles in the context of the history of the city since the 1950s, and Neil J. Sullivan's *The Dodgers Move West* (1987), an equally thorough account of the Brooklyn–Los Angeles Dodgers in the 1950s, are in a class by themselves among team-franchise histories.

On the first avowedly professional club, see, besides Ellard's *Base Ball in Cincinnati*, Joseph S. Stern, Jr., "The Team That Couldn't Be Beat: The Red Stockings of 1869," *Queen City Heritage*, 46 (September 1988), 50–58; and on Cincinnati's first National League entry, see William F. Hugo, "The 1876 Cincinnati Red Stockings: Charter Members of the New National League," *Queen City Heritage*, 46 (Summer 1988), 59–68.

For minor-league history, see Robert Obojski, *Bush League: A History of Minor League Baseball* (1975); Neil J. Sullivan, *The Minors: The Struggles and Triumphs of Baseball's Poor Relation* (1990); Bill O'Neal, *The Texas League* (1987) and *The Pacific Coast League* (1990); and Ken Brooks, *The Last Rebel Yell: The Alabama-Florida League* (1986). By far the best item on the Federal League is Marc Okonnen, *The Federal League, 1914–1915: Baseball's Third Major League* (1989).

Most firsthand accounts have been ghostwritten ephemera of little lasting value, intended to capitalize on the contemporary (and often very temporary) fame of a particular baseball celebrity. Notable exceptions include Ty Cobb, with Al Stump, *My Life in Baseball* (1961); Christy Mathewson, *Pitching in a Pinch* (1912); Connie Mack, *My 66 Years in the Big Leagues* (1950); John McGraw, *My Thirty Years in Baseball* (1923); Ted Williams and John Underwood, *My Turn at Bat* (2d ed., 1988); Bob Feller, *Now Pitching: Bob Feller* (1990); Dick Bartell, with Norman Macht, *Rowdy Richard* (1987); Frank Frisch, *The Fordham Flash* (1962); Jim Brosnan, *The Long Season* (1960) and *The Pennant Race* (1962); Edwin D. "Duke" Snider, *The Duke of Flatbush* (1988); and Hank Greenberg (ed. Ira Berkow), *The Story of My Life* (1989).

Earl Lawson, *Cincinnati Seasons: My 34 Years with the Reds* (1987); Fred Lieb, *Baseball as I Have Known It* (1977); Red Barber, *The Broadcasters* (1970); and Ernie Harwell, *Tuned to Baseball* (1986) are the most useful memoirs by newspaper and radio-TV veterans. Bill Veeck's spirited *Veeck as in Wreck* (1962) and *The Hustler's Handbook* (1965) and Harold Parrott's *The Lords of Baseball* (1976) provide inside views of baseball ownership.

Lawrence S. Ritter's *The Glory of Their Times* (rev. ed., 1984) has become a classic—a splendid oral history. Less-celebrated but valuable similar works are Donald Honig's *Baseball: When the Grass Was Real* (1975) and John Holway, *Voices from the Great Black Baseball Leagues* (1975). See also John P. Carmichael, *My Greatest Day in Baseball* (1946); Anthony J. Connor, *Baseball for the Love of It: Hall of Famers Tell It Like It Was* (1982); Rich Westcott, *Diamond Greats: Profiles and Interviews with 65 of Baseball's History Makers* (1988); and Mike Bryan, *Baseball Lives* (1989).

Among the numerous biographies of baseball people, the following are the most valuable: Robert Creamer, *Babe: The Legend Comes to Life* (1974) and *Stengel* (1984); Marshall Smelser, *The Life That Ruth Built* (1975); Lawrence S. Ritter, *Babe: A Life in Pictures* (1989); Murray Polner, *Branch Rickey* (1983); Eugene C. Murdock, *Ban Johnson: Czar of Baseball* (1983); Charles C. Alexander, *Ty Cobb* (1984) and *John McGraw* (1988); Blanche McGraw, *The Real McGraw* (1953); Joseph Durso, *The Days of Mr. McGraw* (1969); Frank Graham, *McGraw of the Giants* (1944); J. G. Taylor Spink, *Judge Landis and Twenty-Five Years of Baseball* (reprint, 1974); Harvey Frommer, *Rickey and Robinson: The Men Who Broke Baseball's Color Barrier* (1984);

Maury Allen, *Roger Maris* (1986); Joseph T. Moore, *Pride Against Prejudice: The Biography of Larry Doby* (1988).

Also: Peter Levine, *A. G. Spalding and the Rise of Baseball* (1985); Arthur Bartlett, *Baseball and Mr. Spalding* (1951); Don Warfield, *The Roaring Redhead: Larry MacPhail* (1987); Robert S. Boone, *Hack* (1978); Tom Clark, *One Last Round for the Shuffler* (1979) on Phil Douglas; Frank Graham, *Lou Gehrig: A Quiet Hero* (1942); Ray Robinson, *The Iron Horse: Lou Gehrig in His Time* (1990); Donald Gropman, *Say It Ain't So, Joe: The Story of Shoeless Joe Jackson* (1979); William Brashler, *Josh Gibson: A Life in the Negro Leagues* (1976); Donald Honig, *Mays, Mantle, and Snider* (1988); James A. Riley, *Dandy, Day, and the Devil* (1987) on Negro-league stars Ray Dandridge, Leon Day, and Willie Wells; Curt Smith, *America's Dizzy Dean* (1978); Jack Moore, *Joe DiMaggio: A Bio-Bibliography* (1986); and John M. Murphy, *Napoleon Lajoie: Modern Baseball's First Superstar* (entire issue of *The National Pastime*, Spring 1988). Harold Peterson's *The Man Who Invented Baseball* (1973) would elevate Alexander Cartwright to the legendary stature Abner Doubleday once occupied; for a corrective, see Zoss and Bowman, *Diamonds in the Rough*.

Worthwhile biographical sketches include David L. Holst, "Charles G. Radbourne: The Greatest Pitcher of the Nineteenth Century," *Illinois Historical Journal*, 81 (Winter 1988), 255–268; James A. Cox, "When the Fans Roared 'Slide, Kelly, Slide' at the Old Ball Game," *Smithsonian*, 13 (October 1982), 120–122 on Mike Kelly; Charles C. Alexander, "The Tempestuous Texan: Rogers Hornsby," *Legacies*, 2 (Spring 1990), 28–35; Andrew Kull, "Baseball's Greatest Pitcher [Radbourne]," *American Heritage*, 36 (April–May 1985), 102–106; Steven P. Gietschier, "The Short, Sweet Indian Summer of Satchel Paige," *Timeline*, 6 (April–May 1989), 44–53, and "Bill Veeck: Indian Chief," *Timeline*, 7 (April–May 1990), 28–39; Ray Robinson, "Lou Gehrig: After the Ball Game," *Columbia*, 14 (April–May 1989), 13–18; Richard Egenriether, "Chris Von der Ahe," *Baseball Research Journal*, 18 (1990), 27–33; and the sketches of Harry Grayson, *They Played the Game* (1945). David L. Porter, ed., *Biographical Dictionary of American Sports: Baseball* (1987) is indispensable.

On black baseball history, which has generated huge interest in the past twenty years, see Robert Peterson, *Only the Ball Was White* (reprint, 1984); Jules Tygiel, *Baseball's Great Experiment: Jackie Robinson and His Legacy* (1983); John Holway, *Black Ball Stars: Negro-League Pioneers* (1988); James A. Riley, *All-Time Stars of Black Baseball* (1983); Donn Rogosin, *Invisible Men: Life in Baseball's Negro Leagues* (1983); Rob Ruck, *Sandlot Seasons: Sport in Black Pittsburgh* (1987); and John B. Holway, "Cuba's Black Diamond," *Baseball Research Journal*, 10 (1981), 139–145, on Jose Méndez. Sol White, *Sol White's Official Base Ball Guide, 1905* (reprint, 1984) was the earliest effort to chronicle black baseball history.

For the umpires, Larry Gerlach's *The Men in Blue* (1980) is oral history of a quality rivaling Ritter's *The Glory of Their Times*. James M. Kahn's *The Umpire Story* (1953) and Rich Eldred's "Umpiring in the 1890s," *Baseball Research Journal*, 18 (1990), 75–78, shouldn't be overlooked. Baseball play-by-play announcers are compendiously treated in Curt Smith, *Voices of the Game* (1987).

For ballparks, three helpful guides are available: Philip Lowry, *Green Cathedrals* (1986); Michael Benson, *Ballparks of North America* (1989); and Lowell Reidenbaugh, *Take Me Out to the Ball Parks* (1983). Also pertinent are Richard Miller and Gregory L. Rhodes, "The Life and Times of the Old Cincinnati Ballparks," *Queen City Heritage*, 46 (Summer 1988), 25–41; Robert F. Bluthardt, "Fenway Park and the Golden Age of the Baseball Park, 1900–15," *Journal of Popular Culture*, 21 (Summer 1987), 43–52; Bill Price, "Braves Field," *Baseball Research Journal*, 7 (1978), 1–6; and Richard Lindberg, "Yesterday's City: The Southside Baseball Factory," *Chicago History*, 28 (Summer 1989), 60–72.

On particular games, seasons, and periods, see Robert Obojski, *All-Star Baseball Since 1933* (1981); Joseph L. Reichler and Ben Olan, eds., *Baseball's Unforgettable Games* (1961); John Thorn, *Baseball's Ten Greatest Games* (1982); Michael Seidel, *Streak: Joe DiMaggio and the Summer of '41* (1989); G. H. Fleming, *The Unforgettable [1908] Season* (1981); Ken Coleman, *The Impossible Dream Remembered: The 1967 Red Sox* (1987); David Halberstam, *Summer of '49* (1989); William B. Mead, *Two Spectacular Seasons: 1930, the Year the Hitters Ran Wild; 1968, the Year the Pitchers Took Over* (1990); William B. Mead and Harold Rosenthal, *The Ten Worst Years of Baseball* (1982); Harold Rosenthal, *The Ten Best Years of Baseball* (1985); Richard Goldstein,

Spartan Seasons: How Baseball Survived World War II (1980); and Harvey Frommer, *New York City Baseball: The Last Golden Age, 1947–1957* (1985). Fred Lieb's *The Story of the World Series* (1965) is still useful, while Jerry Lansche's *The Forgotten Championships: Postseason Baseball, 1882–1981* (1989) focuses on the original World Series in the 1880s, the Temple Cup series in the 1890s, and the numerous "city series" in the twentieth century.

Eliot Asinof's *Eight Men Out: The Black Sox and the 1919 World Series* (reprint, 1988) comes as close as anybody ever will to fathoming that incredibly confused and murky episode; but see also Robert I. Goler, "Black Sox," *Chicago History,* 17 (Fall–Winter 1988–89), 42–69.

Two special books: Roger Kahn's *The Boys of Summer* (1972) deals poignantly with the early 1950s Brooklyn Dodgers and their later lives, and Mike Sowell's *The Pitch That Killed* (1989) is a fine dual biography of Ray Chapman and Carl Mays, the man who threw the pitch that ended Chapman's life.

On aspects of the game on the field, consult William Curran, *Mitts: A Celebration of Fielding* (1984) and *Big Sticks: The Batting Revolution of the Twenties* (1990); Jim Kaplan, *Playing the Field* (1987); and John Thorn and Pete Palmer, *The Pitcher* (1987).

Efforts to get at baseball's larger social significance include Richard C. Crepeau, *Baseball: America's Diamond Mind, 1919–1941* (1981); Steven Riess, *Touching Base: Professional Baseball and American Culture in the Progressive Era* (1980); Tristram Coffin, *The Old Ball Game* (1972); and Ron Briley, "The Times Were A-Changin': Baseball as a Symbol of American Values in Transition, 1963–1964," *Baseball Research Journal,* 17 (1988), 54–60.

For the legal and business side of baseball past and present, see Paul M. Gregory, *The Baseball Player: An Economic Study* (1956); James B. Dworkin, *Owners Versus Players: Baseball and Collective Bargaining* (1981); Lee Lowenfish and Tony Lupien, *The Imperfect Diamond: The Story of Baseball's Reserve Clause and the Men Who Fought to Change It* (1980); Benjamin R. Rader, *In Its Own Image: How Television Has Transformed Sports* (1984); and especially Gerald W. Scully, *The Business of Major League Baseball* (1989).

Some of the best examples of appreciative writing about the sport include Donald Hall, "Baseball and the Meaning of Life," *National*

Review, 33 (September 4, 1981), 1033–1044; A. Bartlett Giamatti, "Baseball and the American Character," *Harper's*, 273 (October 1986), 27f., and *Take Time for Paradise: Americans and Their Games* (1989); James T. Farrell, *My Baseball Diary* (1959) and "Baseball: A Fan's Notes," *American Scholar*, 48 (Summer 1979), 391–394; George Will, *Men at Work: The Craft of Baseball* (1990); Thomas Boswell, *The Heart of the Order* (1989); and Roger Angell, *The Summer Game* (1972) and *Season Ticket* (1988).

The two foremost statistical compilations are Joseph L. Reichler, ed., *The Baseball Encyclopedia* (8th ed., 1990) and John Thorn and Pete Palmer, eds., *Total Baseball* (1989). Since the first edition appeared in 1969, "Big Mac," as *The Baseball Encyclopedia* has come to be nicknamed (because the Macmillan Publishing Company puts it out), has affected everybody's knowledge and understanding of teams' and ballplayers' past performances. *Total Baseball*, besides offering far more and better historical treatment in essay form (on everything from the All-Star Game to "Mascots and Superstitions") than does *The Baseball Encyclopedia*, incorporates new statistical categories developed by Society for American Baseball Research "SABRmetricians." The user of *Total Baseball* should determine for him/herself how valuable such "newstats" really are.

Finally, the contents of this book rest largely on close reading of a vast quantity of contemporary periodical material, especially such sources as *Sporting News*, *Sporting Life*, *New York Clipper*, *Baseball Magazine*, *Sport* magazine, *Sports Illustrated*, *Life*, *Time*, *Newsweek*, *Collier's*, *Saturday Evening Post*, *Everybody's*, and *Literary Digest*.

Index